WHITEY
FROM FARM KID
TO FLYING TIGER
TO ATTORNEY

TO: Ken
Best wishes

a Memoir by
WAYNE G. JOHNSON

LANGDON
STREET
PRESS

with love from Nancy
NOTE: Wayne D. Johnson
spoke @ Memorial Day
Service @ Sunrise Memorial
2012

Langdon Street Press
212 3rd Avenue North, Suite 290
Minneapolis, MN 55401
612.455.2293
www.langdonstreetpress.com

ISBN-13: 978-1-936183-89-0
LCCN: 2010938405

Cover Design and Typeset by Nate Meyers

Printed in the United States of America

ACKNOWLEDGEMENTS

Many thanks to my family, friends, and colleagues for encouraging me to record incidents of my life that may remain in their memories and may be of interest or inspiration to others. In particular, a special thanks to my wife Delores for her patience, support, and understanding while I spent countless hours at the computer, in researching, writing, and revising this memoir. Also thanks to Judge Mark Munger for his encouragement and advice; my law partner, Pete Morris, and my dedicated legal secretary Lin Elizondo, for their help in editing; my brother, Edgar Johnson, for remembering incidents of our youth; and my friend Oliver Bateman for helping me recall happenings while we served together in the Army Air Corps in WWII.

There may have been some experiences and escapades that I should have left out, but I was counseled to give an accurate and honest recording, and tell only the truth. Thomas Jefferson wrote many years ago, "We should never be afraid of the truth, regardless where it leads us." That observation is as applicable today as it was more than two hundred years ago.

I have made every effort to accurately portray my life experiences. I quote extensively and verbatim from my World War II diary. Any errors in spelling, punctuation, sentence structure, or other grammar structures have been left in the original text of the diary, which was handwritten more than sixty years ago.

INTRODUCTION

My life's story, *From Farm Kid to Flying Tiger to Attorney* consists of three basic parts. As the eleventh child of emigrant parents, I describe my Norwegian heritage and growing up on a farm in rural Minnesota during the Great Depression in a large family.

The story then goes into my military service, training as a fighter pilot, and shipment to China in WWII to serve with the famed *Flying Tigers*.

Returning home at the end of the war, I attended college and law school in order to become an attorney. I established a law practice in the small Minnesota towns of Beaver Bay and Silver Bay, both on the north shore of Lake Superior. In addition to my private law practice, I served as city attorney for both Beaver Bay and Silver Bay for more than fifty years, setting a record as the longest serving city attorney in the United States.

I continued to be active in aviation and was named "Mr. Aviation of Minnesota" in 1968. In 2001, I was inducted into the Minnesota Aviation Hall of Fame and in 2005 the Silver Bay Municipal Airport was renamed the *Wayne Johnson Airport.*

FOREWORD

I have known Wayne Johnson for more than sixty-five years. We first met in the Army Air Corp Cadet during WWII. We went through pilot and fighter training together and were assigned to the same Flying Tigers squadron in China. For the better part of a year, we lived together in tents as our squadron moved from base to base, engaged in combat. We formed friendships in adversity that has withstood the test of time, lasting to the present day.

"Whitey," as we all came to know him, has captured in his Memoir the grim realities of war, the joys and sorrows of young men far from home, triumphs and tragedies, courage in the face of grave danger, and dedication to duty. It was a lasting experience where young men, no more than boys, grew up quickly and formed close bonds of friendship that are eternal.

Whitey developed his character early, growing-up in a large family during the heights of the Great Depression. With the experience of war behind him, he forged ahead to become a successful attorney, earning many honors in his field—but Wayne's passion for aviation never ceased.

After WWII National Guard service, Whitey continued to pilot his own plane well into his eighties. During his lifetime, he spent countless hours promoting aviation. He is a dedicated lecturer and writer. As Editor of the four volumes "Chennault's Flying Tigers," he kept that remarkable history alive. Being named Mr. Aviation of Minnesota, inducted into the Minnesota Aviation Hall of Fame, and having the city's airport re-named the "Wayne Johnson Silver Bay Airport" are testimonials to his contributions to aviation—honors few airmen enjoy.

Whitey has courageously overcome personal tragedies that would overwhelm men of lesser character, and has proven an inspiration to friends and associates throughout the nation.

Wayne's story is a great read, written by an exemplary American patriot and airman.

(Signed) "Oliver C. Bateman

Former Fighter Pilot and Minority Leader of the Georgia State Senate"

Chapter -1-

The Farm Kid Meets the General

What's a farm kid from Minnesota doing in the ancient city of Kunming, China, in 1944? As was his custom, General Claire Lee Chennault, commander of the famed *Flying Tigers,* came down the line to meet the new pilots that came to China. He would stop briefly to talk to each pilot. The guy next to me whispered, "Stop shaking, you look like you are scared shitless."

When the general stopped before me, he looked at me with those piercing eyes for what seemed like a long time. My first thought was that he had been

Gen. Claire Lee Chennault
Commander-Flying Tigers

Whitey

informed of my *mischievous conduct* in India and was going to have me shot. Finally, he asked where I was from and what I had done before I got in the service.

I stammered that I was from a farm in Minnesota. He said, "Good farm boys make good pilots, they know what the sound of an engine means. I was a farm boy myself." He then turned to his aide and said, "Jeez, they are sending me some young kids these days." I looked like I was about sixteen. I had very blonde, almost white hair, which earned me the nickname "Whitey."

I was a farm kid. I was born in the rather poor farm district of Artichoke Township about fifteen miles east of Ortonville, Minnesota, on 8 July, 1921. When my mother

1

went into labor, my father walked to a rail station about six miles from our farm to telegraph the doctor to come out to the farm and deliver me. He walked because he didn't have a car then. The doctor didn't get there in time, because I didn't wait around. With no midwives nearby, my father, with the help of my sister Korty, only twelve years old at the time, delivered me. I was told she boiled the water!

My mother was staying at the Lovaas place about one-half mile west of our farm when I was born. She may have been at the Lovaas place because there were ten kids in our house and she needed a little privacy while giving birth to number eleven.

My birth certificate reads:
Physician or Midwife: Father Jentoft Johnson.

Quite an auspicious entry into this world!

The doctor, Bert Karn, finally arrived later that night, although too late to deliver me. He came out from Ortonville, I believe in a Model T Ford, although he frequently traveled by horse and buggy. On the way he nipped at his bottle, so by the time he got to our farm, he was quite inebriated. My father threw him in the cattle tank to sober him up so he could drive back to Ortonville.

I was the eleventh of fourteen children, most of whom were delivered by midwives at home, except for the oldest brother Villy (Willie), who was born in Tromso, Norway, and delivered by our grandmother, Louise Valine *(Jorgensdatter)* Johannessen, a professional midwife. One in our family, Baby Boy, died at birth, a year before I was born. The child was not given a name since it died at birth. The death certificate just shows "Baby Boy." All the other children lived to ripe old ages. And even with all those kids, my mother lived to be ninety-six.

Chapter -2-

My Norwegian Heritage

My father, Jentoft Kristian Blom Johannessen, was a fisherman out of Tromso in northern Norway. His father, my paternal grandfather, Soren Johannessen, had a fleet of fishing vessels and a fish processing factory on the islands of Ljoso (pronounced *lis-seh)* and Vengsoy. In the old Norwegian patronymic custom, boys were named *sen (*son) after their father's first name and girls were named *datter* (daughter). My great grandfather was Johannes Jensen, so my grandfather Soren became Soren Johannessen, which meant the son of Johannes Jensen

My grandmother's family, the Jorgensens, came from a farm near Nordeidet, a little village on the island of Reinoy, about fifty miles north of Tromso. They eked out a living on their small farm and supplemented the family income by fishing. The patriarch was Jorgen Kristian Gram Hanssen, thus the children became Jorgensen or Jorgensdatter, the sons and daughters of Jorgen. In 1880, because that method of naming children became quite confusing, the Norwegian government declared that henceforth the family name would not change with each generation.

By the early 1900s, the entire Jorgensen family, except my grandmother, immigrated to America. She finally immigrated in 1917, after she had made a number of trips to America. Because of the hard life they lived, many families from that part of Norway emigrated from Norway to America.

One of my maternal cousins, Rev. Hans G. Jorgensen, wrote of the hazards of North Sea fishing in his family *Genealogy:*

Our ancestors were hardy people who eked out their living mainly from the cold and turbulent sea at the expense of much suffering and loss of many a life.

An experience in Sivert's life as a fisherman is worth repeating. [Sivert Jorgensen, was my great Uncle]. *It happened shortly before his emigration from Norway in the late summer of 1891. Sivert, with two of his neighbors, Hans Hansen and Hans Martin and his younger brother Lars* [Jorgensen] *occupied one of the fishing boats that were after herring.*

One night, while they lay at anchor in the Mageroysundet between North Cape and the mainland, a terrific snow storm arose, while they were sleeping in their boat, and pulled the anchor loose from its mooring and carried them to sea.

When they hoist sail to cruise back to the harbor the boat capsized but remained afloat. In this precarious position, in the middle of this dark and stormy night and soaked to the skin by the ice cold water of the Arctic Ocean, they managed to cling to the boat. When morning light dawned three men were dead from exposure to the elements. In his sorrowful and weakened condition Sivert managed to fasten two of the corpses to the boat with ropes he cut from the shrouds. One of them was his own brother Lars, who so recently had said goodbye to his young wife and two children before setting out on this expedition. When the third man died Sivert was not able to reach any more rope to tie him to the boat, but had to let him float away after holding him by the hair as long as he was able.

After an almost superhuman struggle, Sivert was finally able to reach the yawl by which he managed to get to the nearest shore, barren and uninhabited. [a "Yawl" is a small two-masted sailing vessel.] *The only food in the yawl that was not spoiled by the sea water was a chunk of goat cheese, which he ate to revive his strength. He then cut the toes off his boots to let the water out and started to walk in the deep snow along the coast until he was discovered by other members of the fishing fleet. The boat with the two corpses was recovered.*

[Cutting the toes out of his boots seems a strange remedy. I would think he would just take his boots off and dump out the water, unless he couldn't get them off.]

Before taking passage back home he sent the following telegram to his father: "Kullseilet I Magersoysundet. Tre man dod. Lars Jorgensen or Hans Hansen gjenfundet medbringer jeg om otte dager." [Translated it reads: "Capsized in the sound of Mageroy. Three men dead. The bodies of Lars Jorgensen and Hans Hansen recovered, which I will bring with me after eight days."] It was not long thereafter that Sivert gave up this hazardous occupation and immigrated to America with his family.

Regardless of the hazards of North Sea and Arctic Ocean fishing, fish was a critical component of their diet. The fish diet of these Norsemen was supplemented by raising a few sheep and goats, a cow or two, and sometimes farming potatoes where they could find enough soil for that purpose.

These were the type of conditions in which my father grew up. He fished with his father from the time he was about fourteen until he left Norway at age twenty-five. It was under these Spartan living conditions and engagement in hazardous occupations that induced a large Norwegian emigration to America.

The Jorgensen branch of my family can be traced back to Peder Madsen Gram, who was born in 1515. He was a Lutheran minister in Gudbrandsdalen, in the southern part of Norway. We had a number of preachers among my ancestors and relatives, but apparently their lessons did not always rub off on all of us!

The story goes, however, that the Rev. Peder Hansen Gram, a great-great-grand-son of Peder Madsen Gram, also a Lutheran minister in Gudbrandsdalen in the late 1600s, was accused of trifling with one of his female parishioners. He was banished by the bishop to the remote and barren island of Karlsoy, north of Tromso, where he started a church. It appears that throughout history, the cloak of the divine did not protect them from the temptations of the flesh. My grandfather Johannessen and grandmother were married in that Karlsoy church that the Rev. Peder Hansen Gram had started centuries before.

My father's family came from the small island of Ljoso (pronounced *lis-seh*) in the Lofoton chain of islands west and northwesterly of Tromso, Norway, where my father's grandfather, Johannes Jensen, had a fishing operation. Johannes Jensen's children were then named *Johannessen* or *Johannesdatter*, the sons and daughters of Johannes, as was still the custom in those days.

According to the official *Folktellinga* (census) of 1875, my forebearers lived on the island of Ljoso. The census gave the name, relationship, occupation, and year of birth for each ancestor. My great-grandfather was listed first:

Johannes Jensen, Husfar, fisker, gaardb. 1824 [house father or head of house-hold, fisherman, farmer].

The census then listed his wife and seven children, one of which was my grandfather:

Soren K. Johannessen, sen, *Fisker Hjelper Faderen,* 1855 [son, fishermen help-er for father].

Soren Kristian Blom Johannessen married my grandmother Lovise Valene Jorgensdatter (pronounced *lew vee seh - vah lee neh - yorgensdottor)* in 1878 and lived for a time on Ljoso.

Soren and Lovise moved to the city of Tromso in 1881, where Soren developed a substantial fishing and fish processing business and Lovise became very active as a midwife. My father Jentoft Kristain Blom Johannessen was born in Tromso in 1882. Soren and Lovise only had two other children, Hanna and Constance, although they did have an adopted son.

It is said that Lovise probably delivered most of the children in Tromso from about 1881 to 1917, when Soren died, and she left Tromso permanently. She was called *Lovise paa bakken,* "Lovise on the hill," for she lived on a street that ended at the top of a hill. When I visited Norway with my family in 1971, there were old timers that still remembered her with affection and a twinkle in their eyes. It was rumored that besides being a good midwife, she was not bashful about dispensing other *favors,* particularly when my grandfather was out to sea on extended fishing trips, although she professed to be a devout Baptist. Even Baptists might get a little passionate at times.

Norwegian Baptists are very conservative. They do not approve of card playing, dancing, and similar types of frivolous conduct. One of my smart-aleck brothers, Roy, once said, "Baptists never make love standing up. They're afraid someone might see them and think they are dancing." That was probably not a new joke.

Although my grandmother Lovise attended the Baptist church faithfully after she came to America, and visited us often, my mother was not overly fond of her mother-in-law. She said Lovise was a "bad woman" because she "liked men too much." Although Mother was always civil to her, she was never enthusiastic about Lovise's visits. But the kids loved Grandma Lovise. Whenever she came to visit, she would bring us some of her delicious gingerbread cookies or my mother would reluctantly let her use the oven to bake some.

My mother's family lived on *Gronneg gate* (Green Street) in Tromso. The *Folketellingen (*census) in the city of Tromso for 1902 lists the family starting with the father:

Ole B. Olsen: Hf. Bryggeformand 1847 [house father, wharf or harbor foreman].

It then lists his wife and five children, one of which was my mother:

Aasta K. Olsen, datter 1881

My father, Jentoft Kristian Blom Johannessen, married my mother, Aasta Karoline Olsen on November 9, 1904, in the State Lutheran Church in Tromso, Norway. In our 1971 visit to Norway, my family visited that church. It looked unchanged from my parents' wedding photographs. Mother had been christened and confirmed there.

For a time after my parent's marriage, they lived at Soren and Lovise's home.

That arrangement did not endear my mother to her mother-in-law, who she grew to dislike. In particular, Mother resented Lovise's constant urging that Jentoft should take his family to America. Mother did not want to leave her dear Tromso and go to a foreign land.

However, Lovise was successful in convincing my father that he should give up the hard life of a fisherman and move to America. Fishing was a very hazardous occupation, and serious injuries were commonplace. Many lost their lives in the vicious storms of the North Atlantic and Arctic Ocean.

On one occasion, my father was cleaning fish and just as he brought his knife down to cut off the head, the ship rolled violently. The knife sliced through his hand between the index and third finger and became lodged in the cleaning table. Fortunately the blade missed his tendons. After the crew had pulled the knife out and stanched the flow of blood, they smeared the wound with butter. It was the only "salve" on board. Apparently it was effective, since Father did not get an infection and the wound healed before they made port. The injury did not affect the use of his hand. However, he bore a purple scar on his hand (noted on his citizenship papers) as a constant reminder of the episode.

Father once shared with us an interesting remedy for chapped hands, as chapped hands were commonplace among the Nordic fishermen. He said the fishermen would pee on their hands, which he claimed was effective in controlling chapping. I haven't tried Father's remedy as yet, but I'm tempted to do so. Think it would certainly leave a distinct aroma on one's hands.

Bowing to his mother's constant urging, and the lure of riches she described, my father decided to immigrate to America with his wife Aasta and their little son Villy. Grandfather Soren was much opposed. Although Soren had a large fishing fleet, fish processing factories, and was considered well-to-do, he was reluctant to finance his only son's departure.

Soren knew he would never see his son and only grandson again if his son immigrated to America. Soren was heartbroken when they left Norway. His two daughters also immigrated to America, leaving Soren without immediate family in Norway. After his children left, Soren's health deteriorated. It was said he died of heartbreak.

An uncle, Sivert Jorgensen, agreed to pay a part of my parent's fare from Norway, with the understanding that my father would work for Sivert for a year, being in essence a indentured servant.

Despite the fact that Soren did not want his only son to leave Norway, he gave him his telescope and the "Valene" banner that flew on his ship as parting gifts. The banner was three feet in width and twelve feet long. "Valene" was grandmother's middle name, so Soren named his lead ship after her. My father carefully kept the telescope and banner all his life. Mother gave them both to me after Father's death with the hope that I would continue to care for them. I still have the telescope mounted on my living room wall as one of my family treasures. Because the banner was too big to display, I gave it to the Norwegian Museum in Decorah, Iowa, with my mother's consent.

Grandma Lovise was quite a vagabond and was quite the character. She made a number of trips to America on her own prior to the family's emigration. She even experienced the Gold Rush in Alaska in 1898. From that, she had a large gold nugget, which she wore on a chain around her neck. When she died, the nugget disappeared. It was rumored that her son-in-law, Alvert Nielson, Aunt Hanna's husband, took the valuable keepsake.

Lovise moved to America in 1917 after Soren died. She purchased the old Baptist church parsonage in Artichoke, which my father remodeled, and lived there until her death. The house was conveniently located a short distance from the Baptist church that she attended regularly.

Grandma Lovise actually died in the church. It was her custom to sit in the front pew. At the end of the service she would be the first to walk out. The congregation always waited for her to leave. She would sometimes doze off, as some of us may do, but would wake up when the minister would loudly clear his throat at the end of the service.

On the Sunday of her death, she did not get up as usual, despite the loud throat clearings by the minister. Finally the minister stepped down and gently shook her shoulder. She toppled over. She had died. To die in church was certainly convenient since she was close to the next step, whatever that might be.

Other than Uncle Olaf Olsen (Mother's brother) and Mother, none of her family left Norway. If there was any mention or reminder of her family, particularly when she got news that her mother and father had died, Mother would seek sanctuary in her bedroom. She would emerge later with very red eyes. We knew she had been crying but could do nothing about it. It must have been a very traumatic to sail away from your home and family, knowing that you would never see your parents or siblings again.

Chapter -3-

The Emigrants

Just before leaving for America, Grandfather Olsen wanted a photo taken of my mother and little Villy, his new grandson. He knew he would never see either of them again. Because the ship was being loaded, there wasn't much time, but Mother left the dock area to run to the photographer with my father pacing, hoping she'd get back in time before the ship was ready to sail. He said the ship was blowing its final loading whistle when Mother came rushing back. Her father sent the photo to her some years later, and she faithfully kept it until she gave it to me.

Father and Mother with little Villy sailed out of Tromso in June, 1907, for the crossing on the *Empress of Ireland,* a ship jointly owned by the King of Norway and the Canadian Pacific Railroad.

They sailed on a small vessel from Tromso to Trondheim, where they boarded another ship, the British ship, the *Dammino,* for the crossing to England, then embarked on the *Empress* for the Atlantic crossing. Villy was only a little over eight months old when he took that journey.

Mother described it as a terrible journey. After many stops along the Norwegian coast, the first non-Norwegian port was Liverpool, England. My mother recalled "girls" shouting out of windows beckoning boys to come up and enjoy their *hospitality*. "We didn't have that kind of thing in Tromso," she would say. At least that she knew about . . . or would admit to knowing about. But Father allowed that there probably were *those kinds* of girls in Tromso—not that he had ever enjoyed their *favors*!

It was in Liverpool that they boarded the *Empress of Ireland* for the Atlantic crossing. There was a great deal of sickness aboard during their journey. They were in second class and confined by close quarters with the passengers' seasickness, a combination that could make the worst types of messes. Mother vividly described the horrible conditions on the long journey. They endured terrible storms during the crossing. She described how people in the upper bunks would puke "or even worse" on those in the lower bunks.

Although Mother had a vivid memory, neither she nor Father kept a diary. Father was always rather non-committal about the trip. After all, he had endured the hazards of sailing in the North Sea and the Arctic Ocean, waters that produce some of the most violent storms of any ocean.

My great Uncle, Hans Peter Paul Jorgensen, who immigrated to America in 1889, kept a day-to-day diary of his journey in which he graphically described his experience sailing the Atlantic, an account that corresponds almost exactly with Mother's memory.

Hans Peter Paul Jorgensen wrote in Norwegian, but the diary was translated into English (he later dropped the Hans Peter and thereafter referred to himself as Paul Jorgensen). His diary consisted of twenty pages of neat handwriting in Norwegian. I quote from only a few translated entries.

Liverpool, June 26, 1889. We left Tromso on the 13th . . . Many of the passengers got very seasick. . . . We were about 30 altogether when we disembarked in Trondheim. All of which are immigrating to America. . . .

The 18th: We went to the Domirken [Translator's note: the oldest Cathedral in Norway where Kings of Norway are crowned] *It was a beautiful piece of art which is hard to describe. The city is so beautiful and I have never seen anything like it. . . . The ship was supposed to sail at 2 P.M. on the 20th but was delayed to 10 P.M. on account of some cases of salmon which was due to arrive at 10 P.M. . . . We departed from Trondhjem at 11 P.M. We called at Kriestiansund and Aelesund. Iced salmon and halibut was loaded aboard at both places. Storms from north and northeast followed us along the coast . . . There are only 120 passengers aboard. Women with babies and larger children, there are many of. It was terrible to see how seasick the women and children were.*

The 22nd: . . . Norwegian coast and mountains have disappeared below the horizon. Our breakfast are Smorbrod [open faced sandwiches] *and coffee, but there was few that could drink it. Made our own coffee.*

It seems unbelievable that I have left my parents and all my beloved forever behind. . . . it is absolutely beautiful in the whole of England. It was so flat as a calm sea . . . Here in Liverpool have I saw an ass, which our Jesus Christ rode when he arrived in Jerusalem. It looked like such an innocent animal. We left Liverpool at 6 P.M. In the morning we could see the land on both sides. On our port, Ireland, and to the starboard, Scotland. We called at a port in Ireland and took aboard 20 passengers. We had very nice weather the whole night.

The 28th: We left the Irish coast behind in the afternoon and the wind started to shift to the northwest and the sky darkened.

The 29th: It started to freshen up with . . . wind. The sea came across the bow. I have never . . . seen so much misery. . . . Wherever I go, I see people . . . laying like half dead. Many have not eaten for several days. I can hear crying and misery wherever I go. I, for my part, do not think it was . . . rough sea . . .

July the 4th: . . . it started to get foggy again and the ship is proceeding with half speed. It is dark and then we had started to meet ice. It is very large pack-ice and the ship is now laying dead in the water. It is impossible to proceed with the ice and fog.

July 5th: The fog started to lift and the ship started to move. We could see the pack-ice as far as our eyes could see. We saw land on our starboard side. It is called Labrador. . .   We raised Newfoundland in the afternoon on our port. There is about 300 passengers aboard. After breakfast, everyone had to go up on the deck while the cleaning was going on.. . . Fresh wheat bread is baked every day. Butter and bread and tea for breakfast. Soup and potatoes and once in a while pudding, and not even fish for lunch. Butter and bread and tea for supper.

July 6th: . . . It is the river going up to Quebec - St. Lawrence River, and it is very wide.

July 8th: At 2 A.M. arrived in Quebec. After breakfast we went ashore and all the luggage was brought to a large house. We had to change tickets again, and at 11 A.M. we boarded the train. The train . . . is very fast. Looking through the windows, I can see it is a very beautiful country . . . . We have arrived in Montreal.

July 9th: The train has been running all night. . . . Today we have been moving along an inland sea for several hours. It is tremendous large lake. [Lake Huron] *. . . We arrived in a big city called Toronto.*

July 10th: Today we arrived at the border of the United States of America. The train and wagons were taken aboard a ferry and transported across the river. . . . We are now close to a city called Chicago. I have seen more flat land since we arrived at the border, and I have noticed many places the farmers have harvested their wheat . . . I also noticed that they drive their wheat binders with 3 horses . . .

We brought coffee and bread. It was very good coffee . . . we paid 5 cents per cup.

July 11ᵗʰ: Yesterday afternoon we boarded the train and proceeded on. It was heavy fog all night long, and we could not see as for as the road was wide. When the sun came up, it cleared away the fog and it was clear sky again. We arrived in a small city in the vicinity of St. Paul. It is called Minneapolis. When the train stopped it was dark. We [next] *arrived in a small town called Benson and here we had to get off and wait until 7 A.M. in the morning, for a train that was bound for Appleton. At 9 o'clock we arrived in Appleton. . .We met many Norwegians. In the afternoon we caught a ride with a man who lives 2 miles from H-Guard.*

The H. Guard farm was their final destination. This is the end of Paul Jorgensen's diary. Paul was to marry a Gaard girl.

At some point (probably when they got their citizenship papers) the Jorgensen family changed the sen to son. Thereafter the family name was Jorgenson.

When my mother read the diaries, she cried for a long time. The experiences related by Paul in his diary mirrored events Mother experienced when she and my father sailed from Tromso to America.

Chapter -4-

America—At Last

When Father and Mother arrived in Quebec, Father went searching for milk for baby Villy. Father could speak very little English, so had difficulty finding people who could understand what he wanted. He didn't realize until later that most of the people were jabbering in French. He met a Norwegian who could speak English and French but that didn't help much. That man told him that these people did not speak English but spoke a brand of French "that nobody could understand."

With a lot of hand gestures and pointing, Father was finally able to buy some milk, although he considered it very expensive at "ten cents a quart." My parents had exchanged their Norwegian *kroner* for dollars in Liverpool. A lot of conversation during the crossing, with some passengers and crew who had been to America before, they had learned to convert the value of the *kroner* to the dollar.

After the unpleasant journey across the Atlantic, it was a great relief to be on land. Another new experience awaited my parents. A train ride to their destination. Neither had been on a train before.

After a railroad trip from Quebec to Sault Ste Marais, Michigan, and through St. Paul and Minneapolis, Minnesota, my parents arrived in Correll, Minnesota, in the very western part of the state. There they met Sivert Jorgensen, who took them on a ten-mile wagon ride to his farm. Mother was devastated. She had grown up a city girl. Tromso was, and still is, a picturesque city on the ocean in northern Norway. At the time, it was a city of twenty thousand people.

Arriving in western Minnesota, she found her life defined by a small farmhouse on a barren prairie. There were no trees and no water in sight; no water or any plumbing except an outside well and a two-holer out back. She had brought some beautiful clothes from Norway, but there was no place or any reason to wear them. Mother begged my father to take her back to Norway, but that was not to be. Father had no funds. He also had an obligation to his uncle. Soon after their arrival in America, babies started being born.

For my father, it must have been equally a difficult transition to go from deep-sea fisherman to farmer with no experience behind a plow.

After a year, he found a job on the railroad in Ortonville, Minnesota, and moved his family there. This too required the family making a transition. He had no experience with railroad work, but he studied all he could about railroad maintenance and made a point of talking to men working for the railroads, before he applied for a job with the station.

He was hired as a section foreman, because of his self-taught knowledge of the work and his proficiency in English. He would work for the railroad as section foreman for seven years.

The salary was $60.00 per month to start with. He worked on the railroad until he earned enough money to make a down payment on a farm in Artichoke Township near the Jorgensons' farms.

Chapter -5-

A New Occupation.

The family moved to Artichoke Township in 1914. They stayed and farmed with John Jorgenson while my father built a house, barn, and other buildings on his property. Mother was not enthusiastic about their prospects, but reconciled to the fact that Artichoke was where she would raise her family. Despite her acquiescence, Mother always talked longingly about Tromso.

Father bought his one hundred and fifty acres from Randal Hanson, a distant relative. Father bought the land on a contract, although no contract was ever filed. The transaction was likely just an oral agreement between the two men. Father didn't get a warranty deed from Mr. Hanson until May 10, 1920. The price he paid was $8250.00, about $50.00 an acre for the bare land. At the time, it was a very substantial amount of money for that type of farmland, but he had yet to learn the true value of unimproved land.

The property was in Big Stone County, in Artichoke Township, in western Minnesota, on the county line between Big Stone and Stevens County, about fifteen miles east of Ortonville, Minnesota. It is interesting to note that my brothers (Clarence, born in 1915, and Roy, born in 1917), were both born in Stevens County. Mother was obviously staying at a farm in Stevens County, probably at the John Jorgenson's farm, likely due to Father not having built our house. Brother Arnold was born at home in Big Stone County in 1918, so Father must have completed our house by that time.

Although Artichoke Baptist Church was one–half-mile away from our farm, Mother refused to attend services there. She was a committed Lutheran. Because the closest Lutheran church was four miles away, the family trudged that whole distance, which was a long walk for children and was difficult while carrying the little ones. Trudging to and from church took most of a Sunday. Sometimes Father would put the entire family in a wagon and drive to church behind a team of horses. Father didn't like using horses on Sunday. He felt they were also entitled to a day of rest. When we moved to the Hulby farm, a short walk to church, north of Chokio, this saved us and the horses many extra miles. Like most children, we loved it when it rained or stormed on a Sunday, so we could miss church.

Father was determined to be an American. He studied hard to learn English. He learned by listening to others and reading newspapers, books, and magazines, with the help of Norwegian-English dictionaries. His already-fluent uncles helped him and Mother understand the new language. Uncle John Jorgenson had worked for an English-speaking farmer after he arrived in Artichoke and became very proficient in English. Father learned a lot of English from Uncle John.

Father and Mother often conversed in Norwegian between themselves, and therefore most of their children, including myself, learned some rudimentary Norwegian. When they didn't want us to know what they were talking about, they would switch to Norwegian, but we were adept at figuring out what they were saying, even as we pretended not to.

Norwegians, particularly those from northern Norway, are rather phlegmatic. They do not openly show their feelings or emotions. I never saw my father and mother show much affection toward each other, except small pecks on the cheek or touching of or brief holding of hands. But every time Father would go by my mother, he would, with a mischievous grin on his face, pinch her on the rear. She would switch to Norwegian and say: "*Jentoft, hva er uret med du?*" (Jentoft, what is wrong with you?) Though I suspect they both knew what was "wrong with him!"

Chapter -6-
An American Citizen

When Father applied for his citizenship papers, the clerk of court told him no one could pronounce Johannessen, so if he wanted to be an American, his name should be Johnson. Father became Jentoft Christian Blom Johnson. Although Father did not drop his middle names, he usually signed his name Jentoft B. Johnson or Jentoft C. B. Johnson. There were occasions when he forgot he was a Johnson and signed his name Johanson. In any event, Father obtained his citizenship as Johnson in 1912.

Babies came into our family on a regular basis, generally a year or two apart. The first born in America was Orla Margaret, born on August 11, 1908, a little over a year after my parents arrived in Minnesota. The next in line was Korty Aasta, born May 8, 1910. Then along came Roald Jonnie Blom on October 11, 1911. Roald was named after the great arctic explorer, Roald Amundsen. Next, the twin boys, Floyd Jentoft and Myron Aage, arrived November 6, 1913. Clarence Blom was born August 28, 1915, followed by Roy Siggur on April 3, 1917, and Arnold Stanley on September 28, 1918. My parents lost a baby boy during childbirth on June 20, 1920. That child was not named, but merely listed as "Baby Boy" on the death certificate. Then I came along on July 8, 1921. Another set of fraternal twins, Opal Minnie and Edgar Carl, arrived on November 3, 1923. My youngest sister, Gwendlyn Jane, was born on the Hulby farm on February 28, 1928.

It is interesting to note that both sets of twins: Floyd-Myron and Opal-Edgar were both born the first week of November. The month of conception nine months earlier must have been a fun and particularly virile month. Father would say that producing twins just took a little more effort. That remark would earn him a little cuff on the head from Mother, if he were within reaching distance.

Life on the farm in Artichoke was tough. The well was a good distance away from the house. Our "plumbing" was a three holer referred to as the "backhouse," and was some distance from the house. This frequently-used little building had two regular sized holes and a smaller one for little kids.

Our home was quite small, and it was packed full with thirteen kids and Pa and Ma. A couple of the older boys slept in the attic. We used to call our folks Pa and Ma, then Father and Mother, but later in life switched to Dad and Mother.

The soil at the Artichoke farm was quite good, but the fields were full of rock. Willie claimed you could pick a rock one day and it would grow back the next. He should know: he started working the fields when he was twelve years old.

The first school that Willie attended was very unique. It was eight sided. No one knew why it was built that way. Perhaps the builder thought the shape gave the students a better view of the teacher's desk. In later years, the octagon schoolhouse was moved to a museum in Ortonville.

Willie had a tough time when he started to school. He could speak only Norwegian. But since the Artichoke area was primarily inhabited by Norwegians, most of the kids could speak only Norwegian. The teacher was a master at translation, so the kids all became proficient in English in a short time and helped their parents with English lessons. I was about three years old when we moved from the Artichoke farm, so I have little recollection of the life there.

"Baby Wayne about two years old, taken at our home in Artichoke"

Chapter -7-

A Lesson in Finance

Because of our growing family, Dad needed to add onto the house. On September 9, 1922, Dad got a loan of $3,000.00 from the Farmers & Merchants State Bank of Correl, Minnesota. In return, the bank took a mortgage on the farm. Dad faithfully made the payments to the bank and also opened a savings account.

In March of 1925, Dad received bad news. He was served with a notice of foreclosure. He insisted he had only received $3,000.00 from the bank, but the mortgage that bore my parents' signatures was for $4000.00! Dad went to the bank for an explanation. The bank president claimed Dad had made no payments on the mortgage, had no bank account, did not have a savings account, and that the loan was indeed for $4,000.00.

The banker apparently found it was easy to cheat a trusting Norwegian farmer who had basic English skills and no knowledge of banking practices. Dad couldn't believe that a banker would cheat a customer. He never forgot that experience. A number of other Norwegian and Swedish farmers in the area had similar experiences with the same banker and ended up losing their farms to the bank.

A sheriff's sale was held on the 28th of March, 1925. With interest, manipulation of figures by the bank, and foreclosure costs, my parents now owed the bank $4,925.60. My parents did not have that kind of money, so they lost the farm. Dad knew he could not pay off the mortgage in a year, which was the period allowed to reclaim the property, so he rented a farm, the Hulby farm, north of Chokio, Minnesota, and we moved there after the foreclosure sale.

Since my parents, the owners, had a right of possession of the Artichoke farm for a year, they were able to work the farm for the year after the foreclosure sale. Willie and Roald, along with Dad and some of the other kids, would go down to Artichoke on a regular basis to take care of our farm there while also farming land on the Hulby property. Dad was determined not to let the bank fleece him out of his redemption rights. Consequently, my parents planted and harvested a crop on the Artichoke farm in 1925.

The house and other buildings that Dad built are still standing but run-down. No one lives in the buildings now. Dad apparently did a good job, because the buildings are still intact after more than ninety years and have not been occupied for many years. A neighbor now farms the land so has no use for the buildings, but does not want to devote the time and expense of tearing them down and disposing of the debris.

Chapter -8-

A Farmer for Life

Dad worked various farms as a tenant farmer from 1925 until early 1940, when he bought a farm near Wheaton. He farmed that property in partnership with my brothers, Willie and Edgar, until his death in 1951. Not surprisingly, he didn't trust banks; he only dealt in cash. Although farming was completely foreign to him until he came to America, he learned the craft well from his uncles, by reading farm magazines, and from experience.

In any event, Dad was more than an ordinary farmer. He became a good mechanic. He could fix all of his farm equipment, including his Model T Ford.

One of the early Model Ts Dad had was a 1917 model. He probably acquired it in the early 1920s. He kept it in perfect running shape for many years. My sisters loved to use the "T" as a background for photos.

"Wayne about age 4 on 1917 Model "T" with sister Korty dressed in the highest fashion of the day. Photo taken at the Hulby farm in 1925"

Dad was also a good carpenter. He remodeled a house for his mother when she came from Norway, as well as built and remodeled the many structures on our farms.

I may have inherited some of his carpentry skills. After I got married, I built most of my own home with my wife's help, and some years later also built a log cabin on our inland lake property. Dad also became a competent veterinarian. We often observed him reach into a cow up to his armpits to pull at a stuck calf during birthing. He also helped sows deliver their piglets. Dad was a competent barber as well, and cut his children's hair until we left home. In addition, Dad was a credible shoemaker. He had an iron shoe "Last," which was about eighteen inches high with an iron removal shoe on top. The iron shoe came in several sizes. It was used to slip shoes on to repair. Dad would re-sole and repair all of our shoes. He would buy large sheets of leather and cut out pieces for the soles and other parts of the shoes that needed repair. I still have his shoe "Last." I also have our old *bak huse lykt* (back house lantern). The lantern was something Dad had made. It was a tin box about six inches square with isinglass sides, a handle, and a place for a candle. We used it to go to the backhouse (toilet) at night. These are wonderful reminders of the many crafts immigrants learned as part of their struggle to survive.

"Dad's Shoe Last and homemade lantern"

With nine boys, Dad handled his often unruly sons with tact and diplomacy. He seldom used force: a stern look was usually sufficient to bring the most boisterous son into line. He did give me a good smack once when he heard me swearing. He didn't approve of profanity. I had stepped in a fresh cow pie (manure) with my bare feet and said, "Damn cow shit." I was just close enough to him to give me a good cuff on the side of the head.

Although Dad suffered a terrible loss when we moved from the Artichoke farm, he took such defeat philosophically. "Forget our loss, we are lucky, we now have a better farm where we can start new."

We grew to love the Hulby farm, which was called the "Hulby" farm because that was the name of the owner. The house was much bigger. The farm had a huge barn, storage sheds and other outbuildings, and the school was less than a mile away. The soil in Hulby was very good, less rocky, and produced good crops.

A photo taken at the Hulby place by sister Korty depicts four children: Clarence, Roy, Arnold, and me. The interesting thing about the photo is that all four kids are wearing the same kind of coveralls of the same size, and the same kind of caps, although I had lost mine. Mother sewed each pair of coveralls from the same pattern. Clarence's are too small, Roy's are also small, Arnold's are about right, and mine are way too big. The clothes were sewn from black denim, a cheap but durable cloth of that time. They were good, sturdy clothes, but not too fashionable.

"The happy farm kids in homemade coveralls.
(Left to right) Wayne, Arnold, Roy & Clarence. "

When I was six years old, I joined my brothers and walked the mile to the one-room school. Our teacher was Miss Bumback. She was a chubby, smiley little lady, and a great teacher. She was the school's only teacher, and taught all eight grades.

One-room country schools were great educational institutions. As the younger children listened to the lessons being taught the older students, they learned beyond their grade level. I attended one-room schools through the eighth grade.

My sister Orla married Bill Lange in August 1928. The entire family went to the wedding even though my mother did not approve of her daughter marrying a German boy. It was a sacrilege for a nice Norwegian girl to marry a German boy. It was almost as bad as a white girl marrying a black man. But it happened again. In April 1929, Korty married a German, Oscar Lange, the brother of Bill.

Orla and Bill had a wedding reception at Bill's father's farm. Bill's father, Gustav Lange, brewed beer that flowed freely at the party. This was during prohibition, so other than "home brew," there was no liquor, except for homemade "moonshine," to be had for the celebration. Moonshine was potent illegal liquor, but usually the sheriff looked the other way if it was dispensed at a party or dance. Some guy who had a hidden still usually made it.

Gustav Lange was a cigar smoker. Some of the kids discovered his cigars. And of course, we discovered his beer. I was only seven, but I got in on the party with my older brothers and some neighbor kids. We celebrated Orla's marriage to Bill Lange by smoking cigars and drinking beer behind the Lange barn. It wasn't too long before we were throwing up. My dad didn't have much sympathy for us.

In 1928, Mr. Hulby told Dad he was raising the rent starting the next year. The economy was getting bad, and grain prices were dropping. Dad did not agree to a raise in rent. He found another large farm, the Frank Laveen farm, southwest of the village of Johnson, Minnesota, where he negotiated for a better rate. It was typical of some landlords to give a tenant farmer cheaper rent to get him on the farm, and then try to raise the rent.

By the time we moved from the Hulby farm to the Laveen farm in early 1929, we had accumulated quite a number of horses and cattle. We had seven heavily loaded wagons and hay-racks pulled by horses. We had just acquired a tractor, a 1924 Fordson, from which Willie pulled some of the machinery. As the tractor had iron wheels with iron lugs that made big tracks in the dirt or gravel roads, we left quite a physical trail during our move. Fortunately, there were no blacktop or cement roads in the area at the time.

Brother Willie with our first tractor a 1924 Fordson at Hulby farm -1928.

"Brother Willie with his just-purchased 1924 *Fordson* tractor moving to the Laveen farm in 1929"

We tied the bull and some cows to the hay racks. The other cows and calves followed along nicely. I was only eight years old, but drove one of the procession's middle wagons, so I didn't have much to do. My horses just followed along behind the wagon in front. For me, at that age, to be driving a team, I thought I was quite important. It was a fifteen mile trek between farms, which took the better part of a day. Dad and Mother and some of the little kids, Opal, Edgar, and Gwen, led the way in the family Model T.

The Laveen farm was a great place. It had two large barns, a number of storage sheds, and a large house with about fifteen rooms, as well as a huge dining room that could seat the entire family of fifteen at one large table. We lived there for about two years, before Dad got into a dispute with Mr. Laveen about a raise in rent. With the economy getting worse and grain prices falling more, Dad could not afford an increase in living expenses.

There was an exciting experience there that I recall vividly. Dad was a very easy-going man and slow to anger. But when he did get mad, he could be explosive. He was a rather small man, five feet six inches tall and one hundred and sixty pounds, but all of it was muscle. One day, Dad noticed our cattle were missing. He checked the fences and found someone had cut a hole in the pasture fence and let the cattle out. Later, a neighbor, John Sims, came over to our place. Sims claimed our cows had broken out and gotten in his corn field, so he had impounded them. Sims wanted $500.00 for the claimed damage to his corn and a reimbursement for the impounding fee. Five hundred dollars was a huge sum in those days. Sims had a very poor corn crop, so he thought collecting damage compensation for his neighbor's escaped cows would be a good deal. But his scheme backfired.

Dad told old Sims he knew it was a lie, and a big argument took place. John Sims and his sons were big men, all over six feet tall. As I've said, Dad was a short man, so the top of his head came to old Sims' shoulder. When Dad accused Sims of cutting the fence, Sims took a swing at Dad. That was a mistake. Dad easily ducked, leaped up like dynamite, and hit old Sims in the jaw, knocking him flat. Like a whirlwind, he also decked the two Sims boys, laying out all three on the ground.

Dad let Sims know that if they didn't release the cows and fix the fence, he would get the sheriff. The Sims left meekly. Dad and most of us boys followed them to their farm. There, the Sims helped us herd our cows back into our pasture and then they mended the fence.

Because of this encounter, word spread quickly throughout the neighborhood that Jentoft Johnson was not a guy to fool with. After that, to my knowledge, Dad never got in another fight, and we became good friends with the Sims family.

Another incident that I recall from this timeframe involved the linoleum in our kitchen. New linoleum had just been laid and Mother was very proud of the imprint. When Mother and Dad went to town, my brother Clarence got the bright idea to bring one of our favorite horses into the house. The horse was very tame, but when it walked through the kitchen, it left hoof marks on the new linoleum. Mother didn't notice the marks on the floor when she and Dad came home later that day, as it was dark.

The next day, she was mopping the floor as she did every day, and she noticed the marks on the floor. She was really puzzled. She returned to town a few days later and complained to the owner of the hardware store who had sold her the linoleum about the strange indentations on the kitchen floor. The hardware man came out sometime later, took a look, and was equally puzzled. Being a fair shopkeeper, he replaced the linoleum at no cost, although he did send a sample of the damaged linoleum to the manufacturer. The manufacturer reported that they were unable to solve the riddle as to how the marks had occurred. They had never seen its product experience a similar deterioration, and I thought they probably would never see it again either. Many years later, we revealed to Mother the cause of the strange marks. Dad piped up that he'd always suspected that we "innocent boys" had been responsible for the damage. In truth, very few things we did escaped Dad.

Chapter-9 -

A Near Tragedy

While at the Laveen place, we experienced a near-tragedy. Mother and Dad went to town in the old Model T, shopping for Christmas presents. A snow storm started in the early afternoon and turned into a howling blizzard. In the flat country that defined the Laveen farm, there was nothing to slow the wind. On my parent's return drive, the Model T became stuck in a big snow drift a half-mile away from the house. My parents started to walk homeward over a snow-covered road. In a short distance, Mother collapsed. She could not go farther, and was too heavy for Dad to carry, so he tried dragging her. With a quarter mile or more to go, he realized he could not pull her all the way home by her arms.

Dad covered Mother with his overcoat, left her in the road, and made his way as fast as possible to the house. He explained the problem and made it clear he needed immediate help. The boys in the family donned heavy clothes. The temperature was now well below zero. We found two of our sliding sleds and tied everyone together with long ropes, so we wouldn't get separated in the storm. Dad led us through the ever-deepening snow. We were amazed he was able to find his way back to Mother. Perhaps it was his instinct developed over years of living on the sea that led him back to Mother through a snowstorm in which we couldn't see but a few feet ahead.

We found Mother covered with snow, but, thankfully, the snow had drifted over her and kept her warm. We loaded her onto the sleds and towed her back to the house, where we took turns rubbing her feet and hands. Fortunately, by the next day, she had recovered and not sustained any permanent frostbite. She was up early baking cookies and other goodies for Christmas. Only tough old Norwegians could survive such an ordeal.

The storm let up the next day. We hitched up a team of horses to a big sled and shoveled a path to the Model T. It took most of the day to dig through the snowdrifts and pull the car home with the horses. The car didn't have glass windows, but the side curtains were down, so there wasn't much snow on the inside. The presents our parents had purchased were in good shape.

Mother thought we should all go to church and thank God for saving her, but it would be many days before we could travel from home. In our view, since God whipped up the storm, we didn't think He deserved much thanks. But Mother said a prayer anyway.

Chapter -10-

Another Move

When Mr. Laveen insisted on increasing the rent, Dad negotiated a better deal with Andy McLean, who owned a farm five miles duc south of the village of Johnson. The family moved there in 1931. The children were never happy on the McLean place. The house was small and had no insulation. The kids slept upstairs. Most were in one big room, but the two youngest girls, Opal and Gwen, had a separate room, and so did Willie.

With no heat upstairs, it would get miserable in the wintertime. We slept with our winter underwear on and sometimes sweaters, pants, and all the blankets we could pile on. There were no pajamas in those days. We slept three or more in a bed. When the one on the outside would get too cold, we would switch with the guy in the middle.

On cold nights, the bathroom pots would freeze solid. We had to pour hot water in them to empty the pee out. When we were very young, we weren't allowed to poop in the pots, and were expected to go out to the backhouse. That was a tough chore in the winter-time. Usually the boys would go in the barn, since the animals' body heat kept the building's temperature at quite a comfortable level. It didn't make much difference what we did, because it mixed with the cow and horse manure.

We had a coal stove in the living room downstairs and a wood stove in the kitchen, but very little heat leaked upstairs. Mother usually burned corn cobs in her kitchen stove. We had lots of shelled corn cobs that made great heat. When the price of corn was near zero, we would burn the unshelled corn corns. They made even better heat than the shelled cobs. In the other extreme, during the summertime, it

31

would get stifling hot upstairs. The boys would usually go out to the barn and sleep in the hay loft, where it was much cooler.

Chapter -11-

Coping with the Depression

Things got real tough on the farm. It was the Great Depression. Crop prices fell. Oats sold for as low as one or two cents per bushel. Corn prices were just as bad. Dust storms were common and destroyed much of our crops, but the dust storms in our area weren't as bad as in the Dakotas or in Oklahoma, where everything blew away and dust piled up like snow banks.

Dust storms were terrible to experience. Besides blowing away crops, fine grit would get into everything. It would sift into the house and leave a film of dust everywhere. Regardless of how much we dusted and cleaned, the dust was ever-present. When we went outside for a while or walked to school, we would put wet rags over our face. By the time we got inside, the rags would be caked with mud.

Living on a farm, we were poor but didn't know it. We had cows, pigs, and chickens, so we always had fresh milk, beef, fresh eggs, and pork or chicken every day. We raised corn, wheat, oats, barley, and flax, so there were always grains to make bread and porridge. Although the dust storms cut down on our yields, we had enough for our use. We separated cream from the milk on our cream separator to make butter, and drank the fresh whole milk. We milked the cows by hand and would often squirt milk directly into our mouths, which was fun until Dad walked in.

We usually had at least a dozen cows that we milked by hand. The boys were the milking machines. Each one of us had designated cows to milk. We also raised potatoes and had a garden where we grew radishes, turnips, carrots, cabbages, and other vegetables.

The only things purchased were staples like coffee, sugar, salt, spices, Karo-white and dark corn syrup, and occasionally white flour, although most of our bread was made from home-ground wheat. On special occasions, Mother used the white flour to make buns, cinnamon rolls, and sometimes angel food cake. At Christmas time, she needed white flour to make cookies and other Norwegian goodies.

Dad had a gasoline-powered hammer mill, a small grinder that ground wheat, corn, and oats. Oats have hulls, so they had to run through an oats huller that pulled the hulls off the oats before the grinding stage.

Mother made whole wheat bread, corn bread, and oat meal porridge, all from our own grain. She baked every day to feed her hungry family. The kids would fight over who got the end piece when the hot bread came out of the oven. Mother would allow only one of the hot breads to be cut, so the end piece was a real prize.

We usually had home-ground oatmeal, whole wheat mush, and whole wheat bread for breakfast, without knowing how healthy it was. We would have eggs, usually boiled, and whole wheat pancakes.

At times, we had a typical Norwegian dish called *laphaus* (pronounced lups-cows) for dinner. *Laphaus* was a filling stew made with chunks of meat, potatoes, carrots, and any other available vegetables. Everything was cooked until it blended together like a thick soup.

We didn't have a refrigerator, so all our meat and vegetables were canned, except for potatoes, carrots, cabbage, and a few other vegetables. "Canned" does not mean they were in metal cans. Before canning, the meat or vegetables were cooked under high heat, and then sealed in glass Mason jars.

We had a root cellar, where vegetables, particularly potatoes, carrots, radishes, parsnips, and cabbage, would be kept for long periods of time. In the winter, Dad would butcher a steer or pig. The meat would hang in a cool place to keep it fresh, or Dad would let it freeze and then cut off frozen chunks. Mother didn't like pork, so we didn't have that too often. Mother made much of our clothing. There were a lot of hand-me-downs. As one kid grew out of clothes that weren't too worn out, they were handed down to the next child. They sometimes had a lot of patches.

We had a lot of chickens, so we had eggs to sell. Mother used the egg-money to buy necessities. We separated milk with a hand-cranked separator and sold the cream that we didn't use. Mother got the cream money too. We churned all of our own butter. I still have a hand-cranked churn from the farm. If I could get pure cream, it would be fun to try to churn butter!

Mother was very careful with what she bought. Sometimes she'd buy white flour in fifty pound bags. She would also buy staples like coffee, salt, pepper, sugar, cocoa, spices, and *Karo* syrup, both white and dark. Karo syrup on warm bread was very tasty.

There was certain brand of flour that came in patterned bags that Mother preferred. This flour was very popular because women could make nice aprons, dresses for their daughters, and even pillow cases from the bags.

Sometimes, when Mother and Dad went to town, the kids would make candy. We made a delicious caramel candy from the syrup, sugar, and cocoa. We'd clean the pots and pans very carefully, so Mother wouldn't be the wiser. Mother pretended she didn't know what we'd done. But she made sure the ingredients were always there for us to use. They couldn't drag a bunch of kids along when they went to town, so for us to have a little treat of our own when they were gone was alright.

Farming was not allowed on Sundays, except for milking cows, picking eggs, and feeding the animals. No field work was allowed, except in an emergency. Willie liked to get field work done, so he might even sneak out on a Sunday. If grain was ripe and a storm was imminent, then we were allowed to harvest.

We attended the Norwegian Lutheran Church in Chokio very faithfully, until after each of us were confirmed. The first minister that I remember was Reverend Reese. He was a large man, and wore a corrugated collar like the old-time Norwegian preachers. He had a loud voice that shook the building. He preached hellfire and brimstone. If one strayed from the straight and narrow, he'd let you know in no uncertain terms that you'd burn in eternity. He'd draw a graphic picture of Satan wielding a whip as you desperately shoveled coal. If a girl got pregnant without the benefit of a husband, he would not allow her into church. Rev. Reese's God was a demanding and ferocious God. It must have been the same God that caused that terrible snow storm when we lived on the Laveen place!

Our next minister, and my confirmation teacher, Rev. Hal Rasmusson, was of a different school than Rev. Reese. He was very mild-mannered and preached of an all-loving God and a loving and forgiving Jesus. He was a handsome fellow and very popular. The ladies flocked to his sermons. His conduct was always very proper. There was never any rumor that he engaged in any misconduct. But even while men of the cloth might be tempted to partake of the forbidden fruit, there was never any such accusation against Rev. Rasmusson. His wife was a beautiful lady who was very active in the church, and they were always a very loving couple.

Chapter -12-

Church Scandal

Our church in Chokio was forced to deal with a scandal that shook the building to its very timbers. One of the elders, who were in church every Sunday, was the subject of the scandal. He was a deacon in the church and appeared straight laced, the "perfect" Christian. That is, he appeared perfect until he was charged with molesting his daughters. He had six daughters and was accused of molesting them all. One daughter, who would not succumb to his aggressions, turned him in to the sheriff. The man usually waited until a daughter was past puberty to "break her in." The mother knew about his misconduct, but was so terrified of him that she did nothing about it.

The man claimed he didn't do anything wrong. Most of the girls were timid, but they did have enough courage to testify against him. He was so arrogant, he sealed his own fate. He testified that he was only teaching them the facts of life so "some boy would not lead them astray." He had not let any of the girls go out on dates with boys.

He was sentenced to a long term in Stillwater prison. When he got out of prison, he returned to the church in Chokio and wanted to resume his role as a deacon. Despite years in prison, he had no remorse for his conduct. He was politely told he could come to church and pray for his own forgiveness, but he could not play any role in the church. From his return on, he occupied an otherwise empty pew. No one would sit next to him. Mother made sure we sat as far away from him as possible. In the end, he got the message and stopped coming.

Chapter -13-

Sundays Were Special Family Days.

Sunday after church was a special family day at our house. Bill and Orla, Oscar and Korty, with their kids, and some of the other married children, would always come over after church for Sunday dinner. Mother would cook a big dinner for twenty people or more. Orla and Korty helped by baking cakes or pies.

The Sunday dinners included roast beef, oven-baked chicken, or fried chicken, and gravy, mashed potatoes, carrots, peas, buns and pie, or cake. Sometimes we would have chocolate or tapioca pudding, or would make our own ice cream. Dad would get ice from the ice-house in town, but otherwise we had all the necessary ingredients. We had a hand-cranked ice cream freezer. The kids would take turns cranking the freezer until the ice cream was done. The one who cranked the freezer last got to lick the can.

If there were too many people to be seated at our large table, the men would be served first, and then the women. Little kids were served in the kitchen to get them out of the way. This arrangement continued for a number of years.

Chapter -14-

Kids Fun!

We made our own fun. There were quite a few neighbor kids that would come over to play. We made up our own versions of games like "ollie, ollie oxen free." This was a popular game when kids would run and hide, then the leader would call out "ollie, ollie oxen free" to call us to come in, and someone would try to catch each one as we emerged from our hiding places. In the winter, we played hockey on frozen ponds. We had strap-on skates. No shoe-skates like those today. The skates had a wooden bottom that the steel runners were attached to, or they were all-steel snap-on skates.

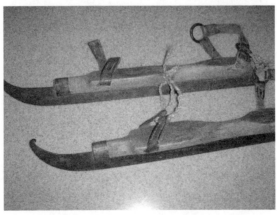

"Our home made strap-on skates"

We made our own hockey sticks from tree branches, and pucks were frozen horse turds. As we grew a little older, we played a lot of softball. We had a Johnson team with six or seven brothers that beat all other teams in the area. I was the youngest and usually played left short stop, although I doubt I ever stopped much.

"Wayne the 'short stop'all dressed up to play ball"

One happening at a ball game was not easily forgotten. One of the batters let go of his bat while swinging at the ball. The bat went flying towards the crowd that was sitting on the ground. There were no protective fences, so it was quite hazardous for onlookers. The crowds would usually stand behind the catcher or sit along the first and third base-lines. My brother-in-law, Bill Lange, a big man, was seated in front of a rather large crowd, consisting of many children. He reached up to grab the flying bat, but only caught the end of it. The bat spun around and cracked him in the head. He was laid out cold. Someone ran and got what they thought was a bucket of cold water and dumped it on him. After several splashes, Bill slowly revived, with a huge lump visible on his forehead. Despite the near tragedy, it caused quite a round of laughing when it was discovered the bucket did not contain water, but lemonade.

Chapter -15-

the Loss of Innocence

There were quite a lot of kids in the neighborhood who liked to come to our farm to play. One neighbor kid, I'll just call him John, who was about 14, taught us something that some of us had not experienced before, and probably should not have been taught. Five or six neighbor kids about my age were visiting and we were playing in the barn. I was about twelve or thirteen at the time.

Farm kids learned early about sex, since we watched animals mating all the time. We also overheard our big brothers or big neighbor boys talking about when they "did it" with girls when they went to dances or went out on dates. They would talk about which girls they knew that would "go all the way." We knew that when a girl would "go all the way," it didn't mean she was going to take a long trip. We knew those were the girls that "did it."

John had us to sit around in a circle in a game he called a "circle jerk." I leave it to the reader's imagination to figure out what that meant. We found it to be great fun, but knew it was something we were not supposed to do, or do only in secret. My brother Willie caught us one time and ended those little parties. He apparently knew John was the ringleader, since he was the biggest boy. He booted John in the rear and told him not to come back. It was more interesting when we discovered girls later. A girl, Blanche, taught me a little more about sex. She showed me the meaning of what she coined "to run my car into her garage." That was pretty much a complete loss of innocence.

Chapter -16-

Some Near -Tragedies

I had a near-tragedy when I was about twelve. I had a ladder running behind a Model T Ford, driven by my brother Willie, pretending I was a trailer while he didn't know I was there. It was a goofy and dumb thing to do. I didn't know until an instant later how dangerous it was. He was moving the car to another spot to load up some stuff. He suddenly stopped and started to back up. My leg became caught under the ladder and the angle stretched the muscles, so I could not straighten my leg. It was cocked at about a forty-five degree angle and stayed that way for months. Dad would put warm and cold compresses with weights on them, to no avail. After several months, he knew his remedies were not helping, and he took me to Doctor Cummings. There was no money for doctors, so going to a doctor was a last resort. Doctors were frequently paid with food from the farm. For people he knew that were strapped for money, Dr. Cummings accepted food products as payment for his services. The doctor worked miracles. He gave us a special cocoa butter salve to rub on many times a day, and told us to continue with the weights and try to straighten the leg.

Dad, or one of my brothers, would also pull on my leg until I would scream from the pain. After several months of this home-therapy, my leg straightened and I could walk and run without ill effects.

There were many hazards on a farm that could get us in trouble. One time, one of my brothers was after me for some kind of mischief. He started to chase me and I knew he could whip me if he caught me, but I was a good runner and was staying well ahead of him. I made the mistake of looking back to see if he was gaining on me and ran smack into a barb wire fence. The barbs hit me in the chest. I went flying backwards and crashed to the ground. Blood was flowing out of all the holes and rips made by the barbs. My brother helped me up and got me to the house. My mother stanched the flow of blood, but when she learned I had been cut by barb wire from a rusty fence, she was concerned about infection. The only medicine she had was a bottle of liniment, which she poured liberally on the open wounds. I'm sure my howling could be heard for miles. Her remedy was effective, since I healed up quite well with no infection. If I look closely, I can still see some of the scars.

On another occasion, I made a little mistake. I was about thirteen at the time. My brother Roy, who was about four years older than I, had an old Buick. The seats were all rotten, so he had pulled them out and replaced with a couple of wooden boxes. He was out working in a field where I didn't think he could see me, so I decided to take it for a little ride. I started it up and my two younger sisters came running, because they wanted a ride. I only knew one speed, which involved the accelerator going to the floor. As I came to a tee in the road, I was going much too fast to make it around the corner. As I tried to turn, I slid off the box and was lying on the floor trying to steer. The car went down into a sloping ditch that was quite muddy and filled with grass. The car went through the ditch into a field, back through the ditch, and back up on the road, then lost its speed and rolled to a stop. I carefully and slowly drove it back to the farm. The girls were in the still intact back seat. They had been bounced around, but weren't hurt except for a few bruises. After they got over the scare, they both started laughing.

When Roy returned from the field that evening, he saw his car splattered with mud, and grass hanging from the underside. He demanded to know who was driving and what had happened. I lost my ability to talk, but one of my sisters, who had gotten over her fright, blurted out, "Wayne was like a race track driver, we really had a fun ride." That was all Roy needed to hear. He tore into me and bruised me more than I had gotten bruised during the ride. I didn't try to drive any of his cars without his permission for a long time after that.

When Dad came in from the field, he saw me bruised, with a bloody nose, and blood on my front, he asked me what happened. I was going to tell him I fell out of a wagon, but I knew that wouldn't sell, because he could spot a lie for a mile away. I told him Roy beat me up. He had seen the car, so he probably had a good idea why, but he asked me why. I told him what I did. His only comment was, "I guess you have learned how not to drive a car." It was a lesson I remembered. He did talk to Roy and told him if there was any discipline to be handed out, "Pa will take care of it— and no beating up other kids." He told me to go down to the water tank to wash off the blood on my face and shirt, and to stay out in the sun until my shirt had dried. He didn't want Mother to see what happened and get all excited.

One other time, we were playing hide and seek and one of the kids had climbed up in a full hay rack in front of the barn and dug himself down into the hay. About that time, one of the men, unaware that there was a kid in the hay, dropped the big grappling hayfork that ran on a rope through the hay loft door pulley. A long rope ran out to a team of horses, which were used to pull the hay-filled fork up to the loft. Without anyone the wiser, the kid was in the bundle of hay being hoisted up to the loft. Fortunately, when they opened the fork to drop the hay, the kid came tumbling out, none the worse for wear. It did scare him a bit, for he crapped and peed in his pants. I don't recall who the kid was, but it wasn't me.

Chapter -17-

A Near-Fatal Escapade

My brother Ed and I were involved in an escapade that was almost fatal. We were out in the pig yard, watching the boar pig mate with a sow. The boar was a big fellow, at least three hundred to four hundred pounds. We thought he had been doing it long enough, so I took a board and cracked him on the rear. He let out a roar and climbed off. He was one mad boar pig. We took off in a run for the fence. The boar stumbled when he got off the sow and fell down, which was lucky for us, so we had a head start. We barely made it over the fence before he was nipping at our heels. He started to butt against the fence and we were sure he'd get through, so we raced as fast as we could to the nearest building, which was a corn crib about twenty or thirty yards away. He did get through the fence, somewhat bloodied, and headed after us, roaring wildly.

The corn crib was a small building, about eight by twelve or fourteen feet. It was built out of heavy wooden boards, with about an inch of spare space between each board to let air in so the corncobs would dry. It was empty at the time.

We barely got the door shut before the big boar was right there, butting against the door. When he couldn't break it in, he went around the crib, butting at the sides, foaming and roaring as he went. He finally gave up, but lay down right in front of the door. Whenever we would move, he would let out a snort. We were trapped. We were in the corn crib for about four hours, and when some of the older boys came in from the fields to do chores, someone spied the boar lying in front of the crib, and realized we were inside. They managed to get the boar back into the pig yard, and fixed the fence.

Dad gave us a lecture on the dangers of interrupting animals while they were mating. He didn't say if that applied to humans too, but we were learning!

Chapter -18-

A Father's Character

When the rural school was being used for an election in 1932, Dad had an experience that demonstrated how determined he could be. When he and Mother came to vote, a fellow by the name of Ginty, who was an election judge, denied them the right to vote. He claimed they were not citizens. Ginty had a first name, but everyone just called him Old Ginty. He was a grizzled and stooped older man, who always looked like he needed a shave, and had a snooze stain on his chin.

Although Dad and Mother both claimed they were citizens, Ginty insisted they could not vote. Voting to Dad was an important part of being an American, and he always voted at every election. Dad had taken some of us kids along so we could learn about the importance of voting. Mother wanted to go home without an argument, but Dad told her to stay. He jumped in his old Model T and raced home to get his citizenship certificate. When he returned with the certificate proving they were naturalized citizens, the other judges agreed Mother and Dad were entitled to vote.

Dad demanded that Ginty apologize for questioning their status as citizens. Ginty refused. Dad told Ginty he did not think Ginty was a citizen since he came from Ireland. Ginty always bragged about his Irish heritage, so Dad demanded Ginty produce his citizenship papers. Ginty insisted he was born in the United States. Dad demanded Ginty go get his birth certificate proving he was a U.S. citizen, or he couldn't serve as an election judge. Ginty said he didn't have a birth certificate at his home, for he had no reason to have it there.

The other judges told Ginty he could no longer serve as an election judge. I don't know if the judges had that right, but old Ginty stormed out. Needless to say, Dad was no friend of his after that experience.

Chapter -19-
School Discipline

Ginty was also on the school board, and through that, he tried to get even with Dad by trying to have all us kids thrown out of school. The school, district number thirty-five, was a one-room school house. In those days, people who wanted to be teachers could, after high school graduation, go to a higher education school called Normal School for one year to become a teacher. The teacher was a young girl just out of Normal School and this was her first teaching job.

The kids learned early that the new teacher lacked discipline abilities. Some of the older kids became quite unruly and disruptive in class. Some even brought corn kernels or spit balls to school and shot at each other and the teacher, using sling shots. The spit balls were pieces of chewed paper soaked with spit until they could be rolled into little balls like marbles, which made great sling shot ammunition. Sling shots were made from a forked branch with half-inch-wide rubber bands stretched between the fork, with a leather pouch in the middle to hold the ammunition. The rubber bands were usually made out of old inner tubes from cars, and were about a foot long. The leather tongue from old shoes made a perfect pouch. Sometimes the shoes were not that old and it was a little difficult to explain how the tongue could break off and disappear.

One time, some mischievous kids locked the young teacher in the school. The school had a porch with a trap door that opened onto a basement. By opening the trap door, the entrance to the school was blocked so she couldn't get out. When all the kids were out of the school at the end of the day, the mischievous kids opened the trap door, blocking the entrance. I know who the "mischievous kids" were, but I am not telling.

The school didn't have any lights, so when the sun went down, the poor girl had to sit in the dark. Sometimes she would stay after school to correct papers and clean up the mess, but those activities never went that late. Late at night, when she didn't return to the place where she was rooming, they went to look for her, and brought her home. She was so upset, she could not teach the next day.

The school board held an investigation, but nobody, not even the littlest kids, would reveal the identities of the miscreants. Ginty insisted it was obviously the Johnson kids and they should all be thrown out of school, permanently. Other board members said there was no proof as to who was causing all the trouble, so they could not agree with Ginty. Ginty resigned from the school board which didn't hurt anyone's feelings.

A few days later, the county superintendent got word of the disruptive behavior and made a surprise visit. He stepped into the room, which was littered with corn kernels and spit balls. No one would admit to the identity of the culprits. He removed the teacher immediately, sent all the kids home, and said a new teacher would be sent in, one who could control unruly kids. That didn't sound good to us.

A few days later, he called the school back in session and introduced the new teacher. Her name was Miss Earrion. She was about six feet tall and skinny as a rail. Her hair was pulled back in a bun, and her smile could crack ice. She stood at her desk, tapping a big round stick. We all knew there was going to be a change.

My brother, Roy, thought he would test her. He made some smart comment, which was a mistake. Miss Earrion picked up a big dictionary and walked casually down the aisle until she got to Roy. She smiled one of her "sweet" smiles, and then clobbered him with the book, knocking him out of the seat. He landed on the floor, very dazed. Too bad teachers don't have that same right to discipline today. The rest of the school year went without any discipline problems. Although a tough disciplinarian, she was an excellent teacher.

The building had one classroom, and an extra room that served as a library and reading room. When Miss Earrion taught the upper grades, she encouraged kids in the lower grades to listen to the lessons, or sometimes she would send kids to the library to study.

We always carried our lunch to school in little tin boxes. In the winter, the teacher suggested we bring potatoes and bake them in the ash pit of the stove, so that we could have something hot. The school was heated by a big round stove that sat in one corner. By putting the potatoes in the ash pit when we got to school in the morning, they would be nicely baked and hot by lunch time. She usually had butter and salt handy.

The school was about two miles from our house. We walked to school every day in a group, except when it was pouring rain, freezing cold, or snowing. Then Dad would haul us to school in the lumber wagon. The wagon had high sides, so some type of cover, usually a blanket or tarp, could be put over the top. He would sit on a seat up front, driving the horses. We had a Model T, but couldn't use the gas unless absolutely necessary. When the road conditions permitted, and weather was bad, Dad would pile us all in the Model T to take us to school.

Sometimes bad things would happen that weren't supposed to happen. One of the girls in the eighth grade got pregnant. She was about fourteen. We called it "knocked up." It was rumored that their hired man was the father. He was quite an old guy, but he disappeared quickly when the sheriff came out, so no one really knew the scoundrel who had caused her condition. Some suspected her father, but she would not tell.

When her belly started to grow, it was obvious that she was pregnant, and she had to leave school. In those days, it was a not permitted for a pregnant girl to attend school, because she could "contaminate" others. Since she could not attend school, her father had her herding cows. She would frequently pass by the school. Kids could be very cruel. When they saw her during recess, some would run out and make nasty comments about her. They would poke her in the stomach and ask her if she swallowed some watermelon seeds or ate too much oats. She was really a very nice girl, and we felt sorry for her, so some of us would go out, chase the nasty kids away, and talk to her. The welfare department made her give the baby away. Some years later she married a neighbor farmer. They became a very devoted couple, but she was not able to have any more children.

Chapter -20-

A Kid's Remembrances.

I got a job during the summer, when my brother-in-law, Bill Lange had me come to his placc to herd cows. I would bring the cows out to the ditches along the road, where there was nice, lush grass. I was scared to death of the bull. I would throw rocks at him to keep him at a distance. One time when I got the cows into the pasture, the bull came up and snorted at me, through the fence. I knew that if he ever got through the fence, I'd be a goner. I hid in the corn field next to the pasture until Bill came and found me.   For a kid who was about thirteen, it was a scary job.

Bill had a big barn with a nice loft. He would take the hay out of the loft and have barn dances. The hay made the floor nice and slick for dancing. The dance would draw big crowds, since he hired good bands. There was a neighbor that furnished the potent illegal liquor known as moonshine, for about twenty-five cents a quart. They would mix it with it with Orange Crush that he sold for ten cents a bottle, while it cost him less than that since he bought it by the case. I was curious to know what it tasted like. One time Bill mixed up a drink and told me to drink it down fast. I did, but it came right back up. I couldn't understand how people could drink that horrible stuff and still laugh and have fun. I did learn a little later.

I was staying at Bill's when my niece, Doris, was born. I was sent to a neighbor about half mile away, who had a phone to call the doctor. When the doctor arrived, I was sent out to the barn until the baby was born. Apparently it was something I was not supposed to see. Even at that young age, I knew what it was about. I had seen calves, pigs, and other animals being born, and imagined this could not be much different. I did wonder how a big baby could get out of that little crack.

We didn't have a bathroom in our house. Everyone took a bath in a big square washtub. The smallest kid was bathed first, and then up the line it went. The water in the tub would get a little ripe after washing a few bodies. Mother would change it after a few baths, but it was quite a chore to go out to the well to get water and then heat it.

Chapter -21-

Brother Willie's "Romance"

My brother, Willie, had quite an experience when we lived at the McLean place. He became very interested in a neighbor girl who lived about six miles away. One night he took her to a dance or show, in Graceville, about twenty miles from the girl's farm. Going home, he had a flat tire on the old Model T, but didn't have a spare. Since it was after midnight, there were no service stations or garages open where he could get the tire fixed. So he drove on the flat until that tire finally came off. He continued driving on the rim until that came off. It was slow going, but he continued until the frame of the wheel came off. Then he was driving only on the spokes. About all he could make were a couple of miles per hour jolting along on the spokes, until each broke off almost down to the hub.

It was probably four in the morning when they finally got to the girl's place. According to Willie, as he drove into the yard, the girl's mother, who was a big dragon and meaner than a wild boar pig, came tearing out of the house, screaming like a banshee. Besides being mean, she was homelier than a mud fence and about one hundred fifty pounds overweight. It was said that, from five miles away, she could scare the neighbor's cattle into a stampede. Her husband was a very nice guy, but always looked like he was about to be led away to the gas chamber.

She threatened to kill Willie if he ever came within ten miles of her "virginal" daughter. What the old lady didn't know, or at least pretended she didn't know, was that her virginal daughter was well-known to have spent more time in the back seat of a car than she did in the front. She had a reputation of having very loose elastic in her drawers. In other words, her underpants slipped off rather easily. Whether they came off for Willie, we will never know, although he walked around for several days with a big grin on his face.

He was not able to drive the car out of the yard. The old Model T sat on the remaining hub and refused to go any further. Willie had to walk home the six or so miles, and arrived in the late morning hours. He and Dad and some of the boys got our truck and went to the garage in Johnson, to get a wheel.

When we went to the girl's farm to replace the wheel, the old lady stood on the porch, shaking her fist and making dire threats in language that would embarrass a lumberjack. She used words that we didn't know had been invented. She also described vividly what she would do with a certain part of Willie's anatomy if she ever caught him near her daughter.

Needless to say, Willie never courted that "sweet young thing" again. If he saw her at a dance or tavern, he would leave in a hurry. He knew the old lady was capable of carrying out her threats. That experience probably convinced him to be a bachelor for the rest of his life. Although he frequently enjoyed the company of other women, he was very careful to not let anyone become too permanent, and he made sure they didn't have a battle-ax for a mother.

Chapter -22-

More Depression Experiences

My brother Roy had gone off to the Civilian Conservation Corps (CCC) sometime during the Depression. The CCC had been organized by President Roosevelt to relieve some of the hardship of the Depression. Roy went to a camp up north in Two Harbors, Minnesota. The camps were run by army officers, and the men built all types of public works, although many were teenage boys. They built road, bridges, and all sorts of public buildings. The camp workers were paid $30.00 per month each. Twenty-five dollars was sent to the parents and each guy at the camp was allowed to keep $5.00 to spend for personal things. They could buy a glass of beer for a nickel. Liquor became legal after Roosevelt took office and repealed the National Prohibition Act at the end of 1933. Tobacco for cigarettes was very cheap. Most sacks of tobacco like Bull Durham or cans like Prince Albert and Velvet, came with cigarette paper, so the guys that were, or wanted to be, smokers, learned to roll their own. A six month enlistment was mandatory, but some re-enrolled for two years because they couldn't get a job on the outside that paid better. They also got free room and board, free uniforms medical and dental care so it was quite a profitable occupation for them during the Depression.

Two of my brothers, Roald and Myron, had heard of opportunities in Iowa for work. The corn crops there had survived the drought and sand storms, and they were good crops. Iowa farmers were looking for men to pick the corn. The technique of picking ripe corn involved horses pulling wagons between the cornrows. The wagons had a high board on the right side, called a bang board. It was designed so that the picker would not throw the cobs against the bang board so they would fall into the wagon and not go over the wagon.

The picker, or husker, wore a glove on his left hand, with a flat spike about one half inch wide and three to four inches long with a hook sewed into the glove. He would pull the ripe corn ear off the stalk, rip the husk off with his right hand against the spike on his left hand, and throw the clean cob of corn into the wagon in one fluid motion.

A good husker could pick several hundred bushels worth of corn a day. Roald was one of the best, and Myron was close behind. Their farmers actually paid them a premium for the amount of corn they picked in a day. They were paid about a penny per bushel. Top huskers could make up to $2.00 per day. Both Roald and Myron would usually exceed that. If they picked more than two hundred bushels, they were paid a little extra.

Both Roald and Myron met lovely girls whom they married and remained with in Iowa. Myron's bride was only about sixteen when they met. Althea was a lovely girl and we all loved her. Roald's bride was a little older but equally lovely. Althea and Margie became good friends of the family, and a source of joy. Mother and Dad were delighted with both of them, and, of course, their children.

Floyd married Margaret Leuthard some years later, I believe in 1940. She was a local girl who lived on a farm near Chokio. Floyd was a farmer and some years later had a repair garage in Chokio. He was a good mechanic and could fix almost anything. He and Margaret had six really nice children, four boys and two girls. Mother and Dad had no favorites among the host of grandchildren, as they were all favorites. The Johnson boys and girls all had quite prolifically sizeable families, but none as large as my parent's brood.

We lived on the McLean farm until 1934. Andy McLean lived in Graceville about fifteen miles from the farm. He was a bachelor and was always impeccably dressed in a black suit, white shirt, black tie, and a black hat. He would come out to the farm on a regular basis to see if we were doing things right. During harvest, he would come out every day and stand on top of the threshing machine and count the loads of grain. He would make sure he got his share, because we were on a share-crop basis for rent. It really irked my Dad that anyone would question his honesty.

When times started to get better, McLean decided to raise the rent. There were plenty of good farms for rent, since so many farmers had lost their farms to mortgage companies. Insurance companies bought up many of these distressed farms, one of which we moved to.

Dad found a nice farm a few miles northeast of Johnson, owned by the Aetna Insurance Company, which gave him a good deal. It was a nice house with a big barn and lots of outbuildings, including a nice two-holer not far from the house.

We kids went to school in Johnson, which was about a three-mile walk. The Johnson school was a two-room schoolhouse. The upper grades were in the top level and the lower grades on the bottom level. I graduated from the eighth grade from that school. Up until that time, none of my brothers and sisters had gone to high school. Since we lived in rural areas where there were no school bus services, it was difficult to go to high school. Besides, the kids were needed to help on the farm.

Chapter -23-

Family Farming

We were required, even when very young, to help with farming and do chores. We usually had a dozen or more cows to milk every morning before going to school, besides feeding all the animals, cleaning out the barn, picking eggs, and other chores. Cleaning the horse and cow manure from the barn wasn't too bad. We hated cleaning the pigpen and chicken coop because the pig and chicken shit stunk so badly.

While quite young, around twelve or thirteen, we learned to drive horses, and later on run tractors, in order to do field work. During harvest, horse-drawn binders or tractors cut the grain. The binders would cut, bind, and tie the grain into bundles with twine, and drop them out in rows. We had to follow along, pick up the bundles, and put them into shocks. That is, stacks of six to eight bundles in a pyramid, with the butts on the ground and the grain at the top. Nowadays, powered combines do all that work.

Prisoners at the Stillwater State Prison made the twine and some machinery. It kept the prisoners occupied and taught them how to do some productive work. They did produce good machinery, which the state sold to farmers at a reasonable price. Too bad the state doesn't promote the same type of work ethnic training instead of coddling them and letting them sit around watching television.

We hated shocking barley or bearded wheat. The barley and wheat grain had sharp bristles that seemed to get into or under our clothes and would itch terribly. The shocks would be picked up during threshing season and hauled to the threshing machine in wagons, called hayracks. A hayrack had an open bed with boarded ends. In addition to the guy driving the hayrack, an extra person, called a spike pitcher, would walk from hayrack to hayrack and help load the bundles. Spike pitching was a tough job since the workers didn't get much rest with the continuous hayrack loading.

I learned how to drive a truck when I was about thirteen or fourteen. It was my job to haul the threshed grain to the grain bins at home or to the elevator in town. The elevator was a storage place that bought grain. The loads hauled to our granary had to be shoveled off by hand. It was hard work for a young kid. At the elevator, the loads were dumped off by raising the front of the truck with a lift raising the front of the truck with a lift dumped off the loads.

On one occasion, I drove a little too far towards the shoulder of the dirt road, and the truck tipped over, with a load of wheat in it. They had to shut down the threshing machine while the crew came over to pick up the truck and reload the wheat. Dad stood on the road to make sure we picked up every kernel that we could with shovels and buckets. Needless to say, I was taken off truck-driving duty, and sent out as a spike pitcher! That was no fun.

Threshing was an interesting job. We had our own threshing machine, a Woods Brothers thresher. We threshed not only our own grain, but also that of a number of neighbors. They all got together for the threshing bees. The ladies would cook huge lunches and bring them out to the fields. There was a lot of neighborly friendship and story-telling during rest periods. It was hard work but a fun time. Usually, on the last day of threshing, Dad would bring out some beer, although he normally did not approve of drinking.

My brother Willie ran the Woods Brothers threshing machine that was powered on a long belt by a Fordson or John Deere tractor. He would stand on top and yell at us if we didn't throw in the bundles properly. We liked to quit early on Saturdays, because we liked to go to the town dances, but Willie usually would insist on threshing until dark like he did on other days.

We figured out that if we threw a lot of crosswise bundles in the feeder, it would break off some of the teeth that dragged in the bundles, and jam the thresher. Willie would go wild. We tried to tell him we didn't do it purposefully, but he never believed a word we said. It would usually take Willie several hours to dig out the jammed bundles and fix the teeth. By the time he got it fixed, it would be dark and the rest of us would be long gone. After a few of those incidents, Willie began stopping early on Saturdays.

We wanted to quit early enough in order to go home, do the chores, and bathe, before going to town. In the summer time, we had devised a nice way to take a shower. We had no running water then, so we couldn't shower inside. We built a platform that sat on legs about seven feet above the ground. We put a fifty-gallon barrel filed with water on top of the platform. During the day, the sun heated the water nicely. We fixed up a sprinkler system that would turn the water on with the twist of a valve. It worked great. When I was in China during the war, we fixed up a similar system at some of the airfields.

We gave Willie the nickname "Doc," which most people called him for most of his life. He would usually preface a comment with "in my opinion," so some smart-aleck brother named him "Opinion Doc." The "opinion" part didn't last long, but the name "Doc" stuck. He didn't mind being called Doc, but he always signed his name Willie.

Corn harvesting was another difficult job. Some of the corn was cut for animal feed. A corn binder was pulled down the corn rows, cutting the corn stocks, and we would bind them into large bundles and tie them with twine in a process similar to grain harvesting.

The corn bundles were much bigger and heavier than grain bundles. We would stack them up in shocks and let them stand in the field until they were needed to feed the cows. When winter set in, the shocks would freeze to the ground and be covered with snow. It was a chore to break one loose, put it in a wagon, and haul it home. We tried to get the corn bundles stacked in the yard before winter, but often didn't make it before the snowstorms started. There was also the problem of finding storage for the corn bundles far enough from the fenced-in animals, so they couldn't get at the stack.

As I grew older, I was expected to do more farm work, but I knew farming was not for me. I was determined to go to high school, but didn't know how I could get to do that.

Chapter -24-

School Days & Fun Times.

After I graduated from the eighth grade, I started planning how I could go to high school. The nearest high school was in Chokio, about six miles away, and there was no bus service in that area at that time. My sister, Korty, had started high school in Chokio when she was about seventeen. She lived in Chokio and did housekeeping for a lady for her room and board. Unfortunately, she became pregnant and had to drop out of school. The daddy of her baby, Oscar Lange, with Dad's encouragement, had married her. Oscar was the brother of Bill Lange, who was married to my sister Orla.

Since I had pretty good grades through primary school, I desperately wanted to go to high school. I did not want to be a farmer. Korty helped me out, and convinced my folks that I should attend high school. She agreed I should come live with her and her husband, Oscar Lange, at their farm, which was within walking distance of the Chokio High School.

I agreed to do his farm chores for my room and board. My job was to milk about a dozen cows every morning before I went to school and milk them again in the evening. Oscar would usually feed the animals, pick the eggs, and do other chores. If he went somewhere, I would do that too.

My folks couldn't really give me any money, except for a dime now and then. I applied for and was granted a benefit from the Youth Conservation Program. It was organized by President Roosevelt as one of his programs to improve the economy and help poor students get an education.

Under the government program, I had to work in the school library for certain periods, and was paid $9.00 a month. That was almost enough to buy some nice clothes from Sears Roebuck or Montgomery Ward. I paid seven dollars for the first suit that I bought, on sale, from Sears Roebuck. I was the best-dressed guy in my class and thought I was a real dude. I even bought a very nice hat for twenty-five cents.

I would also work some evenings and weekends at the local Red Owl Grocery Store. I was paid ten cents an hour and a dollar per day on Saturdays. Occasionally, my brother-in-law, Oscar, would give me a little money to go to a dance. Oscar was a great guy and always treated me well. For the four years I lived at his and Korty's house, he acted like a very devoted father.

Some of the other boys and I figured out an economical way we could go to dances. One guy would go in and pay the twenty or twenty-five cent entry fee and get an ink stamp on his hand. He would then go outside, and by licking his hand he could transfer a legitimate stamp to some of the other guys, so they could get into the dance. The dance halls were usually not well lit, so even a smeared stamp would get us in. The guy at the door probably knew what we were doing, but didn't care, and probably knew that some kids didn't have much money. We would then pool our money and could buy beer or some cheap liquor. Besides the dancing, there was always time for a little "romancing" in the backseat of a car!

One of the favorite dance spots was in Alberta, a little town about six miles from Chokio. They usually had dances on Friday or Saturday nights. It was only four miles from Oscar's farm, so I could walk home if things didn't turn out right or I lost my ride. These dances were great places to meet eager young girls. One time, when I was engaged in some interesting frivolities with a particularly eager young lady, my brother Floyd sort of caught us in the act. He demanded we stop whatever we were doing. Sure, that was easy!

Floyd was a rather conservative guy and watched over the younger boys with the hope that he could keep us out of some youthful indiscretions. He made sure we didn't drink too much. He would have two beers at the most and make sure we got home safely. It was difficult to escape his watchful eye. Later, when he had four sons of his own, he probably had the same concerns and discipline problems with what some referred to as "the Johnson hot blood," which ran deep. Some of them probably didn't inherit his strict habit, of limiting himself to two beers.

Chapter -25-

Learning to Fly

When I was sixteen and a junior in high school, I became friends with Archie Burmeister. He lived on a farm a mile west of Chokio, and had an airplane. He gave me a ride in his plane, and I was hooked on aviation. I wanted to learn to fly. He agreed that if I would do some chores for him and milk his cows, he would give me flying lessons. His airplane was an old Curtiss-Robin, which was the same type that Lindberg flew on the mail routes.

When weather permitted, I would run to his place after school and he would give me a flying lesson. I would milk his cows and then run to Oscar's to milk his cows. Oscar didn't care if I milked his cows a little late, because he knew how interested I was in flying.

I didn't tell my folks about the airplane lessons. I didn't think they would approve my frittering away time and money on something that frivolous. Although I think Dad knew, for he usually knew about most everything we did, good or bad, he never said anything about it, until many years later. When I came home after the war, he just casually mentioned that it was a good thing that I had learned how to fly at an early age, so that I had the skills to survive through the war.

Archie was a self-taught pilot who taught himself how to fly by reading a lot of books and manuals. He had gone to South Dakota and bought the plane from a farmer near Sioux Falls, South Dakota. The farmer took Archie up and showed him how to land the plane, and Archie flew it home.

After about six hours of instruction, Archie allowed me to solo, which meant I flew the plane alone. It was on my sixteenth birthday, July 8, 1937. What a thrill that was. Archie stood out in the field and watched me land. After I made three landings, he clapped both hands together and waved me in to park the plane.

Wayne Johnson flying the Curtiss-Robin 8 July,1937. The plane had a 90 HP Curtiss OX-5 engine, cruise at 85 MPH and land at 47

After that, Archie and I went into Chokio to the pool hall. He bought beer for the house, including me, and bragged about his new pilot. The guy who ran the pool hall, Mr. Wagner, didn't care how young we were as long as we could pay for the beer that sold for a nickel a glass, and behave properly. If we got a little carried away, he would escort us out the back door and probably give us a little twist on the ear or a little boot in the rear. That would be all forgotten by the next time we came around. If we swept the place, he would let some of us play pool for free.

There were some other kids who took flying lessons, but Archie didn't want me to tell them about me doing farm chores for lessons. He expected them to pay for their lessons, because he said their dads could afford to pay. He charged just to cover the gas and oil.

Chapter -26-

A Little Religion and a Little Fun

That summer, after my solo, I went home to help on the farm. I was also required to attend confirmation classes several times a week at the Chokio Norwegian Lutheran Church, which our family attended. If Dad or my brothers were busy and couldn't take me in, I would walk the six miles to attend the classes. The minister insisted that we attend every class, or he would require extra attendance before we could be confirmed. The Rev. Hal Rasmussen was a handsome fellow. Some said that he was much too good-looking to be a preacher, as the women flocked to his sermons.

It was about this time that I started going in with my brothers on Saturday night to a roadhouse called Ritters, on the outskirts of Graceville. My older brothers were quite conservative. It was the middle bunch that kicked up their heels a bit. The middle bunch consisted of Clarence, Roy, Arnold, and Wayne. Ed was three years younger than I, so he didn't join the more "liberal" brothers until a little later. Ritters held dances, allowed people to bring liquor, and sold the mixes. Ritter also served beer, excellent hamburgers, and steaks, all for very cheap prices. It was a very popular place and attracted people from a large area. He usually stayed open as long as anyone wanted to stay, which was sometimes until four in the morning, particularly on Friday and Saturday nights.

Mother did not think highly of the place. She referred to any place that allowed liquor, dancing, and other types of "bad things," as *pigpens*, and liquor was known as *poison*. She would caution us to drink lemonade instead of *poison*, if we went out with the *bad boys* to the *pig pen*. We tried to follow that advice by only drinking lemonade. But to take the tartness out of the lemon, we would add a little gin or vodka or even moonshine. I only drink lemonade to this day, with a tad of Bombay or Sapphire Gin to cut down the sweetness. If you went into the local place of conviviality in Beaver Bay and ordered lemonade, you would be served a drink consisting of gin, 7-up, and a squeeze of lime. Very refreshing, but don't have too many! One time a few years ago, my two older sisters, Orla and Korty, came to visit at our home in Beaver Bay. It was an unusually hot day, and they asked if they could have some lemonade. The kind they drank was pure lemonade, as they did not usually drink any alcoholic beverages. But I mixed one of my special lemonades. After several glasses, they were soon giggling and laughing. Then one said, "I'll bet you put something in that lemonade, because I don't feel like this after drinking my own." Of course, I would not admit to any of that skullduggery.

In the early days, when we went out for a night, most guys wore freshly-ironed white shirts. Our younger sisters' job was to iron the shirts. They hated it, because they were too young to go out. Proper young girls were not allowed to go out to nightclubs.

Every time we went out, Mother would worry that we would become bad boys, because she thought our guy friends were really *darlig gutt* (bad boys). Dad would shake his head and tell her *dount plage* (don't worry), and that we would be all right.

The backseats of the cars in Ritters' parking lot, which was very dark, were well-occupied during the evening. When a couple would sneak out, we could tell who was going to "do it." Other curious customers would sneak out, too, and peak in the car windows. Quite a show at times!

Dad had only two instructions: The guy that drove the car was not to drink any beer or liquor. We were not to come home and let our mother see that we had been drinking. It was always a privilege to drive the car, so we would usually draw straws to see who got to drive. We did follow his instruction fairly well.

He had replaced the Model T with a beautiful, 1934 used Chevrolet. Although it was used, it looked brand new. It was tan, with a lot of chrome, including chrome covers for the spare tires on the front fenders. One time we went down to Ortonville with the car, to a roller-skating rink. Ortonville was about thirty-five miles from our house, but was the only nearby place with a good roller-skating rink.

Roller-skating was a great pastime in those days. On one occasion, Clarence won the right to drive, so was not supposed to drink any beer or booze. The roller-skating rink had a beer bar, and also sold mix for those who had jugs outside. Liquor bottles were not permitted inside. There were always crowd-control monitors on the floor, and they would evict anyone who became too rambunctious.

Clarence broke the rule and drank quite a bit of beer. After every few rounds around the rink, he would stop for a beer. He appeared to handle it quite well, and did not attract the attention of the peace-keepers. When we were ready to go home, he claimed he was quite sober and would have no problem driving. But he did have a bit of a problem. All of us fell asleep, including our trusty driver.

About halfway home, Clarence fell asleep and went off the road, into a deep ditch filled with water. We all suddenly woke up from water splashing over the car. It came up to the windows, which we climbed through to get out. We tried pushing the car out of the ditch, but that didn't work. We knew we were in bad trouble. The only way to get the car out of the ditch was to get a tractor or horses. Some of us, soaking wet, walked to the nearest farmyard a half mile away, and got the farmer out of bed. We told him our sad tale.

He was a good guy and got his tractor out and pulled the car out of the ditch. He refused to take any money, although we didn't have much, for he realized we would be in plenty of trouble when we got home. He knew Dad very well and knew he would not be very pleased about what had happened to his nice car.

Amazingly, the car started right up and we drove on home. It was real dark in our yard, as we didn't have electric lights yet. We did not notice the dirty watermark all around the car at window height. We thought we would be safe, since the car ran so well. When Dad came out in the morning to get the car ready for church, he knew immediately that the car had been in deep water. He checked the oil and found it contained water. He got Clarence out to tell him what happened. Clarence didn't admit he had been drinking beer, but I'm sure Dad could smell it. Clarence did admit that he fell asleep because he was tired from roller-skating. He also stated that there was a little water in the ditch, a partly true admission.

Dad made him get under the car and take the oil plug out. Many gallons of water flowed out, mixed with the oil. Fortunately, driving with the water in the oil hadn't damaged the motor.

The whole bunch of kids who had been in the car were routed out of bed, only briefly gotten into, so we could wash the car in time for church. Clarence was banned from driving the car for several months. Again, there was a stern injunction against drinking and driving. Dad let us know we would all be without a car if that happened again. From then on, we made sure the designated driver did not drink anything intoxicating before driving.

Another rule he had was that, regardless how late we stayed out at night or what condition we were in, we were expected to get out of bed and get to work shortly after sunup. Dad was always the first up in up in the morning. He would make coffee and always, during their entire married life, served Mother Coffee in bed. There aren't many guys like that anymore. Then he would routinely get us out of bed. He would holler each of our names several times: Villy, Roald, Floyd, Myron, Clarence, Roy, Arnold, Wayne, and Edgar. As boys left home, their names were dropped from the get-up call.

Dad seldom swore, but if we still weren't up by the second or third call, he would yell one more time, in Norwegian. "Du bedre fa esel ute fra seng," meaning, "You better get your ass out of bed." Then we knew we better jump out of bed in a hurry.

Cartoon by Holdgrafer. Courtesy of the *Chokio Review*

"Getting out of bed into a freezing room was tough"

We would usually hear Mother scolding him, "Jentoft sadan sprak." Meaning, "Jentoft, such language." We would try tricking him by dropping shoes on the floor to make it sound like we were dressing, so we could lie in bed a little longer, but he caught onto that in a hurry.

At our farm near the village of Johnson, we had a very nice neighbor that lived within a quarter mile. Vern Ronning was a really nice guy and we all became great friends. If he wanted to go to town and be home late, we would go over and milk his cows and do other chores for him. There were usually tasty cookies on the table for us.

One time he and Doc went to town to sell some scrap iron that we had picked up from both our farms. They got such a good price that they thought they would celebrate a little, which turned into a little too much. Neither was accustomed to drinking much, so their little celebration really affected them. When they got to our place, both staggered across the yard to the barn.

Mother was looking out the window and was really shocked when she saw them. She couldn't believe her Willie ever drank *poison*. She screamed to Dad, "*Hellid Gud, han er drukken!*" "Holy God, he is drunk." When Mother got a little excited, she would switch to Norwegian. Willie stayed out in the barn the rest of the afternoon, and milked some cows and drank a lot of fresh, warm milk, which he threw up repeatedly. He finally, sheepishly, came in for supper. Mother didn't say a word to him, and piled a bunch of food on his plate and told him to eat. He turned a little green and had to leave the table suddenly. He never came home in that condition again.

One summer, probably near the end of the Depression, my brother Roy talked me into a crazy adventure. We had some cousins out in Montana who he said could probably get us some good jobs. We hopped on a freight train in Graceville that took us to Fargo, North Dakota, where we jumped on another freight that took us to Guilford, Montana. There were still a lot of bums and hobos riding the freights, looking for work, so the railroad cops were quite reasonable and didn't bother us too much. At some stations, we hid from some really tough and mean railroad cops. They carried big Billy clubs and would really beat on guys trying to climb on the trains.

When we got to our cousins' farm, we found things tougher there than at home, so we jumped back on the first freights. I was happy to get back, for I was very uncomfortable riding the train with all the hobos. I was the youngest guy riding the rails, and always stayed close to Roy, who would challenge anybody threatening. Most were harmless but desperate men, looking for work anywhere they could find it.

In 1939, we moved from the farm near Johnson to a farm southwest of Wheaton, Minnesota. It was not a bad farm, but the soil was mostly gumbo, a sticky black loam. The farm had a fairly large house, a good big barn, and outbuildings. No plumbing except the usual two-holer and a well, both some distance from the house.

Chapter -27-

Graduation from High School as the War Clouds Gather

I graduated from Chokio High School in 1939. The war clouds were gathering in Europe. Hitler's Stormtroopers had marched into Poland, Austria, and Czech territories. Hitler proclaimed Germany's need for more living space, which served as a prelude for the invasion of other countries. War in Europe was imminent, and there were rising concerns that we would be dragged into the conflict. It was not long thereafter that draft boards were formed, and a universal draft was declared in the U.S. There was significant opposition to the draft, any preparation for war, or any help for other involved nations.

A group called the America First Committee was the ringleader of the draft opposition movement. Charles Lindbergh, who gained fame as the first pilot to fly solo from New York to France, was its chairman. His father, a Minnesota Senator, was an anti-war spokesman. Charles Lindbergh's anti-war views, earned the ire of President Roosevelt. When America entered into the war, Roosevelt prohibited Lindbergh from entering the military service, although Lindbergh held the rank of Reserve Colonel.

Lindbergh did, however, serve as a private consultant, and spent a lot of time in combat theaters teaching pilots how to fly with minimum gas consumption. Knowing how to conserve gas saved the life of many a pilot on long-distance missions. After the Japanese bombed Pearl Harbor, the America First Committee quickly disbanded.

Chapter -28-

the Grocery Boy

After graduating high school in a class of thirteen, I searched for a full time job. Mother had shopped at the Farmer's Store in Wheaton and asked the owner if he needed any help. He said they had an opening in the grocery department. Since I had some grocery store experience working at the Red Owl store in Chokio, I got the job. I started out with a salary of $70.00 per month, which was quite good pay, and more than twice the amount I was getting at the Chokio Red Owl store. For ten dollars a month, I roomed at the home of the manager of the grocery department, Oscar Schumaker. For fifty cents a day, I ate two meals a day at Mrs. Krenz's boarding house.

The Farmer's Store was open twelve to fourteen hours per day. Chester Johanson, one of the owners, ran the hardware and machinery departments, but also supervised the entire store. Al Ulrick, the other owner, ran the clothing department and supervised the grocery department. On Saturdays, when most of the farmers came in to shop with their wives, the store stayed open until after the liquor store closed at one in the morning. After the liquor store closed, the customers would come over to the store and get their groceries and other purchases.

Many things in the store, particularly canned goods, were purchased in railroad car-load quantities. Groceries like prunes and apricots came in large wooden barrels. Apples, pears, and peaches came in wooden boxes. The pears and peaches, most of which came from Georgia, were packed with colored tissue paper. These tissues were always carefully saved. They made great toilet paper, much better that the Sears Roebuck catalog or corn cobs! Cranberries, pickled fish, and similar items also came in wooden barrels. Peanuts came in big fifty-pound burlap sacks.

Sometimes we would set barrels of free peanuts out, so customers could get handfuls, peel them, and drop the shells on the floor. The floors were wooden, and the peanut shells did a nice job of oiling the planks. Peanut shells would be scattered out on the street as well, and those we had to sweep up.

In the fall, around about Thanksgiving, we would get a large supply of dried cod for making lutefisk, a Norwegian delicacy. The dried cod came in slabs, two to three feet long, which we stacked outside like cordwood. It was said that the dogs would come along and lubricate the stacks generously, but that was probably a rumor from those who didn't care for the delicacy. It did have quite a strong smell while it cooked. Some said it had a stronger smell than Limburger cheese, or even dog piss. Mother would open all the kitchen windows, even in the dead of winter, when she cooked it.

The dried cod from Norway was soaked in a lye solution, called luteing. After it soaked for a while, it would swell into a nice white fish. It would be drained of the lye water several times. In later years, it came to stores already processed and ready to cook. It was cooked in lightly salted water and eaten with melted butter or a white cream sauce. Lutefish was very delicious, but it was said that you had to have Scandinavian blood to really like it. We usually had lutefish dinners from around Thanksgiving until after Christmas. Most of us kids loved it, as I do to this day. Churches [primarily Lutheran] would put on lutefisk dinners every fall, and some still do. Even some non-Scandinavians will eat it!

The Farmer's Store had a huge basement about fifty feet by one hundred feet, where large quantities of materials were stored. One time the other grocery boy, Dave Eckholt, and I discovered a very large quantity of bean cans stored in the basement. The brand name was Asco Beans. We had some of the cans on the shelves priced at five cents a can, but they didn't sell, so we had the bright idea of having a huge special.

We worked almost all of Friday night hauling the bean cans upstairs and piling them into a big pyramid that almost reached the twelve foot high ceiling. We put a big sign on them: "GET ASCO BEANS AND HEAR YOUR ASCO **BOOM** ... FOR A GREAT SAVING --- TWO CANS FOR 15 CENTS." One of us stood on a ladder and tossed the cans down to the customers. Customers swooped all of them up by Saturday night. We learned a lot about merchandising from that.

We had other successful sales after that. Chester Johanson, one of the owners, would go around the store and mark everything up. He did this throughout the store on stuff that wasn't selling and wanted to get rid of. Then he had us go around and put sale signs on the items he had marked up at a sale price that was usually higher than the regular price. Stuff sold like hotcakes. Everybody loves a bargain.

The Farmers Store sold everything from groceries to hardware and farm machinery. On Friday nights we would try to close by six o'clock and then head to Ritters in Graceville. Quite often, we would go out after work to another tavern about ten miles west of Wheaton, near a park that was a great place to *spoon*.

Another great social gathering spot was a tavern and dance hall in White Rock, South Dakota, about fifteen miles from Wheaton. On one outside wall of the hall there was a long metal trough for the guys to pee. It was quite visible from the inside hall. Girls would gather and stand there and giggle at the sight. Probably checking out the men's "equipment" too!

This was about the time my brother Clarence thought he was Romeo going to see his Juliet. One night he climbed the tree to get into his sweetheart's bedroom. Some of us guys watched from below. When he didn't reappear, we drove on home. He had to walk four miles back to the farm some time later. Now, when he is reminded of those escapades, he will only blink and grin in his usual noncommittal way.

Some of the boys in Wheaton caught a "social disease" from none other than the minister's daughter. Such are the results of youthful indiscretions. Fortunately, the good local doctor, Dr. Ewing, diagnosed the problem and treated it with penicillin, a drug treatment that had been recently developed and quickly cured the problem. He lectured us on the hazards of unprotected sex and taught us how to use a rubber (condom.) Although she too was treated, the minister's daughter became less popular after that. The doctor also advised that boys should always use a rubber not only to prevent VD, but also avoid getting girls "knocked up."

The farm we lived on was a typical farm with outdoor plumbing. Dad later brought the facilities inside. Most of us did not have the opportunity to enjoy those amenities because we had left for the service before those installations were made.

Chapter -29-

Seeking my Fortune.

In early 1941, I left the Farmer's Store with two other guys, to seek our fortunes in California. The only ones left on the farm to help Dad were Willie and Edgar, and my sisters, Opal and Gwen. Willie was too old and Ed too young to be called up for the draft. If there wasn't enough help, some farm boys were exempt from the draft. Willie and Edgar finally convinced Dad to buy a farm on a contract. It was a nice farm a few miles southeast to Wheaton. It had a big house and barn, and other outbuildings.

I bought a 1928 Chevrolet from my brother Clarence for fifty dollars to go to California. He didn't need it since he was going into the service.

It was a nice car, but the axles and even drive shaft had the tendency to break if you didn't shift carefully. We always carried a few extra axles and drive shafts in the car.

While heading to California through the mountains,, we broke two axles and one drive shaft. We would push the car off to the side of the road, jack it up, and replace the axle or drive shaft. Ed Drinkwitz and I, as with most farm boys, were pretty good mechanics, so making repairs was no trouble. The other guy with us, whose name I have forgotten, was from Graceville. He had worked in a garage and was a very good mechanic, so would let us know if we weren't doing the job properly. He joined the Navy as soon as we got to California, since he couldn't find a job. He was killed early in the war.

In early 1941, the draft board starting calling up young men, referred to as draftees. Brothers Arnold, Clarence, and Roy were some of the first to be called up in Traverse County, where we lived.

I got a job at a big grocery store in Los Angeles, but didn't last there long. The manager was one mean dude who no one could get along with. When I worked at the Red Owl store and the Farmers Store, I was always treated respectfully and considerately. I was not about to take any abuse from that guy, so I quit. I hated to leave, because there was a nice girl who was fun to work with. Besides, I had become quite fond of her and had enjoyed her "favors."

I was fortunate to get a job with a company that made voice recording machines for the military. It paid much better than being a grocery clerk. Part of my job was to pick up and deliver and pick up parts from various suppliers and distributors. I learned the streets of Los Angeles quite quickly and would race around the city in record time, much faster than other drivers, which pleased the owners. It was important to get to suppliers in a hurry so as to not hold up the plant production. The company paid for the gas, oil, and even tires for my car. One time my immediate supervisor went with me to make sure I was contacting all the suppliers. My driving scared the hell out of him so he never went with me again, but he recommended me for a raise.

I rented an apartment on Hollywood Boulevard with two other guys, Wes Rogers and "Slick" Fowler from Oklahoma. Fowler's father was a traveling salesman called "Slick," so his son ended up with the same nickname. We had a great time together. Wes was a real character and would dream up all kinds of sayings and poems. He and I met a couple of girls called Violet and Genevieve. He made up a rhyme: "When we go out with Vi and Ginney, we don't spend money — cause we don't got inney."

We really didn't have much money left over after paying the rent and buying food, gas, and other necessities. We would save enough to go to dances at the Palladium in Hollywood and dance to the big bands like Mitch Miller, Claude Thornhill, and Tommy Dorsey.

The entrance fee was usually about twenty to twenty-five cents per person. There was a bar next door that sold beer in big glasses for five cents. It was a fun time, but the war in Europe was on everyone's mind, and the dispute with the Japanese sounded ominous. Not only did it sound ominous, but we learned that any vague dispute with Japan had become a reality. I intended to go to college and had registered at the University of California to start on January 2, 1942, but that got put on hold. It was not until the war was over that I could plan for my future.

Chapter -30-

WAR

Pearl Harbor had been bombed by Japanese naval forces in a surprise attack on early Sunday morning on December 7, 1941. It was reported that most of our battleships had been sunk and several thousand people killed. Los Angeles panicked. A blackout was ordered for all cities along the California coast. At that time, I was living in Hollywood. Along with huge crowds, I went out and watched the sky at night.

The National Guard was quickly activated and soldiers from a nearby Army base swung into action. That night they raced around the city and smashed lighted neon signs and any outdoor lights they found burning. The Guard probably did more damage than if the Japanese had dropped a bomb. A few soldiers carried guns, but I doubt many of them had any combat experience or any combat training.

There were continued reports of sighted enemy planes, and searchlights danced in the sky. An Army general later reported that there were no enemy planes in the area and that the Japanese fleet had disappeared after the raid. There were reports of a Japanese submarine that was sighted off the coast of San Diego and had dropped a shell someplace inland with no inflicted damage. There was an immediate reaction to the attack. Young men and women rushed to the recruiting stations to sign up.

Early the next morning, on December 8, 1941, some friends and I went to the nearest Air Corps recruiting station to sign up. There were many hundreds of guys lined up for several blocks, waiting for the station to open. The recruiters were swamped. So many people signed up around the country, some could not be activated for some time. We were instructed to await a call that would order us to report for active duty. I didn't get called until early the following year. Newspapers that came out later in the day ran headlines such as: "Scores Rush to Enlist at Recruiting Stations."

We heard on the radio that morning that President Roosevelt immediately called an emergency session of Congress for a declaration of war against Japan. He stated: *December 7th, 1941, is a date that will live in infamy. The United States of America was suddenly and deliberately attacked by the naval and air forces of the empire of Japan. I believe I interpret the will of Congress and of the people when I assert that we will not only defend ourselves to the uttermost but will make certain that this form of treachery shall not endanger us again. With confidence in our armed forces — with unbounding determination of our people we will gain the inevitable triumph so help us God.* Continual cheering could be heard for blocks, with horns honking and sirens blowing.

The Senate, within minutes, voted unanimously for a declaration of war against Japan. There was one dissenting vote in the House of Representatives by a woman, Representative Jeannette Rankin. When that was reported on the radio, there was booing up and down the street. "What would she do except to go and kiss the Emperor's ass" were some of the nicer comments about her. She had been a Representative since World War I - obviously too long. She had voted against entering WWI as well. The picture of her in the paper reminded one of a dried-up prune.

A great English philosopher, John Stuart Mill, wrote almost two hundred years ago:

War is an ugly thing, but not the ugliest of things; the decayed and degraded state of morale and patriotic feeling which thinks that nothing is worth war is much worse. A man who has nothing for which he is willing to fight; nothing that he cares about more than his own personal safety; is a miserable creature who has no chance of being free, unless made and kept so by the exertions of better men than himself.

Despite politicians like Rankin, and misguided groups like the America First Committee, most Americans agreed with the principle so compelling expressed by Mill. Those scores of young men and women that rushed to the recruiting stations didn't have to be told of their responsibilities.

Since my brothers Arnold, Clarence and Roy were drafted or waiting to be called up, I went back to Minnesota to help Dad on the farm until I was called up.

Chapter -31-

Call to Duty.

When I got the order to report for duty, I was directed to go to the federal building in Minneapolis for a pre-induction physical. That was quite a unique experience. There were fifty or more young guys in a big room. We were ordered to take off all our clothes. I had seen my brothers in the nude, usually only a fleeting glimpse when they were changing underwear or taking a bath, but this was quite different, with all those naked guys standing in rows. If we had had any modesty, we lost it there.

Each new recruit was ordered to step forward before a bunch of doctors. I assumed they were doctors, as they all wore white coats. That was my first experience of someone putting their finger up my rear. We wondered what the doctor was looking for. One recruit immediately got himself in trouble when he told the doctor that he sure "didn't have anything hid in there!"

After we were examined by the doctors and everyone seemed to pass, we went to another area and stood before some sergeants. Several medics in army uniforms had each of us stand in front of one and said, "Skin it back and milk it out." We weren't sure what that meant, so a sergeant explained in graphic detail what we were to do. "Pull the skin back on your cock and squeeze it." In those days, few guys from our area were circumcised. The purpose of this procedure, we learned, was to see if there was any discharge which, if there was, meant the person had a venereal disease. I didn't see anyone rejected, so I guess everyone was clean and hadn't got mixed up with naughty girls.

As soon as the physical was over and we were given a little lunch, we were put on a train for Jefferson Barracks, Missouri, the army's basic training center. That was the first time I had ever been on a train besides the riding on the freight trains, and it was a miserable experience. It took all night. Just as I would doze off to sleep, the train would come to a jarring halt, and it continually blew its whistle. The train seemed to stop at every town and would sometimes pick up more soldiers.

Chapter -32-

Diary of an Airman

I noticed that the guy in the seat next to me on the train was writing in a small notebook. He told me that his Dad told him to keep a diary of his military experiences. That sounded like a good idea. He gave me one of his little notebooks. I titled the first page: "*The Diary of an Airman.*" It was rather presumptuous and optimistic, for I was far from being an airman. My friend on the train let me read some of his pages, and I decided to follow the format of his diary.

I kept a diary from then on. I wrote day-to-day reports for the next four years. I would send pages home on a regular basis so they wouldn't get lost as I was transferred from base to base. My brother Willie would put them in a box that he stored in the basement. He later put them in my footlocker with some of my other military collections.

In 1952, sometime after I got out of law school and had my own residence, I got my old footlocker and went through the contents. I recovered the diary, but many pages were stuck together and could not be read. Unfortunately, the basement at my brother's farm was very damp and many of the pages got so wet and moldy that they stuck together. There were many pages missing. Some, obviously, were missing from the wet and mold, and some may have been confiscated by censors when I tried to send them home.

Later on I will quote from some of the remaining pages. Each page was numbered, so the reader could tell when pages were missing. I note when there are missing pages. Of those pages that were readable, I made copies and preserved them in a hard-bound book. The introduction page, which I probably wrote in the late 1950s, reads as follows:

PAGES FROM THE DIARY OF AN AIRMAN.

I had entitled my Diary with this caption when I first went into Cadet training. The title was most presumptuous since there was no assurance that I would in fact become an Airman. These pages from my Diary of the war years, 1941-1945, *were recently discovered in my army footlocker.* ["Footlocker" was the army name for a wooden trunk where personnel kept their belongings] *The footlocker had been stored in the basement of my brothers' farm since my discharge in 1946. The first 343 pages are completely missing.* [My brother Willie does not know what happened to them. He thinks he saved everything that I sent to him over the years.] *These missing pages would probably relate the experiences since my enlistment in the Army Air Corps until the completion of tactical training in fighters at Key Field, Meridian, Miss. The pages that have been found relate events from that time to my combat experience as a Fighter Pilot in the 14th Air Force in China, the "Flying Tigers" These pages were scattered with other documents, clothing and memorabilia. Many pages were torn, moldy, and unreadable. Some had been wet and stuck together in a pulp. Many pages are missing. The diary had been in loose leaf form but the notebook itself is missing. There has been no attempt at censorship. Much consideration was given to censoring out or deleting those pages that reflect episodes or escapades which one may not now be proud. We decided not to do so after consultation with comrades who served with me. The narration manifests the exuberance of youth, and sometimes indiscretions and lack of restraint. These are signs of the times. The writing is quite amateurish but does give some insight into the feelings, emotions, hopes and concerns of a young man at war, far from home. Most of the original pages are so fragile that they cannot be handled without damage. We are now having them preserved in plastic and suitably stored. Memories fade and events forgotten. Since the Diary restores memories that might otherwise be lost, it was decided to make copies of the originals and preserve them in book form. For accuracy and objectivity, all readable pages have been included. May my family and friends who are permitted to read these pages be understanding and forgiving!* Wayne G. Johnson

Chapter -33-

Army Basic Training

When the trip ended, we were in Jefferson Barracks, Missouri. It was like getting off in a foreign country. It was a huge military base with a long military history, and was one of the army's largest basic training bases in the country. This was to be our home for at least the next six weeks.

Basic training was another shock. The barracks included one big open room with beds for about forty guys. There was a shower at one end with a dozen shower heads, so a dozen guys would be in the shower at one time, and had to be quick so everyone could take a shower. The toilet facilities were in another room with a bunch of stools and urinals. There was no privacy. Privacy and modesty were things of the past.

On the first morning, we were routed out of bed at 4 a.m. with much shouting by sergeants and corporals. One of them would sing out: "Drop your cocks and grab your socks, it's time to get up in the morning." The beds were foldable canvas cots and if a person did not get up promptly, a corporal or sergeant tipped the cot over, dumping the occupant and leaving them sprawled on the floor. After rapidly getting dressed, we were marched in a staggering bunch to get fitted for uniforms. As soon as we got our uniforms, we quickly dressed. We were a strange-looking bunch, for most of the uniforms did not fit. We then went through calisthenics for about half an hour, and then went to breakfast.

The first breakfast was another surprise. They called it "shit on a shingle." It consisted of ground hamburger or chipped beef with a heavy flour and milk sauce on toast. We had to eat everything on our plate or else we got the same plate for lunch.

Immediately after breakfast, we were taken out on the big parade grounds to learn how to march. That went on with few rest stops until lunchtime. After lunch, it was back to marching and learning small arms fire. One guy had the guts to ask the Sergeant why this crap was necessary, since we were going to be pilots. The poor guy had to put on parachute seat pack and march the rest of the day with the chute flapping on his rear. After watching that punishment, no one ever questioned why we had to go through all this routine.

The climate was horrible. It would get a damp and cold at night and very hot during the day. It was always muggy. Almost everyone got colds. Some became seriously ill with pneumonia and there were even some cases of encephalitis. Some died. One who died was the son of a senator, and we were immediately investigated by the Senate. We were told that we would get heated quarters and other better conditions, but as soon as the Senate team left, things got back to how they were. The government had too many recruits to train and no time to build better quarters or facilities.

One morning, when a big formation of us was at "parade rest" after precision marching, I got caught in an offense that the drill Sergeant apparently considered as serious as murder. Parade rest was standing at less than full attention without moving your feet apart and hands behind your back, which supposedly made for a more relaxed position.

The snot was running out of my nose, so when I thought the drill sergeant wasn't looking, I quickly wiped my nose with my glove. He must have eyes in the back of his head, for he came charging over to me, screaming that he was going to kick the shit out of me for moving when I was supposed to be at parade rest. He called me every name in the book, and a lot that could never be printed. He was a small man, not more than five foot seven inches, but he had a voice that could be heard a mile away. He was considered the meanest and nastiest guy on the base. He was the kind of guy not even a mother could love. He probably ate broken glass for lunch. Everybody hated and feared him.

After the sergeant got through dressing me down, he had me run around the drill field, which was about two miles around and a half a mile square, a number of times, until I was just staggering. Then he had me stand in front of the formation of several hundred guys and continually run my glove back and forth, wiping my nose.

When he dismissed the formation, he kept me standing out in the middle of the field all alone, continuing to wipe my nose until well after dark. He would sneak up on me every once in a while to see if I was still wiping my nose. I kept muttering under my breath what I would do to that SOB if I ever caught him off-base, which was wishful thinking.

I tried to wipe carefully and not touch my face too hard, but my nose was red like a beet for days and my upper lip so sore that I could hardly eat. By the time he let me come in, it was near midnight, so I didn't get any supper. It was obvious he was making an example of me to impress on the troops what would happen if they did anything out of line. I was sure he'd be watching me, so I was determined to be the best soldier on the base.

We did have our revenge. He came into our barracks late one night, very drunk, threw some guys out of bed, and started to beat them up. I was designated, or I might have volunteered, to run out and get the M.P.s (military police). I also reported the matter to the Officer of Quarters. He came over with the M.P.s and had the sergeant thrown in the stockade. He also jerked the sergeant's stripes, demoted him to a private, and took him off his duty as drill sergeant. We heard he got his stripes back later, for he was considered to be a very good drill sergeant, but he was assigned to a different part of the field. After the grueling basic training was over, some of us more fortunate were sent to a college for more training.

Chapter -34-

Off to Cadet College Training

At the time, one could not go into pilot training without a college degree. Because the Army Air Corps could not get enough college men, it relaxed its requirements, and only required a limited period of college. So it sent those men that did well on some written tests to selected colleges. I ended up at Michigan Mining and Technology in Houghton, Michigan, for six months. It was paradise compared to Jefferson Barracks.

"Air Corps Cadet Wayne Johnson at Houghton Michigan technical college."

We slept in the college dormitory, two to a room, in nice beds with white sheets. The meals were delicious.

Marching and calisthenics were limited to one hour per day. Most of the day was spent studying. The classes included: geography, history, map-reading, aircraft recognition, Morse code, and the flying basics, which included navigation and aerobatics. The history course was mostly limited to studies of Germany, Italy, and Japan. Lots of time was spent on the geography of those countries, and map-reading. The military wanted airmen to know as much as possible of those countries, in case we were shot down. The instructors did not spend much time on what would happen to a captured airman; except that under the Geneva Convention all a prisoner had to give was his name, rank, and serial number. We, of course, did not know that Japan did not honor the rules of war set by the Geneva Convention concerning the treatment of prisoners of war, and Germany was not great at recognizing them either.

We also got some flight-time in a sixty-five horsepower Piper J-3 Cub and a sixty-five horsepower Aeronca. They were really fun to fly.

"Wayne in the J3 Piper Cub trainer at Houghton College."

Those airplanes flew much like the old Curtiss Robin in which I had learned to fly. I had been cautioned early not to admit that I had taken flying lessons and had soloed, because the Army wanted to teach students their way.

I have never gotten airsick except on this one long-to-be-remembered flight. A bunch of us had gone out one Saturday night and drank quite a bit of beer. Sundays were always a day off at the college, so we expected we could sleep in. This Sunday turned out to be a beautiful day, so the flight instructor decided to take advantage of the good weather and take a few students up. I was selected first and the instructor had me do aerobatics once we got in the air, since he knew I loved them. The instructor sat in the front and I was in the back, as the Cub was a tandem-type plane.

The Cub was not the best for aerobatics, but a good pilot could do a fair job. After a few spins, stalls, rolls, and loops, the results of the previous nights activities started to take hold. I hollered to Clarence Koss, the instructor, that I might get sick and that we had better land. He just laughed, took over, and did another roll. Up came all of last night's beer, the breakfast, and a lot of other stuff. It came out with the force of a four-inch fire hose and sprayed the instructor in the back. The puke was all over the inside of the plane. He quickly landed the plane and we both went in and took showers. We then spent the better part of the day cleaning out the plane. It was a big job since the puke was sticking everywhere. The instructor didn't blame me, and said he should have landed as soon as I complained. The puking incident was indelibly printed on my mind. We went up the next day and I had no problems. Of course, news of the incident circulated throughout the campus. I was one embarrassed guy.

We had a good social life there. We only got twenty-one dollars a month, but that went quite a long way. When we went out in our uniforms, the locals would always buy us beer or drinks. The uniforms attracted the girls like bees to honey.

Chapter -35-

Air Corps Cadets

But the good life soon came to an end. When the course was finished, we were shipped off to Air Corps cadet training at Maxwell Field, Montgomery, Alabama. It was a spit-and-polish, very strict military training base. We learned precise close-order marching drills. One better not miss a step, or discipline was immediately inflicted. Shoes had to be shined without a speck of dust. A missing button or improperly-tied tie resulted in an immediate demerit called a "gig." Too many gigs and out you went.

During mealtimes, we learned to sit on the front four inches of our chairs with our backs rigidly straight. I won a citation for one of the best postures. Meals were eaten on the square. You brought the food straight up from the plate and then at right angles into your mouth. You took a drink whenever the table leader, an upperclassman, directed. Again, the cup or glass was brought straight up and then at right angles to the mouth.

We did a lot of calisthenics. I won a commendation for doing the most pull-ups and sit-ups, and got a pass to go into town for one evening. Needless to say, I behaved perfectly, for I didn't want to risk a "wash-out." I found a girl, took her to a movie, and with just a little touchy-feely—that was it.

If a cadet got too many demerits for various violations, or misbehaved in any way, there would be a "wash-out" or "drumming out" ceremony. For that ceremony, all cadets were routed out of bed a little before midnight. We were required to dress in our full uniforms, including white gloves. We were marched to the drill field. At the stroke of midnight, a bugle would blow, and the captain would read off the name of the violator and his violations. Then the drums would roll in a mournful manner and the poor guy was marched off the field with an M.P escort. He was not allowed to say goodbye to his friends or roommates. Even the toughest guy couldn't hold back tears. He was not seen on-base again, for he was shipped that night to a regular army base somewhere. It was a ceremony we all dreaded, but an acute lesson to not violate any rules or screw up in any way. By the time we got out of that Cadet school, we were supposed to be perfect gentlemen!

It was there that I met Oliver Bateman from Macon, Georgia. We became life-long friends. We went through most of our flight training together and ended up in the same combat squadron in China, the 118th Tactical Reconnaissance *Black Lightning* Squadron. We spent the better part of a year living together in tents as we moved from base to base in China. I believe we were still cadets when we got passes to visits his parents at their farm at Walden, Georgia, a suburb of Macon.

Oliver's father owned large peach and pecan farms. His mother was a most gracious lady and a great cook. I ate okra for the first time there. I had great difficulty swallowing it. It reminded me of something slimy that one uses a handkerchief for. I had to eat it to be polite. Every time I looked away, Mr. Bateman would slide another portion on my plate. He had great fun doing this. I had to really struggle with each bite to keep from throwing up. It was also the first time I had ever eaten pecan pie, it was delicious. I didn't mind when Mr. Bateman insisted I have a second piece.

The Batemans lived in a modest plantation house, built in about 1850. It was well-built and tidy, nestled in a grove of pecan and peach trees. On a field some distance from the house was a row of small, neat houses occupied by black farm-help and their families. Mr. Bateman had quite a few Negroes who worked for him. At that time, blacks were always called Negroes. Mr. Bateman housed them, provided for their meals, and took care of any illness. It appeared that he took care of them from the cradle to the grave, like his own family. There were several Negro ladies working in the house who were treated as part of the family. They helped Mrs. Bateman with the baking and cooking, as well as the cleaning. It was the closest I had ever come to a group of Negroes. We didn't have any Negroes in the areas where I had lived. I found Mr. Bateman's Negroes very happy and they were very friendly towards me. Although Mr. Bateman treated them like he would any white help, they were still segregated in their living quarters.

Arriving in the South was the first time I had experienced segregation. I was surprised to see drinking fountains, public toilet facilities, and swimming pools with "Whites only" signs. Restaurants did not serve Negroes in white establishments. We were told in no uncertain terms that regardless how friendly or how pretty a black girl was, a white boy better not try and date her. There were no Negroes in the cadets. The military, at the beginning of WWII, was completely segregated. The Army Air Corps commanders did not think that blacks had the skills to become pilots, which was the philosophy of all levels of leadership. There was only one Air Corps unit in WWII that had black pilots. The Tuskegee Airmen, who formed an all-black fighter squadron in WWII, proved the leadership wrong. They proved that black pilots had the skills to be excellent pilots, and set a record comparable to the best fighter squadrons in combat.

Recently, the Tuskegee Airmen Association has worked to restore a P-51 in their WWII unit colors, the Red Tailed Mustangs. Two of the Tuskegee pilots, Ken Wofford and Joe Gomer, now live in Minnesota and have become friends of mine whom I often see at air shows and at Air Force Association meetings. Both had distinguished careers in the Air Force. The Tuskegee Airmen paved the way to a fully integrated Air Force.

Chapter -36-

Primary Flight Training

Those who passed the rigid cadet course were sent to primary flight training. I ended up at Clarksdale, Mississippi, where most of the flight instructors were contract civilian pilots with Army pilots as supervisors.

The flight training was the real stuff. The first primary plane that I was instructed in was the Stearman PT-17. It was an open cockpit biplane, which meant it had two wings, one above the other.

Stearman P-17

It was powered by a two-hundred twenty horsepower Continental radial engine. The PT-17 was a great aerobatic airplane. It had rather narrow, fixed landing gear, so was a difficult plane to land. If not set down properly in a three point landing, it would ground loop. A three point landing was accomplished by touching the main gear in front and the tail wheel to the ground at the same time.

A ground loop happened when the pilot lost control of the plane; it would start to turn, one wing would go down, and it would spin around. Sometimes it would flip over.

Another plane used in primary training was the Fairchild PT-23. It too had two-hundred twenty horsepower with a Lycoming engine. It was also an open cockpit, but a low-wing monoplane. It had only one set of wings. It had very wide landing gear, so was very easy to land. I loved both planes, and both were fun to fly.

After logging nine or ten hours, we were expected to solo. If a student didn't do too well, he would be sent up with an army check pilot. If that pilot found the student deficient, he would go up with the senior army check pilot, usually a major, for a final check. That pilot had the absolute authority to send the student back for more training or wash him out. "Washed out" meant the student was taken out of pilot training. Those washed out of pilot training could be sent to navigator, bombardier or gunnery school. If the major thought the student was not aviation material or a real screw-up, he could end up in the infantry.

The flying was very intensive. We learned close formation flying and night flying. We learned to do spins, stalls, forced landings, and a variety of other aerial maneuvers. I was fortunate to get a very good instructor. He was a chubby fellow, very easy going, and had a great sense of humor. His name was Walter Parker. He apparently believed I had some prior flight experience, because he said I seemed to have more knowledge of flying than a new student. He inquired if I had. I was apprehensive in revealing that I had, but I knew I had to tell the truth. He said it would just be our secret. I told him about a farmer who had taught himself to fly and about how he had given me lessons. He was thrilled that I had flown a Curtiss Robin, since he had flown that plane himself. He had soloed in a Curtiss Robin, so we had something in common. I had just less than nine hours of dual training when he took me over to another field. After we landed, he climbed out of the plane and said, "Okay Johnson, if you think you can fly this crate alone, go ahead and do it and try not to kill yourself, because then I have to fill out all kinds of damn papers." I lucked out by making three perfect landings and he waved me in.

When we got back to base, he waved a "thumbs up," which was the signal that I had soloed. The cadets all came running and threw me in the water tank, which was the usual ritual after a guy soloed.

Besides the flying, we had lots of ground school consisted of reviewing all the flying, including aircraft recognition, with greater detail. We had to recognize not only American planes, but also those of our allies and enemies.

One of the courses that most of us hated was Morse Code. It was difficult to learn and we couldn't see that we would have a use for it. The instructor explained that it was important to know the code by heart. In the event you were shot down, or had to make a forced landing in a remote area, it was a good method with which to signal rescuers, using panels or tramping the code out in the ground or snow.

We were going to be hot pilots and didn't think anyone could shoot us down, so we didn't need it, but we learned it. Morse code was also used while flying and approaching airports when under instruments

The food at the base was excellent. They had dietitians who prepared meals and determined the type of foods that would be best for us. The barracks, too, improved. We had two or four to a room, and much better shower and sanitary facilities. However, we had very little time off.

After I soloed, I got a pass to go to town and enjoy an evening. There were plenty of eager young girls around just waiting for a dashing cadet to appear!

The amount of time in the air was critical. If a guy had over forty hours of dual and solo combined, he would always get a check ride with an army pilot. It was at this point where a number of cadets were washed out.

I had just a little over thirty hours of dual and solo at Clarksville when I graduated. From there, I was sent to Greenville, Mississippi, for basic flight training. It was an Army base, and the discipline was much stricter than it was at Clarksdale.

Chapter -37-

Basic Flight Training

Basic flight training at Greenville was in a Vultee BT-13. We called it the Vultee vibrator. The entire airplane shook when first started. It was a closed cockpit, low-wing plane with a four-hundred fifty horsepower Pratt & Whitney radial engine. It had very wide fixed landing gear, so was easy to land. If a pilot ground-looped that plane, he was a lousy pilot and would probably be washed out.

That powerful engine made it a great aerobatic plane. We did slow rolls, a roll around a point; barrel rolls, a roll around a circle in a coordinated roll; chandelles, a steep dive and then a pull-up while turning one-hundred eighty degrees; and lazy eights, similar to a chandelle, except you would continue on around in another type chandelle until you flew a vertical figure eight. We did loops, a steep dive to pick up speed then pulling up until the plane was upside down then around and down into a complete vertical circle. Immelmens were another fun maneuver involving half a loop where the pilot would roll out to a level position at the top.

About half the flying was solo and half was dual instruction. The maximum allowed in basic flight school was eighty hours. If the student had more than eighty hours and not considered proficient by the instructors, he got the army check flight. Two things would then happen: the student either got sent back for a little more dual or he was washed out, most often the latter.

Chapter -38-

Advanced Flight Training

I had 36.55 dual and 33.05 solo, in Basic which was the minimum when I graduated. From there I went to Napier Field in Dothan, Alabama, for advanced flight training. The North American AT-6 was the training plane at Dothan. It had a 600 H.P. Pratt & Whitney engine and retractable landing gear. A student better not forget to put the landing gear down when he came in for a landing or he would be walking from then on with a rifle over his shoulder. His flying days would be over.

The AT-6 was another fun plane to fly. It was the best aerobatic plane of any that we had flown up to that time. It was a very stable airplane and easy to fly instruments under the hood. Under the hood meant that the instructor would cover the student's canopy and he had to fly solely by instruments. We again went through all the maneuvers that we had learned in Primary and Basic but with better precision. By the time I finished training in the AT-6, I had over 200 hours of flight time including that flown at the college training center. We got quite a lot of instrument training (under the hood) in the AT-6.

We also spent many hours in the Link Trainer. The Link was a little model like the cockpit of an airplane. It had a black hood so it was flown totally on instruments. It was used to teach flying on instruments and navigation. An instructor sat on the outside and monitored the pilot's actions. At the instructor's desk, there was a gadget that had an inked stylus that would show the student's maneuvers traced on paper. It was particularly useful in teaching navigation for the route the student flew would be traced in red ink on a map. It would show if the pilot was "on the beam". Most airfields had a radio beacon used for an instrument approach.

The beacon sent out an "A" (a dash and a dot) and "N" (dot and a dash) signals in Morse Code that branched out in legs from the station. It sounded like "dah dit" and "dit dah", a long dash and then a short dot. If the pilot was flying "on the beam" it would show that he was flying on the proper radio beam to bring him to the field. It required real precision flying. More students "washed out" in that part of the training than any other. Because it was so difficult to learn, the military later developed a better instrument approach system. However, the Link Trainer was very useful in teaching pilots to learn to control the airplane totally on instruments and to navigate on instruments without looking outside. The airlines today teach pilots in a similar type of unit.

At the end of advanced training, those that passed were commissioned 2nd Lieutenants in the Army Air Corps. Each military unit, the Army, Navy and Marines had their own air units. It was not until after the end of WWII that a United States Air Force was organized.

Chapter -39-

The Big Time: The P-40 *Warhawk*

The really big time came at Dothan, Alabama, when I checked out in the P-40 Warhawk.

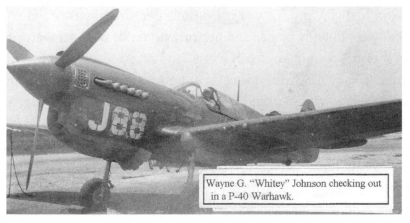

Wayne G. "Whitey" Johnson checking out in a P-40 Warhawk.

"Lt. Wayne Johnson ready for the take-off in a P-40 for the first time"

The P-40 was America's first line fighter when the war broke out, used in every combat theater, and in every Allied air force. The P-40 N had a twelve hundred horsepower Allison in-line liquid-cooled engine. It was a single-seat plane, so there was no room for an instructor. We studied all the manuals very carefully and learned all we could about it on the ground, and then took it up solo. By this time we were expected to be good enough pilots to handle this powerful plane.

It was the thrill of a lifetime to take this great fighter off, and fly it in every maneuver we had learned, and practice gunnery and bombing. The P-40 was equipped with six fifty-caliber guns, fixed in the wings that had terrific striking power. We would shoot at ground and aerial targets in preparation for combat. The aerial target was a brightly-colored sleeve pulled on a long rope behind another plane. We learned various approaches to best hit the target. Sometimes, the target plane pilot saw our approach and would maneuver to see if we could adjust our pattern and still hit the target. An instructor pilot would usually fly above and watch the performance. Back at base he would lecture about the performance of each pilot and what we did right or wrong. It was an exciting time. We were being prepared to be combat fighter pilots.

Towing a target was quite hazardous. If the pilot flying the attacking plane got a little careless, the tow plane might get some holes. Each of us was assigned as tow plane pilots, several times. On one occasion, I recall returning from a towing mission with a number of holes in my rudder. The other pilot got a little talking to! The object was to shoot holes in the towed target, not the towing plane.

Sometimes we had woman pilots from the Women Air Force Service Pilots (WASP) piloting the tow plane. Jackie Cochrane, a famous woman pilot, convinced Gen. Hap Arnold, the Army Air Corps Commander, to form a special unit of women pilots. They could ferry planes and perform all types of tasks that would relieve male pilots serving in combat. It was a great system, and most of the women were excellent pilots. They flew everything from trainers to heavy four-engine bombers and transports. There was a strict rule against fraternizing with these women, although I doubt the rule was, or could be, effectively enforced. Small chance!

Sometimes the girls would add a little humor to their duties. Most single engine planes had a "relief tube," which was about an inch-round hose that come up from the floor between the pilot's legs. It was used when a man had to take a leak. If the pilot did, he would note on the log, as instructions for ground crews, "relief tube used, please clean." One time a WASP brought a single-seat plane in, she had noted on the log "relief tube used, please clean," which caused considerable discussion on how she had managed that!

We not only flew out of the Dothan air base, but also out of a field near Pensacola, Florida, and out over the Gulf. The Navy had derelicts out in the Gulf that we could use for target practice. The training was so intense that we had very little time for any recreation. But every once in a while we were allowed to go into town for some social activities. Dothan had become a military city, but the girls still loved guys in Army Air Corps uniforms. The Army Air Corps officer's uniform was very sharp. It consisted of a dark green blouse and lightly colored pants, called "pinks."

The officer's caps were the typical flat-top caps. It had a wire, called a grommet, inside the top that made it flat. Pilots took out grommet in order to crush the top supposedly to fit earphones over the top. It gave the cap a rakish look.

The next base was Sarasota, Florida, for more tactical training. Flying the P-40, we concentrated more on close formation flying, both day and night, aerial and ground gunnery, and dive and skip bombing. Skip bombing was done out over the Gulf. The pilot would go into a dive towards a target in the water, start to level out just above the water, and try to release the bomb at an angle that would make it skip over the water and into the target. Skip bombing was just like skipping stones over the water when we were kids. It was quite effective and worked well against enemy ships.

Experienced combat pilots at Sarasota trained us for almost two months. Besides the regular training flights, we were allowed to take up the plane whenever we wanted. The commander encouraged us to get in as much time as possible and be really comfortable in the plane. I had over two hundred hours in the P-40 when I left for Key Field, Mississippi.

Chapter -40-

Almost Alligator Bait

I won a special commendation at Sarasota because of one experience when I was flying a P-40 over the Everglades. I was climbing with almost full throttle in order to get to my assigned altitude on time. When I leveled off at my intended altitude, the throttle didn't retract, so the engine was running wide open. It would not take long for the engine to overheat.

I headed back toward base, but knew I could not make it before the engine burned up at full throttle. The only thing I could think of was to turn off the gas so the engine would stop, and glide toward the base. I knew I couldn't make the base, so I would glide for a few minutes and turn the gas back on so the engine would start, but go into full power. I did this repeatedly until I was close to the base.

When I was within landing distance and still had plenty of altitude, I called the tower and told them of my problem. The tower got the base operations officer on the radio. He told me to get away from the developed area and bail out, because, he said I would not be able to successfully land a P-40 with either full throttle or dead stick, which meant without power.. I did not want to join the alligators, so I told him I was landing. The tower cleared other aircraft from the area and I saw the fire trucks and ambulance racing down the runway. They were preparing to pick up the pieces of the plane and the pilot!

I kept up the same technique of turning off the gas to slow down and lose altitude and then turning it back on. When I was in the right position and knew I could make the runway without power, I turned off the gas again and landed "dead stick." I made one of my best landings ever, and coasted down to near the end of the runway. I was sweating just a little.

The operation officer instructed me to start the engine and taxi off the runway. I told him I was sure that with the surge of power, the plane would nose up and hit the prop or nose completely over. He apparently had never flown a P-40. I said, "Why not send out a tow truck and tow me off?" He swore at me, "Goddamit Lieutenant, I'm ordering you to start that plane and get it the hell off the runway."

So I did as ordered. I turned on the gas, the engine started and roared to full power and, of course, it nosed up. The prop hit the hard surface of the runway, the engine stopped, and the plane stayed on its nose. Then a tow truck came out and towed me off. The operations officer came running out of the tower, hollering at me that I had disobeyed orders by landing and wrecked the plane. At about that time, the base commander, I think a general, arrived at the scene. He had been informed of my problem and that I had made a successful landing "dead stick," without any damage, until I was ordered to start the plane.

He congratulated me on saving the plane with only prop damage, and then chewed out the operations officer, a captain, for the dumbness of ordering me to start the engine when I had objected. "Pilots are in charge of the plane and his decision should be superior to that of a person on the ground, unless it was very apparent the pilot didn't know what he was doing. And this pilot obviously knew what he was doing."

The captain was relieved as the operations officer about the lack of damage. He was transferred to be in charge of the mess hall, where he couldn't do much damage except screw up the food, which the mess sergeant could correct. It was not the kind of job a pilot would like.

Usually, when there is a sudden stoppage and the prop hits a particularly hard surface like the airport runway, there would be engine damage. When the mechanics checked the engine, they found it had not been damaged. That Allison engine was one tough engine. All they had to do was put a new prop on it and fix the throttle linkage, and the plane was flyable the next day. The Allison engine was a rugged engine and could take a lot of punishment.

A few days later, the base commander ordered a base formation out on the parade grounds. He called me out of ranks to come up to the reviewing stand. He then narrated my experience in flying and landing the P-40. He talked about how I had saved a valuable airplane with only minor damage done to the craft, and about how would have been no damage if the operations officer had followed my advice. He presented me with a certificate citing me for heroism. I didn't think I was a hero at all. I just hadn't wanted to join the alligators.

With over two hundred hours in the P-40, I really had the feel of it. I loved to fly it. It was a pilot's airplane. You had to fly it all the time to keep it under control. It had a reputation of being a survival airplane in combat. It could get shot full of holes and still fly. Many a pilot struggled back to base with the plane punched with hundreds of bullet holes. After the war, I wrote a tribute to the P-40 that I delivered when a model P-40 was dedicated at the Museum of Aviation at the Warner Robins air base in Georgia.

The P-40 Warhawk

The P-40 . . . a WARHAWK . . . who are you kidding? That old bucket of bolts couldn't get off the ground much less fight a war. But it had to do. When World War II came along, the P-40 was already "obsolete". But it was the only first line fighter the U.S. Army Air Corps had . . . and at first, the only one we had in China. Three red balls up ---- AIR RAID ---- Jing Bao . . . Jing Bao . . . A dash for the plane that scruffy beat up looking craft, perched on its spindly narrow legs, with its grinning shark's mouth . . . drooping and war weary. THAT is what we are supposed fight the mighty ZERO with.

The big Allison engine turned over slowly . . . coughed . . . choked . . . belched smoke and flame . . . a throaty roar and then it settled down to a comfortable purr. Getting off the ground it looked like a ruptured duck one wheel slowly coming up after the other. In the air it whispered like the wind but threw fear into the hearts of the enemy.

Smothered in dust or knee deep in mud, the old Warhawk was eager to get off the ground. Hey . . . this old crate knows what it is doing. It'll get me there and back. And it did. It was heavy on the controls and you had to stand on the rudder to keep it straight in a dive . . . but it did what you told it. Full of holes, it bled with the pilot . . . It struggled mightily to get him back. And most of the time it did.

It was a "crate of thunder" and a pilot's best friend. It stopped the aggressor on all fronts. From the South Pacific to the frozen Arctic . . . over the jungles of Burma and the terraced mountains of China . . . from the desert sands of Africa to the industrial heartland of Germany and the steppes of Russia . . . It held its own against superior odds. One Hundred Forty-five American pilots made Ace in the old P-40 . . . not bad for an "obsolete" airplane!

The poor old P-40, whether called the "Warhawk", "Kittyhawk" or "Tomahawk", did not know it was "obsolete". It wrecked havoc with the Messerschmitts, Fockewolfs, Zeros, Oscars, Tojos, Tonys, Bettys — and ships, trains, tanks, trucks and troops.

*Was it the pilot's skill or was it the **plane**? Perhaps a marriage of both. Loved and hated, the P-40 was a "pilot's airplane". The few that still fly today bring a quickening of the pulse and a tear to the eye. More than any other airplane — the P-40 symbolized the spirit of the **Flying Tigers.** It stands as a monument to the courage and heroism of its pilots. May it be an inspiration to all who view it — re-membering the price of FREEDOM. The P-40 merits its place of honor . . . in the memories of its pilots . . . and a grateful Nation. The sands of time will not muffle the whispering winds of the invincible P-40 WARHAWK.*
wayne g. johnson

Although I bumped its nose and later got a few holes in it, the P-40 was my airplane, and I loved flying it.

Ernest Hemingway wrote of a pilot's love for an airplane:

You love a lot of things if you live around them. But there isn't any woman and there isn't any horse, not any before nor any after, that is as lovely as a great airplane. And men who love them are faithful to them even though they leave them for others. Man has one virginity to lose in fighters, and if it is a lovely airplane he loses it to, there is where his heart will forever be.

The sentiment expressed by Hemingway reflected the feeling of many P-40 pilots. I have flown over sixty different military and civilian airplanes with over seventy-five hundred hours of pilot time. The P-40 was always my first love. Although it could hardly be described as lovely, it was a great airplane. Even after I transited to the P-51 Mustang, I still thought fondly of the P-40.

After the war, I helped form the *P-40s Association* in which pilots who flew the P-40 got together at conventions and told their tales about flying this wonderful bird. Although some of the experiences may have been a little embellished, there was always a great spirit of camaraderie among those who had had the opportunity to fly that veteran of American fighter planes.

One Association meeting was an occasion I will never forget. It was a most emotional experience. Don Chapman, an attorney who lived in Minneapolis, was a member of the P-40 Association, and the Chapmans, father and sons, were all attorneys. I learned that Don Chapman, who had flown P-40s in combat in Europe, had terminal cancer. I called him and asked if he would like to go with me to Dayton, Ohio, to the P-40 Association meeting. The meeting was scheduled during a national Air Force show. It would be a great meeting, not only for pilots who had flown the P-40, but veteran pilots and air crews from all over the country. I picked him up in my Cessna 182 and spent several wonderful days at the convention and air show. Don Chapman died shortly after we returned from the Dayton air show. It was an emotional experience that will live in my memory.

But, back to the war years.

Chapter -41-

More Combat Training - The P-51 *Mustang*

When we had finished the tactical training at Sarasota, most of the pilots were shipped off to Europe. I was transferred to Key Field near Meridian, Mississippi. That base trained in low-level reconnaissance and aerial photography. I don't know why I was sent there. I liked to think it was because I did a good job of low-level strafing and skip bombing — or maybe it was just the way the Army did things.

At Key Field, we practiced close formation flying with twelve to sixteen planes. We also did four plane flight formations, like those used in combat. A lot of emphasis was placed on low-level search or reconnaissance for ground targets, and taking photos of those targets, as well as strafing and low-level bombing. For the first couple of months, we flew the P-40. Then we got a bunch of P-51s, like every single-engine pilot hoped for.

The P-51 *Mustang* was the Cadillac of fighters. It was a beautiful airplane. The A and B models had an Allison engine. Some B models, and the Cs and Ds, had a twelve-cylinder, Packard-built Rolls Royce or Merlin fourteen hundred and ninety horsepower in-line, liquid cooled engines. Although I loved flying the P-40, the P-51 was a pilot's dream. It cruised about seventy-five miles per hour faster than the P-40, and could reach a service altitude of over 42,000 feet. It could reach four hundred and fifty miles per hour in a dive. During training, we continued to fly the P-40 as well as the P-51s.

The P-51 was designed as a high-altitude fighter, but was also used for low-level combat. It was more vulnerable in combat to ground fire at low level, since the coolant lines were in the belly. If ground fire hit the coolant lines and resulted in a loss of coolant, the engine would over-heat quickly and run for only a few minutes.

It could be fatal, since if the pilot had to belly land with the wheels up, or bail out, it would usually be in enemy territory.

While low-level strafing or bombing, we would usually come in from a dive at a very high speed, the faster the better, so the chances of getting hit were much reduced. Getting hit depended upon the anti-aircraft fire's thickness and accuracy. The earlier model P-51s had four fifty-caliber guns, but the later models had six fifty-calibers. The guns were mounted inside the wings, three on each side. It could carry two five hundred pound bombs or two external one hundred and ten gallon gas tanks for long distance missions.

The training at Key Field was very intense. We flew many hours each day, except Sundays. Sometimes we would even have a call-out mission on Sundays, a surprise like that would happen in a war zone. The P-51 was a very stable plane, so it was great for aerial photography. The photo model had a camera fixed in the left fuselage just behind the wing. It was quite easy to line up for a photo target on the ground.

All the flying we did at Key Field was in preparation for combat. When we were not flying, we might do a few things that weren't necessarily in preparation for combat! All our instructors were combat experienced pilots. We had a British pilot who was a real character. He had been a Spitfire pilot, which he bragged about. But he would usually concede that "bloody Mustang might be mite better— in the hands of a good pilot."

Since much of our flying at Key Field was at low level, an engine failure could be quite nasty. One of my good friends, Bill Kenny, had a near fatal accident while flying a P-40. I recorded the event in my diary, as well as our final days at Key Field:

Pages 344 to 419. Bill Kenny piled in to-day. We didn't miss him until we were all in the shower in the barracks and Bill wasn't there. We called ops [base operations] *and finally they decided he was missing. He was on Bill L's wing and just disappeared. Later –ops called Bill* [Kenny] *had bellied in and brought in the medics.* ["bellied in" meant he had landed wheels up or on the belly of the plane, which was a safe way if you didn't have a good surface to land on] *Busted up his leg ---- we all went over to the hospital and the nurses let us in* [it was after visitor's hours] *Bills engine quit and he went into the woods. Climbed through the window of the plane. Didn't know how the hell he could get out the window in the P-40 since his belly is twice the size of the opening of the window.* [Bill was a rather chubby fellow.] *But there he was when rescue got there sitting on the wing with his leg bleeding nothing left of the plane and he cut a swatch about 1/4 mile long. Good thing he did meet some nice nurses and invited* [us] *back tomorrow night — they* [the three nurses] *would unlock the window so we could sneak into Bill's room.*

Damn near got into bad trouble. Snuck in to Bill's room through the window with some "Jordans Delight". [Jordans Delight was an awful tasting cheap whiskey sold illegally in Mississippi that cost fifty cents a pint and "guaranteed to be not more than 30 days old"] *after a few drinks things got rather friendly with the nurses. We blocked a chair under the door* [knob] *so the C.Q. couldn't get in.* [The C.Q. was the officer in charge of quarters. It was his job to see that everything at night was going smoothly and there was no hank-panky going on] *Bill was the only Lt on the floor so was supposed to have privacy. The three nurses; Bill* [Killough], *Bobby, and I were having a great time until that damn Killough knocked over a lamp by the bed — made a helluva crash and heard the head nurse yelling for the M.P.s* [military police]

The nurses had keys to get in the other room but told Bob, Bill and I to get out the window. Landed in a briar hedge with my bare ass — but got my pants on to get back to our barracks. M.P. whistles all over. Next morning — big investigation about whose shoes and shorts in Bill's room. Bill said he couldn't remember anything — good for you Bill- [Jim] *Moran took me down to supply to get pr of shoes— good thing he knew the supply Officer.*

We were getting close to being shipped out and if we get caught we'd probably be Ct. martialed. We are going from here for more tactical training. God it would be awful if I couldn't go overseas for some damn foolish stunt. Ma and Pa wouldn't be so proud if they knew about some of the bad and dumb things I did.

Rumors floating all over the place that we should get our Orders to ship out any day. We are supposed to be through with training but have been flying lots of low level stuff the last few days. They knocked off the dog fights and combat and all missions now under 200 feet — Nobody knows why and even the C.O.s don't know why we are training for low level.

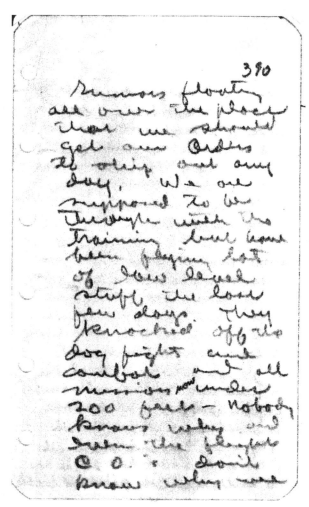

"this is a copy of actual page from Wayne Johnson's Diary"

Flying four + hours per day at tree top level is hard work and we come out dripping wet. What a beautiful airplane that 51 is. Don't know why they call it the Mustang cause its smooth as a kitten. It responds to the lightest touch. We had some mustang horses on the farm once. They were really wild. Course the 51 will race from ground level to 30,000 + in no time. Bet the Japs don't have anything to compare. Rumor is we might go to China. Recent story in TIME that Gen. Chennault wants fighters real bad. What a thrill it would be to fly for the old Flying Tiger.

Diary pages 420 -491. party tonight at the Officer's Club — something is up but nobody knows what — it sound like we are going to get our orders. Sure hope so. We have really been training — flying missions every day—calisthenics more than ever. Start about 0400 —a couple of hours – more calisthenics --fly some more

—but still get in some scr**ing every night.

There must be something up that they let us off base every night to see our girl friends as if it was the last time. I hope these last times keep up. Murph and I have been having a ball with my Billie and his Mary Jo. We found some nice cabins about 20 miles from Key and in Mary Jos old car we can make it there in about 45 minutes. Mary Jo can get good booze through the Officers Club so we don't have to drink that damn "Pride of Anderson" or "Jordans Delight". Don't know how Billie and Mary Jo got together. Billie is so sweet and timid and Mary Jo really talks bad. She embarrasses both of us. She takes all her clothes off in front of Murph, Billie and I. Billie's face gets red and doesn't want to take hers off in front of us. She doesn't mind when the lights are low and just the two of us. She has a much prettier body than Mary Jo. Her tits aren't as big but much nicer. I think I love her but what do I know about love. There is a war on and who is coming back. We are going to win. Our guys are better trained and now finally we are getting better equipment. But what about love. Billie says she loves me and will wait forever – but I don't know. It isn't fair to Billie that I tell her I love her

I don't know what love is. I suppose its two people that really like each other. I can make love to her five times a day but it must be more than that. "Making love" is probably not the right term but it is quite universally used. Probably a more correct term would be "heat of passion" even though we may profess our unending love. We can't talk about kids and the future. We don't know what the future is. Maybe the Nazis and Japs will beat us like they say —maybe we will be their slaves. It can't be. We'll beat them. Our country has learned its lesson. We must be strong to be free. We have to develop the best Military strength — but use it wisely or we will be like ancient Rome — we will waste away until our enemies see all the wealth we have — both in people and material and take us over. But they will not. We have more pride in our country now. With leaders like Pres. Roosevelt, Gen. Hap Arnold and Gen. Marshal we will win and be free and the world will respect us and noone.

Diary page missing. . . . *love. I've talked a lot about love but don't know what it is. Billie really shakes me up. She is the most pretty girl and so gentle and god how she can love! She taught me more than I ever knew about a boy and girl — what wonderful feeling — nothing dirty. How can anything be bad that makes you feel so good.* ----

If I'm in love I can't be. I'll be going to combat soon. My first duty is to do what I have been trained for. I am a fighter pilot. — I might never come back. It wouldn't *be right to let Billie know I love her and let her wait and never see her again. — I like so many things about her. I like her shy smile. I like her Southern lady ways, I like her quite manner. I like her bashful ways. I like the way she looks at me, she's beautiful and I like how pretty she looks even if she does not fix up in fancy clothes and lots of make up like Murphs girl. Looks like she was a bad girl the way she acts and talks and sticks her tits out. Billie looks like an angel, a real horney one, but an angel and maybe some day I'll . . . diary page missing. Every time I saw her or thought about her there would be a stirring in the groin. But it was more than jumping in bed with her, I really cared for her and enjoyed every part of her company.*

---- for loving to be this wonderful it must be love — those wonderful feelings when we are together and the longing when we are apart for just a few days. ---- But I can't fall in love. You can't be a combat pilot and be in love. If I let my concentration stray for just a second in that P-51, I can be dead. You can't think of love if you are to survive in a hot fighter plane. John M. doesn't let girls bother him. He stays in the barracks and makes model airplanes while the rest of us are out drinking and sc------. Maybe he is smarter not worrying about whether some other guy is sc------- his girl friend or worse yet that she is P.G. Anybody that knocks up a girl get thrown out. Maybe I'm not in love. As soon as I get in the plane I forget all about Billie. At 200 feet and 400 mph all I remember is fly that plane — the beautiful roar of the engine and the land going by. Have we got a team — 16 planes in perfect formation for 4 hours and then break off in two plane elements and stick together like we are one. That's the new tactics that Gen. Chennault the famous Flying Tiger in China says is the best way to survive. Two planes like two football players concentrating on the target — hit and run—acrobatics are important and we are the best acrobatic pilots in the Air Corps [sounds like a little bragging] but the team tactics get the enemy and save our lives. Jesus wouldn't it be a thrill to be sent to China to fly with Claire L. Chennault, the Flying Tiger, the man on the Flying Trapeze We've been reading Time about him.

Ralph, Tom, Bobby, Joe and I went into see Col. Peterson if we could get sent to China. He just laughed and said the Army Air Corps didn't do things that way. There doesn't seem to be any chance for China. [for some of us, the dream became true. We did get sent to China and assigned to the Flying Tigers of the 14th Air Force]

We've got a British Commander training with us for the last two weeks. We must be going to England for duty over Germany. He says our new P-51s can beat the piss out of the "Huns" 109s. He calls the Germans "Huns" or "Bocks". I don't know what that means but guess its something left over from the first World War. He really is a character He gets awfully drunk every night but is the first guy up in the morning and can really fly. He told us to breathe pure oxygen for 15 minutes and it would cure a hangover. It does seem to help. His favorite saying is "It isn't the drinkin you know lads – it's the bloody atmosphere" – and Miss [Mississippi] is 100 in the shade and we are soaking wet from sweat every flight. He taught us a lot about tactics and the tricks by the "bosh" pilots. He is a great admirer of Gen. Chennault and teaches team tactics and not dog fights — although he says the 51 can out fight any plane in the air even his Spitfire. We went to New Orleans to night and just got back from the party at 0400 – Spent the night with a beautiful girl good sc------- but feel pretty ashamed — wonder if Billie can tell when I get back that

Pages 477 to 491 are missing.

I had probably recorded the completion of our training and awaiting orders to transfer in those missing pages. My brother Willie later sent me a clipping from our local paper about my graduation from training at Key Field. The Army's public relations department would usually send news of interest to local papers that related to a local man in uniform. The article in the *Chokio Review,* which would be distributed to my parent's home in the village of Johnson, reads:

Graduates from Pilots' School

Second Lt. Wayne Johnson to Be Assigned to Combat Unit

Second Lt. Wayne G. Johnson of Johnson was graduated from the Tactical Reconnaissance Pilots' school at Key Field, Miss., early this week.

The new tactical reconnaissance pilot will soon be assigned to a combat unit. His duties will be to fly camera equipped P-51 fighters over enemy lines and return to his base with photographic evidence of enemy activity. Future operations are thus planned on the basis of what the photographs reveal to trained intelligence officers.

The Tactical Reconnaissance Pilots' School at Key Field is the only school of its type in the United States. Only carefully selected fighter pilots are enrolled as students in this school, graduates of which are currently serving in all theatres of operations.

Graduates from Pilot's School

Second Lt. Wayne Johnson to Be Assigned to Combat Unit

Second Lt. Wayne G. Johnson of Johnson was graduated from the Tactical Reconnaissance Pilot's school at Key Field, Miss. Early this week. The new tactical reconnaissance pilot will soon be assigned to a combat unit. His duties will be to fly camera equipped P-51 fighters over enemy lines and return to his base with photographic evidence of enemy activity. Future operations are thus planned on the basis of what the photographs reveal to trained intelligence officers.

The Tactical Reconnaissance Pilot's School at Key Field is the only school of is type in the United States. Only carefully selected pilots are enrolled as students in this school, graduates of which are currently serving in all theatres of operations.

Because Key Field was a unique training facility, we thought we were pretty hot pilots. We were well trained.

Chapter -42-

Getting Ready to Head Out

Diary pages   *492 - 514. Almost all our group of Tac. Recon. Class got orders today that we would be going to Hunters Field in Savannah, Georgia. For over* [blank space] *shipment. Don't know where we are going but expect England where most of the other guys from Meridian went. Excited about going to combat – but a little worried -- shouldn't be since we are so well trained and we can take care of ourselves. We are bound to loose some guys, but we've got to whip those bastards that are trying to take over the world. Too bad our Country didn't build up our forces earlier and Pearl Harbor, the rape of Poland, France and Norway and all the others worldwide wouldn't have happened. Called Billie, told her Murph and his girlfriend had gotten a couple of days of catching up . . . * * ! ! * * Murph and I went into base for a physical left the girls to <u>rest</u> and clean up the cabins. Capt. McGuire was the Flight Surgeon. He's a nice guy that ran around with us although Captains aren't supposed to go out with 2ⁿᵈ Lts on dates — but we did double date a few times since his girl was a friend of Billie's. He really checked me over but got me worried that I "looked all warn out". He came back with a big grin and paper that said " It is certified that 2ⁿᵈ Lt. Wayne G. Johnson 0-827 442 has been physically inspected 1000 hours and that there is no evidence of communicable disease." Good for me. I'm ready to go.*

Checked out a new A-14 [leather flight jacket] *Oxygen mask and a new helmet —Type ANH-15, size medium. The Supply Officer, a Major Quillen, said we were responsible for them and would have to pay for them if we were shot down or taken prisoner. What an ass – he made us turn in our old helmets and masks. We asked him if he wanted our brown shorts but he didn't think that was funny. He tried to get* *us restricted to base but the C.O. let us go. Murph and I went right back to the cabins. The girls had gone to town to get some booze – so we are going to take a nap til they get back. Need it — because we got a lot of loving to get before we leave —. [* next day] *We are on the train for Savanah. What a helluva day. B.T. came out to the cabin at 0400. M.P.s looking all over hell for us. "Train leaving this morning – not tomorrow." When I ran over to Murph's cabin to get him out of bed I stepped on a big rock and twisted my ankle. I couldn't hardly walk on it so some of my buddies helped me to the train. We pretended we were drunk otherwise the Flight Surgeon would have taken me to the hospital to X-ray my ankle. It was swollen up like a balloon. Good thing we had some booze on the train. I needed a drink to stand the pain. Damn near got drunk before the M.P.s took it away from us. Don't know what will happen when we get to Savannah – can't walk on my foot.*

Medic got on the train thinks my ankle may be broken. What bad luck. If it is I can't go overseas with my buddies and probably end up in some damn training camp. — Savannah, Ga. what a mess, a hangover and maybe a broken ankle. Things looked better tonight. The Medic would not let me walk off the train. They got a stretcher and 4 guys carried me off and through the station. I was in my dress Greens with my pilots cap laying on my chest. I felt like as ass — all the people in the station were cheering

When they carried me by. They must have thought I was a wounded war hero. Ed Mc----, a real character, told the crowd I was shot down over Berlin after shooting down 11 German planes in battle then I escaped from them although one foot was shot off. The damn liar made it sound so good the M.P.s had to hold back the crowd. In fact there was another train with guys coming back from England so it really sounded possible. They X-rayed my leg and decided it was only a sprain so I'll probably be going with the rest of the group. [next day] *Still in hospital but not all bad —*

Got orders to be shipped to Mission Beach [Florida] *that doesn't sound like Europe. Probably Africa. Flight Surgeon said he would send along orders to have my ankle X-rayed in Miami since they have better X-ray equipment there. Swelling hasn't gone down and it still hurts like hell. Hope its not broken or I'll get grounded. Strictly against Orders but nurse arranged for a line to call home. Didn't tell Ma and Pa I was going overseas but think they suspect. With Arnold loosing his eye* [he was hit in the eye by a Jap sniper in the battle for Guadalcanal] *Roy wounded* [in Africa] *and Clarence in combat,* [in the Philippines] *I know they are real worried but proud of all their sons. Pa hates the Germans so bad for the blood bath in Nor-*

way that he'd be proud to send all their sons. They were both very quite and didn't say much but told me to be careful. Ma said to not talk to any bad girls and drink any poison. She calls all booze poison. [She was probably right.] *Brother Willie and little Ed, the kids call him Lefty, said hello too. Opal and Gwenie were not home so didn't get to talk to them. Might be the last time I ever talk to my family. Guess I'm feeling down because of the pain in my ankle.*

Must remember to write Vern R. And thank him for getting folks ready for phone call. ---- three of my buddies came to the hospital and Amy, my nurse friend, lined the guys up with some girls. Amy wouldn't let me pay for the phone call and said she would get her reward. The other guys left at about 0400 and she gently dressed me. First time since I was a baby anybody put on my underpants. Medic wouldn't let me walk so hauled me in an ambulance to the train station. Litter carriers carried me on the train. Even at 0500 there was a big crowd waving flags and cheering. Hope it wasn't the same crowd that saw me carried off the train a couple of days ago. The train to Miami is miserable with my sore ankle. ----- Miami Beach. — I couldn't get off the base. Medics picked me up at the train and hauled right to the dispensary. I had to tell the medics that I had a dripping tool and he wrote "check for V.D." In big red letters. I tried to order him to change it but found the gold bars of a 2nd Lt. doesn't mean a damn thing to a medic. Then of all the embarrassing luck, I drew a woman doctor. I don't mind my girl friend seeing my p**ker but sure didn't want to show it to no women doctor. She said milk it out and took a smear. She came back a little later and said "you're in luck Lt. No spirochetes". I didn't know what that meant so she said "you don't have the clap after all just a strain." She didn't like the looks of my leg but since their X-ray was broken down she had to send me to a hospital in Miami. My orders must have been cut since they assigned 2 M.P.s to take me downtown.

When I started out the door the Doc called in some corpsmen with a litter and had them carry me out. Just when we were going through this big waiting room with hundreds of guys she called out "hey Lt. You better keep that thing in your pants for a few days — you can't get ahead with that stuff anyway." Everybody roared. God I hated that old bag — probably never had a piece in her life. I was so embarrassed I almost cried but glad I didn't have anything.

They were busy at the City hospital so put me in a bed for the night. [next day] *X-rayed my ankle and the civilian Doctor said it was O.K. not broken — but real bad sprain. Soaked it most of day. Tried to get a pass to get out but Army medic – big Major–came in and said I couldn't get out – said I'd screwed up enough — they needed pilots bad and I wasn't getting out of their sight until I shipped out.*

Miami hospital. A Col. with lots of ribbons and wings came in with two Army doctors. I damn near fainted and thought I must have something after all. They talked to the City hospital doctors who said I could be released any time. The Col. showed me a big envelope with a ribbon on it and said it was sealed orders what would be given to me later and I would be escorted to the Floridian Hotel later in the day. [the Floridian Hotel was the official hotel where the military stayed before going overseas] *After lunch 2 young M.P.s came in and said they were to escort me to the hotel that evening. They were real nice guys. One was from Appleton, Minn. Not far from Johnson and one is from S. Dak. Who had been to Louies'* [Ritter's] *Road House in Graceville many times although I didn't know him except by sight. This was his first assignment after getting out of M.P. training and was kind of impressed that he was to escort a pilot although just a 2ⁿᵈ Lt. on some kind of "secret" mission. The officers had not told them what was happening except that I was to be at the Floridian Hotel by 10 that night. I talked the nurses into getting me a jug, they were kind of scared but the Doc said what the hell he's probably going to Africa or some damn place and get himself killed so just as well have a good time. the nurse, Grace McConnville, got off duty at noon — and we went to a room in the basement.---- She lined up two girls for Elmer and Swede, the two M.P.s and made dates with them when they got off duty. We checked out of the hospital about 4 and drove to a deserted point on the beach.*

We both said we loved each other but I knew that was a lie. Sure was fun though. The other girls had some beer so between times we shared the beer. ---- just made it back to the hospital before 10. Grace drove up and we promised to meet again and gave me her phone and address. I was pretty ashamed that I had lied to Grace, maybe it was just a little lie cause I am sure she knew I didn't love her. I guess it makes it easier for a girl to do it if the boy tells her he loves her. That way she isn't doing anything so bad since its alright if you are in love. But Officers are supposed to be honest and truthful at all times. It's honorable to protect another person's feeling but he has to keep his honor too. I'm proud to be an officer and hope I can always be a good one. I know I am a good pilot and hope to serve my Country well. I don't think it's wrong not to want to go to Africa. I want to go to China.

Chapter-43-
Going Overseas

We headed out from Miami in a southerly direction aboard a C-54 four engine transport. We had been told we could open our Orders when wc about one hour out. I don't know who the authorities thought we might tell out there in the middle of the Ocean. The Orders didn't tell me much except that I was to proceed by air direct to Casablanca and await further orders there. ("Proceed by air" ---I'm glad I was on an airplane!) I could be serving in North Africa or somewhere in Europe. The pilot said most guys that went this route usually ended up in India.

Diary pages 516 -518. Over the Bahamas Islands. My first trip over the Ocean but four engines are really purring so no worries. We opened our Orders and still don't know where the hell we are going. ---- the pilots say it has to be China. WHOOPEE. Maybe will get to fly for the great Gen. Claire Chennault after all. Most of the group went to Europe and only about a dozen of us going the southern route. The transport pilots say our first overnight stop will be Casablanca. Started thinking about Billie and kind of ashamed about the nurse at Savannah and Grace McConnvile in Miami. I wonder if I do love Billie sure think of her a lot. Better forget all that since I'm headed for combat for sure now. Troop Commander warned us about Casablanca. Told us to stay in groups and not get mixed up with any women. But he gave us all several packages of rubbers and pro kits.

Condoms in those days were called rubbers. Pro kits that protected against venereal diseases were prophylactic antibiotic fluid that one injected. The "big boys" say it really burns! During most of our military career, we were shown movies of the dire effects of unprotected sex.

Chapter -44-

Casablanca

Diary pages -518 - 541 . . .

How does one stay pure in the wicked city of Casablanca. We were surprised that after we landed and checked in to the B.B.Q - Hotel de gink. they told us we were free to go into the city for a couple of days. [Bachelor Officers Quarters on air bases were called *Hotel de gink*. I do not know the derivation of that term] —

What a god awful place. Beggars, whores, and every kind of terrible looking humans. — solid milling crowds — I've never seen anything like it. I couldn't believe people could live like this. It was much worse than the movies. There were lots of pretty girls but we were to damned scared to try anything that first night. There were six of us in a group and we never separated.

The guys at the base laughed their heads off at us for being so damn scared. Two pilots that had been flying P-39s agreed to take us to some good spots that they knew about. They had been there almost a year and knew where the good Frenchies hung out. It was so hot we stayed in most of the day and then got some sleep. Washed out our shorts and kackies Geo. was at Sarasota when I was there. I had flown a P-39 there — but wanted to get in the air the worse way so I settled for a P-39. Damn old bucket of bolts but it flew pretty good. Nothing like a P-51 though. What a thrill to get in the air again for just a short time. Gas is too valuable to waste. I wasn't supposed to be flying here because I had no orders but Geo. arranged it with the Old Man. He was a war weary old Major now. When I knew him in Fla. He was just a 1ˢᵗ Lt. So you must get promoted fast in this theater. Hoped the Germans or Wops would come over when I was up but no such luck. Probably just as well, how would I explain what

Diary Pages 522 to 531 *Missing. . . .*

Air raid alarms finally died down. Pretty convincing that we are in a war zone. Don't think our guys got anything but they sure scrambled when that siren goes off. Sure wish I could have be with them up there but we are not going to be assigned to this theater for sure. Although I'd like to get into combat I'm sort of glad its not here. What a hell hole – everything stinks and sand over everything. The people are supposed to be our allies but look sinister as hell. There are lots of interesting military though. English, French, Arabs, Indians, black and all shades of brown jabbering away in many different languages. Met an interesting guy in Norwegian uniform. He is only 19 years old. Lars Jensen came from northern part of Norway– Larvik– not too far from where my parents –he knew where Tromso was and had been there. He escaped with Royal forces and went to England then was sent here. He could talk a little English and with my Norwegian we got along fine. He was surprised to find an American kid in Casablanca that could talk Norsk. He told many sad stories about the rape, burning and destruction of entire cities by the Germans. Some of them had been raised there as kids after the first war and now came back as soldiers. What bastards. Many of his friends that had joined the underground had been spied on by the Quislings and turned over to the Gestapo by their so called German friends. [Quisling was a turncoat who took over as Prime Minister of Norway and cooperated with the German occupation forces.] *It is hard to believe that people who had been raised together could turn on their friends and cause such terrible harm. Many of his had been tortured and shot --- He didn't know where his family was. We are starting to learn that war is really hell. It really hits hard when we see the plane loads of wounded and dead coming through. I tried to send part of my dairy home but the censor wouldn't let it through. I have to be very careful with it or they may confiscate it. Glad I sent all that about my stateside service home. Should make interesting reading when I get back. Hope Pa keeps it sealed up like I asked him to. Wouldn't want Ma to see some of . . . .*

Diary pages 536 to 539 are missing.

540. And not the way an Officer and Gentlemen should act. [Don't know what happened to warrant that comment.] *Lars really had fun. He's been here about six months and never got laid before. He was scared as we were of the Arab stuff. I think this is the first time ever for him the way he talked. He and that blond Wac really hit it off great. She's from some place in Wisconsin and of Norwegian descent so they had something in common. Elsie and I hit it off real good to. She had a boyfriend in Nebraska and didn't want to do it at first but Nebraska is a long ways away and so is Meridian — and both lonely. She said this was the first time for her but she really liked it. She said lots of Majors and Cols tried to take her out but she wouldn't go. Its pretty hard for a girl to be good in a place like this were nice girls are one in thousands for all the guys. She could speak a little Norwegian so that is probably why we got to be such good friends. C.Q. just came in with my orders to leave tomorrow, damn just when things were-*

Chapter -45-

Across the North African Desert to Cairo.

I was now on another C-47 transport plane from Casablanca to Cairo. Diary pages 541 to 549 missing.

550-612. . . . desert as far as one can see. wrecks of tanks, trucks, cars, planes and guns all over. Must have been a hellish big war with all the damage. Wish I was out there flying those escort fighters rather than sitting in this crate without protection. Those fighter guys really swarm around us so we should be safe to Cairo. Cairo looks like a green spot in the desert and can see the Nile wandering along with some beautiful green spots. The pyramids look just like a picture post card.

Cairo is a beautiful city. Much nicer than Casablanca but the same milling crowds, lots of beggars but don't go after us so much. The kids are really cute and follow us around and stare. It must be the British influence here. Lots of nice bldgs. The first trip from the air base was awful. The trucks threw up so much sand we looked like the natives when we got to the hotel. Big party by British officers who gave us rooms to clean up in.

And damn lucky to get to share a room with a British Officer and have it to myself when he is gone. It is much better than the banks of the Nile for romance. Still got insect welts on my ass from the first night under the "romantic" Nile moon. Can't thank Jeremy enough for introducing me to Mira – Mira Hertzog from Tel Aviv in Palestine. She is in the British army as a WAAF. [Women's Auxiliary Air Force.] *Maybe some day I can visit Palestine when peace comes to the world. As Christmas gets nearer we think more about the birth of Christ. It's a wonderful experience to meet someone from the land where Christ walked. Mira could be very romantic but she is also very religious. She doesn't think anything wrong with mak-*

ing out with someone you really like. She is younger than me but knows a lot more about life than I do. She is Jewish but knows a lot more about Christ than I do. We'd talk for hours about religion and the Holy Land. She is a real expert on history and archeology. She spent many hours telling me how the Pyramids and Sphinx were built. I didn't know until she told me that it was a Jewish Court and not the Romans that condemned Jesus to death. Pontius Pilot could have stopped the mob but was too weak to be an effective Governor. She knew all about Martin Luther but didn't think he was a saint or anything. We went out to see the Pyramids at night. What a gorgeous sight with the silent stars. How could there be war and destruction in such beauty. When will men learn to live together in peace. I told her I thought I'd be a preacher like my cousin Hans when I get home. She said you Yanks are to horny to be good ministers. Guess she's probably right. ----we spent many wonderful happy hours together. Her leave is about over and I know I'll be getting Orders any day. Mira gave me a beautiful pen last night. We cried a lot and talked about if we would meet again after this crazy war is over. We have to defeat the tyrants and make certain that they can never rise again. Mira says man will always fight but if we had a League of Nations that all participated in major wars could be avoided. [And of course the United Nations became a reality, but that did not prevent wars, for wars have continued on a regular basis from then on.] *What a wonderful girl she is. I call her Cleopatra. She is the most beautiful girl I have ever seen. Billie is pretty but not a beauty like Mira. Can a guy be in love with two women. I think of Billie a lot and do think I love her — but Mira is different – she is like a princess. She can speak 7 languages: English, French, Italian, German, Spanish, Arabic, and Yiddish.---I taught her some words in Norwegian. She calls me her Viking Prince. She said the old Vikings even came to Palestine a thousand years ago – some stayed and there are still descendants of the Vikings there. She said the early Vikings were not circumcised either so I am a Viking. She claims the reason Jew men are circumcised is otherwise the sand gets under their foreskins. ---- The worst day ever. Mira saw me off at the airfield. We both bawled and pledged our undying love and after the war meet in Tel Aviv ----wonder what Ma would say if I brought a dark skinned Jewish girl home for a wife but she would love her too. I know Pa would.*

Chapter -46-
Cairo to Karachi, India

We left Cairo on a C-47 transport that looked the worst for wear. It was obvious it had been flying around in the desert for some time. Most of the paint was well sun bleached with peeling paint and just looked ragged.

The civilian version of the C-47 used by the airlines was designated the DC-3, manufactured by the Douglas Aircraft Company. Everyone in the Air Corps called it the *Gooney Bird*. It was the Air Corps' workhorse, and used by virtually every Allied air force and every civil airline in the world.

. . . We landed in Abadan on the Red Sea. The temperature was 120 degrees What a terrible place. It was so hot we didn't think the pilot could get this loaded crate off the ground. Don't think he climbed a foot a minute. We were out 50 miles at least until we started climbing. God was it quiet in that plane. I think every guy there was praying. I even said a prayer in Jewish that Mira taught me. I think the pilot was drunk he had been making the trip from Abadan to Karachi for months and was getting pretty goofy. Started down for Karachi, India, he yelled out "Now landing at the asshole of the world." There was a Major on board who didn't think it funny at all. He really chewed the Captain out as soon as we landed. The Captain was a southern guy and said "Well maja suh - you all wait till you see the ass wipe they all got heah and you'll agree with me." --- I hope this airbase is not an example — sand and desert and stuff like sagebrush. Guess this was built by the British. It sure as hell is hot just before Christmas. Don't think we will see any snow or Christmas trees. Bet Ma is baking all her good cookies and fattigman and tyttebear. I can just see the house all trimmed with trees and tinsels, and popcorn. Even with a thousand men around this sure is a lonely place.

Fattigman is a deep-fried Norwegian delicacy. It is sweet like cookie dough. It is rolled out like pie dough and cut in triangles, then a slit is made in the middle and one end is pulled through the slit. "Tyttebear" is usually made into a jelly made from lingenberries. Lingenberries are a tart type of berry, like cranberries, grown only in northern Norway and northern Sweden.

Chapter -47-

Not the Exotic Orient

Karachi, India. We saw a lot of camels going into the city. The Indian bus driver drives wide open and just misses the camels and people. Thousand and thousands of people all carrying big loads. What a ride through the dessert. I couldn't believe Karachi. This was much worse than Casablanca. The stink was overpowering. There is no wood around this country so they dry and burn all the shit. I never smelled burning shit before. God is it awful.

The streets were packed solid with people, kids, old, young, girls and women with veils. People carrying loads of hundreds of pounds on their heads. Beggars were everywhere – they would flock around us with outstretched hands and cry out "Bakshees. Sahib" It means give me gift or alms-Sir. The kids are cute but so many pitiful faces. I have never seen so many cripples, poor naked people laying on the ground. I had some gum and coins I started to hand out. A British officer – with a walking stick – no less –told me it was very unwise to give out very much or we would be mobbed – and we were. They crowded around us so we could hardly breath. The British officer beat at them with his walking stick to get them away. I guess that's why so many carry sticks or canes.

The trucks and busses honked horns steady. The noise is unbearable. There doesn't seem to be any regular stores, just thousands of little stalls selling everything one can imagine. Besides the trucks and cars and Jeeps and military vehicles there were Ox-carts. Ox are big brown bulls that move along about ½ mile per hour. Camels – they really are funny looking with huge piles on top of them. They bite at anyone that get in their way. I liked the horse drawn taxi cabs, called "gherrys".

They look much like the old west 4 wheeled buggies except they have regular car wheels.

I really got a bang out of the English soldiers except they didn't talk English. They talked British I guess –many words I couldn't understand. They were very friendly and colorful. I've never seen so many crazy beards and mustaches all sizes and shapes. Their uniforms looked like they had been on an African campaign for two years without washing or ironing. The British officers except the high rank looked rumpled but very-very- "proper". They seemed to have a pained look on their face probably from using that hard brown paper for toilet paper. The paper is worse than Sears catalog or corn cobs we had at home on the farm. I think its part sand paper. We had run out of American toilet paper at the base so have to use theirs. You have to walk straight and careful after using it.

Now I know what the ATC pilot meant. Karachi is not the place Kipling wrote about. No palaces, no elephants with jeweled thrones. We did see some fancy dressed Indians but most seemed to be in rags. Lots of them wore big loose diapers. I think they call it a "dotti". That's all they wear. It's very handy. They just squat down and take a crap anywhere. They are not bashful if they want to take a leak. Even the British just pull it out and piss any place. Nobody seems to notice.

Hundreds and hundreds of different uniforms from all countries of the world. The most soldierly looking are the big Sikhs – huge men in neat British uniforms but with turbans and big beards and foot long mustaches. Fierce looking guys.

A skinny little naked man – chocolate brown– was playing music and this cobra would come out of a basket and weave his head back and forth. Scarey looking thing. It is impossible to explain all the strange sights, noise, stink and variety of clothing. Most of the little kids are naked – very handy –- their Ma's didn't have to wash diapers.

Lots of women wear "bed sheets" some beautiful white–some stinking yellow, some wore veils and some didn't. Those without veils seemed always to carry a big basket or load on their head. Some looked pretty –nice rice brown and others with big running sores. Didn't seem to be any as pretty as Mira or Billie. I don't think I would dare to go to bed with anyone here. The British soldiers didn't seem to be very particular. The men that stunk the worse and were the filthiest and dirtiest were supposed to be their preachers or Holy men. How could anyone like that inspire anybody. This place looks like the Sodom and Gomorrah of Biblical times. This place looks like its hundreds of years behind us. I'm sure there is nothing like this in the U.S. —The most unbelievable sight was little kids and old crippled men making mud pies out of shit. They had baskets full of horse, cow, oxen, camel and I suppose people shit. They had another basket with straw and grass and they would squeeze it all together just like a mud pie. They laid the pies out in neat rows to dry. On the highway leading into the city we saw rows on rows of these mud pies – they even hang them on the sides of buildings and huts where they live. This is their fuel. This is the reason India stinks so bad. I remember Buffalo Bill burned Buffalo dung to keep warm on the western prairie. One of the guys who was from Kansas said his grandparents lived in a sod house and burned buffalo dung. That's probably why they called him "stinkey". Nothing could smell as bad as this. Even our backhouse on the farm smelled good compared to this. I wonder where Kipling lived . . .

Chapter -48-

To China at Last

On a plane bound for China and in bad trouble. I really screwed up bad this time. Screwed up was probably an understatement. I had gotten into a most serious mess that could have had me up for a court-martial. Some of the guys referred to it as *"Whitey's little mischief."* Now I was in China with no orders.

Why no orders? What was the "little mischief" I got into in India? It involved the "liberation" of a jeep, which unfortunately belonged to the commanding general of the area. This happened near an Army Air Corps training base, Landhi Field, about twenty miles from Karachi, India, now part of Pakistan. Three other pilots and I had won an aerobatic competition and were invited to a party at the mansion of the area's commanding general in Karachi. I recorded the event in my diary.

Unfortunately, many pages of my diary have been lost. I note whenever there are missing pages. The excerpt from my diary reads as follows:

Page *577 - 590 - On a plane for China and in bad trouble. I really screwed up bad this time. I better write my thoughts for it might be the last. If Bob's stunt doesn't work I'll probably [come] back in disgrace, if I'm not shot.* [I had known Bob in Sarasota but he was now a major and C.O. of this base] *We were invited to the general's mansion in Karachi. He is. . . the area commander for all U.S. and Allied forces. He must have taken over some Maharajas palace. It was unbelievably beautiful. --- right out of Rudyard Kipling. We rode in an open bus so [were] covered with sand. We had orders to bring our best dress uniforms so we showered and changed after arrival.*

There were lots of high rank American Navy and Air Corps, Marines, in fancy uniforms, and British in snow white dress. The most gorgeous collection of beauti-

ful women I'd ever seen. We couldn't believe our good luck. Four 2nd Lts. In this crowd. The general was very pompous. He never talked to us. Just sent his aide over - a Major Howell, to welcome us to the party. I've never seen food like this before in my life. It was like a scene out of Arabian Nights. There was food I'd never eaten or seen before but we tried everything.

All they served to drink was scotch. I guess that's all the general drank so everyone had to drink scotch except the women that drank some pink stuff that tasted like Strawberry pop but guess it had gin or something in it.

We had to act like gentlemen which was hard to do. About midnight we went out to the garden to cool off and see if we could sober up a bit. [We were not accustomed to drinking scotch, so we became quite boisterous and were escorted out by the M.P.s and a major who told us in no uncertain terms to wait for the truck back to base.]

That's when we did the dumbest thing. I shouldn't say "we" since it was my idea. We decided to take one of the Jeeps parked in the drive. Our bags were stacked in neat rows with our duty uniforms waiting for the bus. We had enough scotch that Ed, Paul and B.T. [Lts Ed McCune, Paul Sheehan and Brundy T. (B. T.) Melvin thought it was a great idea.] *The Jeep was on top of a steep hill by the house so we all climbed in and let it roll down quietly - We must have been going 50 mph when we got to the bottom and through the guard gate. When we got in the light of the guard gate we saw the general's flag on the fender of the Jeep. Jesus Christ we'd stolen the general's Jeep. The guards didn't hear us coming until we were right at the gate. They just jumped up and saluted when they saw the general's Flag waving over the fender. The guards didn't seem excited so maybe we'd gotten away.*

We didn't dare turn back so I threw it in gear and headed for the base. Ed, Paul and B.T. had picked up some turbans in the hallway of the kitchen and were wearing those. Maybe the guards thought the gen. aide was drinking some and taking some dignitaries home. We made the 20 miles to the base in record time. We didn't dare slow down at the gate and I figured the general would never stop anyway. There were big Sikh guards and an M.P. at the gate. They saluted with their mouths wide open when we raced through. The American flag on one fender and the big general's flag on the other were straight out in the breeze. We parked a 1/4 mile from our barracks and ran like hell through the desert. Didn't even worry about any cobras. [We jumped in bed and hoped we wouldn't be caught.]

At 0400 the next morning the shit hit the fan. The C.Q. on duty was standing by my bed. The M.P. s had described me pretty accurately. I'd lost my C. Cap in the ride and my blonde hair was waving in the breeze when we went trough the gate. There were four M.P.s with guns with the C.Q. [The C.Q. is the "Charge of Quarters," the night officer on duty.]

I must have dressed in 30 seconds. They wouldn't even give me a drink of water while my head was exploding from the damn scotch. The C.Q. and M.P. escorted me over to base headquarters. When the major and Sgt. M.P.s walked out of his office all three damn near dropped dead. I was a good friend of Bob's in Sarasota when I saved his ass when I had subbed for him on guard duty and he sneaked into town.

He was so mad he was purple he just screamed at me "Johnson you dumb S.O.B what have you done now." He swore at me for 15 minutes, it seemed like four hours – without stopping. When he ran out of breath he dismissed the four M.P. s and the C.Q. and said I'm going to personally kill this S.O.B myself. I'd never heard an officer talk like that before – even when he was mad. When the C.Q. and M.P. s left he sat down at his desk and I thought he was going to cry. By now he was white as a sheet and shaking harder than I was. I was sober then. Real sober. Although we were good friends in Sarasota I didn't know what he could do. He had his duty.

Bob started talking in a quiet voice – almost a whisper when he read off about 50 charges. One of the charges was transporting native personnel illegally on a U.S. military base. They thought the other guys were Indians. I suppose because of their turbans and the Jeep parked near the mess hall.

The major never asked if anyone else of our group was with me. He told me I'd probably be shot for all those if proven in a war zone or at least a long prison sentence. He said real soft: I know you were drunk or you wouldn't do anything that stupid. You're a good officer and a top pilot. You have to be good what you did with that P-40 at Sarasota. Then he told the Sgt. how I had safety landed a P-40 when the throttle had jammed wide open. The [Operations Officer] *had ordered me to bail out but I kept turning off the gas until I got to base and then landed dead stick.* [Dead stick means you land the plane without power, which is very difficult to do with a high powered plane like the P-40.] *The Sgt. said he remembered he was at the field at the time. Bob sat for 10-15 minutes and never said a word. There wasn't a sound in the room. The sweat was dripping off the end of my* [nose] *- and dripping on my tie. Finally he and the Sgt went into the other room. The clock now read 0500. I think he told me "at ease" but I couldn't or didn't dare to move. They came back in about 15 minutes and told me to sit down. I'd been standing [at full attention] for about an hour but didn't realize I was soaking wet. He was still pale and said "Whitey* [my nickname in the service] *I think the U.S. owed you one. You* *risked your life to save a P-40 when we need every plane — and I'd probably be a buck private if it wasn't for you taking the rap for me that day in Sarasota." He said " I don't know if I can pull it off but I am going to try and Sarge will help — besides being the dumbest bastard — you got to be the luckiest bastard I know.*

We got a radio message that assigns you to the 14th Air Force. Do you know what that means – you are scheduled to fly with the greatest air leader in the world Gen. Claire Lee Chennault. I think his fist was going through the desk where he hit when he said Gen. Claire Lee Chennault. Bang, bang, bang, bang, and each time the top would jump off my skull. "You're going to be a Flying Tiger and I'm going to help you get there." He showed me the radio message dated 22 Dec. 1944, - can't remember it all but remember it said 2nd Lts. Edward L. McCune, Wayne G. Johnson, Paul B. Sheehan, Brundy T. Melvin, having reported this station per orders Miami Beach dated 12 Dec 44 are assigned 14th Air Force and WP via air, rail, or govt motor and report CG 14th AF for further duty. EDC 4 Jan 45 which means no later ---than 4 Jan. 45. He didn't say anything about the other 3 guys. I was honor bound to tell there were not Indians in the Jeep with me. I decided it would not be honorable to volunteer information. Bob stood up from his desk. He was now a Major again. "Lt. Johnson –2nd Lt. Wayne G. Johnson you are hereby ordered per verbal orders of the commanding general to report to the flight line at 0630 hrs to dep 0645 via air to Kunming China Hqtrs 14th A.F. Sgt escort the Lt. to his qtrs for his per. effects and don't let him out of your sight even to take a piss-" his DISMISSED *just about blew my head off.* [I believe he told the Sgt. to put me on any plane that was leaving the base and that he didn't give a damn where it was going.]

He handed the Sgt a written pass to get me on the plane and a copy of the radio message. I asked if I could get very far without formal orders. "Get the fuck out. I think it will work and you got everything to lose." [I left in a hurry escorted back to the barracks by the Sgt. M.P.] *Ed, Paul and B.T. were up - scared to death. When I told them I was being shipped out immediately to avoid a ct. martial they wanted to go and confess and not me take the rap. The Sgt really blew up. "You assholes keep your fucking mouths shut. The Major has his neck out a mile and he doesn't need no more fucking heroes." We all stood with our mouths open — we never heard an enlisted man talk to officers like that before — not even a top Sgt but guess we couldn't be considered officer class for the . . . stuff we pulled. He got not a whisper out of any of the guys and I knew they'd keep the secret. Sgt got me to the plane and insisted on carrying my bag on. He saluted and then said "I'd like --- to shake your* *hand." "Hope we meet in China. . . . With your guts, you'll give the Japs hell. Don't worry about the Major. All the general will ever know is that there were three men with turbans - unidentified - probably Indian service personnel." God – I hope they don't get in trouble – if they do I'll have to go back and take my medicine. Maybe after a while the general will cool off. He's got his fancy Jeep back and besides it was his damn scotch that got us all out of shape. I suppose some camel driver is wearing my C. Cap with 2nd Lt. Bars. I'm so damn hungry and thirsty even the C. rations taste good.* [C-rations were Army dried food packages with no flavor but were designed as survival food.] *The pilot came back and said "You must be on a big secret mission —you are not to get off the plane at any stop until we get to Kunming." So damn cold freezing my nuts off in this plane. These sun tans* [type of summer uniform] *are not designed for high altitude. Pilot brought back a blanket to cover up with.*

[The plane was a C-47 used for hauling supplies and troops but had no heat in the cargo and passenger section.]

If I ever get out of this damn dumb stunt with the Jeep – that's it – on my honor I vow I will never again do anything like that <u>again</u> *that can screw up my career and future. At the time "borrowing " the Jeep didn't seem like a bad idea — if it were one of the Sgt's jeeps might not be too bad —but of all the rotten luck it had to be the general's — once the die was cast we didn't dare to turn back. If other guys get in trouble I have to go back. – they cannot take the rap for me. We were all in on it but I was the ringleader so I must take full responsibility. Never forget Bob saying "what the fuck did you mean* <u>The Vikings are coming</u> *the* <u>Vikings are coming</u> *when you went through the gate." When I explained what it meant, all he said, "oh shit, what next." Bet those Sikh guards still can't figure that out.*

Don't know if the old Vikings got as far as India but I remember Mira saying they raided Jerusalem in about 900 A.D. Don't think Pa would be very proud of my "Viking" behavior but I must have some of their blood. Maybe in a few days I can rectify my mistake and do for my country what I have been trained for. I know I am a damn good pilot and [diary page is missing]

I arrived in Kunming, China, the headquarters of the Flying Tigers in a sweat and more than a little worried. I had no idea how I would explain that I was there without any formal orders.

Diary Page 596 - *When I reported to the 14th A.F. Hqtrs the major in charge said "what the hell am I supposed to do with you without orders." He raved on and on about those dumb bastards in the 10th* [he was talking about the 10th Air Force with headquarters in India] *and stupid bastards in Karachi sending men in without orders. "How the hell do we know you are not a Jap spy." The corporal said he never saw a white headed Jap. He asked where I was from.* [I probably replied that I was from a farm near Wheaton, Minnesota.]

The Major said: "Jesus Christ now they are sending us sixteen year old farm kids from Minnesota." They sure are informal around here - nobody salutes and are very casual. We heard the Old Man is not much for discipline but insists on perfection in the air. No one ever refers to General Chennault. It is always the Old Man. The major said "I suppose the next man we get will have his orders written on ass wipe."

It was told me to go to the hostel, which is what they called the living quarters, and get some rest, then get ready to go out to the combat base. He said that I needed to change clothes for a review by General Chennault, Commander of the Flying Tigers, later that day.

A short time later, a number of other pilots and me were called out in formation and met by General Chennault. As he came down the line he stopped and asked each pilot a few questions. I was scared shitless. I was afraid he had found out about my little *mischief* in India. "Scared shitless" was a common used in the military to describe how frightened a person really was. One of the questions he asked me was where my orders assigned me to. I had to tell him I didn't have any orders yet.

It was a cold day, but sweat ran down my back. Kunming was about six thousand feet above sea level and it was quite cold. I didn't explain why I didn't have any orders. That didn't seem to bother him. He told his aide, "Send him out to McComas, he needs some new pilots." Only a commander like General Chennault, Commander of the Flying Tigers, would make such an order. He made just an off-the-cuff oral order. I learned later that was the type of thing he often did. He was known for not following protocol or regulations. He did what was necessary to get the job done.

The major told me that I was one lucky kid to be assigned to one of the best fighter squadrons with one of the best commanders. He told me to go back to the hostel and wait until someone from Suichuan came to escort me out.

Col. Edward O. McComas was commander of the 118th Tactical Reconnaissance

Black Lightning Squadron, located at Suichuan in what was referred to as "the pocket" in eastern China. The base was surrounded by Japanese troops. A few days later, I arrived at Suichuan. Another squadron, the 74th Fighter Squadron, was at Kanchow, about fifty miles south of Suichuan. The job of these squadrons was to harass the Japanese, to keep them from over running our bases, and to attack enemy shipping. It was from these fields that we attacked Japanese airfields like Canton, Hankow, and Formosa, and shipping in Hong Kong harbor and along the east China coast.

It was several days before I was notified to get ready to leave. There weren't many guys around, so it got rather boring and I was homesick. All the other pilots with orders had left right after the review.

Diary pages missing. . . *what a lonely day. No friends or buddies. Everyone here very nice but I don't know anyone – It takes a while to get acquainted. No other pilots in the hostel.*

I miss the folks, my brothers and sisters and all my friends but I miss Mira too but I miss her in a different way. ---- So peaceful now can not think about Christmas again. What Jesus means to the world. Why do we have wars? I know we have to fight to free people from dictators, but why must there be dictators like Hitler, Mussolini and the Jap war lords. Some day we will have peace. If I have kids I want them to be free. Ran out of my good note paper — borrowed some pages from a newspaper guy that was passing through. Can't remember his name but he wasn't much interested in me since I had not been to combat. He was a real drunk – his nose was red as a beet and he stunk booze all the time. I think he might be a fairy because he looks at me kind of funny. One of the other guys here said he wanted him to go take a bath together some place. Glad I have a room all by myself. I propped a chair under the door knob. Don't want to have anything to do with any fairies. They say he smokes opium too.

The news guy left this morning. God am I glad. Don't really know what fairies do but I don't want any close to me. Ish. There was an air raid last night had to run to shelter but don't think anything happened. Couldn't hear any bombs or guns. -------

Dairy pages missing.   *What will the New Year bring? The Old Man [Gen. Chennault] says we are going to win the war before next Christmas. Hope I get sent out soon.* ------

I didn't have long to wait. I checked out in a nice P-51 and flew out to Suichuan with one of the veteran pilots from the squadron. I started flying in combat the next day.

It was several weeks before the orders arrived that assigned me to the Black

Lighting Squadron. I had already flown missions that were not recorded by the time my orders arrived. My missions were supposedly recorded by the 68th Wing, but those records were never transferred to my squadron. This is what we called "snafu" (situation normal all f......d up)"

I like the Chinese. The kids are really curious. They just grin and stare. They aren't beggars like in India but they accept any kind of treat. I got a Chinese phrase book today. They call it a "Pointee-talkee". By pointing to a phase you are supposed to be able to communicate with the Chinese.

Wherever we went off base, groups of Chinese children and sometimes adults would follow us around. They appeared to be particularly interested in my very blonde, almost white hair. They would point at their own very black hair, then point at mine and giggle. Sometimes, one was brave enough to reach up and touch my hair, which caused uproarious laughter from the crowd.

One day, when four or five guys went for a hike off base, we witnessed an awesome spectacle. A woman was in a nearby field picking up vegetables. She did not appear to notice us, although we were very close. She suddenly squatted down, let out a little moan, and gave birth to a baby in the field. There was a little cry, obviously from the baby. She bit off the umbilical cord, took a shawl-like blanket from around her shoulders, and wrapped it around the baby. She laid the baby on the ground, and went on picking vegetables. I had watched animals being born on the farm, but this was quite an eye-opener. I was amazed that she could go back to work immediately, for I knew that women at home were usually in the hospital and in bed for some days after having babies. Some of the guys turned white and almost got sick from viewing the strange occurrence. We hurried back to camp and that incident was the talk of the evening. Some skeptics suggested we had made the whole thing up, but a sergeant who had been in China for some time said he had witnessed similar incidents. It was quite an introduction to Chinese life.

This is a different country than India. People are poor but not such terrible sickness and cripples. They seem to be very friendly. Whenever we go out they put up their thumbs and say "ding hao" – means very good. Gen. Chennault is their hero. They call him "shen no" or something like that. I learned "meg wah ping" meant American soldier and are the words we are supposed to use if challenged by a Chinese guard.

While still at Kunming, I had written in my diary:

Learning to eat new food. Went to a famous café, "Billies" but it wasn't tops. Sure different though.

[diary page missing] . . . *the city* [Kunming] *is about as crowded as Karachi but doesn't stink as bad. It's a different kind of smell. Don't think they burn dung for fuel. –but they have little buckets. They pick up all the human waste -shit that is - at night and carry it in buckets on a pole across their shoulders. I guess they empty all the pots in the city and trot out to the country to fertilize their farms and gardens.*

They raise the most beautiful vegetables but we are warned not to eat anything fresh. Seems a shame to boil all the nice vegetables.

Some of us had to try the vegetables. The carrots and some of the other vegetables were beautiful but it wasn't long before we got the shits. The flight surgeon was not sympathetic. He said now you will believe us when we tell you not to eat or drink something. *They also warned us about the girls. –the usual lecture about clap, chanre, ziff, elephantitis and all the other things that make your family valuables drop off. I don't care about going to whore houses. Its embarrassing and not much fun. I'm going to wait until I meet a nice girl I know is clean.*

Still worried as hell about that Jeep incident and don't need any more risks. They sent me here to fly fighters and not get screwed up in foolish things. Some of these Chinese girls are real beauties so it's hard not to be tempted.

Learned to drink "jing bao juice" . Jing Bao means air raid in Chinese and its properly named. Its foul tasting stuff like some of the Minn. 13 [moonshine] we had at home but stinks much worse. Never tasted any bad stuff quite that bad. One almost has to hold your nose to drink it. It is not too bad mixed with some lemon powder and water. Dance at the USO but I'm not much for dancing. Too bashful to ask the girls. One took a shine to me and told me how handsome I was and nice build. Guess she's trying to cheer me up. I didn't get shook up by her but asked her if she could go out. She said it was against the rules but we might meet at Billies Café.

Got up this morning feeling good. Did 100 sit-ups and 50 push-ups - still in good shape and have to stay that way to be good in combat. Guy next room had a tape measure. Still have 28" waist and almost 42" chest so am keeping up my condition real good.

Chapter -49-

Who Were the *Flying Tigers?*

The *Flying Tigers* was the brainchild of General Claire Chennault. Chennault, who, as an Army Air Corps captain, had written a series of articles under the name "*The Role of Defensive Pursuit,*" *in which* he argued for fighter plane escorts on heavy bomber missions. He also organized a team of acrobatic pilots called "*Three Men on a Flying Trapeze,*" who demonstrated the versatility of fighter planes. Chennault, with two other pilots, put on air shows around the country, much like the "*Blue Angels*" of today. He incurred the ire of high-ranking Air Corps officers who believed that bombers were invincible and did not need fighter escorts. His concepts were proven correct in the early days of WWII when bomber losses over Germany were staggering, until air commanders started to use fighter escorts.

Chennault was forced to resign from the Army Air Corps because of his criticism of higher authorities. But other nations recognized the validity of his views. He was invited to Russia to advise its air force, but he accepted an invitation to China instead. He arrived in China in 1937 in time to see the destruction of Chinese cities by the Japanese air force. The Japanese had destroyed the Chinese Air Force. It was Chennault's job to advise Generalissimo Chiang Kai-shek on how to protect China from further invasion by the Japanese.

While watching the Japanese air force bomb and destroy China's cities, he carefully studied their aerial tactics. He would later use this knowledge training his pilots. As the Japanese overran China and threatened the free world, Chennault had a vision. He would form a volunteer group of experienced American airmen to come to the aid of China. He sold the concept to President Franklin Roosevelt, who approved Chennault's unique idea.

In April 1941, Roosevelt issued an executive order and the American Volunteer Group (AVG) was born. Chennault was placed in charge. AVG had to be super-secret, since the United States and Japan still had a neutrality pact that did not allow giving armed support to nations at war with Japan.

Airmen from the Army, Navy, and Marines were recruited. One hundred pilots and about two hundred fifty enlisted men, mechanics, radio men, gunnery experts, and all types of support personnel necessary to operate a fighter squadron. The pilots soon found themselves in Burma, gaining the skills of combat fighter pilots and flying the P-40 *Warhawk* under the tutelage of Chennault. The support personnel learned to do their jobs under the most primitive of conditions. The mission of the AVG was to protect the Burma Road, the supply life-line to China. Japan controlled all Chinese ports, so the Burma Road was the only supply avenue to China. The pilots were to be paid $500.00 to $750.00 a month, a huge sum, since 2nd Lt Army pilots were paid $125.00. In essence, these volunteers were mercenaries. But it was the only method of getting experienced pilots to aid China, since we were not at war with Japan at that time.

One hundred P-40s had been sent to Burma for Chennault's mission. The P-40 was a rugged fighter, but considered obsolete by modern fighter standards. The P-40s had been scheduled to go to Britain, but the British air force turned them down. They wanted more modern planes, so the Army decided to give the P-40s to Chennault for his new unit. The AVG pilots, most of whom had never flown the P-40, had to learn its best features. Under Chennault's instructions, they found that the P-40 would challenge and outfight the best of Japanese fighters.

When war with Japan broke out after Pearl Harbor, the AVG was the only effective fighting air unit in the Far East. Most of the unit was moved from Burma to Kunming, China, after Pearl Harbor. Later that month, they surprised a group of Japanese bombers who had previously had no air opposition, and shot most of them down. Ed Rector, one of the AVG pilots on that mission who would later become my 23rd Fighter Group Commander, chased one to the bombers halfway to Hanoi, and finally shot it down. But in his enthusiasm, he did not realize he did not have enough gas to return to base. He ran out of gas and had to "belly in," land wheels up, in a rice paddy. He was found and rescued some days later.

The P-40 was found virtually intact. Mechanics had it flying a few days later. Although they had been training in Burma since early July 1941, the mission in Kunming on 20 December 1941 was the AVG's first combat mission. It was a most crucial mission.

The Chinese, watching the hated Japanese fall from the sky under the AVG attacks, dubbed the American pilots, *fei hu,* or the *Flying Tigers.* A Chinese reporter wrote a newspaper article referring to the Americans as *Flying Tigers.* Spencer Moos, a reporter for the *New York Times,* used the term in his story. The name *Flying Tigers* stuck. Picked up by the American news agencies, it applied to American air units in China throughout the war. To the Chinese, these American pilots exhibited the ferocity and courage against great odds, epitomized by the tiger so idolized in Chinese lore.

Using Chennault's innovative tactics, the AVG compiled a record of aerial victories, unsurpassed in any theater for a unit of its size. It destroyed one hundred and ninety seven Japanese aircraft in the air and many more on the ground, while losing only twelve AVG pilots in combat.

When the AVG was disbanded as a volunteer group on 4 July 1942, it became the nucleus for the China Air Task Force (CATF) - 23rd Fighter Group and later the 14th Air Force. I later came into the 23rd Group as an Army Air Corps pilot. Since America was now at war, it did not want mercenaries representing the military in combat.

Top local military commanders and commanders in Washington made a terrible tactical mistake. General Clayton Bissell, who had been promoted to brigadier general one day of ahead of Chennault, was the top commander in the China-Burma-India theatre. He came to Chennault's headquarters in China and ordered that all AVG personnel would be inducted into the Army, most at reduced rank.

Most of the AVG agreed to stay and become a part of the Army Air Force, but since they had been in combat for months, asked that they be given leave to go home for a rest. Bissell refused and told the men that if they did not stay, they would have to find their own way home and would all be inducted as Army privates on their return. Most of the AVG were furious. They said to hell with it and decided to go home.

Bissell's threats were not actualized, since most of the AVG who went home served their country with distinction and honor in many capacities. A small group of pilots who became squadron commanders in the newly formed 23rd Fighter Group with a number of service personnel, did stay on in China. Tex Hill, who became one of the top aces in China, persuaded a number of pilots and personnel to stay on. He argued that America was at war and that we could not abandon Chennault or China. He foresaw that China would be a critical theatre in the war effort. Chennault gave Tex a major's commission and designated him squadron commander of the 75th

Fighter Squadron. Tex later became commander of the 23rd Fighter Group, where I would be later assigned.

When the AVG was disbanded, the *Flying Tigers* designation followed, and all units that served under General Chennault in China were called *Flying Tigers*. The logo, or official patch, for the AVG was a tiger with wings flying through a "V," for victory. The CATF logo was a Flying Tiger with an Uncle Sam hat leaping through a torn Japanese flag. It showed that the Flying Tigers was an official unit of the United States Army Air Force. When the 14th Air Force was formed on 10 March 1943 from the CATF, its logo was a Flying Tiger against a blue background with the U.S Air Force star above. Chennault personally approved the design.

This was the prestigious *Flying Tigers* unit I was to now join. As my major friend in Karachi said, "I would now be flying for the great *Flying Tiger*, General Claire Lee Chennault." As I wrote earlier, Gen. Chennault gave a verbal Order to his aide to send me out to Col. McComas' squadron. Mc Comas was one of the top Aces in China and one day would become "Ace in a Day" for shooting down five Jap planes on one mission. To be assigned to his squadron would mean some excitement for a "farm kid".

Chapter -50-

Out to Combat

After the short stay in Kunming, I flew a P-51 out to the Suichuan air base with a flight leader that had been in combat for some time. Suichuan was located in the southeasterly part of China and was northeast of Hong Kong. The huge Japanese base at Hankow was only about two hundred miles away and Jap troops were less than fifty miles away. It promised a lot of action.

Diary page 616: *Real nice bunch of guys. Most trained at Key Field. This was supposed to be a Tactical Reconnaissance Squadron but most of what they did was fighter work like the other fighter squadrons.*

Technically, a tactical reconnaissance squadron's function was to search for enemy positions and photograph the installations. The 118th did fly reconnaissance, including typical fighter missions. I knew some of the guys who had left Meridian before I did, and most looked really tired. They had been flying lots of missions. With Japanese bombing almost every night, it was difficult to get proper rest. At page 617 in my diary I wrote: …. *looks like I'm really going to see some action. The C.O. didn't seem a bit concerned that I didn't have any written orders. He asked about things at Key and then a long lecture about combat tactics, team work and how to stay alive.*

The first night after my arrival at the Suichuan base, I got a deathly scare. We were listening to Tokyo Rose on the radio. She always came up with a lot of pro-paganda about how victorious the great Japanese fighters were, and always played some nice music. Suddenly during her program, she stopped the music and said; "Second Lt. Wayne G. Johnson, serial number 0 827 442, who his friends call Whitey, just arrived at Suichuan air field. Hey Whitey, think about some guy screwing your girl friend back home. You will be sorry you ever joined the air corps. You won't last long. Our superior pilots will take care of you and your commander will send a telegram home to your parents that you were killed in action." She said we were all a "bunch of amateurs and wouldn't last long."

Col. Mc Comas told me not to worry. He said that that was the kind of crap she put out all the time. He said that there were Jap spies among the native workers in India and China who are obviously stealing records and sending them to Tokyo Rose. By paying poor natives a small sum, it was easy for Japan recruit spies. He said that our intelligence caught some, but there always seemed to be more. He told us that just a few days ago they caught a Chinese worker with a batch of orders at headquarters in Kunming. The amateur spy was turned over to the Chinese army commander, who had him shot on the spot.

That didn't cheer me up much. I didn't sleep very well that night. This was not the kind of excitement I was looking forward to. For Tokyo Rose, broadcasting from Tokyo, to know the very day of my arrival at this isolated base and even my serial number, was quite chilling to say the least.

Col. Mc Comas took me out the next day on a mission. It wasn't much. We went out, bombed some bridges, and shot up some enemy calvary. I wrote in my diary:

625. Damn Japs get us up almost every night and we have to dive into the trenches. The trenches we used for protection were about four feet deep and about two feet wide. They gave good protection unless a bomb was dropped right in the trench, which never happened as long as I was there.

"Lt. Wayne Johnson in air raid trench at Suichuan Air Base"

Wish we had some night fighters. McComas isn't much for going up in a P-51 at night. We did night training in states but its different here. No runway lights, no beacon, no radio beams. He's probably right it would be more luck than sense if we caught any Japs. They don't do much damage anyway. Mostly drop banana bombs. They make a lot of noise and when AAs open up looks like 4ᵗʰ of July. The Japs don't hit much either.

The "banana bomb" was a small anti-personnel bomb about the size of a banana, hence its given name. The enemy bombers would drop them by the hundreds. Most would not go off, but we had to be very careful about picking them up. They would also drop some big bombs, about five hundred pounds, and sometimes get lucky and hit one of our planes or our gas supplies. They only came over at night, for they knew they would not have a chance against our P-51s during the day. Obviously, part of their purpose was to harass us and keep us awake at night to wear us out.

"Pilots of "C" Flight 118ᵗʰ Black Lightning Squadron. Whitey Johnson is on the right in front row. Oliver Bateman is on the right in the back row."

Chapter -51-

A Friendly Fire Tragedy

One night there was a disaster while we had two night fighters at the base. The night fighters were both P-61 Black Widows, with the latest radar equipment that could spot enemy planes in the air. The radar tower alerted the night fighters about an unidentified target approaching the base and sent the fighters aloft. The Japanese had been on several bombing runs, so it appeared another raid was imminent. The tower directed the night fighters towards the target, which appeared to be a large bomber. The Black Widows shot down the unidentified plane.

I was in the trench with "Vitamin" Pearsall next to me. Pearsall had contracted yellow jaundice and been hospitalized in India for some time. He was given a lot of vitamins, so that became his nickname —— "Vitamin". We still call him that to this day. As we saw the explosion in the air and the debris falling, Vitamin started cheering "we got the S.O.B."

Unfortunately, it was not a Japanese plane. One of our gas transports, a converted B-24 four-engine bomber, was just arriving as the air raid was on. His IFF, a frequency that identified our planes as friendly, must have malfunctioned while the pilot was enjoying the bombing show.

Our squadron flight surgeon had gone up as on observer in the night fighter to witness the effects of night flying. When they landed, he told the C.O. that he thought we had shot down one of our own tankers, since the Japanese did not have twin-tailed planes. It had to be one of our B-24s. He was right. The next day, two of the crew members who had parachuted out of the burning plane walked into base. Six guys, the rest of the crew, were killed. It was a sad day, but one of the mistakes of war. Now when we hit one of our own, it's called "friendly fire." There were other mistakes.

Chapter -52-

Bad Publicity

We were not supposed to keep a diary or journal, but a lot of the guys did, including Col. McComas. On page 626, I recorded:

. . . have to be very careful with my diary. Capt. Watts caught me writing and gave me hell. Gave me a big lecture about danger of recording anything. But C.O. said it was O.K. but make sure not to take any pages with me. Told about Harmon and Scott and harm to air raid net work had on their stories.

Someone contacted Col. McComas about Watt's order, so McComas called the squadron together and told us it was okay to keep a journal, but told us to be very careful with it. He said, "When you guys get home, don't write a damn book with vital information that could be harmful to the war effort." He then described how two officers, who should have known better, wrote some books that disclosed vital military information.

Tom Harmon, the great football player who had just came to China with a P-38 squadron, had been shot down in Japanese held territory not far from our base, but had escaped capture. He was sent back to the U.S. Whenever an airman was shot down in enemy territory and escaped capture, he would usually be sent home or to another theater. Gen. Chennault did not want to risk that person getting shot down again and captured. The Japanese would be sure to extort details about the air-raid warning system from that prisoner, and put a lot of people at risk.

When Harmon got home, he wrote a book called "Pilots Also Pray," and gave speeches about his shoot down and escape. He detailed his mission, being shot down, and how he managed to escape with the assistance of the air-raid warning net.

Col. Robert Scott, who had been commanding officer of the 23rd Fighter Group, wrote "God is my Co-Pilot." In his book, he too described how the air-raid warning net worked, but not quite in the detail that Harmon had. There was a lot of concern that their books might have compromised the air-raid warning system. The publicized release of vital war information was what General Chennault wanted to avoid. It was said that Chennault exploded when he heard of Harmon's book. It was a good thing Harmon was no longer in China!

The air-raid warning net was developed by Chennault in the early days of the war in China. Spotters were posted near Japanese air bases with radios, and when Japanese planes took off, the spotter would flash the news to another spotter in the direction the Japanese were headed. Spotters were stationed on mountain tops and as the planes flew by, would report the number of planes and direction they were headed to the next person down the line. Sometimes they used smoke signals as well as radios.

Each American base had an alert system. When we got word that an enemy flight was two hundred miles away, there would be a "one ball alert," And pilots were ordered to stand by. There was a flag pole where red bamboo balls, about a foot in diameter, were hoisted when the enemy was one hundred miles away. Then, two balls would go up and pilots would dash to their planes.

"Pilots dashing to their planes on air raid alert"

When enemy planes were about fifty miles away, three balls would go up and pilots would get into the air. At night, they would put candles in the balls for visibility.

In addition to the ball alert, Chinese soldiers would have an iron triangle, similar to that used on the chuck wagons in the west, to use as an alarm. They would run around the base and bang on it with an iron rod shouting, "Jing Bao, Jing Bao" to wake every one up, so we would go to the air-raid trenches. "Jing Bao" meant "air-raid" in Chinese. It was a very effective system that depended on the alertness of the spotters, who were very dedicated. Release of any details of the system could be fatal to the spotters and to our air crews.

On page 627, I wrote: . . . *have flown a couple of not very exciting missions. Bombed some bridges and shot up some horse cavalry and trains*. Shooting horses was horrible. As I was a farm boy, I did not like to see animals get hurt. The Japanese had horse cavalry, however, so when we strafed a unit, horses would get killed too. Six fifty-caliber guns had lots of striking power. Seeing horses blown apart or lay kicking in the road were terrible, emotional experience. One could not keep the tears from flowing.

Since my written orders assigning me to the squadron had not yet come though, the operations officers would not record my missions. He said that was up to 68th Wing, where pilots were assigned until ordered to a particular squadron.

I wrote in my diary:

Damn fool won't log it until my orders come. Don't give a damn as long as I can fly —what a goofy war – I fly missions but I am not really flying missions because I'm not officially assigned here yet. I suppose if I get shot down he won't report me missing because I'm not here anyway. It would take a ground pounder to make those kinds of decisions.

Normally the operations officers were pilots, but because all squadron pilots were needed for missions, ground officers were assigned as operations officers. We referred to non-flying officers as "ground pounders," which wasn't very nice because most were very dedicated and competent. Our squadron's operations officer was a friendly fellow, but very strict about regulations and procedure. Because I didn't have written orders assigning me to the squadron, he would not record my presence.

Chapter -53-
The Hell of Ofuna

Christmas was another bad day. Some smart guy in wing intelligence thought the squadron should make a raid on Japanese installations at Hong Kong, which was a highly defended area. He thought the enemy would not be expecting us to fly on Christmas Eve, but he was wrong. The Japanese not only expected us, but knew exactly when the flight would arrive. We learned later that the Japanese intelligence had an exact copy of the order from our bulletin board that stated the number of planes and the names of the pilots, as well as the recommended targets. They obviously had good Chinese spies in our headquarters.

One of the 118th pilots, Max Parnell, had a devastatingly lonely Christmas experience — he became a prisoner of war (POW).

Max Parnell in *Black Lightning* P-51 taken on day of his fatal mission to Hong Kong. He wasn't smiling later that day.

After the war, I interviewed Max Parnell for a story that I co-wrote with him, titled "The Hell of Ofuna," for the fourth volume of "Chennault's Flying Tigers," for which I was the editor. In the story, Max relates his experience as a POW. In part, it goes as follows:

I was flying a P-51 with the 118th Tactical Reconnaissance "Black Lightning" Squadron stationed at Suichuan, one of the few American bases left in the "pocket" in southeast China. Some smart guy [in Intelligence] *thought the Japanese would not expect us on such a holiday. Not so smart it turned out. We came down the slot between Victoria Island and Kiatek airdrome in trail with Col. Ed McComas, our squadron commander, leading . . . I was right on the deck. My two five hundred pound high-explosive bombs hit the Japanese freighter dead center without touching the water. Just the way you are supposed to do it!*

I had to pull up hard to miss the stack. Just as I cleared the center of the ship there was a bomb blast or explosion within the ship. Although the bombs were supposed to have a four to five second delays, they must have gone off on impact. There was a concussion. It felt like I got slapped in the rear with a boat paddle. The cockpit immediately filled with smoke and fire. I was blinded. This was real trouble. Maybe I could make the mainland and be picked up by guerrillas? That was impossible. My first thought was survival and getting out of the plane before it was too late.

I didn't know my altitude or attitude, and didn't know if I was turning, diving or climbing. At 300 mph and about 200 feet something would happen quickly . . . instinctively back on the stick and maybe up to 500 feet, jettison the canopy, and try to get out the left side. But I was in a turn to the right and the only way out was out the right wing. Too much air speed and pinned back in the seat . . . I couldn't get out . . . but my helmet and goggles went flying. Rolling the trim tab full forward I got my feet on the seat and dived out right head first . . . busted my ankle on the tail and hit the water an instant later just as my chute opened.

All quite for a moment, then all hell broke loose . . . Rifle fire and machine gun fire from Stonecutter's Island and Kowloon docks. They were hitting to close for comfort. Those Japanese didn't like me one bit. The freighter that I had hit (about 1000 yards was really burning and throwing clouds of black smoke. All of a sudden the firing stopped. It was 4:40 Christmas Eve. But it wouldn't be peaceful too long.

I lay in the water for about one and a-half hours when a small Japanese gunboat headed out to me at dusk. . . . . I decided my .45 pistol wouldn't do much good so dropped it, holster and knife into the water. They fished me out of the water . . . not to gently and proceeded to "work me over." This is an understatement to say the least . . . they beat the hell out of me. It was approaching dark. They blindfolded me . . . tied my hands behind my back and transferred me to a larger boat . . . That is when the real beatings and brutality started . . . with weapons, boots, fists and the whole ball of wax. These beasts were real pros.

I lost consciousness many times before we got to the docks. They carried me in a van with some Japanese Navy personnel for a most "unpleasant " trip to what I later learned was Stanley Prison, a former British jail. About nine that night they stripped off all my clothes, my flight jacket, pants, shirt, shoes, everything . . . and hauled me up to the third level of the prison to the interrogation room with my hands handcuffed behind my back. This was like a suspense movie. There was a single light suspended from the ceiling. Marble steps led up to what we called the "gon da bow" [(interrogation) area. There was a large table with two high ranking Japanese naval officers and enlisted personnel and an interpreter. They looked like the old sinister movie Japs . . . big horned rim glasses, square face and squinty eyes. They started with the usual propaganda that we were strafing women and children. They asked what unit I was in, where I was stationed, who was my commanding officer, names of other pilots and what type of planes we were flying. I was sure they knew all the answers, but I said nothing except; "my name is Max Parnell, 1st Lt. U.S. Army Air Corps, serial number 0-686010". That did not impress them. If they had heard of the Geneva Convention, that did not impress them either.

They tried to refresh my memory and things got really rough. After working me over with clubs, gun butts and boots, they said I'd been to Hong Kong before, strafing women and children . . . . I had been there before on Dec. 8th, but I denied it.

Then they had a little surprise for me. They presented me with an onion skin copy of the flight schedule of the 118th an exact duplicate of what was posted on our squadron bulletin board for the December 8 mission. My name was there in bold letters . . . they obviously had a spy right in our squadron headquarters.

Then the fun really began. One officer would question me while the other beat me over the head with a bamboo stick . . . Other guards withdrew a large rope from a bucket of salted water and beat me on the back and buttocks. It felt like I was being cut in two.

Parnell relates how they finally beat him unconscious. He awoke on Christmas morning on the concrete floor, in a pool of his own blood. He could see the red ball of the "rising sun" Japanese flag through the high window, and thought, "I'm in bad trouble."

And so he was. He was interrogated at length every day. If they didn't like his answers, they gave him another beating. When asked if he had been on a mission to Hong Kong before, he answered in the negative. The Japanese officer then showed Max an exact copy of a previous order for a mission to Hong Kong, with 1st Lt Max Parnell listed for the mission, along with his plane number. "Then they really beat the shit out of me for lying."

On New Year's Eve, he was given back some of his clothes. He was taken to a ship, placed in a crate that did not allow him to stand up, and put in the hold. He was handcuffed the entire time, except when the guards would loosen them so he could go to the latrine. The latrine sat in one corner of his confined space, and consisted of a wooden bucket that the guard would empty whenever he felt like it. They would shove a small dish of rice or barley through on the floor. He had to eat on his knees because his hands were cuffed behind his back.

After about twenty days at sea, the ship finally arrived in Japan. He was taken to a prison camp called Ofuna. It was not on the list of prison camps disclosed to the Red Cross, but was an interrogation camp for airmen. Ofuna really was hell on earth, as Max described it. He was in solitary confinement for four months. Beatings occurred almost every day. One guard beat a number of prisoners to death with a large club similar to a baseball bat.

They slept on filthy straw mats on the floor. Parnell said, "To say that conditions at *Ofuna* were inhuman is an understatement." The prisoners received no medical treatment during the entire stay. Those who were wounded or sick suffered until they died. Over one-third of the prisoners in that camp died during Parnell's stay.

He stayed in Ofuna until he was rescued at the end of the war. When he was shot down, he weighed one hundred eighty pounds, and weighed ninety pounds when he was rescued. He was wearing the same clothes that he was shot down in. The guards would not allow the men to wash their clothes, so the fabric looked like tattered canvas. We did not know he had been taken prisoner until after the war.

Parnell testified against the camp guards at the War Crimes Trials, a series of criminal trials held after the end of the war. Four of the most vicious guards received long prison sentences, and one was sentenced to death.

It was many years later that Parnell finally agreed to relate his POW experiences and narrated them to me for the story in our history book, "Chennault's Flying Tigers, Vol. IV."

During the war, we did get some information about prisoner mistreatment. Some prisoners escaped and told stories of their abuse. Also we got detailed information about prisoner mistreatment from Chinese or other personnel who were forced to work in Japanese prisons. Tales of Japanese brutality did not help our morale. We knew that if we were shot down and captured, we would be in serious trouble. But that was one of the risks of war.

Chapter -54-

Another Bad Day

After the disastrous Christmas Eve mission, we had another bad day in January that I wrote about.

Diary page *638. 15 Jan. 45 Bad deal today. Got the shit kicked out of our Sqdn. The guys say one of the worse losses in one day. Major Houck, our new C.O. got shot down. Crashed in the Harbor in Hong Kong. Nobody saw him get out and probably KIA. Theobold also went down in the harbor near the shore. They think he's a goner to. Mitchell bailed out some where north of Canton so there is hope for him. Frank Palmer, a nice guy, also*

639. got hit but bailed out in what is supposed to be fairly safe territory. Sure hope they make it. We hear there is a guy that runs a radio station in the interior and gets reports on downed guys through the system and sends help. He's supposed to be a newspaper man that speaks perfect Chinese. . . . what we hear about him these radio guys are real pros and have saved lots of guys. Anyway pretty sad.

Both Mitchell and Palmer escaped from the Japanese ground forces with the aid of Chinese peasants, and the help of a behind-the-lines radio operator. They both had long walks back to our base. We heard later that Major Houck had bailed out into the harbor in Hong Kong, been taken prisoner by the Japanese, and executed.

The radio man in the interior was Malcolm Rosholt. He had been a news reporter for a Chinese-English newspaper in Shanghai. When war broke out, he was inducted into the air corps and commissioned an intelligence officer. He set up a series of radio stations in enemy territory and worked with Chinese troops behind enemy lines. He could speak a number of Chinese dialects and was invaluable in the rescue of downed airmen. He operated a movable radio station, so if the enemy got too close he could quickly move his equipment to another location. The call sign of his station was DS8. After the war, he wrote a fascinating book about his experiences called "Dog Sugar 8 (DS8)."

When we both returned home, we met, became great friends, and both joined the China veterans group, "The Flying Tigers of the 14th Air Force Association." We both became officers in the Association. I eventually became the Association president, and he was the editor of the 14th Air Force Association "Pictorial." His wife, Marge, and my wife, Delores, also became great friends. We made several trips to Taiwan and China together.

Chapter -55-
The Shanghai Raids

We got even with the Japanese while raiding their airfields near Shanghai.
Diary pages 640 -655. 17 Jan. Whoopie – so damn excited I can hardly write. — Got to fly with C. Older the great Tiger Ace. I think he's top Ace in China. I wasn't scheduled for the mission — Mac got sick at the last minute so I was ordered to jump in his plane.

"Mac," whose real name was Jim McGovern and who we called "Earthquake McGoon," had imbibed in too much of his "Jing Bao Juice" and started puking out of his plane. He had set up a still and made potent liquor, like moonshine. The mission commander pulled him out of the plane and ordered me to jump in since I was the closest pilot standing by.

Engine was already running. What a break. This was the first raid ever on Shanghai by our fighters. We caught the bastards by surprise. There were eight from our squadron but Gene Kosa, C. Jackson & Rust had to turn back because of engine problems so only five made it to target. [there were 12 P-51s from the 74th squadron that made it to the target] *Older got three in the air. They just seemed to pop up in front of him and Bang — down they go. He's got to be the best. We were so busy it was hard to keep track what was going on and hard to stay in formation. There were* [enemy] *planes lined up in neat rows. The Japs . . . just stood looking up and didn't start to run until planes started blowing up all over. We made four passes before they started shooting back at us. What a turkey shoot.*

We were down to 50 feet or below on each pass. I hit a big black car that was racing towards the flight line, sent it tumbling, and then it blew up. Those were some Japs that didn't get to use their planes. On one pass, I must have been down

181

to ten feet because I was shooting up at the Japs in the control tower. I blew away much of the top of the control tower. The two Japs came tumbling out. Now I know why we got all that low level training in Miss. On the last pass the smoke was so bad we could hardly see and we were flying through debris from the exploding planes.

Col. Older got the only Nips in the air except Maj. Herbst, C.O. of the 74th, got one. Herbst is another top Ace. Heard he was grounded – don't know how come he was on this mission. All the rest were on the ground. We really wrecked those fields. We could see fires and black smoke for 50 miles after we left the target. The 74th had 12-P-51s. I think one may have turned back.

Because Herbst was the top scoring ace pilot in China at the time, with seventeen aerial victories, General Chennault had ordered him not to fly any more combat missions. Herbst said he only went along as a high altitude "observer." He was at about four thousand feet when he shot down a KI-43 Oscar. That was his eighteenth aerial victory and made him the top scoring ace in China. The Col. Older that I had referred to was Charles Older, who became a judge in Los Angeles after the war. He served as judge on the famous trial of Charles Manson.

The Japs now know we are not amateurs anymore. We didn't loose a plane. A few holes but no problems. Only bad luck I got the shits on the way back and crapped in my pants.

My crew chief, a really great guy, helped me clean up the plane, something he was not required to do. If a pilot, regardless of his rank, crapped or puked in his plane, the unwritten rule was that he had to clean it up himself.

" Crew Chief Sgt. Eston Simmons welcomes his pilot, Lt. Whitey Johnson back from a mission"

Time I got cleaned up I missed the debriefing. [Since I didn't get to the debriefing, the record mistakenly showed McGovern on the mission.] *Most everyone has diarrhea and I just couldn't hold it. The guys said we got 80 confirmed.* [The official count was ninety-four] *Col. Hester said I would get credit for two confirmed on the ground. Hester is with Wing.* [The 118th, 74th, 75th and 76th Squadrons of the 23rd Fighter Group were under the 68th Wing,] *Ray Trudeau and "Balls out" Colleps were the other two guys from our squadron. Col. Older is with Wing too.*

Trudeau was credited with one in the air when his gun camera film was reviewed. Most of our planes were equipped with cameras that were synchronized with the guns, so it was easier for the intelligence officers to confirm kills. Colleps got the nickname "balls out," because he would usually go full throttle over the target. Later, I was fortunate enough to locate some of my gun-camera film from that mission, and preserve it.

What a great day. Everyone really excited. We got extra mission rations so really hooping it up.

"Mission rations" involved two ounces of liquor given to pilots after each mission. It was supposed to calm one's nerves. Rather than drink it at the time, "some guys" would figure out ways to save it, so we could have a party later.

Nobody said anything about my crapping in my pants. I'm sure my Sgt. wouldn't say anything. The word had leaked out because of all the time we took washing out the plane that "Whitey had a little accident."

Still excited about the Shanghai mission. 92 confirmed. . . 3 in the air by Col. Older he must have at least 15 or more. One in the air by Herbst. I think that makes him the top Ace in China if they don't count the AVG. With the AVG Older is tops. That *x*x*x S.O.B operations still won't log my time. Has to wait until he gets my Orders to come in. He says he will send it to Wing and let them log it in since I flew with Wing.

Col. Hester says I'd get credit for 2 confirmed on the ground and one probable. How the hell will ops figure that out if I wasn't even on the mission according to him. I'm not going to worry about it. — the dumb bastard. I shouldn't say that about him he really is a nice guy but feels he has to follow regulations to the book. He just puts up his hands and says "how can I log time for a man that hasn't been officially assigned to us. I got to clear it with Group or Wing." Piss on it. I'm feeling blue today. I was scheduled for another mission to Shanghai but got scratched.

There was a prison camp about one mile off the end of the Kiangwan airdrome runway. We didn't know it at the time. Many years later, I read an article in a magazine by Marine S/Sgt. Charles Holms. He had been a POW in the Kiangwan prison camp after being taken prisoner when the Japs captured Wake Island in December, 1941. In the article, he wrote that he would like to contact some of the pilots that were on the Shanghai raids. I contacted him and we engaged in a correspondence for a number of years. He wrote an article for my book "Chennault's Flying Tigers, Vol. 1." He wrote: *The real thriller came on 17 January 1945. As I remember it was early afternoon and my "Go-down detail" was slaving away digging the tank traps. Suddenly like a bolt of lightning P-51s came zooming over our heads at what seemed like treetop altitudes. They made a turn onto the runways of the Japanese airfields about a half-mile from where we were working. We dived into any hole we could find as the P-51s started shooting up the runways. Back in the Kiangwan Camp the men there cheered and yelled as the P-51s banked over the camp. The cheering Americans infuriated the Japanese guards who tried to make the men get back in the barracks. One guard bayoneted three men, two in the legs and one in the side of the stomach. Some of the 51s were so low we could see the pilot's face. But we were relieved to know that not one round of ammunition fell on the camp. The next day we were put on reduced rations (already reduced) in retaliation for the 14th AF raid. We could still laugh and joke about how the 51s slipped in on the Nipponese and caught them napping. The best I can remember the last raid we saw by the 14th AF came on Easter Sunday, April 1, 1945.*

It took me 35 years to locate any of the pilots who flew in the Shanghai raids. I always wanted to know who those guys were up there in the air. Finally making contact with Mr. Wayne G. Johnson and Judge Charles Older, they were kind enough to fill me in on many of the details of the Shanghai raids that I wondered about for all these years.

I feel that destiny forged inextricable bonds of friendship with the men of the 14th Air Force and the American POW's of the Kiangwan POW camp. Thanks fellows for helping us back to freedom and all the good years since we walked to freedom on 16 September 1945. (Signed) *CWO (W-4) Charles A. Holmes. USMC (Ret)*

Some time later, I got another letter from a Wake Island marine, Sgt. Jessie E. Nowlin, who was also a POW at the Kiangwan prison camp. He wrote: *10 July 1984. Yesterday I was visiting my good friend and former comrade in arms Charlie Holmes. I saw your picture and remembering you flying one of those "Magnificent Mustangs" that shot the ass off that Jap bomber and two airfields in and near Shanghai 17 January 1945. God. The thrill of it all! Remembering you and your buddies flying, shooting and so soundly whipping the ass off those bastards that had been doing the same to us for what seemed like an eternity still makes me tingle. You and your men were absolutely magnificent that long past day over Shanghai. I am convinced that your coming revitalized many a weary heart and soul to extent we could endure the remaining months of the war. You guys emplanted a vision in our minds of a beautiful well fought American airplane and a thrill in our hearts that will endure as long as any of us are still alive and kicking. That Jap bomber you shot down directly over my head had us all standing yelling and cheering and our guards were cringing in their bomb shelters. I was expecting to get the hell knocked out of me again after the raid was over but the only thing the Japs did was to shout "hi-ya-ku, hi-ya-ku speedo-speedo" about your 51s.*

After the 1 April raid, the Japanese first transferred the POWs in the Kiangwan camp to a camp near Peking, and then to Hokkiado Japan, where they were forced to work in coal mines until the end of the war, with just enough food to keep them working. Holmes said that most of the guys were mere skeletons when released. After being liberated, Holmes spent some time in the hospital being nursed back to health. He remained in the Marine Corps and retired as a chief warrant officer. We had many interesting conversations and wrote to each other frequently. Unfortunately, the ravages to his body from the long period of brutal treatment and near starvation as a POW was too much even for a tough marine. He died in his early sixties.

Because of the success of the 17 January raid, 68th Wing Commanders planned another raid for 20 January, despite protests by squadron commanders that the enemy would be waiting and we would lose the element of surprise. And they were waiting.

20 Jan. Since Mac couldn't go on the 17th they decided to send him in my place. I'm happy for him but not so happy for me. — —- Bad news again. Lost two men. Tollet and Geyer. The Nips were waiting this time and shot the shit out of us. Both bailed out and far enough from Shanghai that they might be safe. Williams got his 5th to make him an Ace.

He [Williams] *had about half his wing shot off but the old Mustang brought him home. Mac* [Earthquake Mc Goon -McGovern] *got two in the air. I told him I'd trade my 2 on the ground that he was supposed to get if he'd gone on the first mission and I should get the two in the air since I was supposed to go on this mission. He said he'd agree if I'd give him my share of the mission rations for the next 6 months.* [We told the operations officer and he damn-near had a heart attack.] *But it was a sad day with Tollet and Geyer missing.*

Both Tollet and Geyer escaped capture with the help of Chinese peasants and guerillas. It took Geyer one hundred days to walk back to base while avoiding Japanese troops, who were looking for him. Tollet got back a little sooner. We had a great welcome-back party for them.

Lots of damage to our planes. Almost every one had holes and damage. Lucky we didn't loose more. 16 went out and 14 came back. They got 5 Nips in the air confirmed. There were 12 to 15 Nips in the air so our guys didn't do to bad. They got 30 Nips air and ground confirmed. So the Nips have 30 planes less and we have 2 less. Not a bad percentage. We hate to loose any but we know it will happen. Just out . . .

Diary pages missing.   *. . . four guys that came in from Chengkung day be-fore yesterday have a batch of Orders with my name on them.* [I am now officially assigned to the squadron] --- *glad my Orders are straightened out and think I can forget about the Jeep problem.*

Apparently, we apparently upset the Japanese with our raids on their airfields in Shanghai. We got the word that their troops were on the move and would prob-ably overrun our base in the next few days, so we had better get ready to evacuate. There was quite a large Chinese Army that was supposed to protect our base, but our intelligence had very little faith in them. Most of their troops were inexperi-enced young kids that had been pulled off the farms, picked up on the city streets, or recruited wherever the commanders could find them. That was the Chinese version of a "draft," and the Chinese meaning of "volunteer."

We saw kids who didn't look fourteen years old with guns that were almost big-ger than they were.

"Lt. *Whitey* Johnson at Suichuan with Chinese soldier"

The Chinese did have some professional, well-trained troops, but they weren't in the area. I recorded in my diary:

21 Jan. 45   Bad news. Jap ground troops closing in and no Chinese ground troops to stop them. [As soon as they got wind of the Jap advance, the Chinese army disappeared.]

"Chinese soldier guarding our planes"

Orders to evacuate. Clearing out tomorrow. That's the end of our eastern foothold. But don't think the Nips have much of an Air Force left after our two Shanghai raids. Goodbye Suichuan —we'll be back.

22 Jan. 45. Nips apparently moved in bunch of planes from Formosa after our 17th raid. That's why they were on the ground and in the air on the 20th. We sure as hell got everything on the 17th. Uneventful but sad trip from Suichuan to Cheng-kung. Why couldn't they get us some good Chinese troops and give us some support. With more support we could have held out. The Shanghai raids must have about ruined the Nips air force. Hope we don't sit around Chengkung to long. Started blowing up the base as we left.

Whenever the Japanese chased us out of one of our bases, the engineers would blow up all the buildings and put bombs in the runways to blow big holes, so the enemy couldn't use the field for a while. Chengkung was one of our large airbases in the western part of China not far from 14th Headquarters at Kunming.

Diary page 655 . . . although everyone sad about loosing our forward base we are still talking about the two Shanghai raids on the 17th and 20th. Major from Group Hqtrs brought up an interesting story. He claims the gas we refueled with at Nancheng, the field we staged out of from Suichuan and Kanchow, was gas that had been stored there for the Doolittle Tokio raiders.

Nancheng was located about half way between Suichuan and Shanghai, so was perfect for a refueling stop. There was a small contingent of our engineers and some Navy guys at the Nancheng base. It was interesting to learn that the U.S. Navy actually had a ground unit in China, primarily engaged in intelligence preparing for future navy landings on the China coast. We later learned that Nancheng was one of the fields that Doolittle's group was supposed to land on after their raid on Tokyo. But, because of a longer mission and a screw-up with communications in China, all of his crews either bailed out or crashed.

The Japanese had thought Japan was untouchable since about the thirteenth century. At that time, a large Mongol armada sailed from China towards Japan, and ran into a severe typhoon, which destroyed the attacking Mongol fleet. The Japanese called it a "Divine Wind" that swept the sea clean. From then on, the Japanese were led to believe their islands were invulnerable to military attack.

Colonel James Doolittle, with his flight of North American B-25 Mitchells, proved them wrong. Sixteen B-25 twin-engine bombers flew off the aircraft carrier *USS Hornet* on 18 April 1942, on a mission to bomb Japan in revenge for the deadly Japanese attack on Pearl Harbor.

Unfortunately, the *Hornet* was sighted by a Japanese fishing vessel. The Americans knew that those fishing boats carried radios that could communicate with Japan, so the Japanese boat was fired upon and sunk by the *Hornet.* However, the *Hornet*'s captain and Doolittle did not know if the Japanese had actually been able to send a message alerting the Japanese of the presence of an American aircraft carrier within six hundred fifty miles of Japan. If a message about the American carrier, it could expose the carrier to Japanese attack. Doolittle decided to take off immediately to allow the *Hornet* to get out of the area, which increased the distance the B-25s had to fly in order to reach safe airfields well within China. The planes would arrive over China in the dark of night.

Although the B-25s were all successful in bombing Tokyo, the raid was more symbolic than militarily destructive. It was a blow to the morale of the Japanese people, and changed Japan's military leaders' strategies. They extended their defensive line in the Pacific, which led to the crucial defeat of the Japanese Navy in the Battle of Midway some months later.

Doolittle's planes never made it to Nancheng, or any other Chinese base, because of a bad foul up. All crews bailed out or crashed. Some were taken prisoner by the Japanese and executed. Washington D.C planners "failed" to inform Chennault that the Doolittle group was scheduled to land in China after bombing Tokyo. Chennault was reported to be furious. Had he known of Doolittle's mission, he could have had his radio people direct the planes to safe airfields. The higher-ups in Washington apparently didn't want Chennault to get any credit for making the raid a success. Many wondered how we won the war with our high-ranking military leaders making such stupid decisions.

Chapter -56-
The Philadelphia Story

Diary pages: 660 – 672 . . . everyone sitting around talking all about their – real or imagined sexual exploits. John (Virgin) told us a story that was then called the "Philadelphia Story." John was on leave to Philly and met this good looker that was the wife of a guy flying B-17 in Europe. Since John was in his brand new uniform she said they had something in common so invited him to her apartment to have some lemonade and talk about B-17s. She made some lemonade but John thought she might have put something in it because he started to feel "funny" and warm.

661. She then asked if she could put on something more comfortable on since she was "warm" to. When she came back and sat down all she had on was a open house coat and John "could see everything she had". This got everyone's attention and wondered if John was a virgin after all. "What did you do then John?' "I told her what a bad girl she was acting like that and should be ashamed of herself with her husband overseas flying B-17 and all. I left right away and told my mother about this bad girl I met."

John was nicknamed the "Virgin" after he told that story. It became his aviator call sign on missions. His "Philadelphia Story" became an interesting topic of conversation at many a China base.

That story about tore the barracks down and we resolved to do something about John's virginity. John doesn't drink much so won't be easy to get him out. — Had a big argument with Gus Dinand the ops officer about logging my time at Suichuan. He says its up to Wing since there were no orders for me and Wing would have to straighten that out. He said I could log the trip of evacuation of Suichuan to Cheng-

kung because he now had my orders, what a
Diary pages missing. — — *got John pretty drunk so some of the guys thought this was a good time to take him down to the "House of Soiled Doves" and get him laid. John was not to hot for the idea but was finally persuaded that we couldn't have a Virgin in a hot combat outfit. . . . Don't think John was inside five minutes when he came running down the street hollering "where's the Pro Station – where's the Pro Station".*

The "pro station" was a medical unit usually set up in convenient locations that gave emergency treatment to those who might partake of the "forbidden fruit." Treatment involved an injection of a potent antibiotic, meant to prevent venereal disease, into the penis.

O. C. Damn near fell out of the jeep laughing. [O. C. was Oliver C. Bateman, one of the instigators of John's "education."] *John only had one leg in his pants and trying to run at the same time. . . . took him to the Pro Station and guess he's not a virgin anymore. When we got back to the base and guys learned about what John had done someone asked him how it was. John said, "its overrated". One of the guys told John that the Pro was only good for one hour and talked him to going to get Doc out of bed for another Pro. They talked him into two more Pros that night and by morning his poor dink was so sore he could hardly hold it. He said the clap couldn't be any worse. We felt kind of bad about the trick and it didn't seem near as funny the next morning but John is grinning. I don't care about going to whorehouses it is so damn disgusting and embarrassing. I'd rather wait until I find a nice clean girl. I think guys go more for the challenge than because they want to. There are some real good looking girls around here but real tough to meet them. But laying around the barracks with nothing to do the temptation is bound to overcome especially with —* [Diary pages missing.]

Chapter -57-

A Tragic Accident

Sad day with Chris's funeral. He was a big Swede from Minn. But a good friend. Watts [Captain Watts was temporary squadron C.O] *didn't make things any better after the funeral when he called all pilots out and really chewed us out for dog fighting with the 38's and intend to court martial anyone who does it in the future. I think something happened to his plane because Chris was real good pilot and really could handle the 51.*

There was a Lockheed P-38 Lightning outfit on the field and one of the thirty-eight squadron pilots challenged Chris (Warren Christensen) to a dog fight. The P-38 guy claimed that his plane could out-maneuver the P-51 Mustang. He and Chris went up and started chasing each other around. Chris was doing a great job getting on the tail of the P-38, but when he came around close to the ground and started to pull up, he snapped, rolled, and crashed into the ground.

We think he didn't use the gas from his fuselage tank. The P-51 D model had a forty- gallon gas tank behind the pilot. We were to use that first. If we didn't, in a tight turn the plane would "snap roll." A snap roll was a violent maneuver in which the plane would whip around and the pilot really had to react immediately or the plane would go out of control. Close to the ground, there was not enough room to react and recover.

Chapter -58-

Chengkung and then to Loahwangping and Back to Combat

Since leaving Suichuan and back to this base at Chengkung, there wasn't much to do:

Diary page*: 722. so damn bored with no flying. Wish we could back into combat. Can't win a war with a bunch of highly trained pilots sitting on their ass. . . . We are confident now the Old Man says that we'll whip the Krauts and Nips before the year is out. Rumors are we will be going to another forward base. Most guys are eager to get on good missions where we can see some action. Got a "Dear John" letter from Billie but didn't feel bad. guess I didn't love her after all (or she didn't love me) but sure remember the great times with her. Maybe I wasn't very fair with her. Just made love but no permanent promises.*

A "Dear John" letter was a letter from a wife or sweetheart saying that she had found someone else. In many cases, a "Dear John" letter was a shattering event.

Our barracks at Chengkung was an old Chinese army barracks and was full of lice and rats. If we got lice, Doc. Winkley, the flight surgeon, had some stuff called "blue ointment" that we smeared on to kill the lice. Someone dreamed up a little ditty about the stuff:

"Put on Doc's Blue Ointment,
To the Lice's disappointment
and chase those bastards away."

That remedy worked quite well and also worked well against other types of vermin, like the crabs.

The rats were another matter. They would come out in the evening and run along the overhead beams. Some were as big as cats. One night when I was in an upper bunk, I saw this big rat come out and walk along a beam. It happened to be directly over a table where some guys were playing poker. I took my .45 pistol out, loaded some bird shot, and shot the rat.

It tumbled from the beam right onto the middle of the of the poker table. I don't know what scared the guys the most, the rat dropping on the table, or the gunshot, which had sounded like a cannon in the small barracks. The shot had blown a small hole in the roof. The poker players and other guys in beds all flew out of the barracks and the air-raid warning started clanging because the gunshot was heard throughout the camp.

Cartoon by WWII G.I. artist Bill Mauldin
from *CBI Roundup circa* 1945

When the M.P.s and officer on guard duty learned that the gunshot had came from our room, and of the circumstances, things calmed down. Some of the guys thought it was pretty funny, and I was a hero for a little while. The poker players were a little unhappy, for it busted up their game and they didn't know who the scattered money belonged to.

The C.O. took a bite out of me and made me get out of bed and go bury the rat. Some smart-ass went out and painted a rat representing one of my victories on the side of a plane that I flew. The next morning, the C.O. "suggested" that I climb up on the roof and repair the damage — which I did. It wasn't a very big hole anyway. The CBI Roundup, newspaper of the China-Burma-India Theater, had a Carl Mauldin cartoon which graphically depicted soldier's similar experiences with rats.

We finally got orders to move to a base closer to enemy territory. Some of the guys were to fly the planes to the new base at Loahwangping, and a large truck convoy would move all the supplies. Ron Phillips and I got the nasty job of running the truck convoy. I suspect I got assigned to the truck convoy due to the little rat-shooting episode. Ron had missed a meeting to brief us on the move so was subject to some extra duty. Before we left, we had an enemy air-raid warning. We rushed to the air-raid shelter caves, but it was a false alarm.

Diary pages *749 - 807. One week on the road in this damn convoy is a helluva way for a fighter pilot to travel. I think Gus put me on this to get even for ribbing him so much about his sore p**ker after the circumcision.*

Another interesting event took place when Gus Dinand decided he should be circumcised, because he had a lot of irritation under his foreskin in the hot weather.

Had a circumcision party tonight for Gus Dinand. He decided he should be circumcised and Doc agreed to do it if Gus could guarantee he wouldn't get a hard-on for a week until the sore healed up. He ate a bunch of pills that was supposed to keep it down. His dink was really sore so Doc gave him a pint of alcohol so we mixed that with Jing Bao Juice and some lemon powder and water and had a helluva party. He did look funny as hell with that rag wrapped around it and guess it got pretty sore whenever he sweat. The dust on the convoy is almost impossible to breath. We put soak hankies and put over our nose but they get like mud rags after a while. We have been going for over a week and should get to our new base soon. After a week and no relief in sight I'm about ready to walk. That damn Earl Davison doesn't seem to mind at all and is so caked with mud and dust he looks browner than an Indian.

Earl Davidson was a chief master sergeant, a top mechanic, and a great guy. He was given a field commission as a 2nd Lt. when we arrived at Loahwangping.

Loahwangping. Really tough mission today. — about 4 hours into the Luichow area. — all low level against ground troops, cavalry, trains — lots of AA and got a few holes. The 51 is a damn fine plane and is a beauty to fly but don't think it will take the punishment a P-40 will. The air opposition seems to be all gone. Haven't seen a Nip in the air for months. I like the P-40. We have one used for mail and ferry. They took the fuselage tank and some armament out and put in a seat behind the pilot. Since I like it, that's why I get to fly it when most of the other guys are not interested. Took a trip into town. To see the sights . Loahwangping is a beautiful . . .and even in town has some pretty streets and temples. Got sent on what was supposed to be an easy mission in the two place P-40. Took Earl Davison to see if he could get a plane going at another field. We were tooling along just above the tree tops when the damn engine quit. Scared hell out of both of us. [I had forgotten to switch tanks. In this P-40, the pilot had to switch tanks manually.] *But I managed to switch tanks and get it going again. Had a helluva time trying to switch tanks and keeping that damn Earl from bailing out and . . .* [Diary pages missing.]

197

"Flying the P-40 through the valleys with Sgt Earl Davison when the engine quit."

Many years later at a reunion of the Flying Tigers, Earl Davison was telling guys about an experience in the P-40 when he almost bailed out. He said he would like to meet the crazy pilot who damn-near killed him. I was standing close by when he was telling this story. I told him that I knew who that pilot was and that he was at the convention. Earl said, "Go find him for me. I don't know if I want to kill him or thank him for saving my life." I admitted that I was the pilot, which made for an interesting evening. We were good friends and corresponded regularly until his death.

Went on a mission with Mel Scheer. That damn fool doesn't know when to quit. We did a good job hitting buildings and trucks and started some good fires and lots of explosions. The Nips were getting in some good accurate AA and small arms. I picked up a number of hits and told Scheer I had some holes and lets get the hell out. He said "whitey don't get so excited that old plane will fly with all kinds of holes" and then he makes another pass with me on his wing. Didn't know if I'd make it back or not. We saw no air opposition but their damn ground troops were shooting too close for comfort. I think I got a building with ammo since it really blew up when I hit it. This is the third day in a row I've been on these low level missions. We are raising hell with the troops, river boats and trains but get lots of ground fire back. Maybe get back to some of our old bases before long.

When I told Scheer that we should get out of there because they were shooting at us, I vividly recall his words, "Don't worry, Whitey, there's a war on — they are supposed to shoot at us." That didn't give me much comfort. When we got back to base, the C.O. said, "What the hell have you guys been doing? Your planes look like Swiss cheese." Scheer said it was just a routine day!

```
18th Tac Rcn Sqdn              S E C R E T          SEC T
Laohwangping, China                                By  thority of the C.O.
20 June 1945          FLIGHT INTELLIGENCE REPORT    118th Tac Rcn Sqdn
                                                    20 June '45
                           Report No. 80            Date          Initials

MISSION: Offensive sweep against targets of opportunity along the Liuchow-Pinglo-
         Kweilin roads.

TIME OFF: 1030  OVER TARGET: 1145  LAND: 1420  TOTAL COMBAT TIME: 7:40

NO. & TYPE A/C: 1 P-51K, 1 P-51C

LEADER: Lt Scheer
PILOTS: Lts Scheer, Jonnson

COURSE: Direct to Liuchow 9000'-11000'

WEATHER: Forecast; Clear with 4-5/10's cumulus 4000'
         encountered; Scattered to broken 4500'  VIS unlimited

NO. & TYPE BOMBS: 12 x 100 lb napalm incendiary bombs
AMMUNITION EXPENDED: 2120 rds Cal 50

ENEMY DAMAGE: 5 trucks probably destroyed, 4 bldgs destroyed, several damaged

ENEMY A/A: 40 mm & 20 mm in Lojungnsien area
ENEMY A/C: None

NARRATIVE: Lt Scheer led 2 off on an offensive sweep against targets of opportunity
along the Liuchow-Pinglo-Kweilin roads. Proceeded direct to Liuchow observing
large fires in the town on the east side of the river. Checked over the airfield
and observed that the runway has not been blown. No activity observed in the town
or around the field. Recceed the road north to Lojungnsien observing no activity.
Fairly intense 40 mm and 20 mm AA probably from positions previously knocked out
south of Lojungnsien, was encountered. Checked Lojungnsien over but found no
suitable targets. Scheer bombed buildings in Luchai, starting 2 large fires, one
in south end of town, and one in NW edge of town. Scattered small arms fire was
encountered from the town. Checked road east to Pinglo, observing no activity up
to Lipunsien. Found 3 trucks in two buildings on south side of Lipunsien.
Jonnson scored direct hits on one of the buildings and started it afire. Both
planes strafed the second building finally getting it to burn. Some of the
smoke appeared to be oil or gasoline on fire, indicating all three trucks were
probably destroyed. Some small arms fire was encountered from the town of Lipunsien
Checked road to Pinglo, no activity along road or in Pinglo. Checked to Kweilin
observing no activity. Several barracks areas just North of Yang Tong a/d in
the Kweilin area indicated vehicle parking areas, but no trucks were found when
flight checked over them. Both planes landed safely at base.


                 MARVIN LUBNER            ROBERT C. BURKE
                 Capt., A.C.,             Capt., A.C.,
                 Commanding.              S-2 Officer.
```

The above is a copy of a typical fighter mission report prepared by the squadron intelligence officer after each mission based on information given to him by the pilots.

As a rule, when strafing or bombing ground targets, we were to come in at high speed, make only one pass, and keep going. But not Scheer. He usually made two or three passes, or more. He usually came back with lots of holes in his plane, but was lucky to come back at all.

We are raising hell with the troops river boats and trains but we get lots of ground fire back. Maybe get back to some of our old bases before long. The mission ration sure tasted good tonight.

Another interesting mission was with my friend Ron Phillips when we were part of a flight of four P-51s that took off for a mission against a Japanese base.

We usually flew in flights of four. A flight leader with a wing man, an echelon leader and a wing man called "tail end charley". *Tail end* was an important position. It was his job to look out for any enemy to the rear.

Ron was flying on the flight leader's right wing and I was flying "tail-end Charlie" on the echelon leader's wing, bringing up the rear of the formation. The echelon leader usually flew on the flight leader's left wing. Shortly after takeoff, both the flight leader and echelon leader signaled that they were turning back because of engine trouble.

Since Ron was on the flight leader's wing he should have moved up as flight leader with the echelon leader gone. I turned towards Ron to join him and he turned towards me. I turned away and he followed. Since we were getting off course, I turned back to the course and Ron turned towards me. I finally broke radio silence and asked him where he was going. He replied: "Hell Whitey, I don't know, I'm just following you." I told him I would lead and we did make it to the target and back.

These low level missions are tough. Don't know where the AA [anti-aircraft] is coming from. We don't loose any guys in the air but they clobber us on the ground. Each time we face death we mature a lot. They trained us for low level recon and fighter pilots but didn't tell us about the hazards of low level stuff. But that is what we came over for. We can't expect to fight a war and win without loosing some guys.

We are sure now we are winning the war. The Old Man says it will be over in a few months if we keep giving him good pilots and more planes like the P-51. Boy what an airplane. If I get shot down I did what a good pilot can do for his country. None of us want to die but if it saves our country that's our job.

Hope Ma and Pa aren't worrying to much about us guys. They were pretty worried when Arnold lost his eye [at Guadalcanal] *and with 4 sons in the service that is a real worry. They know we have to fight for our country — —- and what we do. Got some more popcorn from Opal. That's a real treat.*

When we popped the corn, it must have sent a message to the Chinese kids. Although the kids were frequently on the base looking for food and treats, now they seemed to come out of the woodwork. They were fascinated, and watched us popping the corn in the stove. We gave each of them a couple of popped kernels, but couldn't spare too much, for the guys in my tent and others close by also wanted a taste. Amazing what a little popcorn could do for our morale and make some kids happy.

— — Hope the damn Nips come up in the air. Would like to see some air combat. This low level ground stuff is hard work but necessary. Love this flying — — but could use some poontang. Rumor is some one will get a trip to Karachi soon– Hope, hope, hope.

Lubner [our new C.O] *says since I was on the damn convoy maybe he'll send me to India to pick up some new P-51s. He expects to make Major and wants to get some gin and beer back for a party for the 4th. This is beautiful country. Sight seeing is really great. Base isn't too bad. Have England type tents with double canvas so sort of cool.*

I'm in tent with O.C. Bateman and Bob Leavell. Two really great guys. Bob spends most of his spare time writing long love letters to his girl friend in Oxford, Miss. We fixed our tent up. It has a wooden floor with wooden sides and door. We burned a sign on the door –called it –"Fools Paradise".

Diary pages *807-816. To Calcutta on a C-47 –Bad ride over Hump. Didn't think we'd make it but Earthquake* [Jim "Earthquake McGoon" Mc Govern] *kept entertaining us. Sure glad I'm flying fighters rather than these junk heaps. Went directly to Karnarny Estates hotel really beautiful.* [A lavish British Hotel used by transient pilots.] *McGoon went out and got some booze and some dolls----*

Diary pages missing. . . . b*ack in Kunming in two new P-51 Ds. Those 4 days R/R in Calcutta really something. — brought back lots of gin and beer for the promotion party. Picked up promotion Orders. I finally made 1st Lt. rah. Marv Lubner promoted to Major and he's got a big party planned for tonight. He was officially named C.O. to relieve Col. Simpson.*

3 July 45. What a party and what a hangover but still have to fly. Lubner really had a party —dumped all the gin and 5 gals of Docs med. alcohol in 55 gal barrel with lemon powder and a little water and ice –real ice–

We filled a one-hundred ten-gallon wing-tank with water, and Fred Poats took a P-51 up to thirty-five thousand feet and flew around for a couple of hours. When he landed, we had a tank full of ice. We had quite a time chopping it apart. It was quite a novel method of making ice.

. . . tasted mighty good just like old fashioned lemonaide but what a kick. Didn't hit the sack until late and then up before sun-up for a mission. I flew wingman for Lubner and Voznica flew with Hibarger. good mission. blew up buildings and trucks. Also hit the country club. Had been warned not to hit it but Lubner couldn't resist. He skipped his 500# in the front door and I clobbered it with napalm.

As soon as we landed he ran over to me and told me not to mention the country club to Burke. It was a beautiful white castle in a valley on top of a hill but guess the Chinese didn't want it damaged. Lub didn't want Burke told so it would be in the reports.

Burke was the squadron intelligence officer who recorded the results of all missions. I believe that is where I wrote in my diary about the destruction of the country club, but those diary pages are missing. It was apparently owned by a Chinese war lord who wanted to preserve it so he could move back into after the war. It was supposed to be unoccupied. As we flew over it at about one hundred feet, we noticed that there were Japanese military vehicles in the yard, nice cars that were obviously used by some high-ranking Japanese officers and Japanese soldiers standing around.

We went down the valley several miles when Lubner said, "That's a Jap hangout — lets go back and get the fuckin' country club." We turned around and bombed the place. Lubner dropped two 500# high explosive bombs right in the front door. The building blew apart. I dropped two napalm bombs in the yard, both of which set the entire area on fire. Napalm was a sticky type liquid similar to that used in flame throws. We carried it in external mounted wing tanks and could drop them like bombs. When they hit the ground they exploded and spread flame over a large area. The building and surrounding area was completely destroyed. Our intelligence later told us that the country club had been occupied by a half dozen high-ranking Japanese officers, all of whom were wiped out.

The Chinese Warlord who was a general was reported to be furious. Our group commander, Col. Ed Rector, came flying in a little later and told us we couldn't record this mission and we had to deny that we had planes in the air. It became known as a "mission that wasn't a mission."

We released information suggesting that it must have been some Japanese pilots who mistakenly bombed it, because intelligence reported that there were some enemy flying in the area that day, although we didn't see any.

Apparently, the Chinese believed our fraudulent story, because we heard no more about it. Or maybe they thought that the destruction of the country club and the death of several Japanese officers was a good trade-off. Besides, the Chinese warlord was not a very popular guy, so if he lost his fancy estate built with forced slave labor, others didn't feel bad for him.

Diary pages: 816 -853. Another tuff low level bomb and strafe to the Kweilin area. Looks like the Old Man is going to keep the Nips on the run. Haven't seen any Nips in the air for some time. Sure wish some would come up. They don't have anything that will match the 51. Ran into some flak and wasn't sure I'd make it back for my birthday tomorrow. Didn't have any real damage but the plane started missing over the target. Headed for safe territory and got some altitude in case I had to get out. I was really talking to the old bird that I didn't want to walk back. About time I was about ready to leave the engine started to purr beautifully. Must have been a little bad gas.

July 8, 1945. A happy day and a sad day. My 24th birthday today and mess hall baked a nice cake. Lub. shared one of his bottles of gin with me. We were having a good time when the sad news came. Chennault has resigned. Guess Stilwell and some of his pals in Washington got the old Tiger after all.

Stilwell was Gen. Joseph Stilwell, who had been area commander in the China-Burma-India Theater, was always at odds with Chennault. He was strictly a ground general and didn't believe the air force could influence the war. He was still of the old World War I trench philosophy. He was referred to as "Vinegar Joe" for his grouchy demeanor.

Vinegar Joe

"Vinegar Joe Stilwell"

In an argument with Stilwell, When Stilwell said he needed the supplies that Chennault wanted for troops in the trenches. Chennault was reputed to have told him, "Goddammit Stilwell, there are no trenches in China." Generals were not supposed to swear at a senior general, but Chennault seldom followed protocol.

Because of Stilwell's continuing fights with Chennault and Generalissimo Chiang Kai-shek, the President of China and the Chinese armed forces commander, Stilwell was recalled by President Roosevelt and replaced by Gen. Albert Wedemeyer. Chennault was not popular with air force chief Gen. Hap Arnold and Gen. George Marshal, a top military man in Washington D.C. in the war department. They didn't approve of Chennault's lack of military protocol and his tendency to by-pass them and go directly up to Roosevelt.

Diary pages missing. . . . h*ard to believe that our top military leaders can be so small and petty — and stupid. They throw out one of the greatest Airmen in history –and just when it looks like we got the war won. Sure as hell is one big snafu.* ["Snafu" was military slang for situations that didn't go right which literally translated meant "situation normal, all f-----d up."]

When Stilwell left China, when Chiang had him kicked out, the word was he blamed the Old man and would get even. He and Chennault never could agree. Guess Stilwell was a ground pounder but Chennault never could convince him of the value of bombers and fighters. It's a hell of a way to run a war. —— Everyone so damn mad even the Jing Bao Juice tastes good. The rumor is that Col. Rector and other top men who have been with the Old Man for a long time, all were going to resign too but he talked them out of it. I don't understand these politicians and generals in Washington. How can they risk the war effort because of their personal feelings and goals. — — Even after the lift of some good missions and knowing we are still doing our job, morale is horseshit. We hear Chennault is going to fly to all bases and say goodbye personally. Sure hope to get to see him again. He is a true airmen and does more for aviation than all those dudes from West Point and Annapolis put together.

I believe that was the night that Lubner got quite drunk and set fire to our tent. He was out in front singing and wanted Bateman, Leavell, and me to come out and join him. He had been our flight instructor at Dothan, Alabama, and our base C.O. when had we graduated, so we knew him quite well. He was an Ace. (An Ace is a pilot who had shot down five enemy planes) He had been badly burned in an accident on his first tour in China. He was taking off when a plane on another runway was also taking off from an intersecting runway at the same time. Because of all the activity, neither saw the other until too late. They crashed at the intersection and both planes exploded. Lubner survived but was badly burned, and was sent back to the States. After he healed, he insisted on returning to China. He was a real character, and sometimes didn't act like a C.O. was expected to.

When we didn't come out, he set fire to our tent, laughing like crazy. We got out in a hurry, just in our skivies (under-shorts). Fortunately, the night guards promptly put out the fire. The word went out the next day about an accident with a stove that had caused a little fire. Perhaps that type of "relaxation" was necessary to cope with the hazards and stress of combat. At times, there was reason for stress.

Chapter -59-

Some Near Tragedies

A flight of eight P-51s were returning from a skip bombing mission when the tower operator screamed, "Don't land — don't land." One of the P-51s had a five hundred-pound high explosive bomb hung up under his wing. As Willie Nest dove on the target, he released his bombs. One smashed into the target, but the other hung up under this wing. He said he tried everything on the way back, "But the bomb wouldn't release." Coming over the field with the bomb dangling from a hook, the tower instructed him to clear the field area, climb to altitude, and bail out.

Willie was a chubby, easy-going redhead from West New York, with a brogue thicker than a double-crusted pizza. He said, "Hell, I didn't want to lose my nice Mustang, but I didn't want to get blown up either." Willie feared that the bomb might explode if he rolled over to bail out, "I opened the canopy and tried to climb out. The wind pressure was too great and kept forcing me back in. I might not have tried very hard, I don't want to bail out anyway, and I'll take her on in. For some reason I couldn't make out what the tower was hollering about. I touched down as gently as I could and made the most perfect landing I have ever made." His story continues: "A second after touchdown, and going about eighty miles an hour, and not waiting for the damn bomb to blow up, I rolled over the wing and down the runway. Laying cut and bruised and covered with mud, I saw my plane roll to a stop some distance down the runway without the damn bomb. Jeez, where the hell is it — trying to dig myself deeper in the gravel."

When the rescue squad picked him up and took him to operations, he learned that the bomb had dropped off about one-fourth mile short of the runway as he put his flaps down, and luckily it hadn't exploded. "Wow," he said, "lucky me." The doctor patched him up and he was none the worse for his little ordeal.

A few days later we had a near fatality from a similar incident. LeRoy Price came back from his mission with a hung-up one hundred-pound bomb and a bunch of fragmentation bombs attached. The guys in armament had jerry-rigged little fragmentation bombs to the one hundred-pound bomb for low level bombing against enemy troops. Price tried everything to get it released. He did stalls, snap rolls, and spins, but it would not release. The tower thought landing would be unsafe. He was told he should go away from the base and bail out, but he didn't want to do that. After Price explained in detail how he had tried to release the bomb, the base commander decided the bomb was secure, and authorized him to land.

Price put the P-51 down smooth as silk. The instant the wheels of his plane touched the ground, the bombs released and exploded. His plane was in flames. Although he was still going about ninety miles per hour, he had to get out or burn to death. He opened the canopy and rolled out on the wing into the ditch alongside of the runway. He rolled for some distance.

Oliver Bateman and I were sitting in a Jeep watching the landing when LeRoy rolled out in flames. We raced down the runway and beat out the flames on his clothes. He was wearing a leather jacket and gloves, so his upper body, arms, hands, and face, except for an area around his throat, were not burned. He was still wearing his oxygen mask and goggles, which saved his eyes and lungs, but he was still badly burned around the neck and legs. Flames had shot up his pant legs very close to his vital areas; so close in fact, that his only comment was, "Lucky me." If the flames had been a couple of inches higher, he may have ended up with a high-pitched voice!

LeRoy was not seriously injured from rolling out of the plane, except for lots of gashes and bruises from the gravel and grass. After emergency treatment by the flight surgeon, he was flown to the hospital in Kunming. He made a good recovery, except some permanent scaring on his throat and legs.

The flight surgeon expressed his usual sympathy when Oliver and I complained about our burned hands. He slapped on some ointment that we thought it was axle grease, and said, "You'll live. If you got any complaints, go see the Chaplain." They did heal, and the scars went away after time.

The armament section, a terrific crew, worked overtime to correct the bomb hang-up problems. If it wasn't in the manual, they would figure out a way to fix most problems. We never had another hang-up of bombs or tanks after those two incidents.

I wasn't quite that lucky sometime later when I was flying out of another base. I totally destroyed my nice P-51. When I got back and complained to the doctor about my sore neck, he said he didn't think it was broken. We didn't have any x-ray equipment at the base, so he told me to just wrap my scarf tight around my neck for a few days. He put me back on flying status the next day. When we got to Shanghai many months later after the surrender, the Colonel heard me complaining about my neck. He arranged for me to go out to a Navy hospital ship in the harbor that had good x-ray equipment. The doctor there said that I had several healed fractures, but nothing could be done about it. He asked about the sort of treatment I had received when this had happened. When I told him what our squadron flight surgeon had done, he swore so loudly that I think he could have been heard throughout the ship. He said that quack should have been brought up before a court martial. He said with those fractured vertebrae, just the slightest bump could have made me a paro (paraplegic). I should have been taken to a hospital immediately, and my neck should have been put in a rigid cast for at least a month. He told me that I would probably have lots of neck pain as I got older. He was right about that. He advised me to apply for disability, but I didn't want to do that, because then I wouldn't be able to fly.

Chapter-60-
Waiting for the Surrender

Lots of rumors, some wishful thinking and hoping, were floating around, about the surrender of the Japanese. General Chennault had told us as he was leaving China that the Japanese could not hold out much longer and that they would not want an invasion of their homeland, since that had never happened in their history.

Diary pages missing. . . . *been a real let-down since the Old Man* [General Chennault] *resigned. Haven't flown a mission in two weeks. Short of gas. Eager to get back in the air. We hear rumors everyday Japs are going to quit and then we hear they will never surrender until we march into Tokio.*

We should bomb the hell out of them everyday. Burn their damn cities or we are going to loose a lot of troops. They will probably fight harder for their homeland than they did all the islands. The big brass better keep Chennault here and follow his advice. Give us more gas and supplies so we can go all out in bombing the hell out of them.

— — no air activity. The bastards are afraid to come up and meet us. Looks like they are pulling their troops back so we may get back to our eastern bases soon. When we do we'll be back on our way to Shanghai then Tokio. I'd like to tell Tokio Rose "here's old Whitey Johnson that your great superior pilots were going to shoot out of the air." Would like to punch her in the nose — but may be more fun to punch her in the mustache.

Aug 7, 1945. We just heard B-29s dropped some kind of high explosive bomb on Hiroshima. Reports are that one bomb completely destroyed the entire city. And all the people. No survivors. Jesus – I wonder what kind of a bomb can do that kind of damage. They call it the atom bomb. Its something that Einstein invented.

Our Gov't told the Japs to surrender now or all their cities would be leveled. They dropped leaflets in advance but guess the Nips didn't believe we had a powerful bomb like that. Wonder what will happen –will they surrender or will we have to bomb them some more. The Japs are ferocious fighters and won't give up easily. What will happen to wars in the future. Hope there will never be another but if we can wipe out a city with millions of people with one bomb – that is really frightening. What if Hitler or the Japs had that bomb first. We had a bet half the guys in the squadron said the Japs would surrender in a few days and half said they would never surrender. Hope I'm on the right side and the war will be over soon. Seems to be a tragic waste of life when they know they are beat.

Nothing new. Everyone waiting for surrender news. Just walking around looking at the sky – waiting –Even the die hard poker and cribbage players are not at their cards.

8 Aug 1945. a sad sad day in China. The great Flying Tiger left China this morning. Chennault said good bye to his troops — left Kunming home to U.S. Bet Stilwell and some of the other fancy pants out to get Chennault are gloating today.– but to the detriment of the U.S. What a shame – someday history will eventually record that Claire Chennault was America's greatest aviator and our country owes him a great deal for his — [Diary pages missing.]

Wow –another big blast–this time one bomb destroyed a big city called Nagasaki. The reports are that not one building is standing. Everything is burned up. What a shame. Millions of people, women, and children all killed.

The reports were greatly exaggerated. There were not millions involved. There actually were less killed in Hiroshima and Nagasaki than those killed in the invasion of Okinawa. The immediate death tolls in Hiroshima and Nagasaki were, respectively, 78,100 and 23,753, plus an estimated 100,000 immediate casualties in both cities. More than one hundred thousand Japanese soldiers died during the invasion of Okinawa, with many civilian deaths and casualties. Death and casualty numbers vary widely, depending upon the sources.

The Battle of the Philippines was even worse. Two hundred fifty thousand enemy troops were killed, with about eighty thousand U.S. deaths and casualties. As the American forces captured islands on their drive across the Pacific, the casualties on both sides increased as our forces approached Japan. The human loss in the event of an invasion of Japan would have been a catastrophe never before experienced in history. We learned after the war that there were 2.3 million regular army Japanese troops to defend the homeland. There were over four million Japanese army-navy reservists, with over twenty-five million armed civilians. There were one hundred fifty thousand U.S. and allied prisoners, and over three hundred thousand civilian detainees. All those POWs and civilians would have been murdered.

After the end of the war, a copy was found of the order issued by the Japanese high command that provided that all POWs and civilian internees were to be killed if there was a U.S. invasion of Japan.

My friend, Max Parnell, who was in the Ofuna prison camp in Japan, told me later that they had been informed by the Japanese prison commander that he had been ordered by military headquarters to kill all prisoners in the event of an invasion of Japan.

Allied military planners estimated the Allied losses would exceed three million deaths and casualties. Those of us who heard every day of the increasing casualties on both sides were convinced that there would be no surrender by the fanatical Japanese commanders without the compelling use of powerful bombs and the threat of another kind. Throughout the Chinese airbases, we were convinced that we would become a vital part of the invasion forces. We knew that our bomber and fighter squadrons would be moved to air-bases within striking distance of Japan. Whatever the results, that was our destiny. We knew that in order to preserve our freedoms and way of life, we had to win this war regardless of the cost.

History compellingly tells us that the use of the atomic bombs convinced Japan to surrender and that those weapons saved millions of lives. There are still those, more than fifty years later, who argue that Japan would have surrendered without the use of those bombs. They are as misguided and misinformed as those who argue that the Holocaust never happened.

Even some high-ranking Japanese officials expressed the opinion that the atomic bomb was necessary to end the war. During the War Crimes Trials held in Tokyo, Marquis Kido, Lord Keeper of the Privy Seal, and the Emperor's closest agent, testified that the atomic bombing of Hiroshima was justified in that it saved millions of Japanese lives and thousands of Allied soldiers who would have been forced to fight a Japan dedicated to a fight to the end.

Dairy pages missing. *Truman says it is necessary or we will loose millions of soldiers in the invasion. The Jap leaders must be crazy to continue to permit such destruction. Nobody cheered much when we heard the news. We know people must die in a war but why —why can't Nations settle problems peacefully. Everybody looks sad but hope this is the end and the Japs give up.*

Diary pages: *854-864. Rumor – not confirmed – the reports say Japs are suing*

for peace under the Potsdam Declaration. I think that Potdamn means uncondi-
tional surrender. No confirmation by the end of the day. Reports another bomb will
be dropped in a week if no surrender. This time they say Tokio — the Chaplin held
a prayer session that Japan would surrender to save lives. — big turnout so many
of guys must feel the same.

There was continued speculation about surrender. We had learned that the Japanese troops had evacuated the base at Luichow that they had chased us out of earlier
in the war. The Japanese had destroyed everything, so we had to set up army tents
for living quarters. The nice tents we had at Loahwangping with wooden sides and
floors were mansions compared to the army tents.

Headquarters decided to move our squadron to Luichow so we could keep an
eye on the Japanese activities at Hong Kong. In the event of surrender, headquarters
wanted us close by to help the British reoccupy Hong Kong.

12 Aug. 1945. What a crazy war. Sent to India to pick up some new P-51s to
ferry back. Rumors still flying that the war will continue. – that Truman has told the
Japs thru Swiss that another bomb will be dropped in a few days if no surrender.
They claim to have one more powerful bomb than the first two. Picking up some
good British gin and beer. If we are going to be around for a while need some good
refreshments. With all the strain of missions and worry about wars end a little R&R
is — [Diary page missing.]

14 Aug 45. Back over the Hump. Still no news of surrender and no more news
of another bomb. Reports are that diplomats all over the world trying to convince
the Japs to surrender. Some reports say they have surrendered and some say not.

— — — —

Chapter -61-

The War is Over

Diary pages: 865 - 920. 16 Aug 1945. [I printed in large letters:]

WAR IS OVER

*Word is now official. The Emperor of Japan announced the complete and uncon-
ditional surrender of all Jap forces as of Aug. 15th. — — V. J. IS 15 Aug 1945 will
mankind learn before we destroy ourselves.*

Earthquake McGoon was leading a flight of four P-51s back from India out of
Kunming. The others in the flight besides me were Willie Nest and Ben Roberts.
McGoon decided it would be fun to fly to Shanghai, since the war was over. His excuse for not going to our base would be that his compass went out, we had to avoid
bad weather, and he didn't have any maps to our base. It was a crazy idea, but the
rest of us went for it.

1st Lt. James B. McGovern "Earthquake McGoon"
P-51D, Shanghai, China *circa* August 1945

. . . first night in Shanghai is a sensation. Don't know how much trouble we will get into but sure an experience when we followed the advance surrender party in. Noone seemed surprised with 4-P-51s there.–guess they thought we were designated official escort and we were not going to tell them anything different. We might get Ct. marshaled but probably worth it. The ride in the truck from the airport to downtown Shanghai can't be described. Hundreds of thousands cheering and flag waving people. When Earthquake and I landed it was pretty scarey. The Japs were all still armed. We had heard that the Generalissimo had asked Jap authorities to keep weapons until American and Chinese Nationalists could take over and avoid rioting, and not surrender to Chinese communists or guerilla troops. When I saw all those armed Jap troops I started to wonder if Mc Goon's idea of flying right on to Shanghai was such a good idea.

We sat in our planes for a bit to see how the Nips reacted but they just stood back. A little Chinese guy in a black kimono ran up and damn near got his head chopped off by the prop. He could speak good English but we couldn't figure out if he was the Mayor or the Mayor's assistant. He got us to a truck for a ride into the city. Jap troops were everywhere marching in formation but they never looked at us.

Some Japanese had surrendered and were being marched to secure camps. Whenever we tried to take pictures of them, they would hang their heads or look away.

"Surrendering Japanese troops in Shanghai"

The Jap General was really pissed off when we booted his ass out of his fancy suite — — The Park is a beautiful hotel with no war damage. He wouldn't give us his sword. He was not about to surrender to four Lts. and we didn't want to push our luck. The hotel was lavish and don't know where they got all the good steak, fish and fresh vegetables. Didn't look like there had been a war —- After we had a long bath and rub down by some beauties McGoon started to look for poon tang. The masseurs were strictly that and weren't interested in any loving.

"Whitey Johnson enjoying his first beer in the Park Hotel in Shanghai"

Hope J.S. can fix our flight plans and orders. McGoon said we had to divert because of bad weather but 300 miles is a long way to divert. Didn't take McGoon long to be back with girls in tow. They were White Russians and had first been interned in 1937. And after that worked in a hotel as waitresses. They said the Jap officers never bothered them. They preferred Chinese or Korean girls. Something about them being below their station or some damn thing. —— these girls were sure appreciative of us "liberating" them.

More Americans and British arriving every day. Lots of rank coming in. I think our lovely vacation is going to come to and end soon. We don't tell anyone anything except that we were a fighter escort. Gen. Wedemeyer and Gen. Stratemeyer arrived and put a stop to our charging meals, booze and all the goodies. Said the U.S. had no contract with the hotel and didn't know who would pay the tab we ran up. Had to vacate our suite for Gen. Wedemeyer.

When we arrived in Shanghai and taken to the hotel, we were told by the mayor's assistant that we should just sign the bills for food, drinks, and other necessities. Apparently that was the method used by the Japanese officials, and their government paid the bills. Our generals didn't seem to think that was a good idea. Since the suite we had been occupying was the nicest in the hotel, Gen. Wedemeyer took it over. We were placed in other rooms that were nice, but not as lavish as the suite.

Diary page missing . . . *came to a halt with orders to get our asses back to Luichow immediately. Sounds like the shit is going to hit the fan. Now that the war is over hope they don't get too excited about our getting "lost" in bad weather. McGoon says he's sticking to his story that his compass went out. Since he was flight leader the rest of us had to follow.*

3 Sept 45. Complete confusion at the sqdn. Everyone getting orders to transfer or go on ferry missions. Even Mel Scheer [operations officer] *didn't seem much concerned about our absence. He didn't want to hear about our escapade just said "don't give me any of that shit – I know what you f***ups were up to". for your little R&R I am kicking your asses out of the 118th and being transferred to the 75th and can stay in China till hell freezes over. If you like this Chink pussey so well you can stay and enjoy it while we all head for home. Don't know if he was really mad but we were over in the 75th within hours.*

The word got around in a hurry that we'd been to Shanghai but we thought we better not do any bragging and better play it cool. We said we'd been on a secret mission for surrender and wouldn't talk about it. No one in the 75th seemed to care.

McGoon and I found out later that someone had written up an adverse report about us, with the recommendation that our pending promotion to Captain be held up. It was obviously effective, because we never did get promoted. McGoon said: "the Shanghai adventure was worth more than any Captain's bars. They can stick them wherever they want." I met Scheer at a Flying Tigers convention some years later and asked him about the report. He denied making it. He thought it was my old Operations Officer nemesis, Gus Dinand, which had written it up. He told me that Dinand really made a fuss when he learned we had "diverted" to Shanghai and recommended to Col. Rector, the 23rd Group commander, that we should be put up for a court-martial. He said Rector actually thought it was quite a gutsy thing to do and just laughed about it. Rector had a reputation of being quite a maverick himself and probably would have done the same thing himself if he had the chance.

After the war, Ed Rector and I became good friends. Whenever I went to Washington, D.C. I would stay at his house. Rector remained a bachelor but was quite a ladies man. He was quite a handsome guy and had no problem having a beautiful girl friend. Regardless of their name, he would always call them "Myrtle". He would tell them the first girl friend that he had that he loved deeply was a beautiful girl named Myrtle, and "you look just like her and just as beautiful." He told me that was his defense of not calling the newest one the wrong name in the heat of passion. He usually had another beauty each time I saw him. He did not want to get too attached to any one of them for he enjoyed the single life.

After the surrender, we moved from Luichow to Hangchow located about sixty miles south of Shanghai on the east coast. Hangchow had been an elite Chinese cadet school so there were very nice living quarters there. Although there had been some small detachments of Japanese stationed there, the place was never bombed so it was in very good shape.

Col. Rector established the 23rd Fighter Group Headquarters in a nice office building and had his living quarters in a beautiful mansion. There was quite a bit of beautiful young lady traffic to and from his mansion too!

Col. Rector stayed on in China for some time after the end of the war. When the 23rd Fighter Group was scheduled to go home, he turned over command to Col. Clyde Slocum. Rector became one of the Judges on the War Crimes Tribunals held in China.

While at Hangchow we flew some surveillance missions along the coast to watch for any unauthorized Japanese activity. After the Emperor's announcement ordering the surrender of all Japanese military units, some units did not readily follow the Emperor's order. We wanted to make sure they did. We saw a lot of American and British warships patrolling the area in the East China Sea and along the China coast. One of the American battleships on patrol was the *USS Tennessee*.

Some years later, I learned that I, my brother Clarence, and future brother-in-law, Reo Knudson, had been in close proximity to each other but none of us knew it. Clarence was in the 96th infantry that was one of the invading units of Okinawa. Reo was aboard the battleship, *USS Tennessee* that bombarded Okinawa in support of the landing parties.

Reo had been in charge of a gun turret on the *Tennessee* that was hit by a bomb during the Japanese attack on Pearl Harbor on 7 December 1941; He was badly burned and spent about seven months in the hospital. When the *Tennessee* was repaired, Reo was re-assigned to it. The *Tennessee* was involved in almost every major battle in the Pacific, usually bombarding islands in support of our invasions forces.

After the war, Reo married my sister Opal. He had kept a diary of his war experiences that I recently learned about. At Opal's request, I went through the diary, made copies of every page, added comments, maps, photographs and historical material. I them printed and bound it in book form. I entitled it *A Sailor's War -Based on Ensign 2nd, Reo Knudson's Diary*. I had it bound in hard copy for family and friends.

As I was flying patrol above, it is probable that one of the ships below was the *Tennessee,* with my future brother-in-law aboard, and my brother Clarence some miles away sitting in a tent on Okinawa. Such are the strange happenings of war.

We got word about the surrender ceremonies held in Tokyo aboard a Battleship. Lots of high rank attended. It was said that General MacArthur asked the question: "where is Chennault?" Virtually every major commander in the Pacific theater was gathered on the Battleship *Missouri* for the surrender ceremonies, except Chennault. General Chennault was the only air force commander that served in one theater of operations during the entire war.

He should have been one of the principal attendees and signed the surrender documents, since his airmen had battled the Japanese under his leadership for four years. His *Flying Tigers;* the AVG, China Air Task Force, and the 14th Air Force destroyed the Japanese Air Force in China keeping it and large Japanese ground forces from serving in other theaters.

Most of us in the Flying Tigers felt that Generals Marshal and Arnold pulled one of the dirtiest tricks of the war in relieving Chennault of his command a month before the surrender and making sure he was not invited to the surrender ceremonies. They may have been brilliant war strategists from Washington D.C, but one wonders how they reached their high positions with such mean little minds. Roosevelt had the highest regard for Chennault and recognized him as an outstanding aerial strategist. Had Roosevelt been alive, it is certain that Gen. Chennault would have had a part in the surrender ceremonies. ....

Diary Pages: *930-1073:*

Got to fly a P-40 today — went on a mail run – no one else wanted to fly the old P-40. I love that old Warhawk. It's a great airplane to fly – not the Cadillac like the 51 but a good old bird. Mc Goon went to medic with a sore pecker but it turned out O.K. just must have been used too much on the R&R. No V.D. wish we could sneak back to Shanghai but better not press our luck. McGovern's comment: "Just stick with the old McGoon, Whitey, and we'll get back to Shanghai some day."

And in fact we did get back. After we were transferred to the 75th and sent to Hangchow, we made it up to Shanghai several times. But the thrill of the first visit was gone.

Ferried some planes to Loping. Don't know why they are shifting planes around but guess they want to give them all to Chiang's forces so communists don't get them. Don't know much about China politics but some people in the know claim there will be a communist take over soon. Jesus – all we need is a damn civil war before we get out of here. Chennault made many speeches about the danger of Chinese communism but guess no one listened.

Flew an interesting mission today –Sept 20 – flew an L-5 to a little field to pick up a field radio guy – been in the field for a long time. – his radio had been out and just got it fixed and first thing he heard was surrender ceremony on 2 Sept on battleship Missouri. He swore all the way back about rotten brass that didn't invite Gen. Chennault to the surrender. To by pass Chennault was really a disgrace. Marshal should be court martialed for that.

Flew another ferry mission on the 23rd and two more L-5 rescue flights on the 28th. I am getting pretty expert in the L-5. No one else wants to fly it and it's a lot of fun. No one seems to bother logging the time in . . .

4 Oct. 1945. Flew a P-51 K and a few days ago a B.T.-13. Haven't flown one for almost two years. But was great sport. Took my crew chief up for aerobatics. Really enjoyed it. To return the favor he took me into town where he had two favorites lined up!

9 Nov. 1945. Orders to go on "Project Diffenbough" going to ferry a lot of planes from India to China. Nobody knows why. Sure crazy as hell to us. Nov 11th. Departed Hangchow for Shanghai. Got to stay two nights so renewed some old and dear acquaintances. Have flown the BT-13, P-47, P-38 a number of times in the past week. Really love trying out all those ships — — —

26 Nov. 1945 one hell of a trip. Went to Calcutta on 14ᵗʰ with 3 "relaxing" days. Dep. 17ᵗʰ for Panagash, left Panagash on 21ˢᵗ for Chabua to Kunming on 22rd. Kunming to Hangchow on 23ʳᵈ. Hangchow to Shanghai on 24ᵗʰ with 2 wonderful nights in Shanghai and back to Hangchow the 26ᵗʰ. Col. Slocum led the mission. We had no problems but other missions were disasters with many planes and pilots lost. What a tragedy since the war is over. The guys that ordered this mission ought to be shot. The planes had been in India too long with no mechanics available also they had bad weather briefing. What a shame to loose all those men for some damn fool politicians. We would gladly give our lives for our country — but this sense-less waste is in-excusable. We hope there is an investigation and those responsible account. Know Col. Slocum real well. He is a great guy and lots of fun to be with. Made most of the interesting places in Shanghai with him..

It was sometime during this period when I went out to an airfield near Shanghai and met a Japanese officer who could speak perfect English. He had been educated at the University of California, of all places. There was a Japanese Aichi D3A2 "VAL" dive bomber in the hangar. I told him I wanted to fly it. He said, "Hell, the war is over, I don't have the authority to stop you, so go ahead. It shouldn't fly much different than your P-47." He was a pilot that had flown the Val, so I got him to explain its characteristics. The instrument panel was all in Japanese, so he made a card that translated the characters into English. I took it up for about an hour, and had a great time. It had a one thousand horsepower engine, so it really roared. With fixed landing gear it only cruised at one hundred sixty knots. There was an Aichi "Jake" sitting in the hangar as well, so I took that up for a short hop. I didn't think much of it. It had a one thousand sixty horsepower engine but only cruised at one hundred twenty knots. Our military gave American names to Japanese planes. Fighters and dive bombers were named after men, "Val, Jake, Tony, Claude," etc., including one we called a "Tojo." Bombers and transports were given women's names. Their bomber that looked much like our B-25 was called a "Betty." I expect Gus Dinand, our fussy old squadron operations officer, would have had a heart at-tack if he knew that I had flown Japanese planes.

It was at this time that Col. Slocum took me out to the Navy hospital ship to have my neck X-rayed because I had been complaining of constant neck pain.

7 Dec. 1945. Celebrated the 4ᵗʰ anniversary of Pearl Harbor. Lots of firecrackers and dancing in the streets. Shanghai really decked out in flags. A bunch of us drove out where Japs are still kept. We didn't cause any trouble but let them know that Pearl Harbor was a bad mistake. They were sullen and hung their heads. Guess they were pretty scared we might harm them. Hell we are just glad the war is over and the world — [Diary pages missing.]

Chapter -62-

Shipping Out

Diary pages: *1074 -1080. 9 Dec. 1945. Good news and Bad News. We are going <u>home</u>. Orders posted today. Shipment by water. Damn– that means a troop ship. They say a month at sea so we won't be home by Christmas.*

My old squadron, the 118th, flew home on C-54s, but because of McGoon's "diversion" to Shanghai it cost him and me an aerial return home. The remainder of the 23rd Group would go by sea in an old liberty ship – the U.S.S *Alderamin,* and we would be on it.

We all thought our famous 23rd Fighter Group would be flown home. The greatest fighting outfit in China shouldn't be treated that way. The 23rd inherited the traditions of the Flying Tiger from the AVG so in that spirit — [Diary pages missing.]

We left Shanghai on 10 December 1945. Col. Slocum was in command of the 23rd group. I had an extra footlocker full of my gun camera combat film. Unfortunately, some thief got away with the footlocker, which was stored on the dock. Bet he got quite a surprise when he opened it obviously thinking it was filled with nice uniforms but instead found cans of film. He would have had no use for the films, but their loss was devastating to me. Those films would have had tremendous historic value. I did have a few rolls in my barracks bag, so I got those home and made some copies that I have included photos from those in the book, particularly those of the Shanghai mission in January of 1945. Another large chest containing squadron mission reports also disappeared from the dock. That too was a huge loss because many of my mission reports were in those records.

One of the sergeants in the group had befriended a little Chinese orphan boy. He fed and clothed him and kept him well hidden on the base. He had a special uniform made for him. We managed to smuggle the little boy aboard ship, carrying him in a barracks bag. It was no secret once the boy was aboard. We had lots of fun with him on the ship.

The boy strutted around in his uniform on the ship, and saluted everyone he met, regardless of rank. Col. Slocum appeared to have bad eyesight, because, for some reason, he could never see the kid. Even the ship's captain couldn't see him! The sergeant managed to get the boy off the ship without U.S. immigration catching him. He raised the boy to manhood and secured U.S. citizenship for him.

That was my first trip on a ship. We were not far from Shanghai when we started running into bad storms.

Diary page, *1080. 15 Dec. 1945. On the Alderamen going home. Bad typhoon — wish I was flying.*

We did run into a terrible typhoon off the coast of Formosa, also known as Taiwan. We sat for three days, just heading into the wind. Everyone had to stay below deck because waves would wash over the deck. We learned that the ship rolled from side to side up to seventy degrees. Anything that wasn't tied down would go flying. It was almost impossible to eat because the dishes wouldn't stay on the table.

We had lots of seasickness on board. Fortunately, I didn't get sick, but it was a little hard to hold it down with puking guys all around me. It reminded me of stories my mother told, about sailing across the Atlantic from Norway and the experiences my great uncle, Paul Jorgensen, related in his diary.

Diary pages 1081 to 1111 are missing.

We arrived in Tacoma, Washington, on New Year's Eve. They wouldn't let us off the ship and we were to be quarantined for three days. Some of us, including Col. Slocum, slid down an anchor rope while the M.P.s on the dock turned their backs. We got rides into the city and did a little celebrating.

Diary page*: 1112. . . . after spending Xmas on that damn tug the Alderamen we can be forgiven for getting a little out of hand in Tacoma. , even getting thrown in jail for clobbering a Taxi driver after he hit Sloc* [Col. Slocum] *with a wrench was worth it.*

No one ever called Slocum "Col. Slocum." We just called him Sloc. The taxi driver tried to rip us off by trying to charge us ten times more than the taxi fare should have been. We had been riding around to various clubs and knew quite well what the charge should be. Slocum started arguing with the driver about the fare. That was when the driver hit Slocum in the head with a wrench. As Slocum went down, I decked the driver and put him out just as the police arrived on the scene. They kept us at the police station for about an hour and let us go when we told them how the taxi driver had tried to rip us off.

They took a statement from us and said they would file a complaint against the driver, because this was not the first time he had pulled that on servicemen. Sloc had a big gash above his eye. The police called a doctor to patch him up. The police even drove us back to a night club, and cautioned us against getting tangled up with any more taxi drivers.

The police even offered to drive us back to the ship when the bars closed. We decided it would be prudent to stay in a hotel until the quarantine was up, and then we went back and mingled with the troops as they got off. From the harbor, we were taken out to Fort Lewis in Washington, where we took trains to the airbases nearest our homes.

Chapter -63-

Going Home and on to New Assignments

I was designated train commander by Col. Slocum. The train had lots of passenger cars, with hundreds of troops going primarily to Minnesota and Wisconsin.

"Lt. Wayne Johnson with a beer in his hand on the train from Tacoma"

It was my job to keep order on the train and see that all the guys got back on whenever the train stopped. At every stop, they would run to get beer, booze, candy, and other goodies. If they were late, the train would wait until I verified that all were back on board. The final entry in my diary reads:

Diary page un-numbered.

. . . with a sore head, sore knuckles and a sore pecker and rattling along on this old train I'm happy as can be. North Dakota at 40 below even looks beautiful. After furlough going to Santa Anna Air Base so will have to start acting like an officer and gentleman!

All pages of the diary after 1112 have been lost. Although I kept a diary for the rest of my service period, no pages were found, and I didn't keep a personal diary after leaving the air corps.

After being released from the reception center at Camp McCoy, Wisconsin, I went home for a brief furlough. Then I was assigned to a field at Santa Anna, California, on to Luke Field, Arizona, and then to Champaign, Illinois. My final duty station was Kelly Field, San Antonio, Texas, from where I was discharged in November 1946.

Santa Anna was rather boring. There was very little flying, only four hours a month, to keep current. I was named the base's information officer. My job was to give interesting lectures to the enlisted men, supposedly to keep them happy. But we weren't too far from Los Angeles, where there were fun things to do.

My next station was Luke Field near Phoenix, which was more interesting. I did a lot of flying there. Luke Field had been the flight school to train Chinese pilots during WWII. Virtually all the pilots that were in the Chinese-American Composite Wing in the 14th Air Force had been trained at Luke Field. There were still some Chinese pilots in training. Although the war was over, the Communists were becoming a real threat to the Chinese government under Generalissimo Chiang Kai-shek. We assumed these men were being trained to support Chiang's air force. Some of them were advanced enough to fly the P-51, so we taught them combat tactics.

The only shortcoming at Luke was that the temperature would be up in the hundreds almost every day. I was there in July. We had to wear long-sleeved shirts so we didn't get burned when we climbed in the plane, because the metal would get very hot from the planes standing out in the sun. We would run from the pilots' ready room to the plane, and get off the ground as quick as we could. We would try to do most of our instruction above an altitude of ten thousand feet, where it would be nice and cool.

My next assignment was at Campaign, Illinois. It was interesting, but not what I wanted as a pilot. Some bright superior thought I should learn to be an engineering officer. They wanted pilots to know about the different aspects of the air corps. It was interesting to take engines and planes apart and make repairs, but it was not what I wanted as a career. We did get to fly, but it was routine. Chicago was close by, which provided for some interesting diversions.

I got to be good friends with the base commander, who had spent the entire war in the States as an instructor. He was eager to hear about my experiences with the Flying Tigers. He would usually take me to the officers' club after work, so we could visit and have a few beverages. He referred to his favorite drink as "sarsaparilla." He would usually call his wife and tell her he was stopping at the officer's club for a sarsaparilla with some high-ranking visiting officers. There usually were a lot of visiting dignitaries because of the type of base, so that part of the story she could believe. I don't know if she believed his sarsaparilla story, because his sarsaparilla was actually vodka tonic. With the C.O.'s help, I did manage to transfer to Kelly Field in San Antonio, Texas. He had given me a top rating and recommended me for promotion to captain.

When I got to Kelly, the C.O. reviewed the recommendation for promotion and my file. With the adverse report that I had gotten in China after the "Shanghai episode," he felt that the higher authority would not approve my promotion, but he did send the recommendation. Sure enough, I was turned down despite my otherwise good record.

I had seriously considered making the military my career, because I loved flying fighters. Jets were just being introduced to the air corps, and it presented an interesting challenge. But with the war over and a rush to cut down on the military, good opportunities might be few and far between. I knew that being turned down for promotion would be a real obstacle for future advancements. The higher-ups that approved promotions always looked for the slightest blemish on a record as an excuse to turn down promotions. Disapproval became quite commonplace, particularly if one was not a graduate of West Point nor a career officer before the war.

I applied for release from the service in November 1946, which was readily granted.

Lt. Wayne Johnson- flight jacket has 23rd Flying Tiger Grp & 118th Black Lightning Sqdn patches. Kelly Field, TX. 1946

"Lt. Wayne Johnson ready to depart from Kelly Field. He is wearing his leather flight jacket showing the patch of the 23rd Fighter Group on the left and the 118th Black Lightning Squadron on the right."

The Air Corps had many more pilots than it needed in peacetime, so was more than eager to let go anyone who wanted out. In fact, the Air Corps, like all military branches, were discharging many who wanted to stay in.

I got a friend at Kelly Field to agree to fly me and a guy from Duluth home. Because so many guys were getting out and getting planes to take them home, the only plane available was a twin-engine Beech. When we got to the plane, the major said he'd never flown that plane, so I'd have to fly it. Although I had flown twin-engine planes, I had never flown that particular type, but I wasn't going to tell the major that and loose the chance to fly home. We had to get a mechanic to show us how to start it. I managed to get it off the ground without too much trouble. We had a couple of nurses along, both of whom we dropped off in Omaha. There was a "mile high" experience along the way!

We spent Thanksgiving Day in Duluth and went to a famous restaurant, the Pickwick, for Thanksgiving dinner. We were still in uniform, so when the owner saw us, he gave us a most delicious dinner with all the drinks we wanted, on the house.

Maternal Grandparents Ole & Kornelie Olsen
Tromso, Norway *circa* 1904.

The Soren Johannessen home on *Store Gate* (main street) Tromso, Norway where Dad & Mother stayed with Dad's parents for a short time after they were married.

Paternal Great-grandparents Johannes & Anna Jensen on the island of Ljoso, Norway. *circa* 1876.

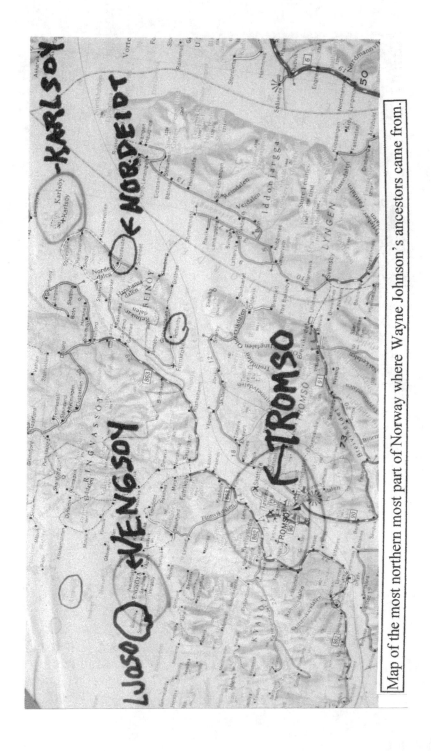

Map of the most northern most part of Norway where Wayne Johnson's ancestors came from.

Photo of Mother & Willie taken the day they left Norway. Grandfather Soren's & my father's were taken a few days before. When they arrived on the barren prairie of western Minnesota, Mother would never wear that beautiful dress again.

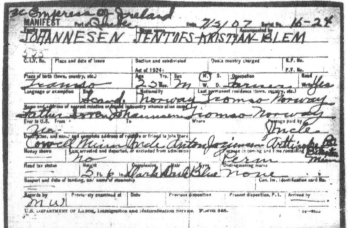

The Manifest of the *Empress of Ireland* as it arrived in Port of Quebec. The agent mis-spelled my father's name. It should have read:

JOHANNE<u>SS</u>EN, JENTOF<u>T</u> KRISTIAN BL<u>O</u>M

Soren Johannessen family.
Standing: Grandfather Soren,
Jentoft, age 14 (my Dad) Constance,
Grandmother Lovise, Hanna.
Tromso, Norway. *circa 1896*

The Jentoft & Aasta Johnson family- *circa* 1935

Back row: Korty, Clarence, Arnold, Roald, Roy, Willie, Orla
Front: Opal, Floyd, Dad, Wayne, Gwendlyn, Mother, Myron, Edgar

Wayne's parents Jentoft Johannessen & Aasta Olsen's wedding in Tromso, Norway 11/07/1904. Wayne Johnson & Delores Christensen wedding 6/28/1956 at Sychar Lutheran Church in Silver Bay, Minnesota.   shown with Delores's parents Laurence & Margaret Christensen & Wayne's Mother, Aasta Johnson

238

The Johnson girls:
Korty, Opal, Gwen, Orla
Circa 1948

The nine Johnson boys all dressed up. White shirts with rolled up sleeves was the fashion. L-R: Arnold, Willie, Floyd, Myron, Roald, Wayne, Roy, Clarence, Edgar - in front *Circa* 1938

Early photo of Johnson boys:
Back: Clarence, Myron, Floyd, Roald.
Frt: Arnold, Wayne, Roy.
Willie took the photo.
Edgar was not yet born.
Clothes were all home made by Mother. *Circa.* 1922

The old farm house in Artichoke
Township that Dad built in 1914-1916

Brother Arnold taking a bath in our "modern bath room" in
the McLean farm house. *Circa* 1934

Threshing was hard work - from daylight to dark - but an interesting and fun time Wayne is pitching bundles of wheat into the threshing machine.

Floyd trying out our almost new 1930 Model "A" John Deere tractor at the McLean farm in 1935 while Arnold, Clarence, Willie & Dad look it over. Tractors replaced horses for farm work. The tractors were also used to power the threshing machines.

Although Dad had tractors he still liked horses for some farming. We liked them for some fun rides. Shown from left are brothers; Clarence, Arnold, brother-in-law; Reo Knudson, and Wayne Johnson at farm southeast of Wheaton, Minnesota. *Circa 1948.*

Wayne Johnson
Graduate Chokio HS.1939

Wayne Johnson with his 25¢ *Sears* hat - looking mighty sharp. 1939

Wayne looking mighty spiffy in his graduation gown.

Rev. Hal. Rassmusson's Norwegian Lutheran Church in Chokio with his 1937 confirmation class. Wayne paid $9.00 to Sears Roebuck for the suit, $2.50 for the shoes and $1.00 for the white shirt.

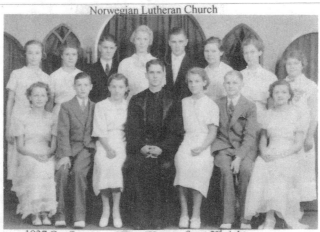

Norwegian Lutheran Church

1937 Confirmation Class: Wayne, front 2nd right

PEARL HARBOR ATTACK: USS *Arizona* sunk and burning. Far left, men on the *Tennessee* are playing fire hoses on the water to force burning oil away from their ship.
Photo courtesy U. S. Navy Photography . Courtesy National Archives.

West Virginia afire immediately after the Japanese attack. USS *Tennessee* is on the sinking battleship's *opposite side. Official U. S. Navy photograph. Courtesy National Archives.*

243

Reprint with Permission

Final.
Edition
Closing Market Price
★★★★

ST. LOUIS STAR-TIMES

7TH WAR
EXTRA

Vol. 56—No. 59

Monday Evening, December 8, 1941

28 Pages

Price Three Cents

WAR DECLARED

3,000 Casualties In Jap Attack On Hawaii

Nearly 1,500 Feared Dead

White House Admits Sinking Of One 'Old Battleship' And Destroyer In Pearl Harbor

MANILA, P. I., Dec. 8.—(U. P.)—Press dispatches reported that 100 to 200 troops, sixty of them Americans, were killed or injured tonight when Japanese warplanes raided Iba, in the west coast of the Island of Luzon, north of the Olangapo naval base.

WASHINGTON, Dec. 8.—(U. P.)—Casualties on the Hawaiian island of Oahu in yesterday's Japanese air attack will amount to about 3,000, including about 1,500 fatalities, the White House announced today.

"We will Triumph—So Help Us, God"

Congress Acts In 33 Minutes

Jeannette Rankin Only Member Of Either House To Vote 'No' After F. D. R.'s Dramatic Request

WASHINGTON, Dec. 8.—(U. P.)—Congressional leaders will take the war resolution to the White House today for the President's signature at 4 P. M. today, St. Louis time, the White House announced.

WASHINGTON, Dec. 8.— (U. P.) —Congress today proclaimed existence of a state of war between the United States and the Japanese empire thirty-three minutes after the dramatic moment when President Roosevelt stood before a joint session to pledge that we will triumph—"So help us, God."

The senate acted first, adopting the resolution by

244

Lt. Wayne *Whitey* Johnson climbing into his P-40 *Warhawk* for a mission with the *Flying Tigers* 14th Air Force, China 1944.

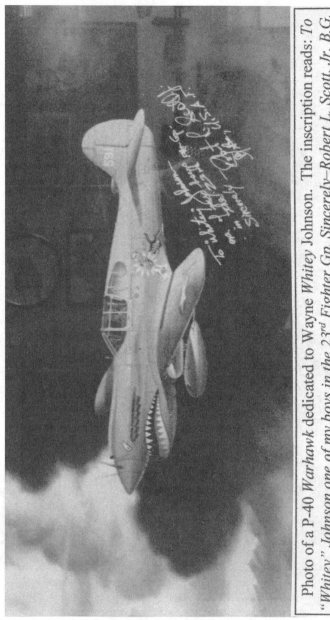

Photo of a P-40 *Warhawk* dedicated to Wayne *Whitey* Johnson. The inscription reads: *To "Whitey" Johnson one of my boys in the 23rd Fighter Gp. Sincerely–Robert L. Scott, Jr. B.G. USAF.* Gen. Scott was the commander of the Flying Tigers 23rd Fighter Group and author of the well known WWII books *God is my Co-Pilot, Five Down and Glory* and many others.

Black Lightning Squadron Tents at Loahwangping Air Base in China. Wayne *Whitey* Johnson's tent was in the back row, 2nd from left. Tents were British style with wood sides and wood floor. These were some of our better living quarters.

Shown on right are Whitey's tent mates, Bob Leavell and Oliver Bateman. Whitey is in the center.

Below are pilots of the 118th Black Lighting Squadron. Whitey in 2nd row 2nd from right. Note the variety of uniforms. Very few are Air Corps regulation. Gen. Chennault did not care how we dressed but required perfection in the air.

American fighter strike on Japanese Airdromes near Shanghai on 17 January 1945 by P-51s of the 118th Black Lightning Sqdn and the 74th Guerilla Sqdn. 97 enemy planes destroyed without loss of any U.S. aircraft.

Lt. Wayne *Whitey* Johnson's gun camera film showing hits on enemy bombers and fighters on the ground.

A Jap *Oscar* in the air takes a hit in the wing and goes down. We didn't see it crash since it went down through the smoke and clouds so was not confirmed as a victory.

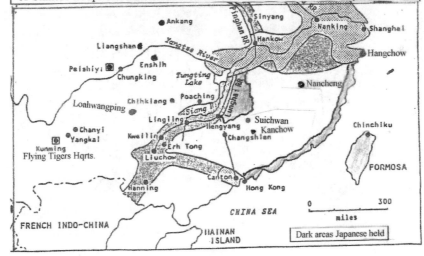

Map of China showing American Air Bases ●
Japanese forces captured Hengyang, Lingling, Kweilin, Erh Tong, Luichow, and
Nanning 1944, and Suichuan and Kanchow in 1945. With air attacks and the aid
of Chinese troops and American Y forces we re-took all those bases by mid 1945

This rescue flag referred to as a "blood chit" was worn on the inside of pilots and air crew jackets that advised the Chinese people that this was an American airman come to help China in its battle against the Japanese invader. It instructed the Chinese to help the American airman that had been shot down back to a friendly air base. The Chinese were very helpful in the rescue of the American flyers at great risk to themselves and without expectation of any reward. The "chit" showed the Chinese red flag with the white twelve pointed Chinese star on a blue background so it was recognized throughout China.

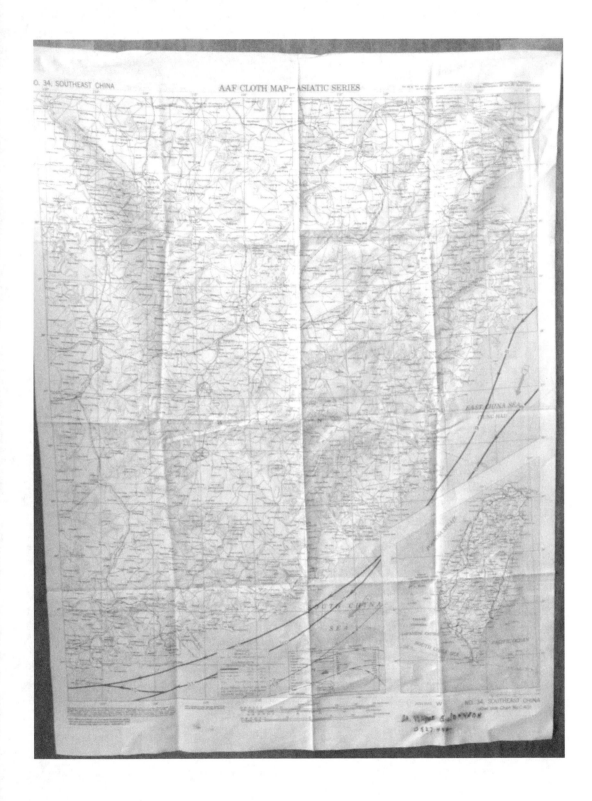

After his forced resignation on 8 July 1945 by Generals Marshal and Arnold, General Chennault made a tour of most of the American Air Bases in China to say goodbye. He would fly in to remote bases and then tour the base in any available vehicle often in a Jeep which he frequently drove himself. There was usually a farewell ceremony which was a most emotional affair because he was such a loved and respected commander. After serving in China for almost eight years battling the Japanese, he was deprived of the honor of accepting the Japanese surrender. He was on his way back to the States when the Emperor ordered all Japanese units to surrender.

Lt. Wayne *"Whitey"* Johnson
Chungking China Air Base, 1945
Dressed for Gen. Chennault's farewell

V-J DAY

Emperor Hirohito of Japan announced the surrender of all Japanese forces on 15 August, 1945. The official surrender ceremonies were held on the battleship *Missouri* anchored in Tokio Bay, while hundreds of Allied planes flew above, on 2 September, 1945. Admiral Nimitz is shown signing the surrender documents. The Japanese delegation had already signed. General Douglas Mac Arthur, Supreme Command Pacific, stands on far left. It was reported that as MacArthur boarded the ship, his first comment was; "Where's Chennault?" Because Gen. Chennault had been relieved of his command by Gen, Marshall and Arnold, he was on his way back to the states and not allowed to attend the ceremony.

Lt. Wayne Johnson flying surveillance in a P-51 over the east China sea while the *USS Tennessee* patrols below. American air and sea units were searching for Japanese that refused to obey the Emperor's order to surrender. *circa* Sept 1945.

A British *Brewster* fighter plane that I photographed from my P-51 over Hong Kong harbor after the surrender. My squadron was based at Luichow about a hundred miles west of Hong Kong. We helped the British patrol around Hong Kong to make certain the Japanese garrisons in the area complied with the Emperor's order to surrender. Some units didn't want to surrender so we had to "persuade" them.

Lt. Wayne *Whitey* Johnson in front of his "Mansion" at Luichow air base.

Lt. Whitey Johnson on transfer to the 75th Fighter Squadron with the logo of the Flying Sharks on a P-51.

Japanese pilot at Kiangwan, Shanghai airdrome after the surrender that coached Whitey Johnson how to fly the Japanese *Aichci* and *Jake* dive bombers.

Japanese Aichi "Jake"

Japanese Aichi "VAL" dive bomber
Flown by Lt. Wayne Johnson 1945

Traverse County Men in the Service

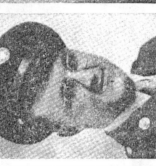

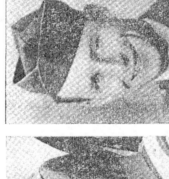

LT. WAYNE G. JOHNSON, son of Mr. and Mrs. Jentoft Johnson of Wheaton. Lt. Johnson enlisted in the army air corps in February of 1942. He is a reconnaissance pilot on a P-51. He was sent overseas in December of 1944 and is now flying with the 14 Air Force in China. Lt. Johnson was employed at the Farmers Store before going into service.

CPL. ROY JOHNSON, son of Mr. and Mrs. Jentoft Johnson of Wheaton. Cpl. Johnson was inducted into the Army in November of 1941. He was sent overseas in April of 1943 and is with the 60 Station Hospital in Italy.

SGT ARNOLD JOHNSON, son of Mr. and Mrs. Jentoft Johnson of Wheaton. Sgt. Johnson was inducted into the Army September 8, 1941. He was sent overseas in March of 1942. He took part in the battle of Guadalcanal and was wounded on November 13, 1942. He has been stationed at Fort Leonard Wood, Missouri for the past two years.

PFC. CLARENCE B. JOHNSON, son of Mr. and Mrs. Jentoft Johnson of Wheaton. Pfc. Johnson was inducted into the army in November of 1942. He was sent overseas in July of 1944 and is with the 96 Division on Okinowa.

For four years, four brothers, sons of Mr. & Mrs. Jentoft Johnson of rural Wheaton, have served in combat in all theatres of war.

258

Attorney Wayne Johnson's first law office in the lumber yard building in Beaver Bay, Minnesota, where he started his law practice in 1952.

Below is the law office building, with a basement apartment for his living quarters, he built in 1953 at the former site of the lumber yard office, financed by a 4% veteran's loan.

Wayne Johnson Family *circa* 1976
Back: Brett (Beaver)   Bruce
Front: Delores   Wayne

Mother Aasta Johnson in her mid-nineties
still looking sharp

Wayne's Cessna 172 in the front yard of his mother's
farm after landing on the gravel road next to the farm.
Mother did not approve of that type of flying.

You can't take the farm out of a farm kid! Wayne acquired forty acres near the airport because of the kids interest in having horses. We built a barn and had a well dug. We bought two Shetland ponies that we named Barney & Hilda. They produced a colt named April. Our boys and their friends had a great time riding them. We also got several full sized horses and some friends brought some so we ended up with a herd of eight horses.

Daughter Margaret had one she called Lady Bird. She loved that horse and rode her often. We cleared some of the land and planted grass. We were able to cut and bail enough hay to feed the horses during the winter. They grazed in the summer.

Shown above is Margaret carrying water into the barn. It fell to Delores and some friends to feed the horses daily and clean the barn.

Wayne Johnson at the Flying Tigers Monument that he helped design and showing the dedication plaque that he drafted at the Dayton, Ohio Air Force Museum. *circa* July, 1992.

Wayne Johnson, Chairman of the Chennault Stamp Committee with Anna Chennault, widow of General Claire Chennault the commander of the Flying Tigers in China in World War II, at the First Day of Issue ceremony in Monroe, Louisiana on 6 September 1990, when the U. S. Postal Service formally issued the 40 cent Chennault stamp.

Shown below is a copy of the First Day Cover, designed by Wayne Johnson, with the 40 cent Chennault Stamp cancelled at Monroe on date of issue with a Flying Tigers special stamp issued by the Republic of China (Taiwan) on 26 September 1990.

Our son, Beaver, loved to take our Cessna 182 up and soar around the clouds. He was an excellent pilot. When he lost his life in a motor vehicle accident it was a devastating blow. In his memory, we inscribed a photo of the 182 on his grave-site monument with the first lines from "High Flight" *I have slipped the surly bonds of earth, And danced the skies on laughter-silvered wings.*

Bruce too is a very skilled pilot having flown many types of planes from small single engines to corporate jets. He is shown below with a *Citation* jet that he flew for several years for a large corporation.

265

Wayne Johnson, City Attorney, supervises Silver Bay City officials: Edward Arola, City Clerk; Melvin Koepke, Mayor; and Earl Carman, City Treasurer in signing Reserve Mining Company Pollution Control Revenue Bonds, Series 1979 for $105 million at the office of Bond Counsel *Cravath, Swain, & Moore* in New York. There were three more issues to add to the total of $450 million Reserve Mining spent to build the on-land tailings disposal ponds at Mile Post 7.

Wayne Johnson, MR. AVIATION OF MINNESOTA 1968 and

Enshrined in the MINNESOTA AVIATION HALL OF FAME 2001

FLY -IN

AVIATION DAY

Silver Bay Airport
Rededication Ceremony

To the

"Wayne Johnson"

Silver Bay Municipal Airport

August 13, 2005
Fly-In 10am - 3pm
Dedication at 1pm

FOOD

ENTERTAINMENT

SKYDIVING

BUDDY JUMPING

PLANE RIDES

DISPLAYS

Fly in to honor Wayne and the Flying Tigers.
A large scale model of Wayne's P-51 will be unveiled.

MODEL AIRPLANE CLUBS

Three old Flying Tigers who flew combat in China with Wayne (shown with
his flight jacket) came to help celebrate dedication of the Wayne Johnson airport.

268

Wayne Johnson, putting on his WWII flight jacket at the Silver Bay *Wqyne Johnson* airport dedication. The jacket shows the logos of the his Flying Tigers 23rd Fighter Group and the 118th Black Lightning Squadron.

Below is the restored WWII Vultee BT-13 plane Wayne flew in pilot basic training almost sixty-five years ago

Dedication of the
WAYNE JOHNSON AIRPORT
Silver Bay, Minnesota on 13 August 2005

Wayne Johnson in his WWII flight jacket and cap expressing his thanks for the great honor of dedicating the airport in his name. Shown with wife Delores at the Dedication Plaques.

Wayne Johnson piloting his Cessna Skylane
at the *Wayne Johnson Airport*, Silver Bay, MN. Aug.2005

US FLYING TIGERS
AND HUMP WW II
VETERANS DELEGATION
TO CHINA

A JOURNEY INTO HISTORY

Wayne Johnson salutes the welcoming delegation of Chinese children during the 60th anniversary celebration of the end of WWII in China. August 2005.

The sign above was at the Beijing airport.

Wayne Johnson enjoying the company of the beautiful interpreters in various cities as well as the delegation of Chinese school children welcoming the Flying Tigers at Kunming.

Nancy at Zhijiang

Susan at Kunming

Anita at Nanjing

Delores and Wayne 50th Wedding Anniversary
28 June 2007

DULUTH NEWS TRIBUNE   Friday, April 20, 2007

CLINT AUSTIN / NEWS TRIBUNE

Wayne Johnson of Silver Bay sits with a model of a P-51 Mustang (left) in the colors of the Black Lightning squadron of the Flying Tigers Army Air Corps, and a model P-40 Warhawk in the same colors. Johnson flew both planes with the Flying Tigers during World War II. After years of pestering the CIA to bring home the remains of fellow pilot James B. McGovern Jr., nicknamed Earthquake McGoon, Johnson will attend a ceremony in May at Arlington National Cemetery in honor of McGovern.

COURTESY WAYNE JOHNSON

A cartoon shows Flying Tiger pilots James B. McGovern Jr., nicknamed Earthquake McGoon, and his tent mate, Wayne Johnson, nicknamed Whitey. The two are leaning against a barrel of Jing Bao Juice, the name given to the moonshine that McGovern made while serving with the Army Air Corps in China. Jing bao means air raid in Chinese.

Man helps bring fighter pilot home

Wayne Johnson of Silver Bay helped recover the remains of James B.
'Earthquake McGoon' McGovern Jr. from an unmarked grave in Vietnam

BY JANNA GOERDT
NEWS TRIBUNE STAFF WRITER

SILVER BAY — Earthquake McGoon was huge for a fighter pilot, well over 6 feet tall and weighing about 260 pounds.

His friend and fellow Flying Tiger during World War II, Wayne Johnson of Silver Bay, recalls James B. McGovern Jr.'s pot belly, dark complexion and penchant for making moonshine out of rice that earned him the nickname of the Li'l Abner cartoon character who shared those traits.

McGovern became one of the first two Americans to die in the Vietnam War when he was shot down while flying supplies to the French garrison at Dien Bien Phu in Vietnam.

More than 50 years later, his remains finally will be laid to rest in the U.S. — thanks in part to efforts by Johnson, who spent a year living in a tent with McGovern.

McGovern will be buried during a memorial service May 24 at Arlington National Cemetery near Washington, D.C. Johnson and a few other surviving members of McGovern's Flying Tigers Army Air Corps squadron will be in attendance.

They will remember a larger-than-life character who was a natural and talented pilot, said McGovern's cousin, Gary McKenna of Atlanta.

McKenna, now 72, recalled how 60 years earlier he watched as McGovern buzzed the telephone poles and church steeples of his hometown in Pennsylvania in a four-engine cargo plane just after World War II.

As McKenna's family watched the derring-do, heads tilted back in amazement, "my dad says, 'My God, that's Jimmy. I know it is,'" McKenna remembers. Sure enough, it was McGovern.

His adventures were so legendary that Time magazine ran an article about his death, and John Wayne called McGovern's parents asking to buy the movie rights to their son's story. The family turned the actor down, McKenna said.

Wayne Johnson was instrumental in bringing home the remains of his fellow pilot James "Earthquake McGoon" McGovern for burial at Arlington National Cemetery. McGovern, who had served with Whitey in the Flying Tigers in China, was shot down by Viet Minh forces on 6 May 1954 while flying supplies to the beleaguered French fort at Dien Bien Phu. Earthquake and his co-pilot were the first Americans to die in the Viet Nam war.

After fifty-seven years in the practice of law, and setting a record as the longest serving City Attorney, not only in Minnesota but in the United States; Wayne Johnson decided to retire. To help him celebrate, a whole bunch of his relatives gathered with his wife, Delores; children Margaret and Bruce, together with Judges, fellow attorneys, and many friends filling the Reunion Hall in Silver Bay to near capacity. Shown below is Wayne with his law partner of more than thirty years, Gerald "Pete" Morris, enjoying a well earned "refreshment".

Chapter-64-

Home at Last. Back to Civilian Life.

The next day, we flew to Fargo, North Dakota, which was the closest airport to my home near Wheaton, Minnesota. By that time, the major was satisfied he could handle the plane and fly back to Kelly Field. He would follow through with me at each takeoff and landing, until he felt comfortable.

My brothers, Ed and Doc, and Dad, came to pick me up. It was great to be home after all those years. I had weighed one hundred sixty pounds when I went into the service, and now I weighed about one hundred forty, so I was quite skinny. Mother immediately started to cook good stuff to fatten me up. I actually weighed about one hundred twenty pounds when we had arrived in Tacoma, but gained some back until I was discharged.

There was big event and a parade in Graceville as a welcome home to the veterans. I was honored to ride in the first car. Afterwards, a lot of the people who had been in the parade gathered at the liquor store, where two young farm boys were complaining about their Model T. Every time they hit a bump, the engine would stop and they had to push it out of the route until they could get it started. It was a 1921 model and didn't look like it had been kept in good shape. One of the guys said, "If someone would give me $50.00 for that pile of junk, I'd take it." I just happened to have $50.00, which I handed to the young man and asked him to get the title card. He protested and said that he really didn't mean it and needed to sell for a higher price.

The bartender said, "You agreed to sell it and the man paid you. You can't change your mind now. That's not the way we operate around here and that's not the way we treat veterans. Now you go home and get the title card and give the man a bill of sale." And the boy did.

We started towing the Model T back to the farm. A short distance outside of town, my brother Doc had us stop, and he looked the engine over. He found a loose wire on the distributor, hanging by just some threads of wire. Apparently, when the car hit a bump it was enough of jar to loosen the wire and cause the car to stop. Doc took his knife, cleaned the wire, and tied it back on. The old T started right up, and we drove it back to our farm.

Years later, when I was living in Beaver Bay, my brother Ed hauled it up for me. My son, Bruce, and I later restored it to look like a factory-new Ford Model T. I still have it, and frequently drive it in parades.

"Wayne with his model "T" ready for a parade"

There was a round of parties. I hadn't seen brothers Clarence, Roy, and Arnold for years. They were out of the service, so some celebrating was in order. We also had to find new girlfriends after our long absence. Most of the girls of pre-war days were either married or had gotten fat, ugly, and much less desirable.

When the "farm kid" met General Claire Chennault, commander of the Flying Tigers, in far-off Kunming, China, the "kid" wasn't too long off the farm. But five years in the Army Air Corps, and a year in combat, caused me to grow up fast.

Chapter - 65 -

the College Years

As soon as I got home, I started to make preparations for college. I had been sending money home on a regular basis, so had a good nest egg that would get me started in college. I had also established a savings account in the Air Corps, which I withdrew upon discharge. I got a letter from the University of California saying that they could re-activate my 1941 application. That sounded attractive, but I would again be a long way from home.

The Agricultural College in Fargo (now called North Dakota State University) which everyone called the "Cow College," sounded okay. It was a general education college, not limited to agricultural studies. It was only eighty miles away from my parents' home. I made several trips to Fargo to check out the college, and decided that that was the best place for me.

Besides, my sister Opal lived in Fargo. She had a boyfriend, Reo Knudson, a retired sailor, who she was madly in love with. He had been badly burned while serving on the battleship *Tennessee* during the Japanese attack on Pearl Harbor, on 7 December, 1941. Although hospitalized for over six months after Pearl Harbor, he was re-assigned to the *Tennessee,* and served there for the entire war.

Another attraction in Fargo was the talk of establishing an Air National Guard there. In fact, shortly after I got there, I helped get a Fargo air guard organized, and we soon got P-51s. I flew for the guard for two years while in college. It was an interesting diversion.

I started a pre-law course at the Fargo College on January 2nd, 1947. It was more than forty below zero, with a wind that could blow off hats. I wasn't so sure that I shouldn't have selected the University of California.

I had decided while in China that if I did not stay in the Air Corps, I would go into the field of law. Bob Leavell, one of my tent mates, talked constantly about going to law school, which influenced me considerably. Also of influence was an attorney in Wheaton. Attorney Al Johanson was the brother of Chester Johanson, one of the owners of the Farmers Store where I worked from 1939 to part of 1941. His law clerk, Dudley Krenz, was the son of Mrs. Krenz, who ran the boarding house where I ate. We often talked about the field of law being an interesting profession. Dudley went on to become an attorney, as I did. Bob Leavell became a highly respected law professor at the University of Georgia. Charles Older, who I had flown a mission with, was an AVG ace pilot and the 68th Wing Deputy Commander in China, also became an attorney, and later a judge in Los Angeles. He was the judge on the famous trial of Charles Manson .

Although I was on the G.I. Bill, I supplemented my income by working part time at Siegel's Clothing Store. The G.I. Bill was passed by Congress at the end of the war to help veterans get an education. The Bill paid tuition, books, and some small amount of cash. Soldiers in WWII were usually referred to as G.I.s (Government Issue), thus the bill to help veterans was referred to as the G.I. bill. I got my clothes for wholesale, and sometimes even less. Jerry Siegel felt that if I was well dressed, I could encourage other students to shop at his store. It worked very well. Reo Knudson, my brother-in-law, had become a tailor, and he designed some interesting clothes for me, in addition to those that I bought at the store.

One year during the early summer, I crop dusted in a Stearman airplane. It was the same type of plane that I had flown in primary training. The crop dusting company had lost some pilots in accidents and was looking for skilled pilots who could handle a plane at very low level. It paid very well.

The part of North Dakota where we did crop dusting was very flat country. The only hazards were the power and phone lines at the roads near the end of the fields. We usually flew under them and made the one hundred eighty degree turn to go back for the next run. We would land on the roads where trucks were parked, and our planes would be loaded with the spray liquid. It was usually fatal if a pilot hit a power line or did a poor job of landing on the narrow dirt roads.

Part of another summer, I did painting. A sugar beet factory was being built near Fargo. It was about a four story high building. The contractor hired guys from the college to paint both the outside and inside. I was almost a fatality there. I and another guy were on a "swing stage," painting the upper level. The "swing stage" was a narrow wooden platform, a couple of planks wide, about twelve feet long, suspended with ropes from the ceiling, near each end of the platform. It was a big, open building with no floors below.

I was standing on one end, reaching out and painting, when the other guy walked towards me to get some paint. I didn't see him coming until the plank platform tipped up and threw me off the plank end. Paint went flying, but I caught onto the rope support and hung there, suspended about forty or fifty feet above empty air. The other guy went sailing off but fortunately landed on a projection about ten feet below. It took some time before they could get equipment high enough to rescue me.

When they got the mess from the spilled paint cleaned up, the foreman wanted us to go back on the swing stage that had been re-rigged. We thought he was crazy and told him so. No way were we going back up there. I told him that I would not paint anything over six feet high. He tried to fire us. We both belonged to the union, so the union agent told him he could not fire us, particularly since it was the fore-man's responsibility to see that we had a safe working environment.

The foreman sort of got even with us. He had us lie on our backs on the floor and paint the underside of a big tank. We decided life was too short for that type of hazardous occupation, so we didn't go back. Jerry Seigel hired me as full time at his clothing store during the summer, and increased my wages, so I was making about as much as I would have at the painting job.

I liked being back in the store. It was a nice place to work. Jerry, who was the boss, was a very nice guy to work for. But his brother Max, who also worked in the store, could be a real ass. If he gave us salesmen too much trouble, Jerry would straighten him out and tell us not to pay any attention to him. Besides being a nice place to work, they had a very lovely bookkeeper, Ethel Werner. We became "very" good friends, and I courted her until I left the college to go to law school in Min-neapolis.

One summer, I got a job as a crop hail insurance adjuster. Since I was a farm boy, I knew about crops and damage from hail. After college let out, we started out in Texas during the early summer and work north as the crops ripened. It was during this season that hail storms would most damage the ripening crops. In areas known for hail, farmers insured their crops against hail damage.

Adjusting hail damage insurance took a special technique. We would go into a grain field and throw our hat randomly into the field and also have the farmer do the same. From those points, we counted out one hundred stalks of grain from the ring we drew near the hats. We would draw a circle about two feet diameter using the hat as the center point. The number of stalks we found broken, unable to mature, or cut off, was the percentage of hail loss we paid. If we found ten out of one hundred damaged, we paid ten per cent, and fifteen broken, we paid fifteen per cent, etc. Company supervisors told us to try to throw our hats into areas that appeared to be less damaged. I didn't think that was fair, so I would just throw my hat out at random. Farmers caught on quickly to a cheating adjuster. There were many different insurance companies so practices varied. The company I worked for (Great American) gave adjusters almost complete discretion.

It was a challenging job because the farmers would usually argue that they had suffered more loss than we had counted. To keep them happy, we would usually conduct a number of tests in each field. Most farmers were very nice to deal with, particularly on farms in Kansas and Nebraska that had large acreage. The most difficult were the German farmers in northwestern Iowa and southwestern Minnesota. They were really tough.

While adjusting in Kansas, I had a partner who was a school teacher. He had a lovely daughter with certain "attractions." She was an only child, and her parents were desperate to get her married. I think they suspected that, with her amorous proclivities, they might become grandparents of a child born out of wedlock. I decided that before I succumbed to further temptation, I had better move on. At that point, I was not interested in strutting down the aisle in front of a double-barreled shotgun.

When I got back to Fargo, I could still fly sometimes. Flying the P-51 for the air guard was a lot of fun. We could take a plane on any weekend and fly wherever we liked. We did have some dangerous flying, too. One winter we had some terribly heavy snowstorms. Stranded cattle couldn't feed, so we would fly out looking for stranded herds in P-51s. When we found a stranded herd we would radio the location to the C-47 plane that was loaded with bales of hay. The C-47 pilot would fly to the herd and the crew would throw the bales to the herd. Unfortunately, sometimes the bale, which probably weighed about fifty pounds, would hit a cow. It was like dropping a bomb on the cow. If the farmer could find it in time, he could probably salvage the meat. It was hazardous flying, because of sudden snowstorms. Our C.O. was killed when he flew a P-51 into a sudden white-out.

One of my friends, Duane Lund, knew a girl in Boston who could line up a friend for me, so we checked out two P-51s and took off for Boston. Our first stop was Cincinnati. It was about nine hundred miles from Fargo. At our cruising altitude of twenty-five thousand feet with a favorable tail wind, we made it there in just two hours.

While there, we ran into a sergeant who I had known in China. He took us to a nearby restaurant for lunch. The place was swarming with beautiful women. The sergeant seemed to know most of them. He introduced us to two lovely young ladies who persuaded us to stay for the evening and enjoy the social amenities of Cincinnati!

Lund called his girl friend in Boston and told her we had some engine trouble with his plane and that my plane had a flat tire because of a bent wheel, so we had to stay overnight in Cincinnati. The next morning, he called her and told her we would be in Boston at a certain time. We flew on to Boston and arrived there as scheduled. The girls were waiting on the ramp in a nice, red convertible. They were two beauties.

Duane's girl friend asked what the problem was with the plane. He told her the same story he had told her on the phone the night before. He said that it was just some fouled spark plugs and that the mechanics had fixed them by morning. She said, "No. there was no engine problem, my daddy checked." Then Duane said that my plane had had a flat tire that had damaged the wheel, so took some time to fix. She again said, "No, he didn't have any flat tire or damaged wheel, my daddy checked." We learned that her daddy was a high ranking Air Force general who had lots of clout, and no problem checking out our story. Of course, he learned that there was no engine problem and no flat tire or bent wheel. We were caught by a little bit of misinformation.

We were standing next to her car wondering how to get out of this predicament when she said, "You guys just missed the best pieces of tail you have ever had." She threw the car in gear and burned rubber out of the airport. She left us standing in the smoke, completely dumbfounded.

Since her daddy was a general, we thought that it would be best to get out of Boston in a hurry. We jumped in our planes and took off immediately. Lund called and asked, "Whitey, where should we go now?" I remembered that the Flying Tigers of the 14th Air Force Association was having its first convention in Dayton, Ohio. We decided it was a good place to go.

We arrived in Dayton just as the banquet was getting under way. Gen. Casey Vincent, who was 68th Wing Commander in China, was the principal speaker. He was elected the first president of the Flying Tigers 14th Air Force Association. I had flown to Washington D.C. on several occasions in an Air Guard P-51 to meet with some of the people who were in the process of forming the Association, so I was well informed about what was to take place.

After the banquet, when he found out I had flown in a P-51, Gen. Vincent took us out to the airport in his command car. He said he hadn't flown a P-51 for a long time and climbed up into the cockpit to have his picture taken. I suggested to him that he crank it up and fly around the pattern. He didn't want to do that unless he could get approval from the commander of the North Dakota Air Guard. No one in Fargo was on duty on late Saturday night, so we could not get the approval of any authority.

At that time, Dayton was headquarters for the Air Corps weather stations. It was supposed to be the most accurate weather forecasting in the country. The major on duty assured us that the ceiling (the bottom of a cloud level) was at about one thousand five hundred feet and not more than five hundred feet thick, and clear above. The ceiling did look lower, but it was hard to tell in the dark. If the major was right, it would be easy instrument flying. But was he ever wrong.

Duane and I took off in formation and were immediately in the clouds. Although he was tucked in on my wing, the clouds were so thick that he was losing sight of me. I told him to turn right five degrees and climb, so we would not run into each other. The clouds were thick and black. We soon ran into St. Elmo's fire, which involves static electricity that dances around the prop like lightning under certain climatic conditions. Flying with it is very eerie.

We finally broke out of the clouds at about forty-two thousand feet, the very limit of altitude for a P-51. The P-51 was really staggering at that altitude. It was beautiful as I broke out of the clouds into dazzling moonlight. I called the base and told them they should advise the weather officer of the true conditions and that should get a new weather officer that could forecast weather better.

Duane had used a little more power than I had, so he reported that he might not have enough gas to make Fargo. He was getting very low on gas, so he landed in Minneapolis. I continued on to Fargo. Because of the hard climb to altitude, I too had used a lot of gas. I thought I could make Fargo, but at about Detroit Lakes, forty miles from Fargo, the gauges were bouncing on empty. Although the gauges were not always reliable, I knew I was very low on gas, but with the time in the air, I thought I had enough to make it to Fargo. Suddenly, the engine started to cut out. I was still at twenty-five thousand feet and knew I could coast to Fargo. I called the tower and tried to tell them of my predicament. Because I had no power, the radio was dead. It was about midnight. I dead-sticked (landed without power) into the

Fargo airport and coasted up in front of the tower. To land a P-51 without power was tough, but even tougher without landing lights even though the runway was well-lit.

The tower operator looked out and saw a P-51 sitting in front of the tower. He came running down and asked where I had come from, for he had not received any message and had never seen me coming. Because the power was off, I had no landing lights. It took a little explaining and then the next day to Col. Neece, the Air Force commander in charge of the Air Guard. The Colonel "suggested" that the next time, I should be more careful about monitoring gas consumption. To say that it was an interesting and exciting trip would be quite an understatement.

Don Sorlie, another pilot in the guard, and me were offered the opportunity to be trained in a new covert governmental space program. We were interviewed by a couple of colonels because of our prior war experiences. They talked about sending people into space, which was beyond our comprehension. It sounded fascinating and challenging. This was Jules Verne science fiction kind of stuff, but in space. But I had decided that I wanted to be an attorney, so I declined the offer. Furthermore, I thought that because I had gotten through one war without getting killed, it would be stretching my luck to do something this far out.

I often wondered what my future would have been had I accepted the offer! Would I have been one of the first guys in space, on the moon, or would I have gotten blown up in a rocket? It was not until 1969 that the space agency actually put two men on the moon. I would have been forty-eight years old by that time, so probably too old to be part of that venture.

My family years from 1947 to 1949 were busy ones. My sister Opal married Reo Knudson on January 15, 1947. Reo had met her at a dance hall in Fargo, The Aquarium, a popular hangout, shortly after he had gotten out of the Navy in January of 1946. He wrote in his diary that he had "met the love of my life" and "I think I'll marry the wench." Mother approved because he was a nice Norwegian boy. He did marry her, but it took him a year to make up his mind.

Then my sister Gwen (Gwendlyn) went and married Harley Rosdahl on March 7, 1947. He too was approved by Mother because he was at least one-half Norwegian. Dad didn't care— he liked them both. My brother Clarence was next. He married his longtime sweetheart, Doris Abraham, on September 7, 1948. Roy wrapped things up the next year by marrying his beautiful redhead, Dorothy Erickson, on October 15, 1949.

I didn't rush into marriage. I waited until June 28, 1957, to tie the knot with my sweet thing, Delores Christensen. Willie, Arnold, and Ed remained bachelors until Ed decided that bachelorhood was not for him. It took him quite a while, and quite a few ladies, before he made that decision. In 2005, he got married for the first time at the age of eighty. Even claimed he was still a virgin!

While in Fargo, I usually had my evening meal with my sister Opal and Reo. They had an apartment near the Bison Tavern. She always had dinner right on the stroke of 6:00 p.m., — and we better be there. Sometimes Reo and I would stop at the Bison Tavern for a little refreshment. One time we relaxed a little too long at the Bison. When we came upstairs a little tardy, she had our food on the table, quite cold and colored green. That was her subtle hint that in the future we had better be on time. Eating cold green potatoes and green chicken with green gravy was a long-lasting reminder not to be late for dinner.

In 1949, I transferred from the Fargo College to the University of Minnesota Law School. Phil Shields, another student, and I rented a house where we could cook our own meals and save some money by not boarding out. Phil was a real character, but fun to be with. He had an old Studebaker car that he usually drove wide open from our house to school. We bought White Castle hamburgers, six for a quarter, for lunch. Since we had a house, we usually had a lot of friends who would visit us for parties and studying. Everyone would bring personal "libations" and chipped in for the food. It was a fun but strenuous time with work and studies.

Phil and I belonged to the same law fraternity. It was off-campus, and did not have a house. We usually met once a month in some downtown bar or restaurant. The avowed purpose was to discuss legal issues that we had in class. After serious discussions, we had a relaxed time when we enjoyed a beer or two and had some humorous discussions.

At most meetings, one of the fraternity brothers was designated to put on some type of program, either a comic skit or monologue. We usually pretended to be co-medians, and told jokes. If some were a little off color, it was okay. Sometimes they got a little ribald. The assistant Dean of the law school would sometimes attend our meetings, as he did with the other fraternities. For some reason, he did not appear to laugh as hard at our jokes and narrations as fellow students did.

One time, we were at a bar in downtown Minneapolis and Phil made a great show of drinking a glass of beer with an expression that clearly showed how much he enjoyed it. A representative of Gleuk's Brewery was in the bar. He came over to Phil and asked if Phil would pose while drinking a free Gleuk's beer. If he liked the photo, he said he would pay Phil $50.00 for it, and he would use it in a beer advertisement. Phil readily agreed. What a nice way to make $50.00. I have a copy of the photo. It looks like he is really enjoying the beer. The bar had a big blow-up of his drinking photo, which hung prominently behind the bar for years. We would go back there quite often and always get some free beers.

Because I needed to work to earn enough to attend law school, I got a job adjusting insurance claims for an independent insurance adjusting company, Main & Baker. I had been working for Title Insurance Company, doing title examinations for realtors and mortgage companies, but that job did not pay much. It was, however, a valuable experience that I used when I got my own law office. In 1950, I graduated from the University of Minnesota with a Bachelor of Law.

With the insurance adjusting job, I could not go to school during the day, so I switched from the University Law School to the night school at the Minneapolis College of Law, which later became the William Mitchell College of Law, to finish my legal education. It was a great school in which all the professors were practicing attorneys. We learned the practical side of law rather than the theoretical taught at the University. It was a great education for an attorney who wanted to go out into general practice, but made for a tough schedule. After working all day, attending classes from about nine p.m. until midnight was quite a challenge.

The adjusting company that I worked for, Main & Baker had a number of offices. It had offices in Iowa, North Dakota, and several cities in Minnesota, including Duluth. I had gone to Duluth on a number of occasions to help out the adjuster there. In my senior year, the agent in Duluth became very ill so the company asked if I would go to Duluth to run that office. They offered me a substantial increase in salary, so I moved to Duluth.

I would leave the Duluth office at about 4:00 p.m. and drive to Minneapolis to attend classes that started at 9:00 p.m. There was no freeway at that time, so all the driving was on old Highway 61. There was not much traffic going southbound at that time of the day, so I could speed just a little.

After class ended at midnight, I would race back to Duluth. There would be little or no traffic, so I could really make good time. I could usually make it in less than four hours. That got me into Duluth at about 4:00 a.m. I could squeeze in about four hours of sleep until I had to open the office. When my secretary went to lunch, we would close the office for about an hour. I would usually bring my own lunch, so I would have a quick snack and take a little nap.

One time while coming back from Minneapolis, I fell asleep and ran off the road on a sharp curve near Rush City. I rolled my car several times. I didn't get hurt except a few bumps and bruises. Because the car did not have seat belts, I really got tossed around. I desperately hung on to the steering wheel for the only support. We had to replace the steering wheel after, because it was all bent out of shape. I walked back to Rush City, about two miles away, and got a guy who ran a garage out of bed. I had adjusted a lot of claims at his garage, so he knew me very well. Since it was about two in the morning, he grumbled a little but got his tow truck out.

The car, a nice 1951 Studebaker Starlight Coupe, was lying on its side. He rigged up some chains and put it back on its wheels. He checked it over carefully and said it looked okay apart from a lot of dents. We had to put in some gas and oil that had leaked out. We started it up and it ran perfectly. I drove it back to Duluth. When I looked at it in the light the next morning, it looked like a real mess. Every window was broken or shattered, and there was hardly a spot that wasn't dented.

I drove it back to his garage the next day. He gave me a car to drive while he fixed mine. He had it all fixed in about a week and it looked perfect. When he found out I didn't have any physical damage insurance on it, he didn't charge me for the repair work. He gave me hell for not having insurance and told me if I couldn't af-ford it, he would advance me the money. I did scrape enough to get full coverage.

I kept up this schedule for almost two years— all of 1951 and part of 1952, when I graduated and was admitted to the bar.

Tragedy struck our family in 1951. My dad had a stroke that proved fatal. He and Mother were coming from town when he suddenly slumped over the wheel, and the car went into the ditch. Mother could not drive, but a neighbor came along and helped her home. Dad died about three days later. He was an easy-going, lov-ing father. He was not very demonstrative, but doted on little children. He was not much of a disciplinarian, but whenever some of us got a little too rowdy, he could be quite stern. He was a man of few words, but we had better listen to whatever he said.

He had written to his cousin Jentoft Johannessen, who had the same name as Dad, in Norway, earlier that summer about his plans for a trip to Norway. Unfor-tunately that was not to be. He also talked about his and Mother's plans to attend my graduation from law school the next year, but that too was not to be, either. Although Dad was gone, Mother did attend my law school graduation at the Min-neapolis College of Law in June of 1952. She was particularly proud because I was the only one of her children to graduate from college and then law school. I offered

Mother "lemonade" that evening, but she very diplomatically refused. She was rightfully suspicious of my "lemonades."

"Wayne Johnson with his Mother at his graduation from The Minneapolis College of Law in June 1952."

Chapter - 66 -

Now an Attorney at Law

I passed the bar and was admitted to the practice of law in 1952. It was a banner year after almost six years of hard study and hard work. That same year, in September 1952, the Flying Tigers of the 14th Air Force Association held their annual convention in St. Louis, Missouri. I didn't want to miss that, because Gen. Chennault, who had been the Flying Tigers commander, was expected to be there. It would be a long drive from Minneapolis to St. Louis. My brother Roy, who lived in Minneapolis, agreed to go with me and help with the driving. We wanted to make it there in one night and one day.

We had a little delay in a small town in Iowa where we were going to stop in for lunch. As we drove though we passed a restaurant, so Roy made a U-turn in the street and parked in front. A cop came running over and started to chew out Roy for making a U-turn, which he said was illegal in his town. Roy told him that you could stand out in the middle of street and piss all day without hitting a car. Roy had the tendency to shoot off his mouth at the wrong time. The cop pulled out his gun like he was Wyatt Earp, told Roy he was under arrest, and started to haul him off to his one-cell jail.

I told the cop I was an attorney (just barely), and because there was no sign prohibiting a U-turn, his arrest was illegal and he was guilty of false imprisonment. I told him I would sue him and the town for false arrest and false imprisonment for at least one-hundred thousand dollars. The town's budget was probably a couple of thousand dollars a year.

The mayor of the town, a guy in a farmer's pin-striped overalls, came out of the café and overheard our conversation. He chewed out the cop and told him he was going to get the town in trouble again for his dumb stunts. He told him to put his damn gun away and let us go.

Roy had to make another comment that almost got us back in trouble. He told the mayor that he should get the cop a new star. He said that the one the cop had on his chest didn't look good because it looked like it was made out of a beer can. He said to the mayor, "You should give the cop a sling shot; he could probably hit something with that." The mayor told me to get this "funny fellow" out of town right away before he did end up in jail.

When I told the mayor where we were going and why, he took a great interest in us. He said he knew an Iowa guy who had been in the Flying Tigers, but he had been killed. He invited us into the café and bought us dinner. He said he had read a lot about the exploits of the Flying Tigers, so was eager to get some firsthand information. The little café was filled with farmers, or at least they all wore farmer overalls, all of whom the mayor insisted on introducing us to. Roy was equally popular after the mayor learned that Roy had been a motorcycle courier and truck driver in the army in North Africa. Roy related the many times he had been blown off his cycle by German bombers. He may have embellished his experiences a bit. I thought he may have gone a little far when he said he almost ran over Rommel, the German general known as the "Desert Fox," with his motorcycle. He said he had made a wrong turn and raced right through the German camp. The audience was wide-eyed, and I suspected our visit would be the topic of conversation in that little town for days. They urged us to come back on our way home. We didn't. We thought we had stretched our luck as far as it would go.

We had a great time at the convention and I got my picture taken with Gen. Chennault and his lovely Chinese bride, Anna. We started back home right after the banquet and got back to Minneapolis late Sunday afternoon, and I drove on to Duluth.

Mr. Baker, who owned the adjusting company, was a very decent guy. After I passed the bar in 1952, he gave me a very nice raise and appointed me the company's claims attorney. He thought that I might lend some prestige to the various insurance companies we represented. My job was not much different except I approved claims handled by other adjusters.

When I first came to Duluth in 1950 to adjust claims, part of my territory was most of the Arrowhead and up the Lake Superior North Shore. I learned that the Reserve Mining Company was in the process of developing an iron-ore processing plant near Beaver Bay, Minnesota, and would be building a town. They had already started constructing a few buildings, and I had always wanted to have a law office in a small town. The town's site and plant reserve was about three miles from Beaver Bay, a little picturesque fishing village. It was established in 1856 by some German settlers from Ohio. It was the longest continuously-settled white community on the North Shore of Lake Superior.

I had stopped at the Beaver Bay Trading Post, a fascinating beer joint. In addition to serving beer and some food, the bartender could usually find a bottle of something a little stronger that he would put in a coffee cup. Serving liquor in coffee cups was supposed to fool any law enforcement officers who might walk in. Of course, they would never think of serving anything illegal! A deputy lived right across the street. Whenever he saw someone who would likely buy him a drink, he would hurry across the street and enjoy a "beverage" in a coffee cup. An interesting bunch of characters always congregated there.

With a newly developing industry and lots of traffic from construction workers, starting a law office in the Beaver Bay area looked like a unique opportunity. As soon as I passed the bar, I started looking for a place where I could start a law office. Space was at a premium. There was a small lumber-yard office owned by Gibson Lumber Company of Grand Marais in Beaver Bay. I heard that the operator might rent me some space.

The building was eight feet wide and sixteen feet long. I worked out a deal with the guy running the yard, George Stapleton, to rent half the space for forty dollars a month. I doubt that he told his boss in Grand Marais about the rental income. Whenever I paid him, he stuck the cash in his pocket.

We hung up a blanket as a divider. It was not the kind of attorney-client privilege space taught in law school. I had a small desk, two chairs, and a book shelf on my side. George had an equally small desk on his side, and while he promised not to listen when I had a client in, I learned at the Trading Post that his promise lasted about as long as it took him to cross the street. I told him I could not operate a law office unless I had privacy. He agreed to an acoustic wall in the middle, with a door into my office. It gave me a little more privacy.

Mr. Baker allowed me to go up to Beaver Bay several times a week in order to get my law office started. Although he knew I would soon leave his employ, he was very considerate while I started my law practice.

My law office in the lumber yard building was quite unique. It turned out to be more than just a law office. When George Stapleton wanted to go somewhere, or make deliveries, I would sell lumber for him. He would return the favor by making appointments for me. I found out that he had even started to interview clients, a practice that I put a stop to.

There was lots of activity, including quite a lot of real estate transactions, because of the Reserve Mining's construction. My work experience examining titles when I was in law school became very valuable. In the early stages, there was no housing for the construction workers. Because many of the construction workers lived in Duluth and elsewhere, there was a lot of traffic on the curvy Highway 61, so there were a lot of accidents. I developed a good reputation for handling injured persons cases, including lawsuits for the families of persons killed in accidents.

I started to develop a good practice, so I left Main & Baker in the Fall of 1952. I lived in an apartment in Duluth. With all the construction traffic, it would take me about an hour and a half to drive to Beaver Bay every day. I still did some work for Main & Baker on a contract basis.

My experience adjusting accident claims for insurance companies became most valuable. Working for insurance companies, I knew their strategy for settling claims, a strategy most helpful while handling claims from an injured person's standpoint. John Hangartner, who owned a lot of land in the area, contacted me about how to best sell some of his land. He wanted to take advantage of the demand for housing plots. I advised him to plot his land into lots so it would be easier to sell, and I did the necessary legal work for the process.

Every time I asked him for a fee, he would say he was a little short and would pay me later. I finally told him that I could not work for nothing and, unless he paid me, I would file a lien against his land. He pulled out a large roll of bills and handed it to me without bothering to count. He said that if he still owed me more I could go pick out any lot I wanted, so someday I could build a house. He said, "A young buck like you will want to get married some day and need land to build a house."

I had walked through most of his land and knew of a nice piece with a beautiful view of Lake Superior. It was heavily wooded, but quite swampy, but I represented an earth-moving contractor, Brown & Toneberg, and Dale Brown looked it over for me. He said that he could remove most of the trees and that there was enough soil on the upper side to fill in the low spots for landscaping. He would do the work in exchange for my legal services for his company. I agreed with John Hangartner that I would take the lot for the rest of my bill, about $3,000.00. A few days later, I heard that John had been bragging at the Trading Post about how he had "snockered" that young lawyer by giving him a mosquito swamp. "Snockered" was a colloquial term that meant he had bested me in a deal.

Sometime later, after Dale Brown and his highly skilled dozer operator, Roy Boen, had cleared and landscaped the lot, John Hangartner came down to take a look. He was amazed. They had built a nice curving road down to the lot, and the landscaped lot was perfect for a building. It had a beautiful view of Lake Superior. It was this lot where I would build my home some years later. The next day, I heard that John had been back in the Trading Post, crying how that damn young lawyer had really snockered him. He complained that I had gotten one of his most valuable pieces of property for a song.

Despite that, we became good friends and I did a lot of legal work for him over the years. He would brag that his lawyer was one of the best, so he was a great source of client business. His granddaughter, Edie Hangartner, later became our babysitter. She said that I was an inspiration for her to go to law school. After graduating high school and college, she went to law school and became a very successful attorney.

The owner of the lumber yard from Grand Marias came to me one day and said he was wanted $500.00 a month for rent. It was ridiculous and I told him so. He then told me to get out of his building. I reminded him that he could not evict me without thirty days proper written notice. He went away grumbling about a damn smart-ass lawyer. He sent me a formal written notice a few days later. Although I had thirty days to leave, there was no other space I could move too.

I told John Hangartner about my predicament. He owned the land where the lumber yard was located and was leasing it to them. John told me to buy the land from him, kick the lumber yard out, and build my own office. I agreed to buy it from him for $3,500.00 dollars, to be paid in fees that he would owe me for present and future legal work.

We then served an eviction notice on the Gipson Lumber Company that said they would have to move their yard and building off my lot by June of the following year. I did not want them to move too soon, because I still needed the little building for my office. I proposed that I would not charge them rent in return for space in the building. Gipson Lumber Company had no place to go, so they agreed to my terms. They even retained me to handle some of their legal work. The owner of the yard told George Stapleton, the salesman, that any guy smart enough to do what I did was the kind of lawyer he wanted. I didn't know if that was a compliment or not, or if it was to butter me up and get a better deal.

In early 1953, I got a veteran's loan to construct my own building. Dale Brown's company did all the excavating work for a foundation and basement, dug a well, and put in a septic tank. His work was to be paid in future legal fees. Because no cash was involved, the arrangements with both John Hangartner and Dale Brown were quite convenient. The arrangements were built on a mutually beneficial exchange of services. I constructed the building on nights and weekends with the help of friends. Many clients who owed me money came to help and work off their bills. The Beaver Bay Lumber Company owned by Les Strand and Ed Shaffer furnished most of the lumber. I had the same deal with them as I did with Hangartner and Brown, so the lumber cost was paid for by legal services.

It was a very nice building, about twenty by twenty-four feet. The upper level was divided into two offices, a large conference room, and library in the back. The lower level had an apartment with a kitchen, bedroom, bathroom, and a small living room with a fireplace.

John Hangartner had a fire next door that burned the garage down. The Standard Oil service man had gone into the garage when the underground tank was filling, instead of standing by the hose. It was cold outside and he thought the hose nozzle would shut off the gas when the tank became full. A bunch of guys were in the garage visiting when they suddenly noticed gas flowing across the ground into the garage. The tank had overflowed. They got out of the garage just as the gas reached the lighted oil heater and exploded. The garage was a large building filled with vehicles and all types of supplies. It was a total loss.

Unfortunately, John had no insurance on the garage. It was a terrible loss. He didn't think anything could be done, but he did ask me what I thought. It was obvious to me that the serviceman was being negligent when he abandoned the gas tank, and that his company would be liable for his actions. I agreed with John that I would handle the case for him on a percentage basis. I would get one-third of any recovery. He agreed. I brought an action against Standard Oil. We started to try the case. The serviceman testified that he had been told by the company that the hose's nozzle shut off automatically, and that he did not have to stand right there and watch it. It was devastating evidence against the company. The judge told the defense attorneys that they had better try to settle the case. The company attorneys asked what we would settle for. We negotiated a settlement that very well compensated John for his loss. He did whine a little bit about my one-third fee, but agreed that he would not have gotten anything if I had not advised him and helped him place a claim against the company. The case was the topic of conversation at the Trading Post that night. My reputation as a competent attorney rose considerably when John related the events. He may have exaggerated things just a little!

One of my early clients was Art Lorntson, who was a well-known business man in the area. He and some others consulted me about organizing Beaver Bay as a village. Up to that time, the community was under the jurisdiction of the Beaver Bay Township Board. The community was growing, due to the influx of people for the Reserve Mining Company development. Since township boards have only limited authority to furnish municipal services, it was necessary to incorporate the area as a village. We needed a water and sewer plant, both of which a township board did not have the authority to build. The individual septic systems were becoming serious health hazards.

I handled all the legal work necessary to incorporate the village, which was completed in middle of 1953. Beaver Bay had been organized as a village in 1856 by the Minnesota territorial legislature, and was the first county seat in Lake County. Some years later, the county seat was transferred to the village of Two Harbors, which was a much larger community, and more accessible to most of the county population. The government of Beaver Bay fell apart and the town board took over jurisdiction. There was an Indian settlement on the point below the Beaver River, but they were only there during the summer months.

My work in organizing the village gave me a lot of exposure to the public, which helped my law practice. I was appointed the first village attorney of Beaver Bay and served in that capacity for more than fifty years.

During that time, a friend bought a WWII airplane. Lots of military planes were on the market for very cheap. This plane was a very nice PT-23, in excellent shape. He had never flown a plane like that, so I taught him. He allowed me to take it on a trip. The Flying Tigers were having their 1954 convention in Toledo, Ohio, on one weekend, and a friend in Toledo had an apartment where I could stay, so I decided to go. I had a great time. I was the most eligible bachelor there! I flew back on Sunday, so was ready for work on Monday.

I had joined the Flying Tigers of the 14th Air Force Association in 1948, when I attended its first convention in Dayton, Ohio. It held an annual convention in different cities around the United States. I could not afford to go to some of the early conventions, but the ones in St Louis and Toledo sounded too interesting to miss.

A few years later, I would begin attending almost every convention until the Association disbanded in 2007. I held almost every office in the Association, including president in 1981-83. I was the legal advisor to the Association for over fifty years. In addition to my law practice, I spent most of my spare time as the editor of the four volume history, "Chennault's Flying Tigers."

General Chennault died in 1958. We held a memorial service for him at Arlington National Cemetery and built a monument, that I helped design, at his gravesite. It set a precedent, and every Memorial Day thereafter we would hold a memorial service at Arlington in memory of General Chennault and had a roll-call of those members that had died the preceding year. It was a most moving and impressive ceremony. I attended every one until the last, in 2007.

In 1955, Jim Lovrien, who had just passed the bar, joined my law practice. We called our law firm Johnson & Lovrien. I had known Jim in law school and also as an insurance adjuster for Allstate Insurance Company. His wife, Arlene, was from Wheaton, my home town, so I knew her family. We were all good friends.

Several years later, we set up a branch office in Two Harbors that Jim was to take care of. He spent a little too much time with some drinking buddies, so that office was not profitable. Spending an afternoon in the Moose Lodge or VFW bars was not the kind of conduct the public expected of their attorney. Two Harbors had a reputation for being a heavy drinking town at the time. Arlene gave Jim an ultimatum— that they would get out of Two Harbors or she would leave with the kids.

Around that time, Jim received an offer from Allstate Insurance Company to be their branch manager on the West Coast. The offer was too good to turn down and would pay a lot more money than he had been making, so Jim took it. With his previous experience with Allstate, he had the qualifications for the job. It not only saved a marriage but saved me the concern of my partner's damage to our profession. He was a good attorney and actually did a very good job in that position with Allstate and gained a reputation as being one of their best field officers.

I had a nice office building in Beaver Bay with living space in the basement. I fixed up a nice apartment in the basement and moved in to it from Duluth in the late summer of 1953. I operated out of that office until 1956 when I moved my law office to Silver Bay in the newly built Norshor Building. Silver Bay, the site of the Reserve Mining plant, was just three miles from Beaver Bay. I continued to live in the basement apartment but rented out the upper level to an insurance agency.

As soon as I moved my office to Silver Bay, I was contacted by a representative of Reserve Mining Company to help incorporate that community into a village. Reserve had built the town and all its facilities, but it wanted the community to become self-governing. With my previous experience in incorporating Beaver Bay, this was an easier task. An election was held and the residents voted overwhelmingly to incorporate the area as a village. Some years later, the Minnesota Legislature changed the designation of all villages in the State so in the future all incorporated communities were called City.

I was appointed as Silver Bay's first village attorney, a position I held for over fifty years. I set a record as being the longest serving City Attorney, not only in Minnesota but in the United States.

Chapter - 67 -

Marriage and Family.

What about the lake lots I bought from John Hangartner and what about marriage? John Hangartner was almost right. I would soon get married. "Soon" was four years after I came to Beaver Bay. I met a beautiful young lady, Delores Christensen, with whom I fell head over heels in love, but it took me some time to get up the courage to tell her so. She was a divorcee and had a little girl.

When I told my mother about Delores and that she had been married before, was now divorced, and had a little girl, Mother was not very approving. She thought I should find another girl. She did not approve of divorce. When I brought Delores down to the farm to meet Mother, she approved immediately. She said Delores was a very nice girl and would make a good wife, but thought Delores wore a little too much "paint." Mother referred to makeup as paint. She never wore any makeup—just a little dab of rouge on her cheeks. Delores has the kind of personality that she fits in anywhere. People immediately like her.

I surprised myself when I became that committed. I had some interesting liaisons with many attractive young ladies over the years, but this was different. The temptations of the past were no longer to be. It was to be a lifelong commitment. We were married on June 28, 1957.

As I look back after more than fifty years of marriage, it was the right choice. There were, as in most marriages, ups and downs, but all in all it was much more complacent and enjoyable than I had expected. Some of my bachelor friends and bachelor brothers had a much lonelier life than what I would have wanted.

Delores' mother was not enthusiastic about our marriage either. She didn't think Delores should marry an "old guy" who had been a bachelor too long. I was eleven years older than Delores. Her mother said, "It will never last." But it did. We have been married well over fifty years.

We had our wedding reception in the basement of the Norshor Building that had a large room used for wedding receptions and public meetings. We had two large punch bowls. One contained pure punch and the other I had laced with a little vodka. The minister and some of the other folks were having drinks from what we had labeled the "liquor free punch." Soon they were as happy as the rest of the crowd. Without anyone knowing, Jim Lovrien had spiked that punch bowl with vodka, too. It made for a merry crowd. Our pastor, Rev. Tibor Hill, told me later that he found out there was liquor in the punch. He said that was the first time he had ever drank any liquor. He was surprised how good it tasted and how good it made him feel. Despite people drinking liquor, he said he was surprised by how well-behaved everyone was. He said he had been at Ladies Aid meetings where they behaved worse.

We had our wedding dinner with family and a few friends at the Flame restaurant in Duluth. The dinners were four dollars a plate, which was quite expensive in those days. We had delicious filet mignons with all kinds of trimmings as the main course, and superb dessert. It was a nightclub type of restaurant, with an excellent band for dancing, and a reputation as the finest dining in the area.

After the dinner we took off on our honeymoon. We ended up at Niagara Falls, which was then a most popular honeymoon destination. On the way back we stopped at the beautiful and world-famous Grand Hotel on Mackinac Island. The island did not have motor vehicles, except for fire trucks. Taxis were horse drawn carriages. We rented a bicycle built for two, and toured the island. We had a lot of fun. Not bad for an "old guy" and his young bride! But then it was back to work.

I moved Delores and her four-year-old little girl into my basement apartment, which was quite cozy. I raised the little girl, Margaret Ann, sometimes called Muggs, and who I usually called Annie, as my own. One day, shortly after our marriage, we were in our downstairs apartment and she became very unruly and spit at her mother. I gave her a little slap on the rear and she started to howl like I had broken some bones. She went into the bathroom, soaked a towel in cold water, placed it on the toilet seat and sat on it, all the while mumbling, "Big bully beat up on a little kid." She became very obedient thereafter. That was the only time I had to "beat" her up.

Our first son, Bruce, was born on June 12, 1958. Shortly after he was born, my building caught fire and was badly damaged. We had been visiting Delores' folks, who lived about six miles away. When we returned, we saw smoke billowing out of the building.

The village did have a small volunteer fire department. Reserve Mining Company also sent a fire rig. They saved the structure, but it was completely gutted and not habitable. It appeared the fire had started in the basement apartment near the fireplace. We assumed sparks had blown out of the fireplace and ignited the area around it, because that appeared to be the most burned. Since I had my office in Silver Bay, I sold the burnt-out building and lot. I felt it would be too costly to renovate it, and since I had already started to build a house, I wouldn't have needed it.

We lost everything. All our clothes, the apartment furnishings and, sadly, most of my World War II keepsakes were all lost. I had to go to Two Harbors the next day to buy a suit, shirt, and tie, so I could at least dress for going to the office. I had built a garage on my lot and started to build a house, but it was far from finished.

We had to live with Delores' folks, Laurence and Margaret Christensen, for some time until I finished a part of the house that we could occupy. Except for the masonry and brick work, I built most of the house myself, on evenings and weekends. Delores did most of the painting and staining. She and her mother did a lot of wall papering. I set up my table saw and other tools in a convenient area that would later become our living room. It was several years before I had enough of the house finished to call it a home.

Brett Jentoft, who we eventually called Beaver, came along on November 25, 1960. As he started to grow, he and Bruce had a good time together. Bruce would put Beaver on the back of his tricycle and paddle around the rooms. Beaver picked up interesting things to say.

When he was about four years old, he was on the toilet. Bruce opened the door and said, "Pew, Beaver, it sure stinks in here." Beaver's response was, "What you expect, woahsis." (Roses) Who could he have possibly learned that from?

Our home was on the shoreline of Lake Superior. It was too cold for swimming. There was a nice inland lake called Lax Lake that was good for swimming and water sports. I had represented Roy Waxlax on some legal matters. Roy owned a lot of land on the lake. The Waxlax family had homesteaded on the lake near the turn of the century, thus the name "Lax" Lake. It was a beautiful lake about six miles north of Beaver Bay. It was a sizeable lake, over a mile and a half long and half mile wide. I was interested in an area on the very west end of the lake that gave a great view of the entire lake and surrounding hills.

The area was rather swampy and covered with black ash trees, which thrive in wet soil. I had my contractor friend, Dale Brown, look it over. He said he could do much like he did on my Lake Superior lot. The lake in that area had a very sandy bottom. He said he could run his dozer and scraper out into the lake and bring sand in from the lake, fill in the low spots, and develop a nice sand beach.

Because of the swampy area, Roy Waxlax didn't think it was worth much. He would give it to me in exchange for my legal fees. I prepared a Deed for title to six hundred sixty feet of lake-front property, which ran about a quarter mile inland, from the shoreline to across the county road. Dale Brown said that his company would furnish the necessary equipment if I would pay Roy Boen, his dozer operator. I made a deal that I would give Boen one of my Lax Lake lots in return for his services. It was a good deal all around with no cash flowing back and forth.

Dale's crew and some of my volunteers removed some of the trees closest to the lake, and used the logs to make a "corduroy road" from the county road through some of the swampy area. It was a technique frequently used by loggers, in which the logs are cut in about ten to twelve foot lengths and laid crosswise in the mud of the proposed road. Gravel or sand was spread on top, creating a good road surface.

Then, Dale brought out his big dozer and scraper. Roy Boen backed the equipment well out into the lake, so that the water came just above the dozer's tracks. He then pulled the sand-filled scraper behind the dozer. He spread the sand throughout the swampy area until he had a nice sandy surface and sand beach. It made a nice lot where I could build a cabin. He did the same with the lot I gave him, as well as the other lots that I would later sell. I divided the parcel into nice, buildable plots with ninety feet of lake-front. I kept three hundred thirty feet of lake-front for my lot.

Reserve Mining had a bunch of cabins that they had purchased from resort owners as temporary housing for their construction workers. Because most of the workers acquired permanent homes, Reserve had no further use for the cabins. There was a rumor that the company intended to burn the cabins to get rid of them. I contacted Ed Schmidt, the Reserve Mining public relations officer, with whom I had a good relationship, and offered to move the cabins for Reserve, at no cost. He contacted the company's president and got approval.

Dale Brown agreed to move the cabins for me if I would give one to Roy Boen for his lot. We put one cabin on my lot and cabins on the other three lots. With the cabins, the three lots sold immediately.

There were ten cabins all together, so I advertised the others for sale. They, too, sold immediately. Dale Brown moved them for each of the purchasers and was paid well for his services. It turned out to be a good deal all around.

The Lax Lake cabin became a fun place for our family. Delores moved up there during the summer months with the kids. It attracted a lot of other kids who would come up to the lake and play with our kids. Sometimes, Delores would have a dozen kids playing in the yard and lake, and, of course, she would feed them. It was a fun family time, but, unfortunately, I could not be part of the fun. I was away too much on legal matters.

After our trip to Norway, Beaver became very interested in learning more about the Norwegian culture. Concordia College sponsored a Norwegian camp where kids learned about their Norwegian culture and living in a Norwegian climate. When the kids arrived in camp, they were given Norwegian names and were allowed to speak only Norwegian. I think he was only about fifteen, but he had a great time. He met a young girl there that he "fell in love" with.

Later that fall, I took my family to the Minnesota State Fair in St. Paul. Beaver spent hours in the hotel looking through the Minneapolis phone book trying to find his Norwegian camp girl friend. He knew her name and her father's name. There were thousands of Petersons in the book and he called many of them. Finally, he found her and asked her to go to the fair with him. They had a great time. She was a very pretty young lady, but like so many young affairs, it ended there. Ah, young love!

We had a fire that destroyed our cabin at Lax Lake. We had an oil burner stove, the bottom of which had apparently rusted out without our knowledge. It was a nice cool day and we were sitting out by the lake. We had left the stove on to keep the cabin warm. We suddenly saw smoke pouring from the cabin. I ran up to the cabin and was able to pull out my airplane skis. The flames were too hot to get inside. There was no fire fighting equipment in the area. The cabin and all the contents were completely destroyed. It was as bad a loss as the Beaver Bay fire.

I built a log cabin to replace it. It took me about two years to build with the help of friends, like Wimpy Knudson and Bob Morrison. Bob Morrison had been in the Navy and was a master at rope work. He lined the stairs with intricate rope designs, all the way to the upper level. After more than fifty years, it is still beautiful. Bob, Wimpy, and I spent many enjoyable evenings together working on the cabin. It is still a great retreat for my family.

Chapter - 68 -

The Lure of the Sky.

My heart was still set on aviation. When I could afford it, I bought a Taylorcraft floatplane with an eighty-five horsepower engine. With that small engine, it really struggled to get off the lake. I later got another floatplane, an Aeronca, with a one hundred ten horsepower engine that preformed a little better. It, too, needed more power in order to be a good, performing floatplane.

One time, me and a friend, Bill Richards, decided to fly up to Canada for fishing. After we loaded the plane with fishing gear, canned food, beer, and a couple bottles of necessaries, we tried to take off from Lax Lake. It was a very hot day and the lake was smooth. These were bad conditions for a floatplane take off. We roared across the entire lake, about eight thousand feet long, but could not get the plane off the water. We returned to the dock and unloaded most of the canned goods. We tried again, but could not get off the water.

We returned to the dock and unloaded everything except a twelve-pack of beer, two loaves of bread, and two bottles that we considered important for relaxing in the evenings. This time, we made it off the water and flew to Clearwater West, a great fishing lake in Canada. As soon as we arrived, we went out fishing for our supper. Fresh fried fish and bread made a delicious supper, with a couple of nips from our "sustenance" bottles.

On another occasion, Delores and I flew up to a friend's cabin on another Canadian lake. Delores was smoking then, and desperately wanted a cigarette. I would not permit smoking in the plane because I was concerned about fire in the fabric-covered interior. We did an interim landing in a lake so she could get a few puffs. We got to our friend's cabin near sundown.

As we started to pull up to the dock, I told her to jump out. She looked at me like I had lost my mind. No way was she going to jump out into the water. I had neglected to tell her that as I approached the dock, I wanted her to open the door and step out on the float so she could guide the plane to the dock. I just assumed that anyone flying in a floatplane would know what they were supposed to do when approaching a dock! The next day, we went out fishing. We brought some bread and beans along, for we intended to have a fish lunch on the shore. Unfortunately, we didn't catch a single fish, and ended up sitting on an island eating beans on bread.

Floatplane flying was a lot of fun, but I decided that a land-based plane would be more useful for my profession. I bought a nice, used Cessna 172, a 1948 model. It had a one hundred forty-five horsepower engine and would cruise at about one hundred ten miles per hour. The identification number was 483E, and the call sign was "483 Echo." I flew that plane for many hours on many trips around the country.

A week after Bruce was born, we flew down to Wheaton to show him to my mother. She did not think much of taking a little baby up in an airplane, what she considered a most unsafe machine. We landed on the road in front of her house, which she didn't consider a safe airport.

We didn't have an airport in Silver Bay at the time. I and another pilot, John Woolever, rented a small piece of hay land from a farmer. We mowed the hay and formed a landing strip. It was only seven hundred feet long, on a slope with high trees on the northwest end and a road on the southeast end. Seven hundred feet was the minimum distance needed in order to get a Cessna 172 off the ground. To get enough speed for takeoff, it was necessary to hold the brakes and run the engine up to full power, then release the brakes. John had a Piper Cub that could easily get off the ground in that distance, and the Jacobson brothers had an old Funk plane that they also stationed there. A few other pilots had planes there.

The field was on a slope up toward the trees on the northwest. Regardless of the wind direction, we would land up the slope and take off down the slope. A road was on the lower end. This system worked fine until the power company built an electric power line along the road. When we took off, we could not get enough altitude to go over the lines, so we had to fly under the line and pull up sharply to miss the trees across the road. The state's Aeronautics Department frowned upon this type of flying. We had a sign made for the field that read "Beaver Bay International."

We decided that we needed a better airport. I became the spark plug for promoting an airport. We found a large, flat area on some farmland several miles to the west of our strip that was owned by Art Lorntson and Dean Anderson. We negotiated the sale of a strip of land sufficiently big enough to build an airport on. The cost of the land we needed was $9,000.00. The Silver Bay Council felt that the city did not have the funds to buy land or become involved in the construction of an airport.

I organized a small group of aviation enthusiasts. We started a campaign to raise the necessary money. We were successful in raising the $9,000.00 and acquired the title to the property, which we turned over to the city of Silver Bay. I worked with the Department of Aeronautics to give the city a grant to build a grass strip. The initial cost was about $50,000.00 to build the first runway, and the city's share was ten percent. We raised that amount through donations. After that, the city of Silver Bay had an airport, built without the investment of any public funds. Several years later, I again worked with the Aeronautics Department for a state and federal grant to put in a blacktop runway and parking ramp for planes. The city's share was five percent of the cost. Again, we solicited private funds to cover the city's share.

Reserve Mining Company had a large metal building about twenty-four by fifty feet that had been used as a wash house, laundry room, and restrooms during construction of its facility. It no longer had a use for the building and put it up for sale. I negotiated with the company's president to donate it to the airport, and the company could use it as a tax write-off. He agreed and had some of the Reserve crew take it down, haul it to the airport, and help us erect it.

One of the local contractors, who was a pilot and owned a plane, poured the concrete floor without cost. Volunteers fixed up the interior of the building by paneling and painting. Another contractor dug in a septic tank for us. We raised enough money to dig a well. It made a perfect administration building for the airport.

We developed quite a unique runway lighting system. We got a number of flare pots from the county highway department. When a pilot wanted to fly in at night, he would call someone local who would go out to the airport and light the pots. We also used reflector posts. It was a rather primitive system, but was sufficient enough so that a pilot could find the airport on the darkest of nights and make a safe landing.

On one occasion when I had been in Minneapolis on a trial, I decided to fly home at night. I called my wife and asked her to go out and light the flare pots at a certain time. She called a girl friend to help her. Unfortunately, they decided to stop at the local "refreshment center" for a few nips while waiting, until it was time to go to the airport. Instead of filling the pots and lighting them, they left me a note: "We couldn't find the fuel so we couldn't light the pots." They obviously were not thinking very clearly, for the note in that dark building would not help me in the air. The fuel cans were in the back room and clearly in sight if they had looked around.

When I arrived in the general area of the airport, I could not see any runway lights. I circled many times until some local residents heard the plane going around. They knew someone wanted to land and was in distress. They called other neighbors and a number of cars rushed to the airport. They lined the runway with their headlights and made a beautifully lit runway for me. It was after I landed and entered the administration building that I found Delores' note!

That incident convinced me that we needed a better lighting system. I had found that the 3M Company produced reflective cones, which were about five inches in diameter and about a foot in length, made out of sewer pipe. They were covered with rows of reflective tape. I bought about a half dozen cones and mounted them on posts about fifty feet apart on the sides of the runway. We first experimented with car lights. The cones showed up brilliantly. I then took the plane up to see if the landing lights would pick up the reflection and show the alignment of the runway. It worked very well. If it wasn't too dark, a pilot could find the field, get lined up with the runway, and land safely. We bought some reflective tape and sewer pipe that came in eight-foot lengths, and made a bunch of cones that we could line up along both sides of the runway. When coming in for a landing, we could pick up the reflections from an altitude of about three hundred feet. It took a little skill to get lined up, but with a few practice runs, it became a good landing system.

When the state commissioner of aeronautics saw our lighting system, he was not too impressed. He had been a Navy pilot and knew the risk of landing on a carrier with limited lighting. He recommended that the city apply for a state grant for electric lighting. The state would provide eighty percent in grant funds, but the city would need to provide the remaining twenty percent balance. The council balked at the expense, so I again solicited funds and raised the city's share by donations from the area's businesses, pilots, and plane owners. We also raised enough to pay the power company to build an electric line to the airport. We not only put in runway lights, but also a beacon. We had a modern airport.

With a good runway, lights, and beacon, and building to meet in, some other people bought planes, so we had six planes stationed on the field. We needed hangars in order to store the local planes, so they would not have to sit outside in inclement weather.

The state's Aeronautics Department had a revolving loan fund to help cities build hangars. The state would loan the city eighty percent of the hangar cost to be repaid, without interest, in six years. So we could cover the city's share, I organized a group of plane owners and pilots into a non-profit corporation. The city advertised for bids, as it was required to do by law, for the construction of a six-unit hangar.

Our new company put in a bid that we were sure would be the lowest, because we intended to donate all the labor ourselves. The only cost to us was for the construction material. We had the lowest bid, by far. The hangar was built by volunteers on evenings and weekends. The loan payment to the state was covered by hangar rental fees. We then donated the completed hangar to the city. I spent a lot of time going to other communities to discuss our unique method of building airports and hangars at little cost.

Because we had a nice airport and quite a lot of flying activity, a number of young people wanted to learn how to fly. I arranged for a flight instructor to come up from Duluth and give flying lessons. Some of the other pilots and I taught ground school, which taught aspiring pilots the rudimentary aspects of flying. One of the best ground school instructors was LaJean Firminhac, a pilot and first grade teacher at the local school.

A few years later, in 1968, I was named "Mr. Aviation of Minnesota" by the governor and the Department of Aeronautics, for my promotion of aviation.

My big year in aviation came in 2001. Each year, the Minnesota Aviation Hall of Fame selects someone they determine to have made significant enough contributions to aviation to merit induction. It is an important event in Minnesota aviation. Usually, at least five hundred aviation enthusiasts gather for the induction ceremony. I was honored to have a large contingent of my family attend, as well as a good turn-out of my Flying Tiger comrades, all to watch my induction into the Minnesota Aviation Hall of Fame. Charles Lindberg was the first enshrinee, so I was among a distinguished group of aviators. It was a most thrilling event.

Both Bruce and Beaver loved to fly with me. When each was about six years old and could reach the yoke, I would put him in the left seat (the pilot's seat) and have him fly the plane. I, of course, sat in the right seat to help them out whenever needed. The plane had dual controls, so I could fly from the right seat as well. I did the takeoff and landings until they could master that aspect of flying. They were not big enough to see out of the window for some years, so learned how to fly the plane purely by looking at the instruments. By the time each got to be sixteen and could solo the plane, they were good instrument pilots. Both of them soloed my

Cessna 172 on their sixteenth birthdays. Both were excellent pilots. Later, when I got a Cessna 182, they both soloed that and flew it a lot.

Bruce became a very precise and methodical pilot. He flew a plane by the book. When he got out of high school, he went to work for an aircraft maintenance facility and became a federally licensed aircraft mechanic. He kept up his flying and later flew jets for Super Eight motels for several years, until he got an offer from an aircraft charter company in Minneapolis, where he serves as chief inspector. The company has about thirty airplanes of all types. His job is to certify the planes flyable. He has about twenty-five mechanics that he supervises.

Beaver was also an excellent pilot, but he had quite the opposite approach. He was a seat-of-the-pants pilot. He just seemed to become part of the plane. He loved to go up and soar around the clouds. Because of his untimely death, at age twenty-one, as a result of a motor vehicle accident, we were not to know what his career might have been.

Beaver was heard to tell one of his friends, "Dad just doesn't want us to be good pilots, he expects us to be perfect pilots. If we get just a few feet off our assigned altitude or a few degrees off course, he'd make remarks like "Why are we wondering all over the sky?"

My wife, Delores, too, learned how to fly. She didn't intend to. One day, I asked her to come out to the airport with me. When we got there, I introduced her to the flight instructor whose presence I had arranged. He told her, "Let's go and I'll show what flying is all about." Her reply was that she had been flying with me for years and knew what it was about. He told her that it was important for her to at least learn to land the plane, in case something happened to the pilot. We had been to a number of Aircraft Owners & Pilots Association meetings in which that was an important topic of discussion. The Association had a special course to teach passengers the basics of landing a plane in the case of an emergency.

Delores finally agreed to go up with the instructor and began to land the plane successfully. After about ten hours, she soloed the Cessna 150. She said her reaction was, "Oh my god, I'm up here all by myself, and I better land this thing." She made three perfect landings. The 150 was a two-place airplane, used for pilot instruction. "Two-place" means there are two seats, usually side-b-side. She later soloed in my 172 and my 182 and did a very good job. But then she dropped out. She felt that she knew enough to take over the plane if needed in an emergency, but was not interested in flying solo. I suspect she thought that if I was stranded someplace, I would expect her to jump in the plane and come to get me. She didn't want to get involved in that!

While I had the 172, I had it put on retractable skis for the winters. The skis permitted landing on frozen lakes, which was great for ice fishing. I had the first 172 plane in the country with skis. Installing skis on a tricycle-gear plane was an experiment by the ski company. The 172 was a little underpowered for ski operation, but worked quite well with only two people in the plane. When I sold the 172 and got the 182, I switched the skis to it. It had more horsepower, so performed very well and could carry some heavy loads.

In the summer of 1973, I sponsored an air tour to Silver Bay. It was an annual aviation event in Minnesota for a number of years, conducted by the Minnesota Aviation Trades Association. Some other pilots and I had helped initiate the tour, which promoted aviation. The tour would usually start in Minneapolis, with about a dozen planes. It would fly to southern Minnesota and stop at airports along the way, where other pilots would join in. The tour would circle over the western part of the state, then northerly through central Minnesota, picking up more planes at airports along the way, and then up over Duluth and along the North Shore of Lake Superior to Silver Bay. By the time the group got to Silver Bay, there were over one hundred planes. Seeing over one hundred planes flying, strung out over a long distance, was most exciting. It stimulated a lot of interest in aviation. Silver Bay was the final destination for that air tour, where we had arranged for ground tours of the area. The group stayed overnight in motels and cabins around Silver Bay and nearby communities. The next day, each left on their own back to their home airports. Sherm Booen, who had a program on a Minneapolis radio station called "The World of Aviation," was on the tour. He also published the "Minnesota Flyer," a monthly aviation magazine. He wrote:

Magnificent is the only way to describe the overfly of Duluth Harbor, then up the North Shore to Silver Bay. The whole town turned out to greet us it seemed and a lunch of FISHCAKES, served in a hangar, was delicious.

Then by bus to the Reserve Mining taconite plant, everyone overwhelmed by the immensity of the operation. RM conducted a fine tour, and most of us came away feeling a special rapport with these people who furnish this nation with one of the products that makes it great. We hope their problems will be solved, and they can go on with the important job of providing America with this necessary product. Then by bus to our quarters spread out in the area. Ours were on a delightful little bay on the rocky, wooded shoreline.

Barely time to change and relax and it was back to SB to the Civic Center for the banquet, short speeches and dancing. There was a starlit, cloudless sky when the music stopped and bus awaited to get us home. Invigorating is the word for the 40 degree temps. And one could see his breath, as he marveled at the beauty of the moonbeams shining on the gentle ways of the northshore bay. Incomparable . . . Another most enjoyable Air Tour. The Minnesota Aviation Trades Association is grateful . . . to the Silver Bay gang . . . headed by Wayne Johnson. We are greatly impressed by the airmen's hospitality.

"Fishcakes" was a special Scandinavian delicacy. We made them with Lake Superior herring. The fish are ground with potatoes and onions, then mixed with eggs, milk, and spices, and made into a batter like soft hamburgers, then fried. They were a great hit.

The following year, we helped arrange another air tour with Winnipeg, Canada, as the final destination. This, too, was a very exciting and interesting tour. The pilots and crews were royally entertained by our Canadian hosts. On the way back the next day, we ran into bad weather. Most planes landed at Baudette on the Minnesota-Canada border. Because it was a small city with limited accommodations, many couples arranged to share cabins. Unfortunately we got housed with a rather nasty couple.

All of us had a few drinks during the evening, but the other couple got quite drunk before we went to bed. It didn't take the other woman long to disrupt the tranquil night. First, we heard her tell her husband, in very descriptive terms, what she was going to do to him if he didn't stop snoring. It had to do with relieving him of some of his vital bodily parts. A little later, she accused me of snoring. I don't know how she could hear above her own eruptions. I thought her own snoring woke her up. She would suddenly stop her window-rattling emissions and wake up swearing. She kept muttering that she was going to "kill all of you SOBs."

As soon as she was snoring loudly, Delores and I grabbed our clothes and sneaked out. We went out to the plane and sat in that until sunup. When the weather cleared, we headed for home. Even with that unpleasant stop, these flying trips were some fun times, a little relaxation from the practice of law.

Chapter-69-
Back to the Law Practice

A few years after Jim Lovrien had left me, another young lawyer, Ron Thomas, joined me. We became Johnson & Thomas. Ron was a big guy, both in stature and heart. He had been a football player at the University in Duluth. He was very easy-going and immediately became very popular. He liked to handle domestic relations type of cases, such as divorce and child custody. His only shortcoming was that he was too easy going. If a client, particularly a woman, complained that she was short of money, he would handle the case *pro bono* (for free).

A law partnership is more stringent than a marriage. Each partner has to dedicate a lot of time to the profession if he or she is to succeed. In a small town, an attorney has to handle all types of legal matters. We usually worked twelve hours or more per day, and often on Saturdays and Sundays. Small-town practice is different from that in a city. In a small town, one gets to know everyone and you are always under the public eye. The practice is built on personal relationships and trust. It is critical that one maintain a reputation for acting with integrity and with the highest ethical standards. Even in private practice, while representing individual clients, one advances the public good by maintaining respect and confidence in the rule of law. I did most of the trial work on accident cases, as well as the city attorney work, while Ron handled divorce and other domestic matters.

A few years later, a young lawyer, Gerald "Pete" Morris, just a few years out of law school, came to the office and asked to join my firm. He was a native of Silver Bay and wanted to practice here. He came in wearing scruffy corduroys and was not very presentable. I suggested that he go home and come in dressed as we believed a professional should dress. He did and we agreed he could join us on a fee basis. We would not pay him a salary. As compensation, he would get a percentage of the fees he generated. The firm then became Johnson, Thomas & Morris. Pete became a most capable and proficient attorney, and always came to work impeccably dressed. He stayed with me for over thirty-five years and continued to run the office after I retired. Lawyers staying partners over that length of time evidenced an amazing compatibility.

Ron was with me quite a few years, until he developed a very debilitating disease, dermomyitisitis, a malady much like lupus. It involved inflammation of the nerve endings, which developed large blisters and became extremely painful. All of his extremities were affected. The bottoms of his feet became so sore, he could hardly walk. He finally had to quit work and died shortly thereafter. It was a sad blow, for we had a very good working relationship and had become good friends.

In the early 1970s, Reserve Mining Company was charged with a violation of their permits issued by the Environment Protection Agency. In its operations, Reserve mined a low-grade ore called taconite. Taconite was a granite hard rock that contained ferric (iron) material. The rocks were shipped from its mines at Babbitt, Minnesota, to its processing plant on the shore of Lake Superior at Silver Bay. There, the rocks were ground to a talcum-fine powder. The iron particles were extracted from the ground rock by a magnetic and washing method. At high temperatures in furnaces, it was formed into marble-sized balls called pellets, which were then shipped to the eastern steel mills.

About two-thirds of the leftover ground rock was waste material. Reserve had permits allowing them to dump the waste material, the ground-up rock called tailings, in a slurry into Lake Superior. It was expected that a density current would carry the slurry to the bottom of the lake, at about six hundred feet in depth.

Under certain climatic conditions, the slurry would stay suspended and form a grey area in the water that was visible for many miles. Commercial fishermen complained that it was detrimental to lake's trout and herring populations. Most of the trout and herring had been destroyed by lamprey, but Reserve's deposits were an easy target because of the discoloration in the lake. There was years of litigation.

The federal government brought an action in a Duluth, Minnesota, federal court, alleging that Reserve was polluting the lake in violation of federal law. It asked that the court order Reserve to cease dumping tailings into the lake, which meant possible closure of the plant. It became the longest environmental litigation in the country. At that time, Reserve Mining had about three thousand six hundred employees. About two-thirds of them worked in Silver Bay. Any action by the federal government would have a dramatically adverse effect on Silver Bay.

As the attorney for Silver Bay, I was asked to join the lawsuit to support Reserve. The entire community depended on the viability of Reserve Mining Company. We had just about worked out an agreement with the federal government, in which Reserve agreed it would build an on-land disposal system, when an environmental group raised the specter of cancer. They claimed that the taconite rock contained asbestos fibers that caused cancer. It threw an entirely different light on the litigation. The court cases lasted for many years. The actual court work was on hold while Reserve and the governmental agencies researched the effect of the plant's emissions on the health surrounding human population. So I decided to take a vacation. It was my first since I started in the practice of law, eighteen years earlier.

Chapter-70-

A Nice Family Vacation

In 1971, the American Bar Association planned a joint meeting with the British Bar in London. Another attorney from Minneapolis, Jack Chapman, and I went as representatives from Minnesota to the convention in London. Deloris and I took Bruce and Beaver, our two boys with us, who were then thirteen and eleven years old. Our daughter, Margaret, did not want to go with us because she was quite enamored with a boyfriend.

The London Bar Association meeting was a unique experience. We attended a meeting of the Inns of Court, a British association organized in the fourteen hundreds to train lawyers (barristers and solicitors) and teach court proceedings. The exact origin of the Lincoln's Inn, and indeed the other three Inns of Court, are not fully known. The extant records of the Lincoln's Inn opened in 1442, the earliest of the Inns of Court, but a society of lawyers by that name was then already in existence. It is likely that it evolved during the later part of the fourteenth century. Much of the procedures were like our courts except with much more formality. The judges in England wore white wigs and robes of various colors, purple for the civil appellate court judges and black for those who handled civil and criminal cases.

Jack Chapman and I decided we should attend the opening ceremonies at Westminster Hall. This was by an invitation only function and only the very highest-ranking American judges and attorney generals were invited to attend. Our entire Supreme Court was there, lead by Chief Justice Warren Burger.

Jack and I had rented some formal suits with striped pants, and canes. We were really "top fashion" dressed. When we got to the gate to the hall, the guard told us that we could not get in unless we had the special invitation card, which was a

319

white, gold-embossed card. We protested that we had picked up the wrong invitations and the other cards were back at our hotel. The guard told us to go to the British Bar Association lady at the gate, who had the authority to determine who would be allowed in.

We got to the door and met the very large woman who was head of the British Bar. She told us in no uncertain terms that we could not get in without a gold invitation card. We explained to her that we had such a card but had picked up the wrong card when we left our hotel. We had a blue card that would admit us to other functions. She told us to go get our proper card. We explained we were staying at Selsdon Park, which was twenty miles away.

She didn't believe anything we said, but probably thought anybody with that much guts should get in. She said that even the queen couldn't get in once the big brass doors were due to close. It was seconds to go before the bell would ring and the doors slam shut. Finally, she told us, "In you go, but if you tell anyone I let you in without a proper pass—I'll kick your ASS." (She pronounced it "Ahass") She was a big woman with about a twelve size shoe —so we would not want to endure that penalty.

Unfortunately, we were seated behind Judge Edward Devitt, a federal Judge from St. Paul, Minnesota, who knew us. He turned around and looked at us with a look, "How did these two peasants get into this prestigious meeting?"

It was a most impressive gathering. First, the House of Lords marched in, then a bunch of the judges of various British courts, followed by a lot of high-ranking American judges, and attorney generals. The final entrance was by the entire United States Supreme Court, lead by Chief Justice Warren Burger. Every time there was an entrance, the bugles blew and an announcement was made, identifying the persons entering. It was a most impressive ceremony to two young lawyers who had no business being there. As we came out of the door after the ceremony, the Bar Association lady leaned over to us and whispered, "What party do you intend to crash next?" We had not fooled her one bit.

The next day, we learned that the queen was having a garden party for distinguished members of the American Bar. Jack and I thought that because we were so successful in crashing the ceremony at Westminster Hall why not go to the Queen's reception? We dressed up in our new tailcoats with canes, and went to the party. We had some white envelopes with us and just flashed them as we hurried through the gate. If the entrance guard wanted to check, we would just explain we must have forgotten to put the invitation cards in. Fortunately, with the large crowd going in, the guards didn't bother to ask us. Every dignitary was there. We mingled with the crowd and everyone was most gracious. No one knew that we were a couple of lowly attorneys who had not been invited.

A long line formed and everyone marched briskly by the Queen with a quick bow or curtsy. Obviously, a farm kid from Minnesota didn't know anything about royal protocol. I stopped before the queen and stuck out my hand. That's the way we did things in Minnesota. We always shook hands with everyone we met, whether we liked them or not. I heard a gasp from the crowd, like I had shot an arrow into Her Highness. The royal guards seemed to snap to even more rigid attention. The queen graciously shook hands with me, but did have her usual little frozen smile on her face along with what I thought was a little twinkle in her eye. I hoped that my brazen conduct was the talk of Buckingham Palace and the pubs of London. It was an exciting experience.

A few days later, the queen had another very special reception for only the very highest-ranking officials of the American and British bars, and top diplomats. Jack Chapman and I thought we had stretched our luck to the limit and decided it would not be prudent to try to crash that party. We had visited a British jail and knew that would not be a pleasant place to spend part of our vacation. We thought it was where we would probably be escorted if we appeared at another function as uninvited guests. In hindsight, it probably would have been fun to try anyway, and we might have gotten lucky and succeeded.

Delores and Mary Chapman stayed with the kids at the hotel. They didn't want any part of our machinations. They were sure we would get caught and probably banned from any future activities, if we weren't thrown in jail.

Some other lawyers and I were invited to attend a British trial. I don't believe that Jack went to that. The trial involved a fellow who was accused of a robbery. The judge asked if I would like to be the defense attorney. The defendant agreed that I should represent him. He had seen Perry Mason shows and knew that American lawyers could always get a man acquitted. It was a most interesting experience. The prosecuting attorney put in the case against the defendant in a very short time. Witnesses in their testimony identified the defendant as the thief. The trial lasted less than an hour. A similar trial in our courts would have taken days. The judge said that although the evidence against the defendant appeared compelling, my "brilliant" defense strategy convinced him of finding the defendant not guilty. Brilliant or not, who could question the wisdom of a prestigious-looking judge in a white wig?

We were invited to attend a dinner at the Inns of Court. It was a most formal affair. The Inns of Court was a British legal tradition dating back hundreds of years as I have described earlier. Lawyers met there to discuss legal issues, dined there, and some resided there.

We went back and forth from our hotel to London almost every day for some function. The train station was a short walk from our hotel. Selsdon Park was a four hundred year-old castle that had been converted into a fine hotel. One of the assistant managers at the hotel took a great interest in our sons, Bruce and Beaver. He told us that if we ever needed someone to take care of them, he would be glad to do so.

After the Inns of Court affair, we were invited to another evening function in London. The hotel's assistant manager agreed to watch the boys, who had become good friends with a boy from Belgium. His parents had been to the hotel a number of times, so he was very familiar with the castle and grounds. He took our boys exploring in the caverns under the castle and through a tunnel that led to the outside by the river. He told them that the tunnel was an ancient escape route for the lords of the castle, when the King would send his troops to arrest some of them. Their hotel official friend would go along with the story and often embellish a bit. I had tipped him quite generously for taking care of the boys, so he became our most attentive friend at the hotel.

We were served two meals a day as part of the hotel charge. Sometimes we would go to the fine dining room and have a special meal. Before we left for London, we told the boys they could go to the dining room, take their Belgian friend along, and order what they liked. We told our hotel friend, who had agreed to take care of our boys for the evening, that he could take the three boys and could pick what he wanted, and the meals were on us. I told the head waiter that their meals should be charged to me.

When we returned that night, I found the bill for the dining room under the door. Surprise. Not only did they all have the top steaks and expensive desserts, but several bottles of high priced wine. I asked the kids about this business with the wine, as "Young boys should not be drinking wine." They said that their Belgian friend told them, "Everyone in Europe, regardless of age, always drinks wine with dinner...." so they had to do the same as he did. It "wouldn't have been polite to let him drink alone." "And besides," they said, "our hotel friend told us it was the custom in England for everyone to drink wine on special occasions." They both chimed in, "We had to drink it because that was the custom." Delores said that she knew exactly who they had inherited that kind of reasoning from!

Our hotel friend was equally attentive to us. A few days after we arrived, he asked us if there was anything special he could do for us. I had quite jokingly said that it would be nice to have a Bloody Mary or nice, cold beer in the morning. On mornings he knew we did not have commitments, we would wake up to find him standing by the bed with a tray and several Bloody Marys, or bottles of beer. Now, that is proper type of hotel service one doesn't often get in even the best of hotels.

Jack Chapman's birthday happened to be during our stay at the hotel, so we planned a surprise birthday party for him. There was a large contingent of International Business Machines (IBM) personnel from a lot of different countries — Norway, Germany, France, Italy, etc. We had met many of them at the bar in the evenings. They were a fun group. So I invited their group of about twenty people to the party. The IBM group was all conversant in English, but sometimes they would switch to their native tongues. It was interesting to hear them chattering in many different languages and then switch to English. It was obvious that most of them could speak a number of different languages. The Norwegian group was quite surprised when I interjected some comments in Norwegian. One of the groups had worked in Tromso, where my parents were from, so that made for interesting conversation. The party was a big surprise to Jack, and a fun time. It went on until the wee hours of the morning.

Jack and Mary were really fun to be with and we are friends to this day. We called him "Sir John" and her the "Lady Mary." They in turn called me "Your Lordship" and Mary dubbed Delores "Queenie." We still greet each other with those fun titles.

When the convention was over, we planned to drive up to Yarm on Tees on the England-Scotland border to visit some of Delores' cousins. When we called them, we learned they were going on a "caravan." A caravan in Britain meant a group of friends would go on a trip with house trailers. Since this had been a long-time planned event for them, we did not want them to cancel. We told them that we would come back from Norway and visit them then. After the visit with Delores' relatives in England, we had planned to go to Norway. We changed our plans to go to Norway first and then visit in England.

We flew to Oslo and then to Tromso, in northern Norway, where my parents were from. I had many relatives in that area. We were met by Inge Mauritz Andressen, a cousin on my mother's side of the family. He was a most gracious host. We stayed in a very nice hotel, the Saga. Inge Mauritz was the district treasurer, but he would take time off almost every day to escort us around the city. We went to the cemetery to see the burial plots and headstones of relatives.

One evening, we were invited to the Andressen home. We had been told by others about the Norwegian custom of an evening invitation that involved light snacks. We had gone fishing that day. When we returned, we were very hungry, so had a big meal. The hotel dining room cooked our fish. When we got to the Andressen home, we found she had prepared more than a full course meal. To be polite, we had to eat it and were stuffed. She brought out huge amounts of deserts, which she kept piling on our plates. Then, to finish the meal, she brought out large bottles of warm Coca Cola and ice cream cake rolls.

I had been told that when visiting a Norwegian home, a gift they appreciated the most was a bottle of liquor. Liquor was very high priced in Norway. I had purchased some bottles in the custom-free place at the airport in Oslo, and presented them to our hosts. After dinner, we had a number of drinks. When we were ready to go back to the hotel, which was about a mile away over a bridge, I asked the son if he could drive us over. The father immediately said, "No, he cannot do that, you must walk." I thought that was rather rude. We learned later that driving laws were very strictly enforced. If a driver is picked up for driving while influenced, (DWI) the driver goes to jail. Regardless of who you are, every person found guilty of driving while intoxicated gets a mandatory jail sentence. Because the son also had a few drinks, the father would not let him drive, which was a wise decision. We actually enjoyed the walk back. It was still the midnight sun season, so it was very light outside. Although it was after midnight, there were a lot of people out strolling.

One day, I rented a floatplane and flew over to some islands. The first island we visited was Karlsoy, where we toured the old church. It had been established by one of my great-great grandfathers, many centuries ago. It was still used on special occasions, such as weddings and funerals, and was in perfect shape. We then flew to Vengsoy, another little island, where my grandfather Soren Johannessen had a fish processing operation many years ago.

I asked a man at the dock in my best Norwegian,"Er der slektning av Soren Johannessen pa den oy?" "Are there any relatives of Soren Johannessen on the island?" After he thought for a long while, he said, "Yah, Jentoft Johannessen han leve oppe der."— ("Yes, Jentoft Johannessen he lives up there.") He pointed around to a nice white house about one-half mile away. I knew immediately he had to be a relative, because before he died, my dad had written to a Jentoft Johannessen about when he had planned to visit Norway.

I noticed a small road that ran from the dock along the waterfront to his house. There was an old pickup truck by the dock that appeared to be the only vehicle on the island. I asked the man if he could drive us up there and said that I would pay him. He kicked in the gravel for a while like he was really studying my request. Finally he said, "Nei du ga." —"No, you walk."

So we did. Delores, the two boys, and I walked toward Jentoft's house. As we neared the area, we saw some people haying. They were cutting hay with scythes and hanging it on the fence to dry. This was typical of the method of haying on small farm plots in Norway. A very blonde little girl, about twelve, saw us coming and ran to meet us. I told her we were Americans and had come to visit Jentoft Johannessen, who I believed to be a relative. She ran toward the house shouting, "Americans! Americans!"

As we got close to the house, a rather small man came out on the porch. I recognized him immediately because he was an exact image of my Aunt Constance, my dad's sister, who lived in the United States. I told him who I was and that my father was Jentoft Johannessen.

He was the son of Johannes Johannessen, a great uncle. The little girl, Trine Hanssen, was his granddaughter. Trine is pronounced "tree-nah." She could speak English so she translated for me. I could speak some Norwegian, but had difficulty with extended conversations. His grandfather was Johannes Jensen, my great-grandfather. So he was a second cousin. We spent a lot of time collecting the names of other relatives.

We had arrived at the house right at the noon hour. Johannes' wife had a big kettle of potatoes on the stove, with carrots and what looked like a meat loaf and brown gravy on the table. We were literally drooling, thinking we would get a good, old-fashioned meal of meat, potatoes, carrots, and brown gravy, since we had been eating only traditional Norwegian "smor brod," meals of open-faced sandwiches and hors d'oeuvres.

I noticed she was taking everything off the stove. She asked Trine to run out and get the "rullepolse." Rulle polse, pronounced "rule eh pull seh," is a Norwegian delicacy. It is made with thin strips of beef, or deer and veal. It is flavored with a variety of spices (pepper, garlic, mace, marjoram, etc.) between each strip of meat, then rolled and tied like a rolled roast. The roll is soaked in brine for about three weeks. It is then boiled until tender. After boiling and while still hot, the roll is pressed under weight. Sliced thin, it makes delicious sandwiches or hors d'oeuvres.

In Norway, after it was cooked and pressed, it was again put in brine so as to last for many months. Whenever they had guests, they would bring out the rullepolse, hjet ost (goat cheese), lefse (similar to a very thin pancake or crepe), open-faced sandwiches, and other delicacies. It was very delicious, but we still craved a meal of meat, potatoes, and gravy.

My dad had brought that rullepolse recipe from Norway, and each Christmas holiday season would always have some soaking in brine. I have carried on the tradition of making rullepolse each fall, just after Thanksgiving, and always send some to other family members and friends.

When I protested to Jentoft that the food she was cooking was just right and not to fix anything special for us, he and his wife would not hear of it. He explained through Trine that we were very special guests and must have special treats. The wife had taken everything off the table and reset it with her fine china, linen table-cloth, and silverware. We spent many hours there, getting information about family relatives. It was a sad departure. Jentoft gave me a picture of my great-grandfather, Johannes Jensen, and great-grandmother. The grandmother in the photo had a very stern look on her face. Later, when the kids looked at the photo they referred to her as "Old Smiley."

Some years later, Trine came to the United States as an exchange student, and stayed with a couple in Washington, D.C. I arranged for her to come and visit us and stay during her school vacation. She was such a sweet girl; we fell in love with her. We took her to Wheaton to visit other members of my family. When we were about fifty miles from Wheaton, we ran into a terrible blizzard. Trine had never seen a blizzard of that ferocity, so was very excited.

Visibility was down to almost zero and the road was becoming almost impass-able, so we stopped in the small town of Herman to wait to see if it would clear. The only place open was the liquor store. There were quite a number of people there taking shelter from the storm and enjoying the "refreshments." Two rather disheveled-looking guys suggested that Trine and Delores could stay at their apart-ment located upstairs of the liquor store. The girls politely declined. The bartender allowed that theirs was a wise decision. He said he would stay open all night if the storm kept up and would get some blankets and pillows to make us comfortable. The atmosphere in the bar looked plenty comfortable to me.

After several hours, the storm did let up a little. A man came in from Wheaton and said the highway was passable, so we headed for Wheaton, seventeen miles away. The roads to my brother's farm, which was only four miles from Wheaton, were blocked, so we had to stay in a motel in Wheaton that night. The next morning the snow plows had cleared the road, so we made it out to the farm where there was a house full of relatives, all waiting for us. Trine was particularly excited about meeting all the relatives. Mother fell in love with her and wanted her to stay for days. Trine said it was a trip she would never forget. We became great friends and corresponded with her through cards or letters at Christmas time. She teaches English to Norwegian children in Tromso, where she now lives.

After our visit with the Johannessen family at Vengsoy, we flew back to Tromso and visited with some other relatives. I met with Johannes Rickardsen, who was Marta Johannessdatter's (my great-Aunt's) son. He was raised by my grandfather, Soren Johannessen, as a member of the family, and my father considered him a brother. He was in the fish-processing business, and shipped his products throughout the world. I was told by others that he was a very wealthy man. He lived in a rather modest house and did not put on any airs. He was not in good health and continued to apologize for not entertaining us more, and for not having all of my family over. He told me how sad he and his father Soren were when my father left Tromso for America. It was an interesting visit. He died several years later.

Instead of flying out of Tromso, we took a trip on the "hurtig ruten," the "swift route," by ship, along the coast of Norway, to Trondheim. We spent several hours there, sightseeing and visiting the old cathedral. From there, we went by hydrofoil to Bergen and on to Stavanger.

At Stavanger, we visited Cousin Harriet. She was a large, jolly woman. She told us of some WWII experiences during the German occupation of Norway. One day, she was going home on a bus when the German guards stopped the bus and inspected the passengers. Harriet had a small pistol in her purse. She kept it at home for protection and often took it with her when she went out, despite the fact that Norwegians were not allowed to possess firearms. If caught with a gun, they would probably be shot. She quickly slipped the gun into her brassiere. She had very ample breasts, so it was not too difficult to hide the gun in her cleavage. The guards inspected her purse. She said that she just smiled at them and thanked them in German, in which she was quite fluent.

We then went to her daughter, Ingride Eliassen, and her family at Sandness. They had twin boys, about Beaver's age. Although Bruce and Beaver could not speak or understand Norwegian, they had a great time playing with Ingride's kids and some neighbor kids, none of whom could speak or understand much English. They were playing hide and seek when Beaver came into the house to hide. When some of the kids came to search the house, he jumped out the window. Harriet saw him do it, ordered him back inside, and really bawled him out. She said, "You could have broken a leg and that would have ruined your family's vacation." She then patted him on the head, gave him a cookie, and told him to be a good boy. She called him "Mr. Show Business" because he was always dreaming up interesting things to do while we visited.

Another second cousin, who lived in a small town nearby, was the sheriff of the area. He had a deputy who had a bad leg and limped quite noticeably. The sheriff jokingly referred to him as "Festus," the limping deputy in the movie "Gunsmoke." He had Festus put the boys in a cell, which they all thought was great fun. He had a copy of one of the "Gunsmoke" movies. It was quite fascinating to hear Matt Dillon, Festus, and some of the other actors speaking Norwegian, which had been dubbed into the movie.

We went back to Bergen and flew to London, then rented a car to visit Delores' relatives, the Bainbridge family, at Yarm on Tees. On the way we visited Shakespeare's birthplace and many interesting sites along the way, including some old fortifications built by the Romans many centuries ago, as well as some old Viking settlements.

Yarm is located near the Scottish border. The Bainbridge family lived in an old brick mansion that was over four hundred years old. Mr. Bainbridge was a pig farmer. The barn where the pigs were kept was as clean as a hospital. He won many prizes for his quality pigs. We spent several wonderful and interesting days learning a lot about some of Delores' relatives, on her mother's side of the family.

As our wonderful vacation came to an end, we flew from London back to Montreal and from there by our own plane back to Beaver Bay. When we had left for our vacation, we had flown in our Cessna 182 to Montreal and departed Montreal by British Airways, and arrived in London. We had left Silver Bay on 6 July 1971. The trip to Montreal took seven and a half hours in my plane, with two stops for gas. We left Montreal and headed home on 12 August 1971, ending a five week-long, memorable vacation.

Chapter -71-

Back to the Law —The Reserve Mining Case

After we arrived safely home, it was back to work and catching up on all the legal work that had piled up. Although my partner, Ron Thomas, did a great job, there were still matters that I needed to handle.

The Reserve Mining case had taken a dramatic turn. After the specter of cancer was raised by the environmental groups, the state of Minnesota, Wisconsin, and Michigan, as well as a number of environmental groups and some pure rabble rousers, like student groups that had no knowledge of the problems joined the case against Reserve. I was asked to join the case as the city attorney for Silver Bay on behalf of Reserve. A number of other governmental and economic units that would be affected by any change in Reserve's operation also intervened on the side of Reserve.

In addition to the cities of Silver Bay and Beaver Bay that I represented, the following cities joined in support of Reserve: Two Harbors, Duluth, and Babbitt, where the Reserve mine was located, the Township of Beaver Bay, Lax Lake Property Owner's Association, County of Lake, County of St. Louis, Silver Bay Area Chamber of Commerce, Duluth Area Chamber of Commerce, the Range League of Municipalities, Northeast Minnesota Development Association, and the Lake County School District. We called the group the Northeastern Minnesota Interveners. All of these units had their own attorneys. However, they appointed me to represent their interests, which I did, throughout the long period of litigation.

This case became known as the longest and most complex environmental case in the country. Scientists, eminent doctors, and experts of every discipline imaginable were retained by both sides in order to prove or disprove the presence of cancer-causing asbestos fibers in Reserve's ore body.

The electron scanning microscope came into play. It was a sophisticated new microscope that could enlarge a fiber smaller than a hair and make it look like a fuzzy quarter-inch rope. The state used it dramatically to show that the minute fibers in Reserve's ore body were hazardous. The microscope was manufactured by a firm in Japan. Reserve's attorneys wanted to learn more about the microscope, so they asked I go to Japan to get firsthand information from engineers at the factory. We contacted the factory and they agreed to meet with me.

I flew to Tokyo and took a number of trains to the factory, located about sixty miles from Tokyo. Officials at the factory gave me precise directions on how to get there. The trains and stations were colored-coded, so I had no problem changing trains and getting to my destination. Japanese passengers were smiling and most courteous. I was given a most hospitable welcome and a tour of the very clean factory. I had to remove my shoes and was given snow-white slippers to wear. They also gave me a long, white coat, so I looked like a visiting doctor. They spent many hours with me, explaining in detail the manufacture and function of the microscope. Most all of the engineers and scientists spoke perfect English. The manager had been educated at the Massachusetts Institute of Technology, and many of the others had been educated in respected American universities. They were all quite adamant that the microscope was being misused in the case. I asked if any of their scientists would be willing to come to America to testify. They declined, saying that they did not think a Japanese scientist would have much credibility in an American court, in view of the recent war. But, they did give me a lot of technical data on the microscope that we were able to put to good use in defense of the case.

When I put on my suit coat to leave, the manager of the plant stared at my lapel pin. It was of a P-40 airplane that I had neglected to remove. He then noticed the Flying Tigers logo on my brief case. It was not very good thinking on my part to have these symbols, both of which might not be appreciated in Japan. He said that I must be a pilot who had flown P-40s in China, because I had these identifications. I could just see myself ending up in a lagoon someplace. Before I could come up with an answer, he told me he had been a fighter pilot stationed in China and had great respect for the skill of American pilots. He then asked if I had ever flown missions near Amoy. When I reluctantly told him I may have, he asked, "Could you have been the pilot that shot me down?" I quickly assured him that was not me, because I hadn't shot down any planes that day. He called in all his staff and introduced me as a daring fighter pilot who "had been his opponent during the war and now we were friends." Instead of going back on the train, he took me back to Tokyo in his personal car, which was a beautiful Mercedes driven by his chauffer, while we sat in the back and sipped some saki. He not only brought me back to my hotel but also bought me dinner. It was a most exciting and fascinating experience. I did write him a letter of thanks but, unfortunately, he died shortly thereafter.

The Reserve trial was a field day for the press. Misinformation became the criterion of the day. At some points, the atmosphere reached near panic. People were concerned about their health and their jobs. Although there was no higher incidence of cancer in Silver Bay or Babbitt than in other parts of the state, demands for the shutdown of Reserve Mining ran rampant.

After months of trial, Judge Miles Lord, the federal judge in charge of the case, issued an order that closed the Reserve Mining plant. The judge ruled that the emissions from the Reserve plant, both the air pollution and discharge into the lake, were critical health hazards. Since all communities along Lake Superior took their drinking water from the lake, he ordered that Reserve Mining must provide specially filtered or bottled water to those communities. Bottled water sales soared. It was a "Black Friday," long to be remembered.

On the day of Judge Lord's order of shut down, the attorneys representing Reserve Mining and the co-owners of Reserve, Republic Steel Corporation, and Armco Steel Company, including myself, rushed to the Eight Circuit Court of Appeals seated in St Louis, Missouri, to seek reversal of Judge Lord's order. We had worked long hours preparing briefs for the appellate court.

The impact on the area and the entire state of Minnesota would be devastating if the plant remained closed. Thousands of people would be out of jobs and lose their homes. Subsidiary businesses that furnished Reserve supplies and depended upon Reserve for their livelihood would go bankrupt. The state of Minnesota and other taxing districts, and the intervening governmental units, would lose many millions in taxes. It would be a disaster of untold magnitude.

We asked the Eight Circuit Court of Appeals for an emergency hearing, which it granted. The case was argued before the court late into the night in a hotel conference room in St. Louis, Missouri. Early the next morning, the Court of Appeals reversed Judge Lord's order. The appellate court determined that there was insufficient evidence to find there was a critical health problem. It ordered the re-opening of the plant. That was not the end of the litigation. It continued on for years. I spent over three thousand hours a year involved in the litigation.

I was away from home for many days, while Delores took care of our kids. The normal work-year is expected to be about one thousand six hundred hours. It was not unusual for the lawyers, during the Reserve Mining litigation, to work three thousand hours or more a year. That meant working sixty to seventy hours a week, rather than the normal forty hours a week. Twelve- to sixteen-hour days were not unusual.

During that period, I was constantly on alert. I always had a bag packed ready for a sudden departure, for a court hearing somewhere or inspection tours to similar types of processing operations. It was not unusual for Keith Sanford, the security Chief for Reserve Mining, to call me in the late hours of the night to tell me that he had to pick me up and I had to attend a court proceeding in Minneapolis, Omaha, or St Louis.

The essence of our case was that the Reserve Mining deposits did not constitute a health hazard. Many tests showed that the fibers in the rock were not asbestos fibers, but did have a somewhat similar appearance under an electron-scanning microscope. One of the issues was whether the tailings (waste rock) deposits would be toxic, especially concerning air quality. The air emissions could be cleaned by new methods of filtering. One of the methods to control air emissions at tailings ponds was the use of vegetation. We made many trips throughout the country, studying how vegetation could grow in tailings and determining that they were not toxic. As attorneys, we had to become experts on every facet of the case.

One night, at two a.m., Keith Sanford, the Reserve Mining security chief, called me and told me that he was picking me up in a few minutes and taking me to Duluth, from where I would take a chartered plane to Minneapolis. It only took me a few minutes to dress, and since I always had a bag packed for an emergency trip, I was ready to go.

From Duluth, I flew to Minneapolis and then to Denver. From there, I and other attorneys took a helicopter to a copper mine to study how they disposed of their waste rock and controlled the dust with vegetation. Then, we flew back to Denver and on to Anchorage, Alaska, and up into the hinterlands to view the above-ground oil fields (tar fields). We were interested in the tar fields' operators' methods to protect the environment. The tar fields' operators had developed a unique system for environmental protection, as it extracted the oil from the ground. They planted grass and trees in the tailing-disposal areas. The lush, green fields attracted deer and other animals. It was good evidence that vegetation could grow in tailings, and would be attractive as a habitat. Reserve set up a similar test plot and planted grass and trees in pure taconite tailings. They grew quite successfully. We presented the evidence to the court to demonstrate that the Reserve Mining's operation was not posing a health hazard and that through the use of proper techniques used by other mining companies, tailing deposits would not be environmental hazards. We argued that Reserve Mining Company could apply those same technologies to its taconite producing facilities. There were many other trips to other areas to study other coal fields, as well as copper and gold mines, and other mining operations.

One of our memorable trips was to Boston and Cape Code to meet with the A. C. Little Company and their team of experts, in every discipline imaginable. Most of the attorneys had their wives with them. My wife, Delores, accompanied me. While the attorneys were at myriad meetings, the wives explored the antique and gift stores. Delores liked to collect flat irons. She discovered an antique store with a trove of flat irons. She bought a suitcase full. When we were boarding the plane to return home, the airline attendant, a small Oriental girl, tried to lift the iron-filled suit case to the loading belt. She could not budge it. She had to call for several men to help her lift it. It probably weighted one hundred fifty pounds. It was before the days airlines limited the weight of baggage.

The litigation went on for years. Reserve Mining Company agreed to stop discharging its tailings into Lake Superior. It agreed to build an on-land disposal tailings pond in an area called Mile Post 7. It was seven miles from the Reserve processing plant. The state Environmental Protection Agency and the various environmental groups would not accept that method of resolving the case. They suggested a number of other sites, far from the plant. The alternate sites were not economically feasible.

Judge Lord became very aggressive in his handling of the case. He became more of an advocate against the mining companies than a judge. He could be very caustic high-ranking mining company officials when they testified, although I'm sure he felt he was acting judicially and in good faith.

Reserve Mining Company and the parties that I represented filed a motion (a legal proceeding that asks the court for certain relief) in the Eight Circuit Court of Appeals to have Judge Lord removed because of his overt hostility toward the mining companies. The case at hand was critical to the welfare of the citizens of Silver Bay, and if Judge Lord issued another order to close the Reserve plant, it would be disastrous. By his rulings and handling of evidence presented by Reserve, he was cleverly laying the groundwork to justify closure. I am sure that he sincerely believed the health hazard was a serious one, for he will argue that to this day.

A hearing by the Court of Appeals was held in Omaha, Nebraska. Attorneys for Reserve Mining Company; led by Ed Fride, Bill Egan, representing Republic and Charles Murnane representing Armco Steel Companies, asked that I, representing the people of northeastern Minnesota who were the most affected, take the lead in presenting the case against Judge Lord.

The removal of a federal trial judge was a most unusual procedure. It seldom happened. Federal judges are appointed for life. The Circuit Court could remove a judge from a trial for bias or misconduct. Otherwise, the only way to remove a federal judge was by impeachment. Impeachment of a federal judge was very rare. We did not want Judge Lord impeached. All we wanted was for Judge Lord to be removed as trial judge, and have another judge appointed. To make matters more difficult, Judge Lord appeared in person. It was also most unusual for a judge to appear on his own behalf as Judge Lord did, to argue his own case as to why he should not be replaced as the trial judge.

I had tried cases before Judge Lord and had a great deal of respect for him. As a young lawyer, he had given me invaluable advice. To ask for his removal as the trial judge in the Reserve mining litigation was a most difficult task for me.

The significant part of my argument was, "Judge Lord had shed the cloak of a Jurist and assumed the mantle of an advocate." In other words, he was acting as a trial attorney rather than an impartial judge. The Court of Appeals removed Judge Lord as the trial judge and appointed Judge Edward Devitt to handle the balance of the case. Judge Devitt was a very strict judge, and handled cases without any variation from the rules of trial procedure.

The litigation continued before Judge Devitt in St. Paul, Minnesota. Since I was the city attorney for Beaver Bay and Silver Bay, it was necessary for me to attend the council and commission meetings of each city. The meetings were usually held in the evenings. I would fly my plane from Minneapolis in order to attend Beaver Bay Council meetings on the second Tuesday of each month, and the Silver Bay Council meeting every other Monday night, and sometimes oftener for Silver Bay Commission meetings. The distance from Minneapolis to Silver Bay was about two hundred miles by air or about one and a half hour flight time in my plane. During the winter, I would land my plane on skis at Lax Lake. The snow on Lax Lake contrasted with the dark terrain, so it was easy to find. We had a cabin on Lax Lake, and Deloris would be there to pick me up. I would usually fly back to Minneapolis after the council meetings so I could attend court in the morning. It was standard procedure during court sessions before Judge Lord, but also during sessions before Judge Devitt. Reserve provided me with an apartment in Minneapolis where I stayed during the litigation. In early 1975, we were in trial literally every day, in federal courts in St. Paul or Minneapolis.

Besides my trial work, another matter concerned me. My mother was in failing health. My sister Korty attended to her every day. Daily, Korty would drive from her home in Chokio to Mother's farm near Wheaton, which was a distance of about twenty miles. She had been doing that for several years as Mother's arthritic conditions got so bad it was difficult for Mother to get around. Also, she started to have some heart problems. Because she was in her mid-nineties, some health problems were understandable.

The doctor usually came out to the farm where she lived to see how she was doing. The doctor in Wheaton was a great guy who agreed to make house calls because he knew it was difficult for her to go to his office. Shortly before she died, after the doctor had checked her over, he told her that she should come in to the hospital so he could examine her better and see what was wrong with her. She told the doctor, "I know what's wrong with me, I'm getting a little old, but I am not going into your hospital so you can get a bunch of my money. When I am ready to die, I'll do it at home." And she did.

One Sunday night in late June, Korty called to tell me that she thought Mother was on her deathbed and that I should try to come home to see her. I flew to the farm, landed on the road in front of her house, and taxied the plane into the yard. When I went into the house, Mother was sitting up in bed. She asked how I had gotten there, as neither of my brothers who lived with her, Doc nor was Ed home to go to the airport. I told her that I had landed on the road and my plane was sitting in the yard. She bawled me out. She said it was too dangerous to land an airplane on the road and from then on I should go to the airport in Wheaton and she would get someone to pick me up.

Although ninety-six years old, she was mentally sharp. I flew to Minneapolis that night. I later got a call from Korty that Mother had died a little after I left.

Giving birth to fourteen children, never in the hospital (most all children were delivered by midwives at home), and surviving for ninety-six years were impressive feats, and evidenced her strong will. She still looked quite young on her photo at age ninety.

She never drank nor smoked, nor did she approve of smoking. The strongest liquor she ever drank was communion wine. Dad seldom drank. He had a small bottle of brandy in the cupboard. It was for medicinal purposes only. If he had a cold or didn't feel well, he would pour a little in his coffee. But he smoked heavily. Mother stoically tolerated Dad's smoking. He would even wake up at night, roll himself a cigarette, and place the smoking butt on the iron rail of the bed below the mattress. He was most fortunate that his habit didn't burn the house down. Fortunately, the roll-your-own cigarettes would burn out rather quickly. But he never smoked in the house during the day.

Everyone respected her opposition to smoking. Doc smoked for some years, but he always went out into the yard or barn. Roald, Floyd, and Myron were the only other boys who smoked, but never in the house. Opal was the only one of the girls who smoked, but never did it in front of Mother. When we visited, Delores would always go outside or upstairs for a smoke. Our sister-in-law, Margie, was a heavy smoker. But when we all came to visit on holidays, Margie, Delores, and Opal would go upstairs to have a puff. Of course, Mother knew what they were doing, but she never said a word.

One time, Beaver, who was just a little kid, caught them smoking. He went downstairs and told Grandma that his mom, Margie, and Opal were upstairs smoking. She told Beaver that they shouldn't be smoking, but he should not be telling things about what others were doing. From her words, he learned a lesson about what to tell and what not to tell.

Mother never went into the barn or fields, but knew what was going on all the time. She knew when the crops were to be planted and harvested, what animals were producing, and the family income. After my dad died, there was no questioning that she was the matriarch of the family. She knew the daily details about how Doc and Ed ran the farm.

She was also concerned about the many hours I was spending away from home, because of the Reserve Mining litigation. She wanted to know why I had to spend that much time away from my family. She often said it would have been much better if I had stayed a farmer. But she understood that law was my career and that it was my responsibility to do my best for my clients.

One of the highlights of the Reserve Mining litigation was my appearance before the Supreme Court of the United States, on two separate occasions. They were thrilling experiences for a country lawyer from a small town. During the litigation, I had made a number of appearances before the Minnesota Supreme Court and Eight Circuit Court of Appeals in Omaha, Kansas City, and St. Louis. The appearance before the United States Supreme Court was by far the most exciting. Time was rigidly controlled. Each speaker was given a specific time-limit. The clerk would hold up a card with the remaining time written on it. He would usually hold up a two minute and a one minute card. When the time was up, he would hit a little bell. The speaker had better stop, even if it was in mid-sentence. After the presentation, the Supreme Court ruled that there was insufficient evidence to establish that Reserve's operation constituted a health hazard.

Finally, after many more court proceedings, the Federal District Court, the Eight Circuit Court of Appeals, the Minnesota State District Court, and the Minnesota Supreme Court all ruled that there was not sufficient evidence to show that Reserve Mining's emissions constituted a health hazard. The courts agreed that Reserve could deposit its tailings in a new, to-be-developed tailings deposit area called Mile Post 7.

To build Mile Post 7 and change its deposit operations, Reserve had to raise approximately four hundred fifty million dollars. The City of Silver Bay, with my advice, agreed to issue revenue bonds in order to raise the necessary funding. Revenue bonds did not require the full faith and credit of the City, but were to be repaid using revenues from Reserve's operations so there would be no risk to the taxpayers of Silver Bay. Revenue bonds would not impose a tax burden on the public. We made many trips to New York to meet with investment and banking firms and New York Bond Counsel.

On some trips, we were allowed to take our wives, because we spent some time in New York. With Reserve, Armco, and Republic Steel Company attorneys, and the Bond Counsel from Minneapolis and New York, there were often forty to fifty attorneys in the room. The bonds were issued in various increments. The first issue was for one hundred sixty five million. Each time there was a new issue, the same procedure took place in New York, which meant additional trips.

At the end of the working day, sometimes twelve hours or more, we enjoyed some of the amenities of New York. We saw a number of Broadway plays, including the very popular "Best Little Whorehouse in Texas." It was always a thrill to seek out some of the more interesting restaurants in New York. We stayed in the finest hotels, such as the Waldorf Astoria and the Plaza, and sometimes a delightful French hotel, all at Reserve Mining's expense of course. On several trips, the mayor, city clerk and city treasurer of Silver Bay went to New York with us to sign bond documents.

Although the court decisions resolved the Reserve environmental case, the eventual costs were still a disaster to Silver Bay. The terrific financial burden of the litigation and the astronomical costs of Mile Post 7 sent Reserve Mining Company into bankruptcy. The plant was closed again and remained closed for some time, until sold by order of the Bankruptcy Court.

Chapter -72-
More Flying Tigers Fun

With the Reserve Mining litigation winding down and other legal matters that I had been working on, I could see a little time for other activities. I was becoming more deeply involved in Flying Tigers Association matters. I attended a lot of the early conventions starting in 1948, up until I got married. Although I continued attending after I was married, Delores did not always go because she needed to stay home with the young children.

One convention we attended turned out to be a disaster. It was the one held in Atlanta in 1981. I was the master of ceremonies and had asked each speaker to limit his or her remarks to no more than five minutes. Those who spoke followed the time, except one. The convention chairman, Al Johnson, had invited a former Chinese general, who now lived in Atlanta, to speak. The general had been in charge of furnishing housing and food for our forces in China. It was said that he had made a fortune by cutting all kinds of corners. I had heard him speak before and was very concerned that he would ramble on for a long time, talking about what a great guy he was and how he had helped win the war. I asked him to limit his remarks like the other speakers had. He promised to do so.

He droned on and on, bragging about his career and eventually went into a long spiel that criticized the United States. After about twenty minutes of the audience getting restless, I pulled on his coat tails and asked him to close his remarks. He told the audience, "Your M.C. wants me to not talk longer, do you want me to stop?" Some damn fools in the audience started to applaud. Although it was just a brief patter, that was all he needed to hear. Despite my efforts to stop him, he kept on for almost an hour, even though many people were walking out. I finally stood up and took the mike away from him. He was very insulted and said that he would never speak at one of our conventions again. That remark resulted in a thunderous applause by the remaining audience. I established a rule that at any future conventions, the M.C. would have a switch to turn off the mike if a speaker went on for too long. The switch worked great, but speakers learned, so we seldom had to use the switch.

After the convention, we took another trip to Taiwan. Because I was president of the Association, I led the delegation. I had a rather unique golfing experience there. I was invited by the vice president of Taiwan to join in for a foursome of golf. The other two people were the Commanding General of the Republic of China (Taiwan) Air Force and another four-star general, who was the golf course manager. I protested that I had not played much golf and would not be a good partner. However, they insisted. I was informed by some of our Chinese hosts that it would have been improper protocol to refuse the vice president's invitation.

They provided me with golf shoes and other golf attire, as well as a fine set of golf clubs, which were carried by a pretty girl caddy. Because of all the dignitaries, a large crowd had gathered at the course as well as a good portion of my delegation. I was asked to tee off first, despite my protests. The girl caddy even placed the ball on the tee for me. I took a mighty swing and missed the ball completely. There was a little moan from the crowd.

The caddy made a great show of wiggling the ball on the tee and looked at me with a big smile. I took another swing and this time just chipped the top of the ball. It rolled about eight or ten feet. The caddy ran and retrieved the ball and teed it up again. She grinned at me and said, is it teed up right this time, Mr. Johnson?" I allowed that it was properly teed. Since I had made a complete ass of myself, I took off my cap and threw it on the ground and laid my sunglasses on it. Pretending that the whole episode had been some kind of a show, I wiggled my club like a pro.

The crowd was completely silent, without a whisper. I did all the proper wiggles and took another swing at the ball. Surprise: I hit the ball the best I ever had. It went sailing out in a straight line, then rose up over a hill about two hundred fifty yards away. I had never hit a ball that well or that far before. The roar from the crowd sounded like one at Yankee Stadium when a player had hit his second homerun.

My ball was right in the very center of a double dogleg fairway. The green was about another two hundred yards out, but behind some tall pine trees. The fairway turned left about ninety degrees where I was standing after my first shot and another ninety degrees left, just short of the green. The caddy politely suggested that I drive the ball straight ahead so I would have a good approach to the green. I agreed that it was a good idea, and took a swing at the ball. I really hit it hard. But it didn't go straight down the fairway. It headed right for the tall trees. My three companions and the caddies all let out little moans. The ball rose high in the air and right over the top of the trees. When we got to the green we found the ball right on the green, a few feet from the hole. My companions and the caddies went wild.

One of the players pointed at me and said, "Arnold Palmer," which got a big laugh from the following crowd. At that time, Arnold Palmer was one of the top golfers in the United States and was known in golfing circles throughout the world.

The next few holes went fairly well, and then I hit one into the rough. My three companions were all excellent golfers and always hit the ball straight down the fairway. I noticed that the vice president turned slightly and drove his ball into the rough, too. Amazingly, the two generals' drives, for some strange reason, also went into the rough. They apparently were going to make sure that they didn't beat me or the vice president. The caddy found my ball buried behind a big rock. While the others were looking for their golf balls, she slipped off her shoes and picked up my ball with her toes and put it in a nice lie, so I could hit it out of the rough, and winked at me with a big grin. Luckily, I hit it out of the rough so I had a good lie on the fairway.

The others all claimed they could not find their golf balls, so the vice president suggested it was getting too hot to play and that we should go into the clubhouse for refreshments. I was sure that his decision was made in order to not embarrass me further, because by that time they knew I was not that great a player. The "refreshments" turned out to be some of their powerful wine, so the afternoon became quite relaxing. It was a great trip. We were treated like visiting royalty.

Chapter-73-

A Family Tragedy

The joy of the trip, and the rest of 1981, vanished a little later. It was by far the most devastating year that any family could experience. Nothing is more traumatic to parents than the loss of a child. Our son, Beaver, lost his life as a result of a motor vehicle accident. He was twenty-one years of age on October 25, 1981. He and some friends were working in the oil fields in Watford City, North Dakota. After working for about twelve hours or more every day of the week, one Friday evening, he and two of his friends decided to drive home to celebrate Halloween and his twenty-first birthday with his family.

Beaver was driving a pick-up truck. His two friends fell asleep. From having no one to talk to and being overly tired from the long days of work, he too fell asleep. He ran off the road near Brainerd, Minnesota. He hit a driveway and the pick-up catapulted into the air over the driveway and landed on its nose. Beaver hit his chest on the steering wheel with sufficient enough impact to bend the wheel. All three boys were thrown through the rear window. All survived, but were cut and badly bruised.

Beaver called me at about four in the morning to say that he had been in an accident but was okay. The pick-up was a total loss and could not be driven. I flew to Brainerd in my plane to pick them up. The boys did look okay, but had many bruises and cuts. They had been patched up at the local hospital. The following day, Beaver called his boss and told him that he had been injured and needed to take a few days off. We took him to the local clinic, where they did an examination and a number of X-rays. The doctor pronounced him in good health, but advised rest for few days. He was home for a week. On the following Sunday, he decided he was well enough to go back to work. He had just been promoted to foreman. He did not want to lose that position, so was eager to get back.

I agreed that he could take my plane to go back to Watford City. Beaver was an excellent pilot. I had complete confidence in his abilities. We went out to the airport and he made several landings to show that he could fly the plane safely. He would fly back home in several weeks to arrange for another vehicle.

He was saying goodbye to his girlfriend at our home when he suddenly collapsed. He was rushed to the Silver Bay Clinic, but died from a ruptured aorta. Unfortunately, the doctor had misread the X-rays. When I looked at the X-rays, even to me as a layman, it was obvious on the X-rays that there was a substantial darkening in the pleural cavity that should have alerted the doctor to a leakage of blood. The rankest amateur should have seen that his condition required immediate surgical intervention. It was operable and could have saved his life. The doctor left the area, which was fortunate, before she could do further harm through her incompetence.

Beaver was a fun guy. He was sometimes mischievous, but a devoted son with a delightful sense of humor. He was sensitive and considerate, and brought much joy to our lives. Although the tragedy happened almost thirty years ago, during this writing we are daily reminded of the loss. We are sustained by his memory, and it gives us some measure of solace. We remember.

Beaver

My brother-in-law, Oscar Lange, died in November of the same year. It was another blow, because of our close relationship. I had lived with him and my sister Korty at their farm for four years while going to high school. He was a kind and understanding man, and overlooked most of my foibles.

But life had to go on. It was the time when I was still immersed in the Reserve Mining litigation and other legal matters.

Chapter-74-

A Time of Uncertainty

I was involved in the Reserve litigation from the early 1970s until the late 1980s, until after Reserve filed bankruptcy. The Reserve bankruptcy was another devastating blow to the community. The plant was stripped and many of its assets were sold off. The population of Silver Bay dropped from 3,600 to about 1,600. Many had to abandon their homes and seek employment elsewhere. Home values dropped to nominal amounts. Nice homes sold as low as four thousand dollars. People from Minneapolis and other areas bought up a number of the cheap homes for vacation or retirement homes. Some residents could not sell their homes at all and just walked away. The shut down adversely affected every business in the area, as well as our law office. They were lean times, but we held on.

The bankruptcy proceedings were held in New York. I made many trips there to protect the interests of Silver Bay and northeastern Minnesota. We wanted assureance that the company that bought the bankrupt Reserve Mining Company would serve the best interests of our community.

Two companies bid on the Reserve bankruptcy — Cleveland Cliffs, one of the largest iron mining companies in America that had other plants in Minnesota, and Cyprus Minerals Company from Denver, Colorado. Cyprus was a gold and copper mining company with little experience in iron-ore processing. But it had the best bid and assured us that it would be a permanent fixture in Silver Bay. Other attorneys and I, supported Cyprus in its bid. The bankruptcy court awarded the bid to Cyprus. It reopened the plant.

With only a few years operation, Cyprus decided it was not a profitable operation. The plant was again closed. An atmosphere of gloom permeated the area.

Those who had opposed the Reserve Mining Company acted with sadistic joy. They thought that finally they would get the taconite processing plant off the shore of Lake Superior. It did not concern them that thousands of people would lose their jobs and many dependant businesses would be forced to close. It did not concern them that people were part of the environment and needed protection in balance with the natural environment.

Then, Cleveland Cliffs stepped into the breach. It purchased the operation from Cyprus Minerals. Cleveland Cliffs was one of the largest iron ore processors in the United States. Brighter days appeared to be ahead. But all those who had invested in the Reserve Mining Company Revenue bonds took a total loss. With Reserve's bankruptcy, the revenue bonds became worthless. Fortunately, since we had insisted the bonds would be revenue bonds rather than the typical government issued bonds, the city did not take a loss.

Iron ore mining and processing facilities traditionally operated by union labor. Cyprus, however, was a non-union operation. When Cleveland Cliffs took over, it hired most of the former Cyprus employees to operate the plant and mine with non-union labor.

This operation was called Northshore Mining Company. Cleveland Cliffs had many mining and iron ore processing plants. The mine in Babbitt and the processing plant in Silver Bay were their only non-union operations. The Steelworker's Union tried to unionize the operation, but were unsuccessful. The employees were generally paid better than union scale, and with better benefits. They also liked the flexibility of not having a specific craft. They could do work in many areas rather than be confined to one particular craft.

After years of uncertainty, we finally had stability in Silver Bay. There were opportunities for well-paying work in the plant. People needed homes, so the real estate market boomed. The influx of workers and the sale of homes was a boon to our law office. Like all other businesses that developed in Silver Bay, our law office profited.

Chapter-75-

A Varied Law Practice

Besides my involvement in the Reserve Mining case, I had a very dynamic law practice over the more than fifty years that I was active. There are a number of cases that have stuck in my memory.

One of the first cases I tried happened to be in the United States District Court in Duluth, Minnesota. Admission to the bar does not authorize an attorney to try cases in federal court. There is a separate procedure necessary in order to be admitted to practice before the federal courts. One had to be recommended by another practicing attorney who had been admitted to federal practice. After an attorney is admitted to practice before the Federal Court, he, or she, is usually appointed to defend a person charged with a crime who can't afford an attorney.

I was appointed to defend a young man who claimed to be a conscious objector and therefore refused to serve in the military during WWII, and claimed he could not afford an attorney. The United States had a special exception to persons who opposed military service because of religious beliefs. They could be exempt from the draft or placed in non-combat positions.

My defendant was a member of the Jehovah Witnesses, a philosophy that opposed any kind of military service. He claimed to have faithfully attended Jehovah Witness meetings and to have been active in door-to-door proselytizing. I thought that I could raise a good defense. Several other young men, who established, to the satisfaction of a jury, that they were true conscious objectors, had been acquitted.

There was, however, one significant obstacle in my case. During the war, my defendant had worked as a sailor on the ore boats that hauled iron ore to the steel mills. That industry was vital to the war effort. The prosecuting attorney made a big point that the defendant had been making big bucks during the war years, working in a vital defense industry, while soldiers were making twenty-one dollars a month.

During final argument, I objected and said that, I as a veteran who had spent five years in the service and a great deal of time in combat, respected the right of one who was opposed to war. It was probably improper argument, because it had nothing to do with the evidence, but the judge let me get by with it, recognizing my inexperience. I said, "Congress in its wisdom had passed a law establishing the right of a conscious objector to not serve in defense of his country." I argued that the defendant, through his religious beliefs, was a bona-fide conscious objector, as defined by Congress, and was therefore immune from military service. The jury didn't buy it. It only took them a couple of hours to find him guilty. I talked to some of the jurors after the trial. They unanimously decided that the man was not a true conscious objector since he worked in, and was making big money while, producing the raw material for the production of steel, a critical component of the war effort. .

The judge told the defendant that he did not qualify for appointed counsel and had sufficient assets that he should pay me. Before he went to prison, my client sent me a book, "God Is Love," which he said paid me in full. I still have the book as one of my "well paid" fees.

Another of my early cases was in the defense of a man accused of murder. He was accused of killing another man in a drunken brawl outside of a tavern. The incident occurred in a rural area in Cook County, about twenty miles north of Grand Marais and not far from the Grand Portage Indian Reservation. My defendant was a small, one-armed fellow of about one hundred fifty pounds. He had lost the other arm in the war. The deceased was a big Indian who probably weighed two hundred and fifty pounds. Because of the defendant's physical condition and war injuries, I felt it vital to his defense that he testify.

The defendant testified that he had gone outside with the Indian to try to calm him down because the Indian was getting too unruly in the tavern. It was a very cold night well below zero with snow and ice on the ground. He claimed that the Indian had started to fight with him and had slipped and fallen on his knife, which my client had just brandished as protection. He stated that the knife had hit the deceased in the armpit when he was on the ground and had raised his arm to protect himself from the deceased's attack. He stated the knife only hit the deceased once in the armpit and that was the only place. The knife had hit an artery, so the Indian bled to death in a very short time. But there were about seven or eight of what appeared to be knife holes in the armpit of the deceased's underwear.

Fortunately for the defendant, the sheriff had cut off the sleeve and upper part of the deceased's underwear to preserve as evidence. He had saved only the bloody upper part with the sleeve. In my pre-trial investigation, the sheriff had said that he didn't want to keep the entire underwear because it had probably been worn for six months without washing, and was not too clean in the seat area. He had burned the other parts.

During our motion (argument) to suppress the evidence, the sheriff testified that the underwear was "ripe," which was probably an understatement. I objected to the admission of the bloody sleeve as evidence. I argued that since the sheriff had mutilated the evidence, we could not show that there might be similar holes created by different sources in other parts of the underwear. The judge ruled in our favor and held the evidence inadmissible.

Cook County is the northernmost county in the arrowhead of Minnesota, adjoining the Canadian border. It is rather sparsely populated, with a substantial Native American population, although there were no Indians on the jury. The prosecuting attorney, Henry Eliasson, was related to many people in the county. His brother and sister-in-law were on the jury panel. I objected to their presence. Henry argued that they were honest and fair folks. The judge told Henry, "You can't have your close relatives on a jury, regardless how honest or fair they would be." He dismissed them from the panel. The sheriff went out on the street and picked up several other residents to be on the panel.

During the trial, I had the defendant lie on the floor with his arm upraised, as I, playing the role of the deceased, lunged at him. The prosecution attorney screamed an objection but the judge ruled that the demonstration was consistent with the evidence. The jury acquitted the defendant, so the judge ordered his release, as the sheriff had put the defendant back in jail during the jury deliberations.

The sheriff was infuriated by the jury's verdict. He took his sweet time letting the defendant out of jail. It was about midnight when he hauled the defendant, who was a free man, to the county line and told him never to come to "my county" again.

It was about thirty degrees below zero. The sheriff left the poor fellow standing out on a deserted road. My client walked to the nearest residence, about two miles away. He called me, told me the story, and asked that I come and get him. I brought him home and the next day drove him to Duluth so he could catch a bus for Arizona, where he had a shack in the desert. He never thanked me for getting him free and never paid me. I never saw him again.

The defendant had a small cabin on a parcel of land near a lake in Cook County, near Grand Marais. Because he did not have any funds to pay me, prior to the trial I had gotten a promissory note and mortgage on the property, to assure that my fee would be paid.

I had to foreclose on his land in the county. My fee in those days was most modest. I had agreed to defend him for six hundred dollars. His father wanted his son's local cabin, so he paid me off and I gave him a deed for the property.

The defendant had called his father, who lived in Grand Marais, from my house before I took him to Duluth. He told his father what the sheriff had done to him. The father trotted down to the local liquor store, called the Power House, and made the sheriff's actions the talk of the town. The news quickly spread throughout the county. The sheriff's conduct was generally considered atrocious. He was soundly defeated in the next election. After those experiences in trying criminal cases, I decided to limit my practice to civil matters.

We made every effort to improve the efficiency of our office. We watched for new technologies and tried to keep abreast of innovative developments that would allow for a more efficient practice. Our secretaries were very proficient in shorthand, but dictating directly to the secretary was time-consuming and not very efficient. However, that was the way most law offices operated. We found a dictating system that was just coming on the market. A small dictating machine was installed in each office connected to a transcribing unit on the secretary's desk. That way, the attorney could dictate at any time and the secretary could transcribe when she had time rather than have to coordinate a dictating session.

We had several other firsts in our law office that helped us prepare documents and gather evidence for cases. We were one of the first law offices in Minnesota to buy the IBM ball typewriter and the punch (magnetic) card typewriter. It was the forerunner of the computer. We bought the first law office computer in the state. It used the Valdocs software. It was very primitive, but permitted us to preserve information in a more usable form. It was in use before Microsoft Word and Word Perfect came on the scene.

During my career, I tried many civil cases. Many of those involved serious injuries and deaths from accidents. I always represented the injured persons. I considered all cases important, for they were all important regardless of the significance to my clients.

Another case of particular interest was one in which my client fell from a fifth floor in a hospital. He survived, but was seriously injured. He had been hospitalized after getting surgery for a medical condition that did not involve injuries from an accident. After the surgery, he developed a psychosis, suffered from weird hallucinations, and became quite violent. He was treated by a psychiatrist and other medical doctors. High doses of Haldol seemed to aggravate rather than alleviate his condition. He became violent and would leap out of bed regularly.

As his condition worsened, restraints were ordered by the doctors. One night, the nurses failed to place him in restraints. He leaped out bed and ran down the hallway with his intravenous tubes dangling from his body. The nurses belatedly gave chase, but he beat them to the doorway leading to a balcony, where he either jumped or fell off. His injuries were so serious and permanent that he would never be able to work again.

He had a previous condition wherein he could not read or write, but was well-spoken and intelligent. He had a good job with the State Highway Department and also had a garbage collection and hauling business.

We brought action against the hospital for the nurses' negligence, not only because of his injuries but also for his wife's loss of consortium. Loss of consortium denotes the inability of the spouse to provide the normal marital benefits, such as financial support and a sexual relationship. In addition to his physical injuries, my client had become impotent. He testified at trial that he and his wife had always had a very satisfying and enjoyable marital and sexual relationship, but now he "could do nothing."

A most interesting little surprise occurred at trial when the defense attorney was cross-examining the wife. He said to her, "It is true is it not that your husband has been impotent for years?" She was not sure what "impotent" meant. So, the attorney explained. "Your husband has not been able to have sex with you for years, long before his injury. His hospital record shows that?" She turned beet-red but blurted out, "No, that's not my John; he could do it all the time and was really good at it. We had it right before he went to the hospital." The defense attorney offered a medical record that showed the patient was impotent. The only problem was that his associate had gotten the wrong record. The record was one for my client's brother whose name was very similar. The brother was an alcoholic, a diabetic, and had many other medical problems. He had been in the hospital many times where the record showed he had complaints of impotency. These were the days before Viagra.

My client and his brother both had similar first names. Somehow the defense attorney's assistant got the wrong records. We had my client's medical records, which showed that he had never had any complaint of impotency. There was no question that the blushing wife's candid and obviously sincere comments impressed the jury.

Another piece of defense evidence that backfired and helped our case was the testimony from the defense employment expert. She testified that even if my client could no longer do manual labor or operate his garbage and hauling business, he could easily handle a sedentary job, such as an operator of elevators in office buildings. She stated he would not need to read or write or do anything physical to be an elevator operator.

During cross-examination, I asked her how many personnel-operated elevators there were in Duluth or surrounding cities. She did not know. Of course the jury knew all the elevators in the area were self-operated. There were none in the area that were operated by paid personnel. There were some personnel-operated elevators in Minneapolis about one hundred forty miles from Duluth. She had to admit that those were all being phased out, so there would be no employment opportunities at that location. The defense attorney was a very competent attorney, so it was surprising that he had made those kinds of trial mistakes.

Jurors remember the types of things that jump out at them. The jury returned a verdict awarding five hundred eighty-eight thousand for the husband and three hundred thousand for the wife's claim for loss of consortium. They obviously felt she had suffered a substantial loss because of her husband's injuries. Although the judge reduced the amount of the verdict, it was still a substantial recovery. We got our clients to agree that we set up an annuity for them from their share so that they would have a good, fixed income for life. We had learned from experience that when people get a lump-size settlement, regardless of size, it is usually gone within two years. If we negotiated a substantial settlement, or got a substantial money verdict, we always counseled our clients that we arrange for an annuity for them.

Another fascinating case was against a dentist. My client had gone in for a root canal. The dentist started drilling in an upper tooth when it should have been the same place on the bottom tooth. Every time his patient would scream with pain, the dentist would tell him, "You are just imaging it because I gave you Novocain, so it can't hurt." He kept drilling. The patient couldn't stand the pain and jumped out of the chair.

The dentist looked again at the X-ray and said, "Oops, I guess I read it upside down. I was drilling in one of your good teeth." He then told the patient to get back in the chair and said that he would do the root canal on the bad tooth. My client would have no part of it and went to another dentist. The good tooth was a total loss because of the drilling and the new dentist could find nothing wrong with the so-called bad tooth. It did not need a root canal. The first dentist refused to compensate my client for the new dentist's bill, and actually had the guts to send my client a bill of his own for the time spent in his office.

We brought an action against him not only for the second dentist's bill but for the loss of the tooth, and the pain and suffering. After about twenty minutes of deliberation, the jury brought in a substantial damage verdict against the negligent dentist.

There had been a report in the legal journals about a big malpractice case. Two men were in the same room. One was to have surgery for prostate and testicular cancer. The other man was to have surgery on his toe. The nurses mistakenly moved the toe man into the operating room where the cancer operation was to be held. The man was given the usual anesthetic that put him to sleep. The surgeon operated on the prostate and removed the patient's testicles, apparently, without first checking his chart. When the toe man woke up he saw that his toe was still inflamed and he had bandages in his groin, he panicked. He learned that his family jewels were missing. Needless to say, he was one unhappy man.

At the end of our dentist trial, the judge said he'd just read that story about the surgery where the wrong patient's testicles had been removed. He said that when he heard about drilling in the wrong tooth, his nuts started to hurt. Even in a sad case, a little humor can develop.

Another challenging case involved a propane gas explosion. The farmer had run out of gas in his farm home. The gas service people came to fill the tank. When the farmer tried to light the gas water heater, there was an explosion that blew the house into small pieces. Parts of the house scattered hundreds of feet away. The farmer had severe burns over a large part of his body.

The unit was equipped with a Robert Shaw control valve. We learned that there had been a number of cases involving defective Robert Shaw valves. Other lawyers had taken many depositions from company engineers and gas explosion experts. We were able to gather hundreds of depositions, so had a good handle on the case in a fairly short time. In every case, the Robert Shaw Company had battled the case and spent thousands of dollars on defense. They were frequently successful in using all kinds of delays to wear down claimants and settle for nominal amounts.

We knew this would be a tough case. Lawyers from a small town would be up against some of the top trial lawyers in the country for the defense. After we started the case in federal court, three of the top executives and their attorneys from Robert Shaw contacted us about a settlement. They flew in from New York and met us at our office. They seemed to be a bit surprised to see our well-equipped office and the large amount of material we had gathered.

Their first comments were that the Robert Shaw valve was not defective and any injuries were due purely to mishandling by the user. But, they said, "We feel sorry for this poor farmer and we are willing to pay some of his medical bills. We have no intention of making him rich." After our client's firm rejection of their nominal offer, they went back to New York.

Engineers determined that the valve was definitely defective. The design of a small slide that controlled the gas flow did not operate properly. It would often stick and allow gas to flow into the room when the unit was off. Company records showed that some of their own engineers had recommended a different design with a different metal. The company chose to not spend the extra money for the design and installation of the better part, even though the cost was quite nominal. However, the company was apparently concerned that a change in the product might be construed as an admission of liability, and that they would have to recall thousands of controls.

Congress had created an agency called the Consumer Products Safety Commission (CPSC) that was responsible for monitoring claims of defective products and ordering recall of those products it found to be defective.

When we started our case, we learned that there had been over seventy deaths and many injures from gas explosions from units equipped with the Robert Shaw valve. Robert Shaw's in-house counsel, their staff attorney, had reported only four deaths and injuries to the CPSC, and stated that all those were caused by customer misuse. With that type of report, the agency apparently decided it had no basis for investigation.

We decided to take the deposition of Mr. Reynolds, the president of Reynolds Metals that owned the Robert Shaw division. We also noted the deposition of Mr. Howell, the in-house attorney for Robert Shaw, and several of their engineers. Through their outside attorneys from a St. Paul law firm, they gave us notice that none of them would appear for a deposition.

The headquarters of their company was in Richmond, Virginia. Our case was filed in the United States District Court in St. Paul, with the Honorable Miles Lord as the presiding judge. The company advertised and sold its products in Minnesota. Virtually every water heater in Minnesota was equipped with a Robert Shaw valve. Since they did business in Minnesota, we could bring the action against them in Minnesota courts.

The defendants argued that Judge Lord did not have the jurisdiction in Virginia, and could not order them to appear for a deposition. We advised Judge Lord of Robert Shaw's executives' refusal to comply with the deposition notice. Judge Lord picked up the phone and called the defense attorneys. He told them in no uncertain terms that, as a federal judge, he had jurisdiction throughout the United States. I could not find any law to that point, but I had to believe the judge knew what he was talking about. He told the defense attorneys that he would hold all of those we had served with deposition notices, and their attorneys, in contempt of court if they did not appear.

Defense counsel apparently believed the judge, because the attorney called me the next day to say that the Robert Shaw people would appear for depositions any place we set them. We agreed to take their depositions in Richmond, Virginia; otherwise, under the rules of court, we would have to pay the witnesses' travel expenses. It was much cheaper for my partner, Pete Morris, and I to go to Richmond than to have them come to St. Paul. Besides, we thought we could enjoy some of the Richmond amenities in our spare time; if there was any spare time.

But, we ran into a problem immediately. Mr. Howell, the in-house counsel for Robert Shaw, kept telling the witnesses not to answer our questions. The St. Paul attorney who represented Robert Shaw sat there, not saying anything. He knew that he didn't want to deal with an irate judge. I called the judge and told him of our problem. He warned opposing counsel about what would happen if they did not comply with the rules for taking deposition.

Under the rules, we were allowed to ask any questions of the witness that might lead to relevant information, whether or not that information was admissible in court. It gives the inquiring attorney rather wide latitude for getting information that might be helpful for the case, and limiting the time at trial.

Judge Lord had told me that if we had any further problems to call him and that he would resolve them. We didn't ask him, but we made a sign by the phone in big letters that read: "The Honorable Miles Lord, Judge of the United States District

Court." Whenever a witness was a little evasive, we would just point to the phone. It usually brought immediate compliance.

"Major" Reynolds, President of Reynolds Metal Company and Robert Shaw Company, was an arrogant, pompous, blustery, little fat individual. All his staff called him "Major." Apparently, he had been in the military in WWII and had wrangled a majors' commission. I thought he was far from officer material.

He started out immediately in his deposition by saying that he was taking the Fifth Amendment and would not answer any of our questions. His attorneys took him in the other room and, I assume, explained to him that the protection of the Fifth Amendment applied only in criminal matters, and was not available as a defense in depositions for civil matters. They probably also explained to him that he did not want to test the judge's ire.

Reynolds was much subdued when he returned to the room. He testified that he didn't know anything about any deaths or injuries that may have resulted from Robert Shaw valves. He did not know that his engineers had recommended changes in the control. He did not know how many deaths or injuries his attorney had reported to the CPSC.

I asked him what he did as president of a world-wide company with a huge salary, when he didn't appear to have any knowledge of what his executives or employees did, and specifically what he did in running his company. He blustered and fumed, but didn't have an answer, except that the information was not the job of a president to know. He couldn't explain what the job of a president of a company entailed.

We had what we thought would be a disaster that night. We had all our documents needed for the deposition of Attorney Howell, and others, piled on the tables and beds in our room. Suddenly, at about eleven p.m., the fire alarm went off. We were on the seventh floor of the hotel. We packed everything as fast as we could in our briefcases and suitcases and carried them down the seven floors, since we knew to not use elevators in case of a fire. We just got to the ground floor when the all clear was announced. It was a false alarm.

We just got back to the room when the fire alarm rang again. This time, I called the front desk. They said that we must evacuate, as there was a fire. Again, we packed all our files and carried them down seven flights of stairs. There were dozens of fire trucks and fireman rushing about. There actually had been a small fire in the kitchen where a cook had spilled some grease. It caused a lot of smoke. The kitchen-help put out the fire with some rags. After getting all our files back up to the room, we decided "to the hell with any further preparation," and went to the bar for a much-needed libation.

The deposition of Robert Shaw Company's in-house attorney "Mr. Howell, Esquire," as he informed us he expected to be addressed, was scheduled for eight a.m. the next morning. He came sauntering in at about eight-thirty, just about the time we were going to call the judge to have him cited for contempt.

He was one arrogant ass. He let everyone know that he was a graduate of Harvard Law School. I let him know that I was a graduate of the University of Minnesota and Minneapolis College of Law, each of which taught lawyers ethical standards and how to comply with federal regulations.

He freely admitted that he had only reported four cases of injuries to the CPSC that might have been caused by controls that customers had abused. Although some of the company engineers had testified about the problems with the control, he was adamant that there were no defects in the control.

After we completed their depositions, we were certain the jurors would not give any credence to the two high-priced executives' testimonies, with their evasive answers and filing of false reports to a federal agency. We asked the court administrator to set the case for trial.

The Robert Shaw control was about four inches square and about two inches thick. The metal slide was about one-half inch wide and a little over two inches in length. It was very thin. We had our engineers make a scale model that was about three feet square, showing a cut out of the control valve. It would operate exactly like the original control. Using the large model would make it easy to demonstrate to the jury how the control would malfunction. The defense attorney objected strenuously to our use of the model. The judge set a hearing in which he closely inspected the model and saw how it operated. He overruled the defense attorney's objection and ruled that the model would be admissible for demonstrative purposes. Building the model had cost us several thousand dollars, so we were taking quite a risk if the judge wouldn't allow it. We did recover our investment by renting the model out to other attorneys who had similar cases against Robert Shaw.

The day before the case was to be tried; the judge called in the attorneys for both sides to see if we could reach a settlement. The big control model was sitting prominently on the exhibit table. The defense attorney kept trying not to look at it. He knew it would be very compelling evidence to the juror. It was a very effective negotiation tool. The judge even stepped down and ran it through an operation.

Some judges act as mediators in order to help settle a case. Judge Lord was very good at that. He had a real knack for determining the value of a case and what amount the jury would most likely award. First, he called my partner and me into his chambers and asked what amount my client would be willing to settle for. He, of course, had read all our memorandums and the medical reports outlining my client's injuries. He thought my demand was just a little too high, but said it was possible in a jury verdict.

The judge then called in the defense attorney in and asked him how much his client would be willing to pay in settlement. That offer was way low and would not be acceptable to my clients. I was not in the judge's chambers at the time, but he must have told defense counsel to get on the phone and get a reasonable offer from his client. The defense attorney came out with a very unhappy look on his face. He went down the hall to a public phone booth and spent some time there. The case was settled for an amount that was close to our client's demand. We set up an annuity for our client that paid all his medical bills and provided a very substantial income for the rest of his life. We would have liked to try the case, since it would have been a real challenge. But the outcome was very satisfactory for our clients and for us. We had taken the case on a contingent basis, and took a risk. If we were successful in settlement or trial, we would get an agreed-upon percentage. If we were not successful, we would get nothing and the loss would be all ours. As a result of the settlement, we were quite well compensated. Investigating and preparing the case for trial did take up a lot of our time over a period of several years. We had incurred substantial expenses that we would have had to bear if we couldn't settle or had lost the case at trial. Those are risks a trial attorney has to take.

Another case that merits mention involved a head-on collision between an ambulance and a semi-trailer truck. The driver of the truck lost control when he swerved and braked to miss a deer crossing the road. The jack-knifed truck was skidding at a ninety-degree angle, blocking the entire highway, when it collided with the oncoming ambulance. The driver of the ambulance and the passenger-patient were killed and the attendant in the back received serious injuries.

We had a ten foot-long scale map of the highway with over-lay skid marks prepared from the state trooper's investigation. We also had scale models of the ambulance and truck. Using this material, our reconstruction expert did a video re-creation of the accident. While watching the video, the jury was able to visualize the accident as if they were witnesses on the scene.

"Attorney Wayne Johnson demonstrating use of the highway exhibit"

We also did a "story of my life" by incorporating home movies showing the decedent's close relationship to his family, both at work and at play.

The defense attorneys objected strenuously to the use of the video re-creation as evidence. The judge viewed the video and agreed that it accurately portrayed the accident and that it would be helpful for the jury to understand how the accident happened. He ruled that we could use the video. It facilitated settlement, so it was not necessary to try the case.

To help make the settlement, we did something else quite unique. We did life stories of each of the decedents, with family photos to show the value of each person's life. Usually, attorneys trying to effect a settlement with insurance companies would prepare a brochure detailing the decedent's work record and earnings. We went several steps further by portraying the person's life and his family ties, in addition to his present and future earning capacity.

We then had the story bound in hardcover book format, which we presented to the insurance company claims department. In one package, they had a complete picture of the decedent, so they could determine how reasonable our settlement demand was. We usually had those settlement books bound in black hardcover, with gold lettering. They made impressive settlement brochures.

We had another case in which we used the same techniques. The case involved a head-on collision between a Minnesota State Highway snowplow and a passenger automobile. The driver of the car saw the wheels of the snowplow turn toward the center. He thought the plow was going to cross the road in front of him. He slammed on his brakes, but because of the snow-covered shoulder and icy road conditions, he skidded into the snowplow. The driver and his passenger were seriously injured. Again, we created scale models, of the highway with the car and snowplow. Our Reconstruction Expert animated the accident using the scale models, moving them at intervals on the scale drawing of the highway in the same path as the skid marks. Watching precisely how the accident happened was most compelling to jurors. That type of trial preparation led to a successful result.

Another earlier case that attracted a lot of local interest was a Breach of Promise case. Rosie had sued Cliff for Breach of Promise. She contended that she was a very virginal young lady and had given in to his amorous advancements on his promise to marry her. With her dyed, flame-red hair and excessive makeup, she could easily have played the part of a madam in a Nevada house of "entertainment." She did not look very virginal! The word spread throughout the small community that there was some titillating goings on at the courthouse. The courtroom became so filled with spectators that there was standing room only in the hallway.

I had taken her deposition in advance of trial, in which she testified that the defiling act had taken place on a boat on a lake in northern Minnesota. She said that the culprit had misled her into thinking it was an innocent fishing trip. She said that he had made sincere promises of marriage as he inveigled her into slipping off her panties as he violated her virginity.

During the trial, she testified that she was visiting friends on Thanksgiving Day when Cliff had coaxed her into "giving in to him" on the strength of his promise of marriage. During cross-examination, I reminded her that she had previously testified under oath that the act took place in a boat while out fishing on a lake well north of Cass Lake, in northern Minnesota. We had her read that deposition to the jury. The jury knew, as along with everyone else in the court room, that at that time of the year, all lakes in the area would be frozen solid. They could just picture these two in a boat on the ice. The judge, who frequently added a little humor to cases, leaned over and said, "Rosie, wasn't it a little cold out there in that boat on the ice?" The comment might not have been according to proper judicial conduct, but it was obvious that Rosie had no case. When the jury retired to deliberate, we could them laughing through the closed doors. It didn't take them long to decide that Rosie was not entitled to any compensation. Shortly thereafter, the Minnesota legislature passed a law that prohibited future Breach of Promise cases.

Some of those cases came to the attention of the American Trial Lawyers Association. The Association holds conventions with seminars each year to keep attorneys abreast of new developments in the law and new techniques for trial and settlement preparations. Several thousand attorneys from all over the country usually attend the conventions. I was invited to the Association convention in Kansas City to give a lecture and demonstrate the use of video showing how motor vehicle accidents happened. I don't know if they were so impressed or just needed another speaker, but the Association invited me to make a presentation at the Association convention in Boston the next year. At the Boston convention, in addition to the video demonstration, I discussed settlement techniques using family stories in hardbound books to fully demonstrate the full value of human life to insurance adjusters and claims departments.

One of the most well-known trial attorneys was Melvin Belli from San Francisco. When he saw my demonstration, he turned to one of his staff and said, "If a small town lawyer can dream up this type of innovative stuff, why the hell can't we?" It was a very nice compliment. He even bought me a drink later and spent some time going over my book. He asked if he could borrow it to show to his staff back at his office, which I agreed to. Sometime later on a trip to San Francisco, I visited his office. It was very impressive. This time he not only took me out for a drink, but also bought me lunch. I hope I can impress more guys like that.

I was not that successful in all my cases. I lost some cases in which I thought I had a slam-dunk guarantee of winning, and I won others I was initially speculative about. Every case presented a different challenge, and needed a different approach.

I did not like to handle domestic cases, like divorce or child custody. It seldom pleased anyone involved in the case. But in a small town, an attorney had to handle all types of cases. Later, we had a young attorney join our firm who loved to handle those types of cases, so I was relieved of that burden. However, there was usually something unique in each case that would stick in one's memory.

In my early practice, a lady came into my office with two black eyes and lots of bruises, and a babe in arms. She was the wife of a logger. They lived deep in the woods in a tar-paper shack. Many of the poorer loggers lived in tar-paper shacks that could be easily moved when the timber in an area was logged away. In response to my questioning, she stated that she got the injuries when her husband beat her up. She had borne twelve children in about that many years of marriage, with most of the kids a year or less apart. I asked if her husband had ever beaten her like that before. She said, "Yah, that old man pounded me up on our honeymoon and he has been pounding me up regular ever since." I asked, "If he beat you up all the time, why didn't you leave or report him to the sheriff?" She said, "Well, the kids kept coming, and I needed him to support us." I asked her why she kept having all those kids if he was treating her like that. Her answer, "They just kept coming." Then I made a mistake. I asked if she didn't know what made the kids keep coming. She replied, "Yah, fuckin." It was rather difficult for me to keep my professional demeanor after that knowing reply. In even the saddest case, some humor could pop up!

Although most aspects of practicing law take place in the office, I did enjoy trial work. Each case in the courtroom presented a different challenge.

I was fortunate when Gerald "Pete" Morris joined our firm. His work was very meticulous. He would review my briefs and writings for grammatical errors, sentence structure, and subject matter. He was an excellent legal researcher and supplied the necessary case law for trials, and was a very able assistant during trial or while preparing brochures for settlement.

After my partner Ron Thomas died, Tim Helgesen joined our firm. He was a well liked and a very competent attorney, but only stayed for a few years, when he decided to accept a position with the Minnesota Department of Human Services. Jeff Dobberpuhl, a very friendly and also very capable lawyer, was with us for over five years. His wife was offered a very good position in social services in Minneapolis, so he moved there with his family. Our last associate was Patrick Dinneen. He, too, was very competent. He only stayed about five years, and then he decided he wanted to be a sole practitioner. Pete and I decided not to have any more associates. Training an associate cost a considerable amount of money and time. If they left to seek what they believed to be greener pastures, their training was a financial loss for our firm.

I think being a fighter pilot was actually great training to be a successful trial lawyer. It was combat on a different level. Combat flying requires skill and concentration if one is to survive. You have to keep your fears under control and stay calm in the face of danger. Under stress, you have to make quick decisions.

There is, of course, no physical danger in the courtroom. Not much anyway. There have been occasions where attorneys and judges have been attacked by disgruntled clients or disturbed individuals. In trial, one has to stay calm and show confidence when things are not going your way. You have to anticipate the other side's tactics. You have to make quick decisions and change your own trial tactics to meet your opponent's challenge. In every tactic, every move, regardless how minute, you have to anticipate the impact on the judge and jury. Every strategy has to be tailored to make sure the other guy doesn't get the advantage. Trial work is interesting, but stressful and ever-challenging.

The military flying experiences were invaluable to my civilian flying. I spent over seventy years in the air as a pilot with few mishaps, although there were always close calls, particularly in combat. On one occasion, a friend, who had a Mooney airplane, was having trouble with his landing gear. The Mooney had wheels that were retracted manually by a spring loaded handle. He said that, at times, it took a great deal of force to pull the handle. I agreed to go with him to see if I could help with the problem. Because I did not think there would be any hazard, we took my sixteen year-old son along for the learning experience. As we took off, the pilot tried to retract the wheels. He used considerable force and the landing gear's handle broke off. The wheels were only partially retracted. We would have to make a wheels-up belly landing. Because there was no safety equipment at the Silver Bay airport, I called the Duluth airport which was fifty miles away about our problem and asked for permission to land there. Duluth had facilities to handle that type of emergency, and could spread a foam and grease-like fire resistant substance on the runway to make the plane slide better and also lower the risk of fire.

As we approached touchdown, I kept turning off the power to get the propeller parallel with the runway to avoid prop and engine damage. Fire trucks and ambulances were in ready position just off the runway. As we touched down, the plane skidded along on its belly. I had told my son, who was in the back seat, that the minute the plane slowed down, I would open the door and he was to get out and jump off the wing and run away from the plane. If the plane caught fire, I wanted him well away from it. He did as told and stood well away from the plane as it came to a stop. As I joined him, his first words were, "Dad, I'm hungry, when can we eat?" One of the firemen standing by commented, "That kid doesn't sound very scared." Bruce had to call some of his friends as soon as we got home to tell them about his "fun" experience. The pilot and I didn't consider it fun, but it was an interesting experience. There actually was very little damage to the plane.

Chapter -76-
Some More Flying Tigers Activities.

I had become very active in the Flying Tigers of the 14th Air Force Association. It was a veterans association for those who had served in the American Volunteer Group (AVG), the China Air Task Force, and the 14th Air Force in China, (Flying Tigers) under Gen. Claire Lee Chennault. Chennault was the only air force commander that served in one theater during the entire war. Since we were a small air force compared with the European theater, we developed an enviable camaraderie and esprit de corps.

To keep that fraternal spirit alive, we organized the Flying Tigers Association in 1948, and held an annual reunion every year thereafter until 2007, when we formally disbanded. In addition to our annual reunion, we held a memorial service each year from 1958, when Chennault died, until 2007 at Arlington National Cemetery in memory of General Chennault and other Flying Tigers who had died in the preceding year.

We had a convention in New Orleans in 1975. The most memorable event was that which we would like to forget — the disaster at a famous restaurant called Antoines. It was advertised as one of the finest French restaurants in New Orleans. They served us an inedible dinner on paper plates, with plastic forks and knives. It was like a bad picnic. The only things missing were the ants. Most everyone walked out. We did, however, enjoy some of the other famous eating and entertainment places in New Orleans. Antoines apparently had a bad chef on that occasion, for we tried their restaurant on another occasion and had excellent food and service.

New Orleans was the first convention for which I had taken the family. It was a fun time. One of the highlights for the kids was a cruise on a paddle wheel boat up the Mississippi. They really enjoyed riding on a small river craft though narrow rivers into the Acadian parishes. The Acadians in this area were descendants of French-Canadians who had been forced out of Quebec. They lived in this swampy area and made their living primarily from fishing. The kids enjoyed seeing alligators and other strange creatures they had never seen before. Most of the houses were on stilts. People would sit on their porches and wave at us as we floated by. We heard a lot of music and singing in the more populated areas.

The next year, Delores and I went to the Flying Tigers' convention in Tucson, Arizona. Immediately after that convention, we took a group trip to Taiwan, where we were royally entertained. We had fabulous dinners with top-ranking air force generals, as well as Chiang Ching-kuo, the President of the Republic of Taiwan. We still have many valuable gifts that we received on the first trip, and other trips. One very interesting side trip was to the island of Kinmen. The island was located just off the coast of mainland China. The communist military on the mainland were constantly trading shots with the Taiwan forces on Kinmen. They never seemed to hit anything on either side, or even want to.

Kinmen was an island fortress for Taiwan. They had built huge underground caves to secure island operations. The main cave was well-equipped as a military headquarters, and had all the amenities of a first-rate hotel.

We flew over to the island in one their passenger planes, escorted by a number of Taiwanese fighter planes. It was a very hot day, so the cave was a welcome and cool place for the visit.

At dinners, the Chinese traditionally toast the guests with little glasses of their potent wine as they salute with *gam bey* (bottoms-up). The commanding general of the military installation at Kinmen went around to each table and gave the toast. We, in turn, would toast him. Since there were usually eight of us at each table, he drank a lot. He would get more smiley at each table, but seemed to handle his liquor well.

When we went outside into the hot air, it hit him. He started to stagger around until some of his aides got on both sides to hold him up. He insisted on going to the plane to see us off. By that time, his feet were dragging as he was pulled along by his two muscular aides. He gave us a very happy send-off.

The 1977 convention was in Portland, Maine. One of the highlights there was a lobster feed on a nearby island. The lobsters were boiled in large vats, and cobs of corn boiled in other large kettles. It was a memorable feast, sitting on the rocky shore of the Atlantic.

I hosted a convention in Duluth in 1978. When I proposed Duluth as a convention site, the reaction of the Board was, "Where the hell is Duluth?" The members who attended soon found out. They were delighted by all the amenities that they could enjoy. We made a tour of the iron range, an area about fifty to seventy miles north of Duluth with a large number of iron ore mines, and for the first time at any convention, a parade was held for us.

The parade was sponsored by the city of Chisholm. It appeared that every man, woman, and child in the city was along the parade route. After the parade, they organized an ethnic dinner of exotic foods that many had never tasted before. I had invited the governor of Minnesota, Rudy Perpich, to attend the festivities. Since he was a native of the iron range, he readily accepted. It was the first time a governor had attended one of our conventions.

The Chisholm Free Press carried a story on July 27, 1978. It is worth repeating and worth remembering because it epitomized our philosophy.

JUST ONCE IN A WHILE, Once in a while, in these troubled times, we should pause for a few moments to read . . . to digest . . . and inhale deeply a part of America's history that strengthened its sinews to make men free.

Its all in the history books, written with authenticity, a flare for detail, an ingredient of greatness that far surpasses the muck and rot that fills the news today. They were daring that breed of another generation. They wore the Khaki, the Brown, the Navy and the Green with a pride that makes your heart swell and your eyes dim. They had grown up in a time of hardship, unemployment, deep Depression. But they never gave up, and when the call came, they took up the banner for freedom and carried the Stars and Stripes with sacred honor. No burning or shredding here, for they were proud to be Americans.

THIS WASN'T A TIME FOR CRYING: In the fox holes, from the battleships and the crippled planes came the clarion voices that ALL MEN SHOULD and MUST BE FREE. They're free to peruse the libraries of our vast nation. Try them for challenge and thought-provoking moments! "From Corregidor to Bataan"; "Days of the Ching Pao"; Dog Sugar Eight"; "D Day"; and "The Anzio Beachhead." THEY MAKE YOU REALIZE: Those books make you realize that our birthday is the Declaration of Independence. We are a fabulous country of many things and many people. We are the United States of America.

We are the William Penn and Paul Revere. We stood on the Lexington green and fired the shot heard round the world. We are Washington, Jefferson, Hale, Patrick Henry and Lincoln. Bunker Hill. Valley Forge, Yorktown, Iwo Jima, Corregidor and the Philippines are a part of our heritage. We are the John Paul Jones, Daniel Boone, Davy Crocket, the Doolittle Brigade and the **Flying Tigers.** *We are Generals Lee, Grant, Eisenhower, Patton, MacArthur and Chennault.*

We remember the Alamo, the Lusitania, Pearl Harbor and Iwo Jima. Whenever Freedom called, we answered that call. We left our heroic dead in Argonne Forest, Flanders Field, on the rock of Corregidor, the Burma Road, and on the cold, bleak slopes of Korea and the swamps of Viet Nam. We are the Golden Gate Bridge, the wheatlands of Kansas, the farmlands of Idaho and the fabulous forests of the Northwest. We are the Grand Canyon, a small village in the hills of New England, and the open pit iron ore mines of Minnesota.

Yes, we are the United States of America and these are the things that we are. May we always possess the integrity, the moral courage and the strength, and the spirit of the **Flying Tigers** *to keep us unshackled, to remain the stronghold of freedom, and a beacon of hope to all the oppressed throughout the world.*

It was written by Veda Ponikvar, the publisher of the Chisholm Free Press.

The next day, we made a trip to Silver Bay to enjoy a golf outing. We were escorted on the route by the Minnesota Highway Patrol, which was another first. Again, the group was most impressed by the challenge and the beauty of the Silver Bay golf course, and the hospitality of the Silver Bay residents.

Tours of the Duluth harbor and views of the iron ore carrying ships, as well as dinner aboard a cruise ship, were most impressive and enjoyable events. There was no question from then on about "where the hell Duluth" was. Some members were so impressed that they took two more private tours of the harbor.

Besides my family, my law practice, and flying, my role in the Flying Tigers of the 14th Air Force Association became my passion. I believed that it was imperative that veterans of the Great War preserve and perpetuate the history of events so present and future generations could learn and profit by their experiences. I became a member of the Board of Directors, and after I passed the bar, legal advisor to the association.

We took another trip to Asia later on. Bruce and Margaret went with us. We flew from Minneapolis to Chicago to Anchorage, Alaska, and then to Tokyo, where we stayed overnight, then on to Taipei, Taiwan. There, again, we were treated royally. Because I was the President of the Association, Delores and I were treated like high-ranking diplomats. We were given a beautiful suite in the newly remodeled Grand Hotel, one of the world's most beautiful hotels. I had made several trips to Taiwan that year in order to help plan the convention, and worked closely with my Chinese counterparts. Three Taiwanese former air force generals were on the planning committee. This time we visited more interesting places throughout the island.

One of the highlights of the trip was the dedication of the Flying Tigers Monument that I had designed. It was placed in a beautiful park, New Park, next to the Chennault statue. It was a hot day, well over one hundred degrees Fahrenheit. An honor guard of about one hundred Chinese Air Force members in shiny silver helmets stood rigidly at attention. Unfortunately, as so often happens when speakers get "diarrhea of the mouth," a Catholic priest who had been a military chaplain droned on for over half an hour.

Much like my experience with the long-winded guest at Atlanta, this guy would not stop talking. I handed him a note saying that he must limit his remarks, but he kept on until the commanding general stood up and glared at him.

The poor guards had sweat running off their noses. I suggested to the general that he allow the men to stand at ease or parade rest. He told me that it would not be appropriate. I said that some of them might faint. His reply was, "No, they are not permitted to do so." I didn't know what would happen to the poor guy who did faint. Judging by the stern face of the general, anyone that had that misfortune would probably face a firing squad.

That night, our hosts put on a lavish banquet. We were seated at a table with the vice president, the commanding general of the Air Force, and several other high-ranking cabinet members. Again, there were many *gam bey* toasts with their potent rice wine. We were presented with a number of beautiful gifts, including a delicate china cup from President Chiang Ching-kou.

We visited a number of historical and fascinating sights, including Taroka Gorge. Taroko Gorge was in a mountainous area and looked much like the Grand Canyon. The ride in the bus was breathtaking, not only for the scenic beauty, but also because it was roller coaster of a ride. The driver raced around hairpin turns with apparent reckless abandon. I was seated in the front seat next to the driver, and could look over the cliff at nothing but air for thousands of feet. As I looked back at the other passengers, there were many wide eyes and I'm sure a lot of prayers. The tour guide's only comment was a very quiet, "He good driver."

Besides the scenery, Taroko Gorge was famous for its marble deposits. The marble factory and adjacent store did a brisk business from the eager tourists. The next day, we departed for Hong Kong. At that time, Hong Kong was still in British hands. It was one of the most fascinating cities in the world.

Landing at Kiatek Airdrome was another adventure. I think the pilot had taken lessons from the Taroko bus driver. The airport was located very close to the downtown area. As we whizzed by tall buildings at window height, the pilot overshot the runway and had to come around for another pass. I think most passengers were praying, some quite loudly. When the wheels touched down, there were loud cheers from the passengers.

We were housed in a beautiful and most lavish hotel, and started several days of touring. We were treated to visits to Victoria Peak, which had a magnificent view of the city, then to Repulse Bay, Aberdeen, Tiger Balm Gardens, and the Yau Ma Tei Typhoon Shelter. Last but not least, we took the Star Ferry boat ride to the one of the world's most famous floating restaurants. And, of course, there was bargain-shopping of all kinds. The hand-tailored suits that would have cost four to five hundred dollars in the States were snapped up for as little as one hundred dollars.

A few of us elected to take a side trip to Canton. It was the only city in mainland China that we were allowed to visit at that time, under very close supervision by Chinese Communist authorities. They escorted us to a show-case farm, which they tried to convince us was typical of a farmer's life in China. We could just look out the train or bus windows and see farmers toiling in the fields behind oxen, and know what life was really like. Several of us managed to sneak a peek into some nearby one-room shacks with large families gathered around a little stove in the middle, much like we had seen in the country fifty years before.

Dan Mitchell, from my squadron, had been shot down while strafing the airdrome near Canton. He wanted to see the spot where he landed with his parachute and had escaped capture. He and I wrangled to get permission to rent a car and drive out to the airdrome, with a security guard in tow. Seeing the hill on which he had landed less than a mile from the then-Japanese occupied airdrome was an emotional experience. It was amazing that he had managed to escape, even with the help of some Chinese peasants.

We were allowed to walk short distances from our hotel. When we did, large crowds, with many curious little kids, would flock around us and want to hear us speak English. The tour was all too short, but we had to get back to Hong Kong to catch our plane to Bangkok.

Bangkok was another fascinating city, with the world's worst traffic jams. It was a real challenge to try to cross the street even with traffic signals, which few drivers seemed to obey. Because I was president of the Association, we were given the presidential suite at Bangkok's top hotel. A river tour was quite sobering, and we saw little children in rags sitting on outcroppings and small houses on stilts. The men and women, many in small boats and fishing in the muddy water, were equally as ragged. It was quite a contrast to the well-dressed people in the hotels and stores, and gold-plated shrines and temples of the cities.

From Bangkok, we flew to Singapore, another fabulous city. There we enjoyed a reception by Peter Fong. Fong had been a fighter pilot in the Chinese-American Composite Wing and was well known to many of us. He had become quite wealthy in the shipping and oil business. Unfortunately, I could only enjoy his hospitality for one day. I was called back to Taipei on an urgent matter by my Taiwan counterparts, who required my personal attention for an easily solved mix-up about some hotel reservations. I then flew back to Singapore to meet my family. They said that I had missed the most fabulous banquet of the entire trip.

Bruce didn't care that I hadn't been there because he had met a lovely young Singaporean girl who he had become quite interested in. She was the daughter of Weng T. Ho, an associate of Peter Fong, and former fighter pilot in the Flying Tigers. She wrote Bruce many perfumed love letters after we got home, but his interest apparently waned when separated by half the world. The perfumed letters aroused his mother's curiosity, but Bruce never revealed their contents.

Singapore was a superbly clean city. There was absolutely no trash on the streets. Gum-chewing was not permitted outdoors. Throwing a cigarette butt or any kind of waste on the street was a serious offense. Punishment was usually a whipping with a bamboo cane. It would be considered cruel and unusual punishment in the U.S. yet it was certainly effective.

We made three more trips sponsored by the Flying Tigers Association to Taiwan, in 1985, 1987 and 1990, all equally fabulous and hosted by the same generous people. On one trip, when we left Taiwan, we went to Japan and spent several days there. The Japanese appeared very friendly. Delores and I took one of their high-speed trains to Kyoto. It was a fascinating city that had not been damaged by WWII. We visited beautiful shrines and temples, and strolled through the streets without any concerns. We had been told it was a very safe city. We found a man who could speak very good English, and asked where we could find a good restaurant that served traditional Japanese cuisine. He escorted us through small alleys. We weren't sure about his hospitality until he led us upstairs to a little café and left us there. We were the only white people in the place, but the waiter, with a little English, made us feel comfortable. The menu was all in color, with photos of the various types of foods, so we had no trouble ordering. It was quite a unique experience and our presence was a curiosity to the local diners.

Besides the wonderful trips sponsored by the Association, there were some time-consuming activities that kept me rather busy. I was elected president of the Flying Tigers of the 14th Air Force Association in 1981, and served through 1983, and then became a permanent member of the board. When I was the executive vice president, I had persuaded the Board that we should do a history of the Flying Tigers. The board asked that I serve as editor. I became more than the typical editor and became the author of a good portions of the history books.

It took me about two years to collect photos and historical material for the book. Some others on my editorial board and I made a number of trips to Dallas to work with Taylor Publishing Company, which produced the book. I wrote in the preface to volume one of "Chennault's Flying Tigers - A Commemorative History of the American Volunteer Group, China Air Task Force, 14th Air Force 1941-1945," published in 1982:

The Association's purpose in publishing this book is to preserve a "Page in History" for future generations, and to pay tribute to those who participated in the events. It is not intended as a comprehensive history of America's role in the air war in China in WWII. We hope this small effort may serve as a useful source book for historians and students of history.

In some small measure it reflects the drama and excitement, the joys and sorrows, and the fear and courage of young men and women at war — far from home.

In the dedication portion, I wrote:

Meeting in a time of adversity, those who served with Lt/Gen. Chennault developed a most unique camaraderie and esprit de corps.

To preserve that unique bond, and to perpetuate our contribution to the cause of freedom — we dedicate this commemorative history.

We look back with nostalgia but more importantly we look back to learn from the lessons of history. We were touched by glory and are enriched by memories of the past. We are not reliving the past — but remembering that we were a vibrant force in history — our group exemplifies the tradition which instilled pride in ourselves and pride in country.

Liberty and Freedom were not easily won. They are not easily preserved. It takes dedication and belief in a cause — the conviction that all peoples have a right to live in peace and dignity. We cannot impose our way of life on others but we can be an inspiration to others. We must maintain our traditions as defender of human rights and the champion of the cause of freedom.

May remembered efforts to liberate the oppressed give hope to those threatened by the yoke of tyranny. The lessons of history must never be forgotten. If history teaches us anything, it is we must be strong, prepared and ever vigilant. Always the defender —never the aggressor.

For if we remember and learn the lessons of history, our Nation will maintain the world's respect; Our Flag the emblem of freedom of all peoples; and AMERICA the hallmark of Liberty and Justice.

I thought that it would be of great interest if I could get some high-ranking government officials to write a blurb for the book. I thought, "Why not go to the very top and try President Ronald Reagan?" I wrote the President a short letter with a very brief explanation of our proposed Flying Tigers history book. A week or so later, my secretary, Marge Johansen, came rushing into my office and said, "The President's on the line." I said, "How can that be? I'm the President of the Association." She said, "No, it's the President of the United States." I decided to answer just to find out who was pulling my leg. The voice said, "Please hold for the President." A new voice came on the line that I recognized immediately. It was President Ronald Reagan. I damn-near fell out of my chair. He said that he was very happy to hear I was doing a history of the Flying Tigers. He said it was important for the American public and future generations to know about the sacrifices made to protect their freedoms. He asked if I could send him a little more information concerning exactly what I wanted, so that he could write a proper statement. I sent him some more details. About two weeks later, I got President Ronald Reagan's response, with a photo that I could use for the book. He wrote:

To the men of the Flying Tigers of the 14th Air Force Association: Throughout the history of this great Nation, men of courage have set an example for others to follow. America's own triumph over tyranny was realized more than 200 years ago; many times since then, our people have been called upon to defend our ideals and institutions with our toil, blood and treasure.

World War II was perhaps our greatest challenge. Our destiny then, as it has been in all wars, was determined by the will of our people and the strength of our Armed Forces. We owe it to future generations to remember those who defended and preserved the gift of freedom.

Your efforts to record the lives and accomplishments of the men of the Flying Tigers will serve as a reminder of past sacrifices as we work to honor their commitment to America as the last, best hope on earth. [Signed] *Ronald Reagan*

Wow, that worked great. Why not get some high-ranking military? I contacted General Albert Wedemeyer, who had relieved Gen. Joseph Stilwell as China Theater Commander, and asked if he would write something for our book. I had given him an outline of the proposed book and what we wanted to accomplish with it. We wanted to preserve and perpetuate the illustrious history of the Flying Tigers and get his view as the area commander. I got his answer about a week later. He wrote the following:

TRIBUTE TO THE FLYING TIGERS: During the Second World War, a noble generation of young Americans, laying all else aside, went bravely and buoyantly off to their duty, as they understood it. It is my good fortune to be associated with that assemblage of men and women in the United States and in various battle areas of Europe and especially the Far East. It was reassuring to Generalissimo Chiang Kai-shek, the President of China, and to me, the China Theater Commander, that the 14th Air Force, under the intrepid and inspiring leadership of General Claire Chennault, was always ready, eager, and highly competent to meet any challenge. All ranks and commands of that valiant band of flyers compiled a distinguished record of which they can be justifiably proud — their exploits adding illustrious pages to the annals of American Military history.

I welcome this opportunity to salute you, comrades and friends of World War II days. I hail you as veteran survivors of that legendary organization which is heralded and respected throughout the United States and China. As I reminisce and relive those demanding days of yore, I am confident that you will do your outmost to preserve and pass on to your heirs and those some ideals, dedication, patriotic zeal, and gallant spirit which characterized your loyal service to our beloved country. [Signed] *A.C. Wedermeyer, General, U.S. Army. (Ret.) China Theater Commander.*

He also sent me his photo to be included with his tribute. I was on a roll. Why not get the top man at the Pentagon? I wrote to General Lew Allen, United States Air Force, Chief of Staff, and gave him some details about our book project. He answered very promptly, and included his photo. He wrote:

TO THE MEN AND WOMEN OF THE FLYING TIGERS OF THE 14TH AIR FORCE ASSOCIATION. More than 40 years ago, Americans first witnessed the daring exploits of the Flying Tigers. Even before Pearl Harbor, that exclusive group of volunteers was contributing to the defense of free peoples of the Far East. Following our entry into the war, they became the core of one of the most distinguished units in the Pacific Theater. The courage and dedication set by Claire Chennault and those who served with him continue to inspire guardians of liberty everywhere. The accounts of their actions will serve as examples for generations of airmen to come.

[Signed] *Lew Allen, General, United States Air Force, Chief of Staff.)*

I used the letters just as each had written with each of their pictures in the very first part of the book.

One of the more interesting men I interviewed for the book was General Jimmy Doolittle, who had led the famous raid on Tokyo in the early days of the war and was one of America's outstanding aviators. I had written him requesting an interview. His secretary called with permission to come visit him in his home in Carmel, California. When I asked if I could take his picture, he graciously assented. Unfortunately, the battery on my camera was dead. He asked his secretary to get his camera. The battery on that was also dead. He then asked his secretary to go downtown and buy one of those ready-to-shoot cameras. He insisted that I join him for the photo.

Wayne Johnson, Gen. Jimmy Doolittle -1981

Although I had read everything I could about the famous Doolittle Raid on Tokyo, I asked if he might give me some personal views. He went into considerable detail about the meetings with Roosevelt, General Arnold, and General Marshal about the planning of the raid. He also told of the training for the men who had volunteered for a mystery mission. All they were told was that a mission was being planned in which B-25s would fly off an aircraft carrier. They would have to learn to make short takeoffs on a field the length of a carrier deck. "I told the men that this would be a very hazardous mission, and none of us might come back, so if any of you don't want to get involved, step forward now and it won't be held against you. Nobody stepped forward. I knew I had a dedicated crew."

He said, "Everyone was sworn to secrecy." They could not tell anyone, including their wives, family, or sweethearts about what they were training for. The low point in his life, he said, was after he bailed out in China, when he learned that every plane was lost and that most of the crews had to bail out. Some were killed and some captured by the Japanese. He said that he was sure he would face a court-martial and be thrown out of the air corps in disgrace, or sent to prison. "Can you imagine my surprise when I was informed that I was being promoted to Brigadier General and awarded the Medal of Honor?"

He also told me about giving Chennault his general's stars that Doolittle had just received. Col. Clayton Bissell, the commander of the 10th Air Force in India, had been promoted to brigadier general one day ahead of Chennault. He came to China and presented Doolittle with his general's stars. Because Col. Bissell was promoted to brigadier general one day before Chennault, it made him a superior officer. Chennault's promotion to brigadier general was on the same order as Doolittle's. Doolittle said that when he met Chennault later, he noticed Chennault still had his colonel's insignia on his collar. Chennault said that there were no general's stars in China. "I took off my own stars that Bissell had given to me and pinned them on 'Claire's' collar." Claire was Col. Claire Lee Chennault. "I didn't tell Claire that I had gotten my stars from Bissell, I knew Claire had a very low opinion of Bissell, and probably rightly so." Doolittle said that he was very upset when he learned that Chennault had never been informed of his mission. "If Chennault had known about it, he could have brought my planes to safe landings." Bissell had been told about the Doolittle mission but he "failed" to tell Chennault.

I had agreed to an hour-long meeting with Gen. Doolittle. I ended up being there for over four hours. It was by far the most interesting experience I had while producing the Flying Tigers' books. I made sure that the photo of me with Doolittle appeared in the book. I sent him a complimentary copy of the book. He wrote me a nice letter expressing his appreciation. He also gave me a copy of his biography: "Doolittle A Biography" written by Lowell Thomas and Edward Jablonski. He autographed it, "To Wayne Johnson With Sincere Best Wishes. J. H. Doolittle." It is a book I most treasure. Later that year he sent me a Christmas card signed "Jim Doolittle." That is one Christmas card I have kept.

I did three more "Chennault's Flying Tigers" books over the next fifteen years. The final three books were published by Turner Publishing Company of Paducah, Kentucky, which meant many trips to Paducah. Volume four was produced in 1995, so we had a four-volume history of "Chennault's Flying Tigers." Volume two was primarily a pictorial history, with emphasis on the American Volunteer Group (AVG), the first air unit that earned the sobriquet "the Flying Tigers." For some time, the Japanese Air Force had been bombing Chinese cities at will. They had destroyed the Chinese Air Force, so there was no opposition to their bombing raids.

But when the AVG arrived in Kunming, China, with their brightly-colored P-40s with the shark's mouth illustrations on the sides, the scene changed. On 20 December 1941, the Japanese sent a fleet of ten bombers to attack Kunming. A flight of American P-40s rose to meet them. They shot down most of the Japanese bombers. When a Chinese reporter saw the American pilots shooting the hated Japanese raiders out of the sky, he wrote that the American pilots were like "fei hu," translated as "flying tigers." In Chinese lore, the tiger is an animal of great ferocity and courage. The reporter attributed these qualities to the American fighter pilots. Spencer Moos, a reporter for the New York Times, picked up the story and from then, the Flying Tigers became legend. After the disaster at Pearl Harbor, the AVG was, at that time, the only effective fighter force in the Pacific theater.

In my fourth book of "Chennault's Flying Tigers," our fiftieth anniversary edition, published in 1995, I wrote in the dedication:

V.J. DAY - September 2, 1945. Fifty years ago, World War II, the greatest conflagration the world has ever known, came to an end. At the surrender ceremonies aboard the Battleship Missouri, Pacific Theater Supreme Allied Commander, General Douglas MacArthur said: "Today the guns are silent. A great tragedy has ended. . . . It is my earnest hope, and indeed the hope of all mankind, that from this solemn occasion a better world will emerge out of the blood and carnage of the past — a world dedicated to the dignity of man and fulfillment of his most cherished wish for freedom, tolerance and justice."

These hopes have not been realized for tyrants still deprive peoples of their freedom and wars abound. The human race has not learned from the lessons of history.

We have attempted to gather here a bit of history that the world will remember the cost of freedom. It is not the intent to glorify war, nor live in the past, but to remember the heroism, dedication to duty and the sacrifices of those who fought to liberate the oppressed.

We hope and pray that intolerance and oppression will disappear and that peace will prevail among all nations. This volume is dedicated to that goal and to those who made the supreme sacrifice in the cause of freedom and to honor those who served their country.S/ Wayne G. Johnson, Editor. September 2, 1995.

Dave Turner, President of Turner Publications, that produced the books, wrote:

Looking back over the scope of United States History, one can see many honored and respected individuals and groups. But among these people, one group holds a special place in history: Chennault's Flying Tigers of the 14th Air Force.

Throughout our existence as a nation, we have never been afraid to take risks necessary to guarantee the freedoms and principles for which we stand. Members of the Flying Tigers exemplify these ideals, as they took to the skies to defend China from the Japanese Air Force. First as the American Volunteer Group, and finally the 14th Air Force, their dedication never failed, their vigilance never waned.

We thank the Flying Tigers of the 14th Air Force past president Wayne Johnson for his dedication to the completion of this project; his historical materials and willingness to help scrutinize the manuscripts helped to insure the accuracy and relevance of this book for years to come. I have had the privilege and honor to work with Mr. Johnson on two previous Flying Tiger book projects. It has been my pleasure to work with such a fine gentlemen and historian as Mr. Johnson.

S/Dave Turner, President.

I wanted to get the input of a Chinese officer who had served in WWII. I knew Huang Hsien-yung, who had been a major in the Chinese-American Composite Wing in WWII. He was now General Huang Hsien-yung, Commander-in-Chief of the Republic of China (Taiwan) Air Force. I wrote to him about our Flying Tigers book and asked if he would be willing to make some comments that I could use.

As his tribute to the Flying Tigers, he wrote, in part:

To the Chinese, the Eight year of the War of Resistance against Japan is not only a Holy War, but was a glorious and tragic epic event. . . . The American-Chinese cooperation to fight against Japanese aggression is, without a doubt, worthy to be praised and a memorable event in WWII. With a small number of personnel, aircraft, equipment and scarcity of logistic supplies, the Flying Tigers, nonetheless, complied an outstanding record of downing Japanese airplanes and steadily gained air superiority in the Chinese theater. In addition the 14th AF was remarkably successful in drawing Japanese ground forces and provide Chinese armies with invaluable close air support, which contributed to far-reaching inspirations on the morale of the Chinese people.

In memory of the meritorious achievements established by the early martyrs, together with those Chinese and American pilots who served in the holy war, we commend the 14th AF Ass'n. For publishing this historic book. While we celebrate the 50th victory anniversary, this is a work that all members can be justifiable proud. In remembrance of the War, our friends coming from afar against Japanese aggression surely attests to the old saying 'misfortune tests the sincerity of friends'. May we always remain friends. [Signed] *Huang Hsien-yung*

Because the history books were so well received, I recommended to the Flying Tigers Association Board that we should put out a calendar showing aircraft we used in China during the war and other historical events. I believed the inclusion of daily historical events would be an attraction not only to our members, but to historians and students of history. The Board agreed that it would be an interesting project. Since it was my "brilliant" idea, I was elected to handle the project.

I contacted Turner Publishing Company, the world's largest publisher of historic material and the producer of our history books, to see if they could produce the calendar. I furnished all the photos for the facing pages and the historical material for the daily pages. The material consisted of mission reports, individual victory records, and interesting personal experiences. The calendars sold very well and more than covered the cost of production. The profits help fund our Flying Tigers exhibit at the Museum of Aviation at the Warner Robbins Air Base in Georgia.

The books and calendars were a labor of love. The long-time secretary of our Association, Duayne R. Huston, once commented that my participation with and contributions to the Association were not only passions, but compulsions. When he received volume one of "Chennault's Flying Tigers," he wrote: *The 14th Air Force History Book arrived a couple of days before Christmas. What a beautiful work of art. Every spare moment I get, I have the book in my hands. You should be proud of this great accomplishment and contribution you have made to the 14th Air Force As-*

sociation and to the history of the United States Air Force. Many Thanks. [Signed] *Duayne Huston*

Milt Miller, the editor of the Flying Tigers of the 14th Air Force Association bimonthly newsletter, the Jing Bao Journal, wrote of my various activities and contributions, he wrote:

WAYNE G. JOHNSON

Contributions to the Flying Tigers - 14th Air Force Association

Official Positions:

President   Executive Vice President

Vice President - Duluth Convention

Board Member - 1976 to 2007. Legal Advisor to the Association for over 60 years, without charge. Editor - Four Volume History of "Chennault's Flying Tigers." Wrote many of the Articles and designed the covers and many of the inserts. Secretary - Dayton Memorial Committee. Secretary - Museum of Aviation Committee, Warner Robbins Air Base Georgia. Chairman - Nominating Committee.

Chairman - Convention Committee

Chairman - Air Force Fifty Anniversary Committee. Chairman - Taiwan Tours.

Chairman - Chennault Stamp Committee. He designed the Programs and First Day Covers (envelopes with the first day of issue of the Chennault Stamp) and attended the U. S. Postal Service First Day of Issue ceremonies at Monroe, Louisiana; New Orleans, Louisiana and Dayton, Ohio. He handled the sales of First Day covers with a substantial profit to the Association. Made a number of trips to Washington, D.C. to meet with Postal Officials to urge issuance of a Chennault Stamp. Contacted all State Governors, every U.S. Senator and all members of Congress, either in person, by letter or phone, to support issuance of a Chennault Stamp.

Designs and Art Work: Designed the Association Membership card and Pin. Designed the Following Plaques for the United States Air Force Academy, Colorado Springs, Memorial Wall: 14th Air Force Plaque. 23rd Fighter Group Plaque. 118th Tactical Reconnaissance Black Lightning Squadron Plaque.

Designed the 14th Air Force Association commemorative Plaque for the Tomb of the Unknown at Arlington National Cemetery. Designed the Dedication Plaque for the Dayton, Ohio, Flying Tigers Memorial Monument as well as the inscriptions and designs for the logos and planes. Designed the Dayton Memorial Pin. Designed the Taiwan Memorial Pin. Designed the Ceramic Cruses for the 40th Anniversary Celebration of the end of WWII, in Taiwan. Designed the Flying Tigers - 14th Air Force Memorial Monument placed in New Park, Taipei, Taiwan, and attended the dedication ceremony as Chairman of the American delegation. Designed the Flying Tigers watches. Designed the Empty Cockpit certificate for the Arlington Cemetery Memorial Services. Drafted the inscriptions for the gifts to President Chiang Ching-kuo and other dignitaries for the 1985 Taiwan tour.

Prepared the eulogies for Tom Corcoran, General Charles Stone, Malcolm Rosholt, Duayne Huston, George Hightower and many other officials.

Helped in the designs and prepared inscriptions for the Flying Tigers Exhibits at the Museum of Aviation in Warner Robbins Air Base, Georgia, with numerous trips to Georgia to help prepare the Exhibits. Prepared the Flying Tigers History brochures. Arranged for reproduction of the Chennault Medallion.

Designer and author of the "Chennault's Flying Tigers" Calendars and handled the sales.

Prepared and delivered the "Salute to the P-40" for the dedication ceremonies of the Flying Tigers exhibit at the Museum of Aviation.

Other Activities:

As Attorney for the Association collected substantial sums of disputed estates for the benefit of the Association, without charge. One recovery alone was over $30,000.00.

Collected and had bound (over twenty volumes) all issues of the Jing Boa Journal. And

placed copies of the bound volumes at the National Air & Space Museum in Washington, D.C.; the United States Air Force Academy at Colorado Springs; the Museum of Aviation at Warner Robbins Air Base, Georgia; and Planes of Fame Museum at Palm Springs, California. He has also collected and had bound (over twenty

Volumes) of the Ex-CBI Roundup. Donated large amounts of artifacts and memorabilia,

Including his original leather Flight Jacket, to the Museum of Aviation.

Written numerous articles for military and aviation magazines and lectures widely on the role of the Flying Tigers in WWII. (And many other activities too numerous to mention.) AND HE NEVER ASKED FOR NOR EXPECTED ANY CREDIT OR THANKS. This is my way, on behalf of the Association, of Thanking Wayne Johnson. Call this bragging or an inflated ego, if you like . . . but these are all FACTS.

[Signed] Milt Miller

Milt had posted this on a bulletin board at one of our conventions. He told me that he intended to run it in the next issue of the Jing Bao Journal, which was our Association's bimonthly newsletter. I begged him not to, because I felt it might be misconstrued, and, although factual, could be interpreted as my bragging. Milt was not the kind of fellow who could be told about what he could write in his newsletter. He reluctantly agreed not to publish it but said that he intended to send it to all members of the board and selected members of the Association. It was a wonderful tribute.

While producing the books and calendars, I felt it important to record as much history as possible, looking at it from the view of those who participated in the events. We learn from the lessons of history. What we learn from experiences of the past guide us in the future.

One of my activities became a compulsion. I wanted to bring my friend Jim McGovern's (Earthquake McGoon) body back from Vietnam. After the end of WWII, Earthquake went back to China to fly for Chennault's airline. When hostilities ended, Chennault had started an airline called Civil Air Transport (CAT), the purpose of which was primarily to supply Chiang Kai-shek's Nationalist Army troops who were fighting Chairman Mao Tse-tung's Communists. By that time, the Chairman's troops were overrunning China. McGovern, or "McGoon" as he liked to be called, became a legend and volunteered for the most hazardous missions. I had written an article about Earthquake McGoon that appeared in volume one of "Chennault's Flying Tigers." It read in part: *The communists shot down McGoon's cargo plane near Kunming and held him for five months.* [McGoon loved to eat and by this time weighed well over two hundred fifty pounds.] *When the communists released him, he refused to walk and convinced his captors to provide litter bearers to carry him out. They had to carry this behemoth half way across China from Kunming in the far west to Nanning* [in the southeast near Hong Kong.]

Earthquake McGoon made his last flight on 6 May, 1954. Chennault's CAT Airline had been commissioned by the CIA to transport supplies to the beleaguered French garrison at Dien Bien Phu. McGoon had volunteered to fly one of the huge cargo planes, the C-119. He had flown forty-five missions to Dien Bien Phu. This would be his last. Each mission got tougher as Ho Chi Minh's troops drew a tighter circle around the French holdout. McGoon's big C-119 had to let down to below 1500 feet to make accurate drops within the small fortress. The big birds were sitting ducks. McGoon's plane took a direct hit from the communist gunners in one engine and another in the rudder. He had no control. Another pilot in the area heard the calm voice of Earthquake McGoon over the radio "it looks like this it son" . . . his last words as his plane cart wheeled down the mountainside and exploded. The final irony — the French surrendered Indo-China to the Viet Minh the next day. Earthquake McGoon and his co-pilot were the first American casualties of the Vietnam War.

Natives in the area had buried Earthquake, his co-pilot, and several crew members, and had informed CAT Airline authorities of the location of their graves. Earthquake's family wanted his remains brought back home, as did many of his friends who had flown with him in the Flying Tigers and CAT Airlines. Felix Smith, who had flown with Chennault, had made some contacts with government agencies, and gave me some information about where to start. I contacted CAT to see if they could arrange to bring his body back. By this time, the Vietnam war was in full force and it was not until after the end of the war that Americans were allowed in to search for soldiers who were missing and killed in action. I wrote many letters and made many calls to the CIA, the graves registration commission, and other governmental agencies to bring James McGovern's body back. It took almost fifty years of pushing and pleading with government bureaucrats to get any action. The Duluth News Tribune carried a front-page story about my efforts to bring Earthquake home. Finally, his remains were taken to Hawaii for identification, which was positive. We in the Flying Tigers organization, and his fellow pilots, felt that Earthquake should be interred at Arlington National Cemetery.

With the help of Senator Ted Stevens and Gary McKinnon, one of Earthquake's cousins, we finally got permission from the cemetery superintendent for an Arlington interment. It helped that Ted Stevens was a fellow Flying Tiger who had flown cargo planes during the war in China. It also helped that I had developed a friendship with the cemetery superintendent. I had known the superintendent for many years, as he always helped make special arrangements and would attend the Flying Tigers' memorial services held at the cemetery each year since 1958, after Gen. Chennault's death. I met with him a number of times to make the necessary arrangements for the funeral. In 2007, we had a full military funeral for Jim "Earthquake" McGoon Govern, with a horse drawn caisson, a large air force marching unit and military band, and many hundreds of Earthquake's fellow airmen, relatives, and friends in the procession. It was a fitting tribute to a great pilot and a dedicated patriot who made the supreme sacrifice for the cause of freedom. It was a very emotional moment.

Although my participation in Flying Tigers Association activities took a great deal of my leisure time, I was actively engaged in my law practice, my duties as city attorney for two cities, and the Reserve Mining environmental case up until mid-1986.

The Reserve case in particular imposed a heavy burden on my wife, Delores, who took care of the children during my many absences from home. There was sufficient time between trial schedules for us to take a number of trips, flying to various places in my Cessna 182. Most of our vacations were usually three or four day affairs, during Flying Tigers Conventions. Because our conventions were held in a different city each year, we flew to many parts of the country.

We had a convention in Reno, Nevada, in 1980. After the Reno convention, we flew up to Salem, Oregon, to visit Jim Lovrien, my former law partner, and his family. When we were ready to leave Tucson, I found that the battery on my plane was dead, so I could not start it with the battery. Because it was Sunday, there were no facilities open that could charge the battery.

It is possible to start smaller airplanes by hand propping. To prop an airplane, one swings the propeller by hand. As you pull the propeller through a rotation, you quickly step back out of range of the spinning propeller as the engine starts.

In the early days of aviation, small planes did not have batteries, so the only way to start a plane was to spin the propeller by hand. The first plane that I learned to fly in, the Curtiss Robin, had to be hand propped, so I did have some experience in that regard. It was not very difficult with planes that had low horsepower engines. The bigger the engine, the more difficult it was to hand prop. The Cessna 182 had a two hundred thirty-five horsepower engine. It took a lot of strength to hand prop it. But I did get it started while Delores held the brakes. She didn't think much of the idea. Her feet were shaking so bad that she had trouble holding them on the brakes.

We arrived in Oregon the day after Mt. Helena erupted. Smoke and ash were still billowing out of the top. For miles around, the terrain was covered with a fine talcum powder like sand.

After visiting with the Lovriens, we flew to Vancouver and then across Canada, with stops at Abbotsford, B.C., to attend a Lawyer-Pilots Association meeting. From there, we flew to Chilliwack, Lethbridge, Regina, Winnipeg, and back to Silver Bay. It was a long but exciting and interesting trip.

In addition to flying to Flying Tigers convention, we often flew to Lawyer-Pilots annual meetings. They would usually be held at interesting resorts. I knew a number of attorneys who were pilots and had airplanes. Some of us got together and discussed the need for an association, where we could not only have fun flying and socializing, but also a forum in which to discuss aviation law. I helped organize the Lawyer-Pilot's Association and became a charter member. The conventions were very family-oriented. Many came with their children, which we frequently did.

After our Flying Tigers convention in San Antonio, I had a once-in-a-lifetime flying experience. That most exciting flight was a flight in the space shuttle simulator on 18 May 1988. My good friend, Dan Mitchell, who was in my squadron in China, was a very close friend of the manager of the Houston NASA (National Air & Space Agency) station. He arranged for me to be checked out in the space shuttle simulator. It was the unit that trained all NASA pilots until they went into orbit. My log book reads:

DATE; 5/18/88; AIRCRAFT MAKE AND MODEL: Space Shuttle; AIRCRAFT IDENT: OV-104 Sim. FROM: KSC; TO: Earth Orbit and Return: REMARKS, PROCEDURES AND MANEUVERS: One very successful Ascent, Orbit of Earth, One manual landing at Cape Canaveral:

Brian Duffy, Col. USAF: Certified by D. Mitchell, Shuttle Check Pilot.

Delores and a number of other friends were in the NASA control room, watching my flight on the control room screen. They could see my takeoff and flight circling high above the earth, and the landing at Cape Canaveral. They said that the Earth looked about the size of a basketball as I circled around.

My landing at the Cape was particularly interesting. I started the approach at eighty thousand feet. I had to zigzag to slow down enough to lower the flaps. (air brakes) The runway appeared on the screen in the cockpit. It was necessary to keep the instrument course indication needle exactly in the center, and the descent indicator right on the bar.

As we flaired for the landing, I had to use considerable force in order to bring the nose up high, so the main gear would touch the runway first. The flight instructor, Col. Brian Duffy, commented, "I could tell you were a fighter pilot, you really greased it in." What a thrill. The buttons popped right off the front of my shirt!

But the shuttle experience brought back some memories. I vividly recall being glued to the television as the first space shuttle landed on the moon on 20 July 1969. Could I have been on that most exciting mission?

I was interviewed while flying for the North Dakota Air National Guard to see if I could join the space program, but we had no concept of what the space program meant. No one we knew had ever heard of it. We were only told that we would be trained to participate in a new adventure to explore space, and that it might mean many years of highly intensive training.

It was not until the late 1950s that the public learned of space exploration. Russia started the "space age" with the launch of *Sputnik*, a space module that orbited the Earth. Then, in 1961, Russia actually sent a man into space. Yuri Gagarin, made a full orbit of earth. It challenged America. We could not let the Russians beat us. NASA sent Alan Shepard for a suborbital ride around earth to the edge of space.

It was in May of 1961 when President John Kennedy told Congress that he wanted to appropriate funds for a bold commitment to land a man on the moon before the Soviets. Unfortunately, President Kennedy did not live to see his wish to put a man on the moon come to fruition. He was assassinated in 1963, long before the space program would develop a realistic lunar project. We had an interesting experience with President Kennedy. He was in Duluth, Minnesota, on a campaign for re-election. A large crowd had gathered at the airport to welcome him. I was near the front line with my little son Bruce who was then about four years old. As Kennedy came down the fence line shaking hands, Bruce shouted out "Hi John F. Kennedy." Kennedy, with a big smile, reached for Bruce's hand. Just then, someone pushed in front and Kennedy missed Bruce's handshake.

It was not until 1969 that NASA was ready for the great space adventure, and carried out Kennedy's plan. It was a year of national discontent and turmoil. War protestors to the Vietnam War were marching in the streets, burning the American flag.

America needed something that would lift it out of the depressive climate and again assure the world that its flag was a symbol of world peace. America had to win the space race and beat the Russians to the moon. The world was getting smaller, and the moon was getting closer within our reach, metaphorically speaking. The "man in the moon" had to be an American.

Along with millions of other Americans, I watched on television as the *Saturn* rocket blasted off from Cape Canaveral, Florida, carrying *Apollo 11*, the *Columbia* spacecraft with the lunar module, and *Eagle*, that was to put Neil Armstrong and Buzz Aldrin on the moon. Eight days later, on 20 July 1969, the *Eagle* sat down in cloud of dust on the moon. The *Eagle* was a strange looking craft. Some wag said it looked like a gold-foiled cement mixer.

As Neil Armstrong descended from the *Eagle*'s ladder and got one foot on the moon surface, he said for the world to hear, "That's one step for man . . . one giant leap for mankind." The simple wording on the plaque the astronauts left on the moon carried an impressive message: "Here men from the planet earth first set foot on the moon. We came in peace for all mankind."

Along with many other people around the world, I sat transfixed as we watched these two astronauts walk on the moon. How many of us had often sat outside on a moonlight night and watched the face of "the man on the moon?" As I watched, I wondered, "Could that have been me?" Had I accepted the offer, while flying for the North Dakota Air National Guard in Fargo, to join the fledgling space program, could I have been one of those to first land on the moon? Or would I have suffered a fiery death, like the astronauts Chafee, Grissom, and White, of Apollo 1. Probably not, since the moon venture was twenty years after the Guard interview. It was interesting to speculate about what might have been, but I believe making my career in the field of law was the right choice for me.

After that thrilling flight into space in the space shuttle simulator, it was quite a change to get back in my 182 and fly home.

One of my passions in the Flying Tigers was promoting the issuance of a Postal Service stamp in honor of General Chennault. Several of our members had worked very hard trying to convince the Postal Service to issue a Chennault stamp, without success. I wrote to every member of Congress and all the governors for support. I made a number of trips to Washington, D.C. to meet with Postal officials.

At a function at the Air Force Academy in Colorado Springs, I met with Senator Barry Goldwater. When he learned of my efforts to promote a Chennault stamp, he said that he would personally help. He was an admirer of General Chennault. In WWII, he had served in the Air Transport Command, flying supplies from India over the Hump to China. Goldwater apparently had a lot of clout with the Postal Service, for I was informed shortly thereafter that the Postal Service would issue a Chennault stamp in 1990, on the one hundredth anniversary of Chennault's birth. Although many military records showed Claire Chennault's year of birth as 1900, his birth certificate correctly shows the year of birth as 1903. His son Max Chennault told me that his dad had purposely predated his year of birth so that he would not be younger than his wife, Nell.

The dedication ceremony for the Chennault stamp was held at Monroe, Louisiana. I flew down in a 182. My plane was in the mechanic's shop for its annual inspection. My friend, Jerry Kelly, allowed me to take his 182. What a wonderful gesture by a great friend. Anna Chennault, widow of General Chennault, with many other dignitaries, was in attendance. At the dedication of a new stamp, interested parties prepare First Day Covers. First Day Covers are specially designed envelopes with the new stamp. The envelope was cancelled by the Monroe post office with a "first day of issue" notation. There are many stamp collectors that specialize in collecting First Day Covers. I had designed several versions of the Chennault first day cover that sold very well.

I contacted Ambassador Konsin Shah, former air attaché to the United States from Taiwan and a Flying Tiger member, to see if Taiwan would issue a Chennault stamp to coordinate with the U.S. issue. Shah agreed and was successful. Taiwan issued a Chennault Stamp a few days after our issue. One of the first day covers that I had designed had the Chinese Chennault Stamp as well as the U.S.-issued Chennault stamp. The unique cover was of particular interest to collectors.

I flew around the country a lot, not only on legal matters that I handled, but also for Flying Tiger and Lawyer-Pilots functions. I put my plane on retractable skis in the winter, which made it much more useful. It was great for northern Minnesota flying.

I had retractable skis for my 172 and later put them on the 182. The skis were designed so that the wheels sat on a retractable plate, using a hand-actuated hydraulic pump. I could take off at the airport on wheels and fly to a frozen lake and land on skis. It was great fun in the winter for ice fishing. Also, I could fly down to my folks' farm and land on snow-covered fields.

One time, me and a friend, flew to New Orleans for the Mardi Gra in early February. I had the retractable skis on the 182. Flying with the skis slowed down the air speed about five knots. It took about one-half day to remove or install them, so I decided to leave them on. When I landed at the New Orleans waterfront airport, the ski-equipped plane attracted a lot of attention. A man from the tower came down to look them over, and a lot of line boys came out to really make a careful inspection. Line boys were airport employees who would meet and park planes, and do necessary servicing. It was obvious they had never seen an airplane equipped with skis before.

Finally, one curious black fellow who seemed to be in charge of the line attendants asked, "What are them things for?" I knew they would all be familiar with floatplane operation and water-skiing, so thought that I would have a little fun. I told him they were "water skis" and that I could land on water and ski along just like a water skier would do.

There was an opening in the bottom middle part of the ski where the wheel would go through. He got down and looked the ski over carefully and then said, "But don't water come up through that hole and she sink when you slow down?"

I said, "I do just like a water skier would do. I ski along at high speed and when I come up close to land, I zoom up on the beach." By this time, quite a large crowd had gathered and begun listening to our conversations. The line man was scratching his head and finally said, "Man that sure is something, I done never seen anything like that before."

I decided that I had kidded them enough so I said, "Actually, I can't land on water with these skis, they are for landing on ice or snow." The crowd all looked puzzled and finally the spokesman said, "Now you're joshing me, ain't you." None of them had probably ever seen ice or snow, and could not picture a plane landing under those conditions. My friend was in near-hysterics while listening to this exchange. But it was fun and put us in the mood for a good time. We spent four days enjoying the revelry.

Chapter -77-

Some Sad and Some Not so Sad Happenings.

But there were always sad happenings that took the joy out of life. A particularly sad year for our family was 1995. Our sister, Orla Lange, died in August, 1995, sister-in-law Margie Johnson (Roald's wife) died in November, and my brother Willie (Doc) in December. Roald, Roy, Floyd, and Myron had died a few years earlier, so our family was gradually fading away. Of the original thirteen, there were only four boys and three girls left.

Although I missed them all, I particularly missed Doc. Whenever we visited him on the farm, he would have something interesting to tell us that caused a few chuckles. He was a dedicated Democrat and a devoted member of the National Farmers Organization (NFO). The NFO were a group of farmers that were organized much like a union. Their purpose was to control production and sales so that their products would bring in a reasonable price and not be subject to the prices offered by large companies and chain stores. Brother Ed became an officer, and was a dedicated member. He still attends their conventions. Doc had suffered through the Depression's rock-bottom prices, so he had no love for Republicans, who he held to be at blame and had no love for large chain stores that controlled prices.

Because the Wheaton area where his farm was located was an excellent pheasant-hunting area, hunters would frequently come to the farm and ask permission to hunt there. When pheasant season opened, the corn crops had usually been harvested, but there was always corn on the ground, which attracted pheasants. It made a good hunting area. He or my brother Ed, who farmed with him, would always give permission to hunters, except for a certain few. One time, Doc had put up signs saying who was allowed to hunt:

The signs attracted a lot of attention and were a great topic of discussion and objects of humor in the area's liquor stores among gathered farmers.

Chapter -78-

A Banner Year.

2005 was a banner year for me. The Silver Bay Airport Commission and the Silver Bay City Council decided to rename the airport the Wayne Johnson Silver Bay Airport in my honor for my "dedication to aviation and community service." We had a huge fly-in for the airport dedication.

The Minnesota Commissioner of Aeronautics, a state senator, the district state representative, two former commanders of the Minnesota Air National Guard, General Ray Klosowski, and General Wayne Gatlin, and many other dignitaries attended. A number of my Flying Tiger friends came from Florida, South Carolina, Georgia, and Missouri. Ted and JoAnne Connolly came from Miami. Ted had flown cargo planes in WWII over the Hump (the eastern end of the Himalayan Mountains), bringing supplies to our airbases. Oliver Bateman from Macon, Georgia, and Ron Phillips from Butler, Missouri, who were in my squadron in China, were in attendance.

Seldom in an airman's lifetime is he granted the honor of having an airport named after him. Usually, airports are named after the airmen are dead. I was glad they named one for me then rather than waiting until I no longer was around to care!

The Commission had arranged for some World War II aircraft, of the type I had flown, to come to the function. Pilots from the Commemorative Air Force from St. Paul flew in with an L-5, the liaison plane used in China for rescue work. They also had a Vultee BT-13 basic trainer and a North American AT-6 advanced trainer. The BT-13 was particularly interesting; because we learned that the same airplane had been stationed in Greenville, Mississippi, and had been flown by cadets. I checked the serial number of the plane and found that it corresponded with the number in my pilot's log-book. I had flown that identical plane for fifty minutes while I was stationed at Greenville for my basic flight training, almost seventy years earlier.

The Commission, by its airport manager, Dick Morris, had a large model of a Mustang P-51 of the same type that I flown in combat and painted in my squadron colors, the 118th Tactical Reconnaissance Black Lightning Squadron. The plane was mounted on a pole in front of the administration building as a wind vane. It was designed so that it would always point into the wind with the propeller turning. They also had a plaque mounted on a large taconite boulder directly in front of the airport administration building.

My son, Bruce, and I met the planes in Two Harbors, which was prearranged, and then flew in formation to Silver Bay. We led the formation in our Cessna Skylane 182. Oliver Bateman's daughter, Edna, flew with us and took aerial photos.

Oliver Bateman brought my original leather flight jacket from the Museum of Aviation at Warner Robbins Air Base in Georgia. I had donated the jacket some years ago to the museum's Flying Tigers exhibit. I was challenged to put the jacket on. My friends and the crowd were certain that it would no longer fit. I was a little concerned because I was afraid the leather might have "shrunk." I did manage to get it on, but for some reason it would not zip up.

After the ceremony, we adjourned to my home in Beaver Bay for a most relaxing time. A crowd of well over one hundred enjoyed a lunch of homemade fish cakes and other goodies. Some even imbibed a little in some "refreshments" that seemed to flow freely.

Delores and some other ladies had spent most of the previous day making fish cakes. Fish cakes are a particular delicacy of ours. They are made with fresh Lake Superior herring. The fish is ground with onions and potatoes, and then mixed into a batter with eggs, milk, and spices. Salt is put in last, which thickens the batter to a hamburger-like consistency. The batter is spooned into an oiled pan and fried until golden brown.

Several weeks after the airport dedication ceremony, I had another very pleasant surprise. I was invited, along with sixteen other former Flying Tigers, to go to China, as guests of the Chinese government, for celebrating the sixtieth anniversary of the end of WWII. In addition to the members of the Flying Tigers, there were some members of the Hump Pilots Association. They were the pilots and air crews that flew supplies from India to China over the high Himalayas that were called the Hump. Also included were some Doolittle Raiders, who were the survivors of the famous raid on Japan lead by Col. James Doolittle in retaliation for Japan's devastating attack on Pearl Harbor.

I flew from Duluth to Los Angeles a day before the scheduled overseas departure. I wanted to be well rested before the long journey to China, so I checked into a hotel near the airport. I also surprised my brother Clarence, who lives in Encino, a suburb of L.A. He was celebrating his ninetieth birthday, so there was a large gathering of relatives and friends.

Chapter -79-

A Journey Into History.

This was truly a journey into history. It was a long trip from Beaver Bay to Los Angeles and then a thirteen hour plane ride on China Airlines to Beijing, China. We arrived in Beijing about five-twenty in the morning. The arrival was spectacular. We were given a most royal welcome. We were first met by a group of high-ranking government dignitaries. They arranged for us to bypass customs so we had no delay when we arrived. The entry to the terminal was lined with several hundred young school children who were probably eight to ten years old and dressed in bright blue and white uniforms. At the end of the reception line, we were met by thirty to forty of the most beautiful women in China, in splendid Chinese gowns, lined up in two perfect rows, holding huge bouquets of flowers that they presented to each of us.

We were then taken by bus to the Jinghou Garden Hotel, a magnificent hotel comparable to the most luxurious five-star hotels in the United States. It was a big difference from when I was in China sixty years ago. Each person was assigned an interpreter, usually a college student or teachers who were very conversant in English. We were allowed to rest until the noon luncheon. The luncheon was a fabulous layout of all types of exotic foods.

At 1430 we were on the bus to attend the Chinese and American Veteran's Reunions at the Great Hall of the Peoples. All events were noted in twenty-four hour time rather than a.m. or p.m. So, 1430 was therefore 2:30 in the afternoon. The Great Hall was one of the most magnificent buildings I have ever seen. I doubt that any ordinary people were allowed within blocks of it. The hall was closely guarded by military police and city police officers. We were treated to a tremendous show and, of course, a lot of long-winded speeches by Chinese officials.

The next day, we were taken to the China Aviation Museum, housed in a cave in a mountain. The museum had a spectacular collection of virtually every aircraft ever flown, as well as a wealth of aviation art and historical displays. We rode slowly through the museum in large open vans. When the vans stopped for photos, my friend, Ron Phillips, and I decided to walk. There was a lot of shouting by the Chinese tour guides that walking was not permitted, but we just strolled away, pretending not to hear. We got to the exit just about the same time the vans came racing around from the far end. We were cautioned to stay with the group.

From the museum we went to a section of the Great Wall. It was most awe-inspiring, seeing the Wall winding through the valleys and mountains. One wonders, while observing the huge wall with great watch towers, how such an engineering marvel could have been constructed with human labor, centuries ago.

By 1600 hours (4 p.m.) we were back in our hotel, getting ready for a banquet at 1700 hours (5 p.m.) at the Great Wall Sheraton Hotel, another superb five-star masterpiece. The banquet was hosted by the Chinese People's Association for Friendship with Foreign Countries. It was a most impressive title for an association, and they did exude friendship. The banquet consisted of a variety of Chinese cuisine, with many toasts with a potent Chinese wine, which in WWII we had called *jing bao* (air raid) juice. The toasts were *gam-bey* or "bottoms-up." The imbiber had to be careful, or he would be bottoms up.

The following day started with a typical Chinese breakfast of a nice variety of interesting foods. Then, we got on a bus for a quick visit to the Temple of Heaven, an impressive edifice built during the Ming dynasty and age of Confucianism. The next affair was one of the most impressive. At 1330, we were on a bus for a one-hour, riding to the ceremony of the Beijing Peace Declaration and the opening ceremony of the Peace Wall, located in a beautiful park near a nice lake.

The Peace Wall was a magnificent edifice with plaques from all Allied nations. It depicted the struggles and sacrifices of those involved in WWII, and China's struggle against Japanese aggression, tied together by the theme of future peace among all nations. Besides the United States, there were representatives from Australia, Canada, Britain, France, India, New Zealand, Russia and a host of other nations to sign the Peace Declaration. There was a huge audience in attendance, with an estimated crowd of over one hundred thousand people.

I was asked to give a speech on behalf of the American veterans. They had prepared a speech for me. The Communists still wanted to control what people were supposed to do or say. I told them that I preferred to make my own comments to better express our true feelings of friendship. There was much chattering amongst the host committee. Finally they turned to me with big smiles and said, "Okay, you give talk." They gave me the traditional Chinese salute of approval, the thumbs-up. They only asked that I pause regularly for translation of my remarks into Chinese. The symbol *** denotes a pause for translation to Chinese by interpreter Lui Yan-ling.

My comments were:

*Today, we are pleased to attend this signing ceremony for the Beijing Peace Declaration together with old friends and veterans here. This is a very important event for us that participated in World War II, and it is of special significance in our lives. ****

*Over sixty years ago, we came to this land in flames of war far from our country and fought with the brave Chinese people in the cause of Freedom. Sixty years later, we are on this land of an old civilization again doing our bit for sustaining world peace. ****

*This year marks the 60th anniversary of the victory of the World War against Imperialist aggression. ****

*Many commemorative activities have been held in places like Normandy, France; Moscow in Russia and in London, Great Britain. Now we are gathered by this serene lake at this beautiful park in Beijing, the capitol city of China, *** signing the Beijing Peace Declaration in order to express the sincere wishes for peace of those who witnessed the smoke of battle, suffering and death. ****

*We wish that world peace will last for generations to come just like this great Beijing Peace Wall behind us. We trust and hope that peoples of all Nations may live together in peace and friendship. Thank You. ****

Wayne Johnson addressing the Beijing
Peace Declaration Conference

At the end of the ceremony, hundreds of doves were released as symbols of peace. I was given a standing ovation. My extemporaneous remarks appeared in the Chinese newspaper the next day. They delivered a translated copy to me.

There was a Russian general with a decorated chest full of medals who wanted to tell me about his experience on the Russian Front against the Germans. It didn't seem to have anything to do with the war in China or why he was at this function, because Russia didn't get into the war with Japan as an ally of China until a few days before the surrender. His English was so broken and I could only understand a few words, but I listened politely.

When the ceremony was over, we went back to the hotel for a little rest and dinner. Later that evening, we again went to the Great Hall of the Peoples to participate in the 60th Anniversary Performance for Victory of the "World's Anti-Fascist War and the Chinese People's Anti-Japanese War," sponsored by the President, or Chairman, of the People's Republic of China, Hu Jingtao and the Government of China. The Mainland of China is called the "People's Republic of China," while Taiwan is just called the "Republic of China". It was a stunning performance by a troupe of over three hundred performers. I doubt that Hollywood or Las Vegas could put on anything as impressive.

The next morning, we were taken to Tiananmen Square. Large crowds of well-dressed people were strolling about. Our tour guide made no mention of the massacre that occurred there when unarmed protesters were gunned down by their own troops. When one of our curious members asked about the killing of protestors, the guide quickly went on to another subject. The tomb of Mao Tze Tong was located in a large marble building on one side of this huge square. I didn't bother to go see his tomb. The body of this cruel dictator was of no interest to me. It was bad enough to see his picture plastered all over the city.

That afternoon, some of us were selected to go to a television station for interviews. A most gorgeous young lady conducted the interviews. She asked me to describe a mission that I was on. The mission had been mentioned in one of our brochures and was the first fighter strike on Japanese airdromes near Shanghai. She kept insisting that I give her the details of an accident that I had mentioned happening on the way back from the target. I finally told that on the return from the mission I had shit in my pants. She lost her aplomb for a moment and quickly went on to the next interview.

That evening we again went to the Great Hall of the Peoples for a reception by Chairman Hu Jingtao. This again was a most impressive affair. There were over five thousand people in the great hall from nations around the world. There were several Russian generals who, as usual, were weighed down by medals.

The Chairman made a point of coming around to some of the tables where the American veterans were seated and giving each at the table a special toast. There were lots of long-winded speeches by high-ranking government officials. We were getting a little weary of these speeches. We have some long-winded speakers in the United States as well, particularly in our Congress, but I have found that the shorter the speech, the more effective it is. They all emphasized the importance of the American contribution to victory over Japan and our efforts in promoting peace among all nations. It is quite a switch from a few years ago when their history books had made no mention of the American forces' presence during the war. When I visited China in 1980, we were only allowed to go to one Chinese city, on a strictly regulated tour from Hong Kong to Canton. At that time, there was never any mention of America's participation in the air war against Japan that lasted four years, or that the American air forces were the only active air units during that period. Each of us was presented with a beautiful book entitled "American Airmen in China during World War II." The book contained biographical sketches and photos of those of us on the trip, but all in Chinese.

The next day, we started a tour of China and went to some of the cities where we had bases in WWII. We flew from Beijing to Changsha. For some reason, the Chinese government never changed the spelling of that city, like they did most others when the Communists took over. We were met by another fantastic reception with bands and huge crowds. Most were waving American flags and shouting "Welcome, Flying Tigers." We were only there long enough to enjoy the reception and eat a box lunch.

From Changsha, we flew to Zhijiang (pronounced "she-jung"). This city was called Chihkiang (chee-key-yang) in WWII. We had a fighter strip there. The government had just built a new airport and beautiful terminal building on the site of the WWII airport. They had planned it so that our plane was the first plane to land at the new airport.

The 75th Fighter Squadron and some squadrons of the CACW (Chinese-American Composite Wing) were stationed there. I could not recognize anything about the area. It had changed dramatically since WWII. It was from this base on 2 April 1945 that the 75th had made a raid on Japanese airfields near Shanghai. We had raided those airfields a number of times since our first raid on 17 January 1945. The plane of the commander of the 75th Fighter Squadron, Major Clyde Slocum, was hit and on fire, so he had to bail out. He landed in downtown Shanghai, a Japanese stronghold since 1937. It was obviously not a friendly place to hop into. He was rescued by local Chinese residents and hidden from Japanese troops. He got back to his base several months later. Although I didn't recognize anything about the area, it was still a thrill to be back there.

Since Zhijiang did not have a large enough hotel to accommodate our group, we took a thirty minute bus ride to the city of Hauihua (pronounced "how-we-how") to stay at the Xian ("she-ahnn") Hotel. Large crowds, many thousands of people of all ages, lined the bus route for much of the way, cheering and waving as we passed. The population had obviously been informed that American veterans were visiting.

Then we were treated to another fabulous reception with another delicious banquet. I was assigned to another beautiful interpreter. We usually got a new interpreter in each city, but some did travel with us. My interpreter, Yang Chuanmei ("yang chew-anne me") was a lovely girl, very proficient in English. She was a teacher in the local school. Her English name was Nancy. After I returned home, I corresponded with her quite regularly. I sent one of our Chennault's Flying Tigers books for her school.

Nancy knocked on my door at 0530 the next morning so I could get ready for breakfast at 0600. We were scheduled to take a bus trip at 0700 back to Zhijiang to attend the China Zhijiang International Peace Culture Festival at the Zhijiang Airport. The Chinese are great at having long-winded names for their activities. Just like their speeches. I shouldn't criticize them for their long speeches, for they obviously wanted to convey their hospitality.

Starting at 0800, we enjoyed a fabulous opening ceremony and a large-scale theatrical performance. We were met by twenty high-powered government officials, all of whom had highly formal titles like the "Party Secretary of the Party Standing Committee of Zhijiang Dong Minority Autonomous County" and the "Vice Chairman of the Standing Committee of the National People's Congress," and many more with equally impressive titles. Surprisingly, there was the "Director Assistant, Taiwan Affairs Office of the State Council." It was surprising to us that there was an interchange of officials between the Republic of Taiwan and the Peoples Republic of China and that a Taiwan representative would appear at such a public function. All the high officials stood in a receiving line to meet and be introduced to each veteran. Each was asked to tell what he did in China in WWII. Late that afternoon and evening, we attended the International Peace Forum and a signing ceremony of the Zhijiang Peace Declaration and the Sino-American Veterans Re-union for the 60th Anniversary of the WWII Victory. That was enough to wear out the hardiest, but that was not enough for the day.

As soon as those festivities were over, we got on the bus back to Huaihua City for another reception by the Zhijiang County and Government of Huaihua City. The theme of the reception was based on the construction of a peace monument with soil from provinces all over China. They had small sacks of soil from around the country, so each veteran was asked to place the soil in a vat near the stage, representing the soil of China to build a peace monument.

I was asked to sit on the stage with the mayor of Huaihua City and about a dozen government officials. Each official gave the usual long-winded speech, which was translated into English. One was so long-winded that the mayor sent a message to him to end his talk. He kept talking, so the mayor, with a mean look on his face, started to get up—then the speaker quickly ended his speech that, when translated, sounded like he quit in mid-sentence.

I had been asked to give a speech as representative of the American veteran's delegation. I was told I could speak for one hour, but I thought five or ten minutes would be long enough. My comments were:

Sixty years ago we came to your country to help in your War of Resistance against Japanese aggression. *** We came as young men from the farms and factories, from schools and universities, from small towns and large cities — but we came with one purpose, to help the Chinese people defeat a vicious enemy that was bent on enslaving your nation. *** We fought in the air -side by side- with your brave young men. We came to an ancient land with a different culture. *** But we quickly adapted to that culture and learned to become part of it. *** We came to accept and enjoy the foods so different from our own. We learned to live in Spartan conditions and to suffer with your people as we lost our comrades in combat. *** But most importantly –we developed friendships that survive to this day. *** We were impressed by the friendliness of the Chinese people then as we are welcomed here with such open friendliness and good will. *** I was a farmer before I became an aviator. I was close to the soil. So your use of the soil to build a peace monument seems so appropriate. *** The soil to build your Peace Monument is symbolic of our effort that binds us together to build peace among all nations. *** May the leaders of our Nations be inspired by the friendships of the peoples of China and America, exhibited here tonight — and throughout our visit in China with the out-pouring of friendship and goodwill. *** May our leaders resolve all disputes and differences in the spirit of diplomacy that the peoples of all nations may live to-gether in peace and harmony. (*** represents a pause for the translator to translate my remarks into Chinese)

I didn't think my talk was that great, but I got a standing ovation that lasted for some minutes. I was told by one of my friends who timed me that my speech, with the translation, lasted just five minutes. Perhaps the extended applause was in appreciation of my short speech compared to those of our Chinese hosts. My speech made the newspaper the next day – but all in Chinese. They did send me an English translation, so I knew what I said, as I have recorded above.

After another day of sightseeing, speeches, and banquets, we flew back to Changsha for a trip to Kunming. Kunming had been the headquarters of the Flying Tigers during WWII. We were greeted with another fantastic welcoming ceremony at the airport. During WWII, Kunming was fairly small city with ancient gates and one-story buildings. Now it was a city of over seven million people, with huge sky-scrapers. Our hotel, the Kai Wah Plaza, was another first-rate hotel, more superb than any we had seen before.

The ancient city had become so modernized that we could recognize very little of WWII days. Ron Phillips and I found a bar called The Hump that we had sometimes frequented during the war. It looked exactly like it did sixty years ago, both inside and out. It looked like some of the same cobwebs hanging from the ceiling and the glasses were the same dull color from years of use and obviously infrequent washing. We had a beer but drank it out of the bottle.

With just a short rest, we attended another sumptuous banquet at the beautiful Golden Hall of the Green Lake Hotel. As we went from city to city, each banquet seemed to be in a contest to be the best. This banquet was sponsored by Mr. Wan Wen Tao, mayor of Kunming, and Mr. Qin Guangrong, Executive Governor of the province. There was the usual collection of many high-ranking officials with impressive titles, and again, some long-winded speeches. It did not appear that Chinese officials had the ability to make a short speech! I was given a beautiful certificate by the mayor that named me an "Honorary Citizen of Kunming for services as a fighter pilot in the Flying Tigers of the 14th Air Force."

The next morning, after a Chinese breakfast, we left for the Kunming International Convention and Exhibit Centre for the opening ceremony of a Memory of History and the debut of the book, "When Tigers Roared." The book featured the WWII experiences of most of the veterans on the trip. I had a little difficulty reading my section because it was all in Chinese, but I did recognize my picture. They promised an English version, but that still has not come out. We were taken to a book store and spent a good part of the day autographing the books for eager buyers.

Another group of big-wigs were present, with even longer titles like Ms. Yan Younqiong, "Director-General of the Publicity Department of Yunan Provincial Committee," and Mr. Xu Kemin, "Vice-Chairman of the Yunan Provincial Committee of the Chinese People's Consultative Conference."

That afternoon, we went out to Dianchi Lake on the outskirts of Kunming. In WWII, this lake was always a landmark for navigating to Kunming. We took some launches out to the middle of the lake where there was a salvage operation going on. In the very early days of the war an AVG pilot had gone down in the lake in his P-40. His body had been recovered at the time but the P-40 rested on the bottom of the lake for over sixty years.

The Chinese salvage crews had located the P-40 and were in the process of trying to raise the plane. Although the lake was the graveyard of a number of planes that had crashed into the lake, the salvage crew was certain they had located the AVG P-40. The old runway at Kunming leads directly toward the lake, so if a pilot had a problem on take-off or landing, he usually got very wet and sometimes permanently so.

The next day, we were scheduled to go to the old headquarters of the Flying Tigers- 14th Air Force and the residence of General Claire Chennault, the commander. That function was cancelled because road construction in the area did not permit access. Instead we went to Chenggong (Chengkung), an old WWII airfield about twenty miles away from Kunming. We drove through some scenic country of rice and wheat fields that I recognized. Farmers were still plowing with water buffalo, just like they had been doing sixty years ago. Again, there were large crowds and government officials to greet us as we arrived at the old airfield.

My squadron, the 118th Tactical Reconnaissance Black Lightning Squadron and the 308th Bomb Group, a B-24 heavy bomb outfit, had, at times, been stationed at this field. It was a particularly exciting part of the trip since it brought back a lot of memories.

The old barracks buildings, alert shack, and headquarters building were all gone, but the runway of crushed rock was much as I remembered. There was an old concrete roller still lying in the grass near the runway. All airfields in those days were built by human labor. Thousands of workers, from young children to old grandpa and grandmas sat all day, breaking rocks and pounding them into gravel-like particles. The runways were designed to carry the weight of heavy bombers, so they were usually at least eighteen inches deep. That took a lot of rock. Big rocks were hauled in by little carts, pulled by donkeys or people, and placed on the bottom, then smaller ones on top, until the surface was quite fine, crushed rock. Huge concrete rollers, pulled by as many as ten thousand coolies (laborers), were used to pack the runways. The smaller rollers, like the one in the grass, were used for the smaller areas, like taxi strips and parking ramps. I asked one of the officials why the roller was still there. He just shrugged and said, "We don't have any use for it." He didn't mention that it was quite a tourist attraction.

The field is still apparently used by the Chinese Air Force. There were about a dozen old planes on the field that looked like some old, Russian trainers, but we were not allowed near them or to take photos. The planes apparently had some purpose, because they were well-guarded by Chinese troops who kept us at a distance. They sure didn't look like any type of secret weapon that required all those surly-looking guards!

When we got back to the hotel in Kunming, I decided to shop around to see if I could find some unique gifts for Delores and the family. Monique, the assistant manager of the hotel and incidentally a real beauty, offered to help me shop. I wanted to buy some jade. She dissuaded me from several items that I thought looked great – but she said were not good jade.

She agreed that I should buy a jade tiger pendant that she said was of the highest quality. When I saw the price tag, I rebelled. The price was marked $400.00. Monique got into a spirited discussion in Chinese with the salesperson and then the manager of the shop. She told me that she could get it for $40.00, which was her wholesale price. I grabbed that. After looking at a number of jade bracelets, which she rejected, she picked out one I really liked for a present for my daughter Annie (Margaret Anne). But again, the price of $250.00 was a little much. After another spirited go around in Chinese, the price came down to $25.00. It turned out to be a great day of bargain-shopping with one of the most beautiful ladies in Kunming.

The next day, we went out to Yunan University, a beautiful campus with modern buildings, nestled in a wooded area. It looked like a fine American campus, as picturesque as Harvard or Princeton. Students were scattered around the campus at tables in secluded spots and under shady trees, obviously studying. When the bell rang to come to the meeting hall, they all came running. Banners of "Welcome Flying Tigers" and "Welcome American Heroes" were prominently displayed.

Several hundred students gathered at the campus auditorium to participate in a most interesting cultural exchange, "The U.S. Veterans and Undergraduate Symposium." Some of the veterans were asked to make brief comments about their WWII experiences, and impressions of China in WWII. Students responded enthusiastically, with many questions. I felt that the students were more interested in our impressions about their country than combat stories.

My brief comments were much the same as those in Zhijiang:
We came to your country more than 60 years ago to help the Chinese people in their struggle against Japanese aggression. We were impressed by the friendliness of the Chinese people. We came from a different culture but soon learned to adapt to yours. We learned to enjoy your food – probably because that was what we had to eat, but more importantly we developed friendships that endure to this day. It is hoped that as we develop new friendships today, it will help to secure peace between our two nations.

Other speakers and I received long, standing ovations. As we left, students gathered around us for photos and sincere shows of affection. There were few dry eyes on our part and those of the students. We were asked to autograph the "Roar of the Tiger," which many of the students had. The "Roar of the Tiger" was a brief history of the Flying Tigers, with a biographical sketch of each veteran on the trip. The meeting at the college was another unique experience.

After lunch at the hotel, we went to the Jimbi Square and Yunan Ethical Handicraft Market, where we observed the displayed work of various Chinese artists and designers. A local band played Forties and Fifties tunes. One of the members played on a saw, much like some guys at home. They sounded more like one of our bands back home than the typical Chinese music. I enjoyed a dance with one of the attractive young lady interpreters, which drew loud applause from the locals and the band. It was a fun and fascinating three hours.

After dinner we were treated to a cantata called the Green Path of the Rainbow or Rainbow over the Green Dyke, depending upon the translation. It told the story of the adventures of Flying Tiger fighter pilots, as well as those who flew the Hump. It was an awesome performance with many hundreds of singers and dancers in gorgeous costumes. Although we didn't get back to the hotel until almost midnight, it seemed like a short day with all the exciting events.

Early the next morning, after a hasty breakfast, we were taken to the airport for a flight to Nanjing, formerly Nanking. (Nanking). A bunch of high-ranking officials were there to see us off. Again, there were a number of "Director-Generals," which China seemed to have a large supply of. Among the high-ranking officials was Mr. Zing Ming, "Director-General of Information for the Government of Yunan Province;" Mr. He Mingsheng, "Deputy Director-General of The Department of Foreign Affairs for Yunan Province;" Mr. Ha Kebin, "Director-General of the Office of the Kunming Municipal Government;" and a host of other dignitaries and well-wishers, including a large group of perfectly dressed little children waving flags and banners.

The arrival in Nanjing Lukou International Airport was another spectacular affair. Again, we had a group of high-ranking government officials, bands, children, and a group of beautiful ladies as greeters, with large crowds of military and civilians cheering widely.

Nanjing was the site of the horrible Japanese slaughter of over three hundred thousand Chinese men, women, and children in the early days of the war. It was called The Rape of Nanking. After the airport reception, we were taken to the Nanjing International Conference Hotel, another five-star service, gleaming structure. We had been checked in already, so were taken directly to our rooms. I was assigned to another lovely interpreter named Liang Cao, with the American name of Annette.

We had another bountiful lunch, and then took a trip to the commemorative ceremony at the Aviation Martyr's Monument. It was a magnificent monument, with huge statutes of an American and Chinese airman in the foreground, and soaring columns. Black marble walls in the background were inscribed with the names of the two thousand eight hundred American airmen who lost their lives in China during WWII. The black marble walls were similar to the Vietnam monument in Washington, D.C. The monument sat on a high hill and was reached by many hundreds of stairs. I was asked to lead the delegation up the stairs to the monument. It took a little huffing and puffing before reaching the top. There were some who couldn't make it.

The monument was spectacular up close, as well as from a distance. It was a great tribute to those American and Allied airmen who made the supreme sacrifice during China's War of Resistancc against the Japanese invaders. The Chinese call the conflict that started in 1932 with Japan's invasion of Manchuria its War of Resistance. Standing at the impressive edifice was a most sobering and emotional experience.

That evening, we werc welcomed by Mr. Liang Baohua, (pronounced "bow-how") Governor of Jiangsu Province where the city of Nanjing is located, with yet another fabulous banquet at the Nanjing Peace Hall. They handed out beautiful books to each veteran. The presentation of unique gifts was a typical gesture in every city we visited. Most of us had to buy extra suitcases to bring the gifts home —and pay extra luggage charges!

The trip the next day was one of the most sobering. We were taken to the Memorial Hall of the Victims of the Nanjing Massacre by the Japanese Invaders. Rooms were filled with photos and statues of victims, over three hundred thousand names emblazoned on the walls . . . signifying the number of victims of the slaughter. We spent almost two hours there, mostly in silence, reminded of the Holocaust, except that this atrocity took place in a matter of weeks rather than over many years.

From there, we went to the Nanjing New District Planning Showroom, a series of architectural displays, which showed a miniature model of the city of Nanjing. It was a truly impressive display of many architectural marvels. The display was a pleasant relief from the depressing Victims Monument. Nanjing was the capitol of China prior to the Japanese invasion. During the invasion, the government had to flee to Chungking. Nanking was an ancient city established in 472 B.C. Most of the early dynasties made Nanjing (Nanking) their capitol. It was one of the most picturesque cities we visited. The ancient Taicheng City Wall was one of the most impressive city walls in China, and one of the best preserved in the world. The Sun Yat-sen Mausoleum, old Presidential Palace, the Ming Tomb, and many other historical sites, are located in the city. Our stay was much too short to enjoy all the amenities of the beautiful city.

After the usual meeting with government officials at the Mandarin Garden Hotel, we were treated to an outstanding, and the very best, banquet we had been to so far. Each city seemed to outdo the others. The hotel was located in a remote park area. It was a most delightful spot. Too bad we didn't get to stay there, although I did not think it was any more fabulous than our hotel. It was an international meeting place. We saw lots of BMWs and Mercedes parked there. Then, we had another treat. We went to the Nanjing Culture and Arts Center to see a musical and dance drama, "The Charming Jinling." It was another superb Las Vegas type of show. The one and one-half hour performance seemed to last only a short time. The cast, costumes, and staging were magnificent. It was a fascinating and most enjoyable day. Fortunately, we got back to the hotel by 2130, so the bar was still open for a little relaxation.

We were scheduled to depart Nanjing by bus for a trip to Shanghai, the final destination of our China tour. Caroline had been my interpreter in Nanjing, and as usual when we parted with our interpreters, there were many tears. The interpreters, mostly college students, became like best friends. It was always sad to leave them. The trip on the buses to Shanghai, about a distance of one hundred thirty miles, was on an eight-lane super highway for much of the way. We had one rest stop that was quite interesting, as the men's rest room was most unique. The urinal was a concrete trough about a foot square that ran the length of the building for several hundred feet against one wall. With other traffic besides our buses, there were hundreds of men seeking relief in this community urinal. The toilets were holes in the concrete floor with a spray nozzle above to wash things down. Quite a sight!

There was a lot of traffic, but mostly heavily loaded, vintage trucks. There were a few big, black sedans with smoke windows, so no one could see in. The interpreter said that those cars were of high-ranking government officials.

The arrival at the Galaxy Hotel in Shanghai held quite a surprise. As I got out of the bus and started up to the entrance, an elderly Chinese gentlemen came running with a package in his hand, shouting, "Slocum, Slocum, Slocum!" Through the interpreter, I explained to him that I was not Slocum, but had known him.

Major Clyde Slocum was my squadron commander in the 75th Fighter Squadron and later C.O. of the 23rd Fighter Group. Slocum was shot down in a raid on a

Shanghai airfield in April, 1945. He bailed out of his burning plane and landed in downtown Shanghai residential district. He was rescued by a lady and her young son. They hid him under the floor in their house until they could spirit him away by floating him down the river on a small boat at night. The boatman turned him over to Chinese guerilla troops, who brought him back to our base. The Japanese troops tortured a number of residents in the area trying to locate Slocum and find out who had rescued him. Despite torture and abuse, no one would tell. The residents hated the Japanese and gave every assistance to downed airmen, despite the hazards of doing so.

Surprise—the Chinese gentlemen shouting "Slocum" was the young boy who helped his mother rescue Slocum. I explained to him that I was not Slocum, but that he was still alive and lived in the United States. He asked me to deliver his gift to Slocum. I told him Slocum lived in Georgia over a thousand miles from my home, and that it would be difficult for me to deliver the gift, but that I could mail it to him. I gave him one of my cards. The man was overjoyed. He grabbed me and hugged me. Such a show of affection was most unusual for a Chinese man. I asked the interpreter to get his name and address, but he had disappeared before she had an opportunity to do so. I mailed the package to Slocum when I got home. He called me and we spent some time going over the incident.

The Galaxy Hotel was another of those very luxurious hotels that would out-shine anything we had in the U.S. My room, about the size of four normal hotel rooms, was on the fourteenth floor, and provided a great view of Shanghai. I don't know if I got such a fancy room because I was a past president of our Association or because I had been on the first fighter strike on Shanghai airfields, but whatever the reason, it was super. There were big bouquets of flowers, fresh fruit baskets, and a bottle of fine wine every day.

We did a bus tour of the fabled Bund waterfront along the Huangpu River, in the Pudong district. It was not like anything I remembered from when I left there in the U.S. Liberty ship, the *Alderamen* in December, 1945. But it was fascinating to stroll along the same streets that I had sixty years ago.

When we got back to the hotel in the late afternoon, one of the other guys and I discovered a well-stocked bar on the first floor. They didn't have my preferred Sapphire gin so we had to settle for the House of Lords brand. We were able to enjoy a couple of "lemonades" before getting dressed for the banquet.

The banquet was another royal affair, with a huge variety of Chinese foods, some that I'd never seen before, and also some American foods. There were piles of fresh shrimp, lobster, oysters, and many other hard-to-describe snacks. A long table was stacked with every kind of desserts imaginable. After the banquet, several of us went back to the bar, since it was too early to go to bed. Besides, we had to let the foods settle.

The next day, we took another tour of Shanghai and visited the Songhu Memorial and the magnificent Pearl Tower. We had another five-star lunch in the revolving restaurant on the top of the Pearl Tower. When we left, there was a crowd of students asking me to autograph cards. I usually had some one-page brochures describing the WWII activities of the Flying Tigers, with my biographical sketch included. They were much in demand by the students wherever we went. They appreciated those more than the candy and gum we would give to the little kids.

After lunch, our next stop was the City Guard Temple, dating back many centuries. We had a long shopping stop in the old Shanghai district. I didn't do any shopping, but the ladies had a ball bargaining for all types of goodies. I did recognize some of the old buildings in the district.

When shopping time was finished and the usual stragglers were rounded up, we were taken to the Dragon Boat floating restaurant in the Huangpo River (pronounced "wung poo") for another fabulous dinner. We then went to another dock for an evening cruise down the river. It was a clear night, but made almost daylight-bright by the hundreds of lighted signs and other cruise ships. It was amazing to see the myriad of signs advertising products from all over the world, many of which were American. There were lots of automobile signs advertising Ford, Chevrolet, Buick, Cadillac, BMW, Mercedes, and many more.

Everyone agreed that it was a fantastic evening. It was particularly enjoyable since this was to be our last night in Shanghai. We regretted that we did not have more time to spend in the cosmopolitan city. We got back to the hotel about 2345. Most people went to bed, but a few of us found the bar still open, with much revelry going on. There was a group of German tourists whooping it up. I met two beauties from Belgium who asked me to take turns dancing with each one. I found that I wasn't tired at all!

There was a wake-up call at 0600. I don't know why so early since we were not due at the airport until 1100 for a 1300 flight to Beijing. At Beijing, we would catch a flight to Los Angeles. Why we didn't fly direct from Shanghai to Los Angeles was a Chinese puzzle that was never answered. When we got to Beijing, the plane to Los Angeles was late, so we sat around the airport for several hours. Then we took a long-long flight to LAX (Los Angeles International airport.)

I had given up my assigned seat in business class to a handicapped person, so was now seated in regular seating. I had the misfortune of getting a seat next to the fattest guy on the plane. He slopped over halfway into my seat. He was a jolly fellow, but that didn't help my rest. He didn't seem to know or care that he was squeezing me out of my seat. The plane was full, so there were no vacant seats that I could move to. I stood up or walked around the plane for most of the thirteen-hour trip.   We landed at LAX (Los Angeles International airport) at about ten thirty p.m. I went back to the same hotel I had stayed at the night before departure from L.A. I was too tired to sleep, so I went to a nice restaurant a few blocks from the hotel, where I enjoyed a delicious steak and a few "lemonades." The restaurant stayed open until four a.m., and was very busy. After a nicely relaxing evening, I went back to the hotel and slept for over twelve hours. The next day, I headed back to Minnesota. The trip was truly a journey into history.

After being gone for three weeks, it took a while to catch up on a lot of law work. My partner, Pete Morris, had done a great job in my absence, but there was plenty of work for me to do.

Chapter -80-

More Tragedies

We had another family tragedy several years later. My sister Korty died in September, 2007. Her death was an acute loss to me. I had lived at her home for four years while going to high school. We were very close, and I miss her a great deal. She lived a long life, reaching the age of ninety seven. She had a stroke and was confined to a wheel chair for almost twenty years, but she remained mentally sharp. Her family asked me to do the eulogy. It was a most difficult task. The eulogy I gave expressed my feelings in part:

Korty Aasta Lange. Her middle name, named after our mother, Aasta, exemplifies many of the traits she inherited from her mother. Sacrifice, Compassion, Understanding, Responsibility, Dedication to family and —Courage.

In most of the things Korty did — she was self taught. She was a cook and baker par excellence — and a concerned and practical nurse. A devoted wife; a loving mother, grandmother, great grandmother, sister and family member —and a friend to many.

It is customary at funerals to say good things about the deceased, even if they might not be true. But for Korty, it is easy to say good things about her, since she was indeed a good person in the truest sense of the word. There are three words that best described Korty: Responsibility, Dedication and Courage.

She knew well and always carried out her Responsibility to her family. To her husband, Oscar, and her children — they came first and she sacrificed much. And to other members of her family she also felt a great Responsibility, willing to Sacrifice and assume burdens that should not have been hers. She was the one that insisted that I attend high school. . . . We lived too far from the closest high school and our parents could not afford to cover the cost of travel or staying over. She solved that problem. She invited –- no directed — me to come to live with her and Oscar at their farm home, two miles east of Chokio, so I could attend Chokio High School.

She became my surrogate mother and disciplinarian. Because of her kind heart and easy going manner she wasn't much good at discipline. Later, she would say with a grin, "you probably got by with a lot more than you should have, but I guess you turned out O.K."

Dedication to a cause became her hallmark. For she felt she had another compelling Responsibility — to care for her Mother in her Mother's later years. As a practical Nurse, she dedicated her talents, time and efforts in caring for her Mother. Dedication to those efforts, she felt, was her Responsibility. She drove from Chokio to Mother's farm at Wheaton, daily for many years. She dedicated herself to being Mother's nurse, caretaker and companion. But Courage — in the face of adversity personified her being. When a stroke more than twenty years ago left her partially incapacitated, she bore that burden like she had so many others — with stoic Courage. One can only imagine the fortitude it would take to be confined to a wheel chair for all those years — but still keep a mental balance.

She was probably deprived of the many things she enjoyed but — still do so without complaint. She maintained her sense of humor and mental alertness. She could remember things most others had forgotten. On a recent visit, she recounted to me that she had helped our father deliver me at birth. . . . She wasn't quite twelve years old at the time but — an example of her future life — of assuming responsibilities well beyond required or expected of her. She was quick to forgive and never held a grudge against anyone with a credo that said "Do unto others as you would they do unto you". She lived the Christian mandate of "Forgive us our trespasses as we forgive those who trespass against us". Regardless of hurt or insult, she always forgave.

In all her 97 years, she lived an exemplary life. She suffered much — which she bore with equanimity. She will be missed by family, friends and community. She may now rest in peace . . . for God will certainly welcome her into his Kingdom.

Chapter -81-

Bad News

After many years of comparative good health, I had a life-threatening experience in 2008. I went to my cardiologist, Dr. Langager, for an annual checkup. I had no symptoms and thought I was in perfect health. I exercised regularly and walked several miles a day, several days a week. I had a treadmill, a NordicTrac, and an exercise bicycle that I used regularly. Delores was an excellent cook and always cooked proper, healthy meals. I suffered a heart attack about twenty years ago, but had made a very good recovery with no ill side effects.

As the doctor examined me, he said that I had some heart murmurs that needed further checking. He ordered an echocardiogram. An echocardiogram generates a series of photographic images of the heart. One can see the heart pulsating and the valves opening and closing. The results were frightening. While looking at the films, it was obvious that I had a serious heart condition. The mitral and aortic valves were not opening and closing properly. Dr. Langager informed me that I would probably die in a few months unless I had surgery to correct the problems. It left me with very little choice. I agreed to surgery.

The heart surgeon informed me that he could repair the mitral valve and replace the aortic valve with animal tissue. Both the cardiologist and the heart surgeon informed me that the success rate of this type of surgery was better than ninety percent. That seemed like pretty good odds to me compared with doing nothing. They said I should be out of the hospital in three or four days.

But things didn't work out quite that well. It turned out that I was in the ten percent unsuccessful category. It was a disaster. I was in intensive care for five weeks, on the brink of death. I developed a rare malady that the doctors said only happened in one-in-ten thousand major surgeries. They called it cholesterol showers. When they removed the heart-lung pump after surgery and gave me a shot of Coumadin, they said the shock to my system made small pieces of cholesterol break loose in the aorta and migrate to the extremities. The fat emboli (cholesterol) went down to my feet and shut off the blood supply, so I developed gangrene.

They had to amputate both legs to save my life. Fortunately, if one can call it fortunate, the amputation was below the knee, so I would still have knee flexion, which would make it easier to walk with prostheses. That meant three months in the hospital with another three months in rehabilitation. What a bummer.

It was quite a shock when I woke up some time after the surgery. As the nurse was changing the bedding, I looked down and my first reaction was to cry out, "Where the hell are my feet? They are gone." My shouting must have been quite loud, because nurses and doctors came running. Although the doctors said that they had discussed the need for the amputation with me and I had given my consent, I had no recollection of doing so. I spent three months in the hospital. There was a long period of therapy while I was fitted with prostheses for both legs during which I learned how to walk, first with a walker and then with canes.

But with the hand that was dealt to me, I had to adapt. Sitting in a wheel chair was not the kind of life I wanted, but I had to accept it. I learned to walk with a walker and with canes. I did become quite self-sufficient, with Delores' help, in learning to take care of myself, despite the handicaps. When I first got the prostheses, it was such a joy to stand up and take a pee, and to be able to sit on the toilet stool. Nothing was more humiliating than having to go in a bed pan.

Chapter -82-

Retirement

Because of my limitations and the burden it would have placed on Delores to drive me to meetings and to attend to city business, I resigned as city attorney of Silver Bay, effective 1 June 2009. I set a record as the longest-serving city attorney in the United States, having served the cities of Beaver Bay and Silver Bay each for over fifty years. I had handled the organization of Beaver Bay in 1953 and served as its city attorney, over fifty-two years. I also handled the organization of Silver Bay in 1956, so served there as city attorney for fifty-three years.

I had many honors for both my law and military careers, and activities after WWII as a member of the Flying Tigers of the 14th Air Force Association.

Martendale-Hubbell, the international rating bureau for attorneys, gave me an "A" (very high) rating for "Legal Ability," and a "v" (very high) General Recommendation "that embraces faithful adherence to ethical standards, professional reliability, and diligence."

Among the awards from the legal bar was one from the Minnesota State Bar Association "for leadership and unselfish participation in public affairs of the community, state and nation and those commendable personal qualities that characterize those who best exemplify the high ideals of the profession as an officer of the courts in the administration of justice." The Wisconsin Bar Association issued an award "for fifty years of Distinguished Service and in recognition of special efforts in the furtherance of the high standards and ideals of the legal profession dedicated to the public service." I was admitted to practice in both Minnesota and Wisconsin.

The Minnesota 11th Judicial Bar Association issued a special citation "for fifty years of honorable service – setting an inspiring example of devotion to the duties of an Attorney and Counselor at law." The Minnesota City Attorney's Association issued a special commendation for "exceptional and dedicated public service." The Lifetime Achievement Award was awarded by the Minnesota Trial Lawyers Association for "outstanding contributions and tireless efforts in promoting the public good."

In 2004, I was awarded the prestigious Douglas K. Amdahl Public Service Career Award by the Public Service Section of the Minnesota State Bar Association "in recognition of his dedication and commitment to public service and the public practice of law." It is the highest award made by the Minnesota State Bar Association. The award is named after the Honorable Douglas K. Amdahl, former Chief Justice of the Minnesota Supreme Court. Douglas Amdahl, as a young attorney, was one of my law professors at the Minneapolis College of Law.

One of my treasured awards was from the Republic of China (Taiwan) Air Force "In recognition of Outstanding Personal and Professional Achievements in Military Aviation."

Being named Mr. Aviation of Minnesota and enshrined in the Minnesota Aviation Hall of Fame and having an airport named after me were among the highest honors that could be awarded to an airman.

Although all those awards and recognitions are most meaningful, the respect and recognition that I have in the community is much more appreciated. The respect and recognition after a lifetime of public service, without any blemishes on my character, is a reward that few enjoy.

In achieving those goals, I have had the support of my ever-patient, caring, loving, and understanding wife of over fifty years, Delores, and members of my family. So too, I have been fortunate to have highly competent partners in my law practice and very dedicated and efficient secretaries. Marge Johanson served as my legal secretary for twenty-five years and Rita Rushenberg for almost twenty years and our last secretary and para-legal, Angela Goutermont, was with us for many years until she decided to leave to have a family.

The *Johnson & Morris* law firm in the Wells Fargo Bank Building in Silver Bay, Minnesota. In 2009 the firm consisted of Attorney Gerald "Pete" Morris; Paralegal, Angela Goutermont & Attorney Wayne G. Johnson. Not shown Secretary-bookkeeper Lin Elizondo

I was also fortunate in the public sector to work with generally very dedicated mayors and council members. Although they did not always agree with me, they accepted my legal advice and abided by it. One of the outstanding mayors was Robert Kind, who I worked with for eighteen years.

With my law partners and staff, I always sought to adhere to the highest ethical standards of our profession. In all the years of my practice in the field of law, although personal rancor between parties often surfaced, I was seldom the subject of criticism. Even those who lost in a case where my client was the victor never held any animosity toward me.

When I decided to retire as city attorney and limit my law practice, my office arranged for a retirement party. I was overwhelmed by the turn-out. Accolades were rendered by judges, and fellow attorneys from many areas, public officials, friends from near and far, as well as family members, all attended.

For those that could not attend, there were many touching messages for a happy retirement. One in particular was most touching. My lifelong friend from Flying Tiger days, Senator Oliver Bateman from Macon, Georgia, who in his inimitable way, could add a little humor to a sentimental message. My birthday happened to be one week before my retirement. He tied the two together in a beautiful manner:

There are no more important events than the birthday and retirement of Wayne G. "Whitey" Johnson; aviator, war hero, noted jurist, raconteur, lemonade connoisseur, and DEAR FRIEND.

How did God let us live to this age? Evidently, it is because of our impeccable conduct!! –or maybe He planned for you to continue to be productive, and a role

model for young and old. He is always right. Thanks to Him, I've been allowed to hang around and cheer you on.

Evidently, He has forgiven us for those days of our indiscretions, if any! Can you remember when our mantra was: "Live fast, Love hard, die young — and leave a beautiful memory?"

Old Friend, we were spared the dying young, but gave #1 (Live fast), #2 (Love hard) our successful effort — and pray that we are indeed remembered beautifully.

The "lemonade connoisseur" refers to is my affinity for a particular libation made with Seven-up, a squeeze of lemon, and a little Sapphire gin. Whenever he and I got together for a relaxing evening, we would both enjoy a "lemonade" or two.

Another message that I treasured was from United States Chief Magistrate Judge Raymond Erickson. Ray had worked with me during the long Reserve Mining litigation. It was the legal expertise he had shown in that case and his brilliant brief writing that later won him the appointment as a United States District Court Magistrate Judge. He wrote:

I send my deep regrets that I will be unable to attend your retirement recognition. . . . I congratulate you on a superb legal career, which has justly earned you the kudos and esteem of your colleagues. . . . We have had many rewarding experiences over the many years, and most particularly, the continued existence of a mining enterprise in Silver Bay, notwithstanding seemingly in surmountable odds that the employment of an entire generation of honest, hard workers, as well as an enviable small community experience for so many fine folk, would come to an end. . . . Needless to say, your accomplishments, in achieving the triumph of a sensible and safe solution, were both ceaseless and inestimable.

So many have gone before, who would have been proud to join your celebration, but you know the great respect that Ed Fride, Ed Schmidt, Ken Haley, and the Presidents of Reserve, Armco ,and Republic, and even the opposing attorneys in the case, held for you. Again, congratulations on an historic occasion — the longest serving City Attorney in the United States is an incredible accomplishment — but what else would one expect except from a Chennault's Flying Tiger.

(Signed: *Ray Erickson, U.S. Magistrate District Judge*)

Ed Fride was the chief attorney for Reserve Mining during the environmental litigation, a master litigator, and someone with whom I worked closely for many years. Ray Erickson was one of his chief assistants and brief writer. Mac Hyde, one of the younger attorneys, contributed a cool professionalism to the case. Bill Egan, who represented Republic Steel Corporation, was one of the stellar trial attorneys. There were many other attorneys on our team who were tops in their profession. Ed Schmidt was the public relations officer for Reserve Mining Company, and an invaluable consultant. Ken Haley was Reserve Mining's research engineer and one of the key, expert witnesses in the litigation. Reserve Mining Company Presidents Ed Furness and later Merlyn Woodle and Matt Banovitz, were stable, guiding forces throughout the entire period of litigation.

I was proud to be a member of that distinguished team. We worked together for almost sixteen long years, coping with a stressful controversy that we were able to bring to a successful conclusion for the benefit of the people of northern Minnesota, the state, and the nation. . The litigation took a terrible toll, not only on those that lost their homes, their life savings, and their livelihoods, but also on the attorneys and others engaged in the day-to-day controversy, most of who have now succumbed to the stress, and few of those team members are still alive.

Delores and I have been blessed with many friends, both locally and from throughout the United States and the world. Our activities in the Flying Tigers, 14th Air Force Association brought us many special friends. The Bateman family from Macon, Georgia, is among our dearest. There are a host of others from virtually every American state and many countries abroad that would take pages to list. Those bonds of friendships, often formed during the adversities of war, live on to be long remembered.

One of my friends, George Harvey Cain, in his book "Turning Points II," published by the American Bar Association, writes about what lawyers can do outside the strict field of law. He illustrates a number of examples. As one example, he sums up my life in a very succinct manner. Although some of his story repeats what I have already recounted, it does reflect a fairly objective perspective of my life:

Wayne G. Johnson: This lawyer is a good example of that saying that "variety is the spice of life." ... This first example is a lawyer with a truly remarkable career with a variety of accomplishments. He will demonstrate that a person with many abilities may put them to good purpose, and not always as an advocate in the courtroom or a draftsman on the side of contract preparation. He gave of his talent to local representation and to ventures of wide geographic significance as well. . . .

I will tell you about "Whitey" Johnson's remarkable life in detail, but know that he started law practice in 1952 — and still practices. When you learn what Wayne Johnson has done . . . you wonder whether he ever had time to sleep. [He] . .

. learned to fly an airplane when he was only 16 years old in high school in Chokio, Minnesota. Wayne Johnson joined the Army Air Corps the day after Pearl Harbor was trained as a fighter pilot and sent to China as a fighter pilot. After World War II, Wayne Johnson pursued a college and law school education in his home state of Minnesota and was admitted to the bar in 1952 and is now the Senior Partner of Johnson & Morris. This activity on the "legal front" did not curtail Wayne Johnson's efforts in a number of other areas. He continued throughout his life as an outstanding pilot . . . became active in the 14th Air Force Association, the unit embracing the "Flying Tigers" . . . Wayne served in a number of positions, including presidency. Somewhere along the line his artistic ability shone, and he created a number of plaques for such facilities as for the memorial wall at the Air Force Academy in Colorado Springs . . . He also designed the "Chennault's Flying Tigers Calendars" distributed by the 14th Air Force Association, including researching and writing the historical material included in the calendars. . . .When doing this, Wayne Johnson became what he terms, an "amateur historian." He edited the four volume "Chennault's Flying Tigers" history. . . . When not thus occupied, he managed to write for military and aviation magazines, and lecture about the role of the "Flying Tigers" in World War II. . . .   His talent as an aviator was the result of military training and wartime combat experience. His legal training brought him a wide swath of knowledge that was useful in creating the cities of Beaver Bay and Silver Bay, in allowing him to deal effectively with people and secure donations of material things and money for museum related to his aviation heritage. . . .

Examine your talents. . . . If you are searching for something different to do, think of what you do best and what you enjoy doing the most . . . You can find people and organizations that have tasks and goals that should fit your likes and can match the criteria you seek. You won't need all of the talent and experience of a Wayne Johnson to launch your . . . career; but a broad look at the broad spectrum of his efforts should demonstrate that there are opportunities waiting — if you only make the effort.

By George Harvey Cain. The excerpt from the article is included with permission of the American Bar Association.

In the "broad look" and "broad spectrum" that the author speaks of, I believe I have done things that I felt I could do best and that I enjoyed the most. Despite the trauma of losing my legs and learning to walk again with prostheses, in the latter part of my life, life has generally been good to me.

Although that event probably precipitated an earlier retirement than I had anticipated, I could not burden Delores with driving me to meetings and other obligations of my law practice. I knew and accepted the hand that had been dealt to me, and the fact that I had to live with and still deal intellectually with the many others assets that life has to offer. Perhaps I will go back to farming in my old Fordson!

"*Farmer*" Johnson with his 1924 Fordson

"Farmer" Wayne Johnson with his 1924 Fordson tractor.

Regardless of whatever humble backgrounds we may come from, if we have the will, each of us can "pull ourselves up by the boot straps" and lead a productive and interesting life. Even though we may not reach or achieve it, most of us have the ability to strive for excellence, and the fortitude to reach for that goal.

Each of us leaves some mark on society, some good — some bad. It is my hope that, with my heritage, I have left some good marks.

I have been very fortunate to have a loving wife who has stood by me for more than fifty years, and fortunate to have a fine family. Except for the usual mischief that young folks sometimes get involved with, my children caused me few problems. Although none followed me in the field of law, they were each successful in their chosen vocations. Margaret Ann, who I usually called Annie, became a physical therapist. Bruce became a commercial pilot, flying jets for a large motel chain, a skilled aviation mechanic, and now chief inspector for an aircraft charter company. Because of his untimely death, we do not know what career Beaver might have chosen. He was an intelligent and ambitious young man, and we had every confidence that he would have been successful in any field he chose. His death was a terrible and lasting loss.

My family was and is very important to me. All of my brothers and sisters were very close. We visited and communicated with each other on a regular basis. Delores' family, too, became a very important part of ours. She was an only child and very close to her father and mother. She visited with or talked to them on almost a daily basis. They only lived a few miles away from us, so we visited frequently. After her mother died, Delores became a devoted caretaker for her father, who lived in quite good health into his nineties. He loved to visit our home, particularly when grandchildren, great-grandchildren, and great-great-grandchildren were there. He was particularly proud that he was the patriarch of five living generations.

Of all the memories of a person's life, the ones most cherished are of lifelong family relationships and friendships.

I considered leaving out graphic language that was a sign of the times, but was counseled not to do so. To do so would not be an accurate recounting of an age in which part of this story takes place. If I have offended anyone by those inclusions, and reports of some youthful indiscretions, I offer my sincere apologies.

APPENDIX

Wayne Johnson's Genealogy

showing his

Johannessen (Johnson), Jorgensen, and Olsen Ancestors

GENEALOGICAL RELATIONSHIP CHART

from third great grandparents

ANDREAS PETTERSEN

to

WAYNE JOHNSON

Relationship Chart

Andreas PETERSEN (1766-1845) **Ane Marie HANSDATTER-MJELDE** (-)	third great grandparents
Jens Wilhelm ANDREASSEN (1801-) **Ingeborg Marie NIENSDATTER** (-)	second great grandparents
Johannes JENSEN (1824-1880) **Anne Cecilie NICOLAISDATTER** (1828-1880)	great grandparents
Soren Kristian JOHANNESSEN (1855-1917) **Lovise Valine JORGENSDATTER** (1850-1937) Married 1878	grandparents
Jentoft Kristian Blom JOHANNESSEN (1882-1951) **Aasta Karoline OLSEN** (1881-1976) Married 1904	parents

Relationship Chart

Wayne Gordon JOHNSON
(1921-   )

This chart through the Johannessen (Johnson)
Petersen line (also spelled Pettersen)

GENEALOGICAL RELATIONSHIP CHART

from tenth great grandparents

PEDER MADSEN GRAM

to

WAYNE JOHNSON

Relationship Chart

14 Jul 2010

Peder Madsen GRAM
(1515-1586)

tenth great grandparents

Mads Pedersen GRAM
(1550-)
NO INFORMATION
(-)
Married 1575

ninth great grandparents

Lars Madsen GRAM
(1577-1645)
NO INFO ON WIFE
(-)
Married 1608

eighth great grandparents

Larsen GRAM
(1610-)
HIS WIFE UNKNOWN
(-)

seventh great grandparents

Hans GRAM
(1645-)
WIFE UNKNOWN
(-)

sixth great grandparents

Relationship Chart

Peder HANSEN (GRAM)
(1677-   )
HIS WIFE UNKNOWN
(-)

fifth great grandparents

Mads PETERSEN (GRAM)
(1717-1787)
Margrete GRONBECK
(1723-1763)
Married 1754

fourth great grandparents

Jorgen MADSEN (GRAM)
(1755-1837)
Beret ENDRESDATTER
(1762-1812)
Married 1787

third great grandparents

Hans Peder (Gram) JORGENSEN
(1788-1858)
Pauline NIKOLAISDATTER
(1803-1833)
Married 1823

second great grandparents

Jorgen Christian Gram HANSEN
(1824-1897)
Hanna Bendikte Molde INDAHL
(1828-1901)
Married 1849

great grandparents

Relationship Chart

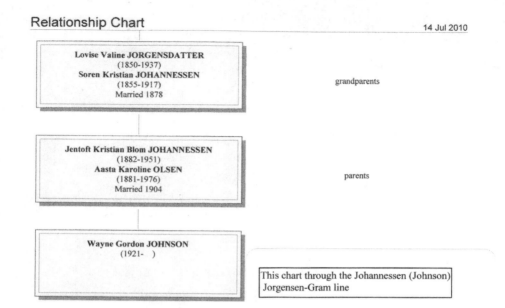

Lovise Valine JORGENSDATTER
(1850-1937)
Soren Kristian JOHANNESSEN
(1855-1917)
Married 1878

grandparents

Jentoft Kristian Blom JOHANNESSEN
(1882-1951)
Aasta Karoline OLSEN
(1881-1976)
Married 1904

parents

Wayne Gordon JOHNSON
(1921-)

This chart through the Johannessen (Johnson)
Jorgensen-Gram line

GENEALOGICAL RELATIONSHIP CHART

from tenth great grandparents

CHRISTIAN HEGGLUND

to

WAYNE JOHNSON

Relationship Chart

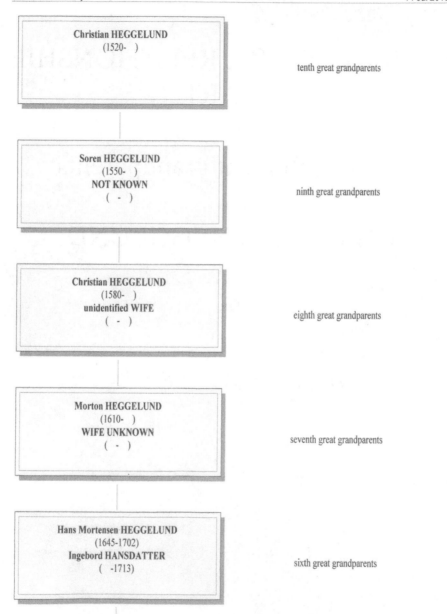

Christian HEGGELUND
(1520-   )

tenth great grandparents

Soren HEGGELUND
(1550-   )
NOT KNOWN
(-)

ninth great grandparents

Christian HEGGELUND
(1580-   )
unidentified WIFE
(-)

eighth great grandparents

Morton HEGGELUND
(1610-   )
WIFE UNKNOWN
(-)

seventh great grandparents

Hans Mortensen HEGGELUND
(1645-1702)
Ingebord HANSDATTER
(-1713)

sixth great grandparents

Relationship Chart

Soren Hansen HEGGELUND
(1682-1759)
Anne Margrethe RASMUSSDATTEER
(1693-1766)
Married 1715

fifth great grandparents

4th great-grandfather Lars Sorensen HEGGELUND
(1726-1806)
Nille Severine Pedersdatter FIGENSCHOW
(1749-   )

fourth great grandparents

Anne Meldahl HEGGELUND
(1774-1844)
Soren Lorentzen INDAHL
(1761-1827)
Married 1792

third great grandparents

Lorentz Fabritius INDAHL
(1792-1858)
Andrianna ANDERSDATTER
(1790-   )
Married 1819

second great grandparents

Hanna Bendikte Molde INDAHL
(1828-1901)
Jorgen Christian Gram HANSEN
(1824-1897)
Married 1849

great grandparents

Relationship Chart

Lovise Valine JORGENSDATTER
(1850-1937)
Soren Kristian JOHANNESSEN
(1855-1917)
Married 1878

grandparents

Jentoft Kristian Blom JOHANNESSEN
(1882-1951)
Aasta Karoline OLSEN
(1881-1976)
Married 1904

parents

Wayne Gordon JOHNSON
(1921-)

This chart through the Johannessen (Johnson)
Jorgensen-Hegglund line

440

Pedigree Chart

Chart no. 1
No. 1 on this chart is the same as no. 1 on chart no. 1

16 Jens Wilhelm ANDREASSEN
b: abt 1801 cont 2
d: unknown

17 Ingeborg Marie NIENSDATTER
b: unknown
d: unknown

8 Johannes JENSEN
b: 26 Jan 1824
p: Movig,Norway
m:
p:
d: 1880
p: Ljoso (Lysoy), Tromsosund,Norway

4 Soren Kristian JOHANNESSEN
b: 1855
p: Ljosoy,Norway
m: 11 Sep 1878
p: Tromso, Norway
d: 1917
p: Tromso, Norway

18 Nicolay ANDERSEN
b: 3 Aug 1798 cont 3
d: 21 Feb 1870

19 Martha OLSDATTER-BULL
b: 1800
d: unknown

9 Anne Cecilie NICOLAISDATTER
b: 3 Jun 1828
p: Logvig, Norway
d: abt 1880
p: Logvig, Norway

2 Jentoft Kristian JOHANNESSEN
b: 19 May 1882
p: Tromso, Norway
m: 9 Nov 1904
p: Tromso, Norway
d: 27 Nov 1951
p: Wheaton, Minnesota, USA,-of stroke

20 Hans Peder (Gram) JORGENSEN
b: 22 Nov 1788 cont 4
d: 12 Feb 1858

21 Pauline NIKOLAISDATTER
b: 1803
d: 12 Nov 1833

10 Jorgen Christian Gram HANSEN
b: 7 Sep 1824
p: Nordeidet, Norway
m: 14 Oct 1849
p: Nordeidet Norway
d: 21 Jul 1897
p: Big Stone County,Minnesota near Ortonville

5 Lovise Valine JORGENSDATTER
b: 25 Sep 1850
p: Nordeidet, Norway
d: 28 May 1937
p: Big Stone County,Minnesota near Ortonville

22 Lorentz Fabritius INDAHL
b: 1792 cont 5
d: 12 Mar 1858

23 Andrianna ANDERSDATTER
b: 1790
d: 16 November, 1972

11 Hanna Bendikte Molde INDAHL
b: 18 May 1828
p: Reinoy, Norway
d: 24 Oct 1901
p: Big Stone County,Minnesota near Ortonville

1 Wayne Gordon JOHNSON
b: 8 Jul 1921
p: Big Stone County,Minnesota near Ortonville
m: 28 Jun 1957
p: Silver Bay, MN
d:
p:

sp: **Delores Evon CHRISTENSEN**

24 Christian OLSEN
b:
d:

25 UNKNOWN
b:
d:

12 Ole CHRISTIANSEN
b: abt 1800
p: Tonsvik or Sletten
m: 10 Nov 1841
p: Tonsvig, Norway
d: 28 Sep 1876
p: Tonsvik, Norway

6 Ole Bertin Edvard OLSEN
b: 29 Aug 1847
p: Tonsvig, Norway
m:
p:
d: 20 Sep 1929
p: Tromso, Norway

26 Johan Christian ANDREASSEN
b: abt 1789 cont 6
d: 11 May 1861

27 Martha WILLUMSDATTER
b: 9 Jan 1789 cont 7
d: 11 May 1861

13 Anna JOHANNESDATTER
b: 25 Jul 1816
p: Stakkevolden, Tromso, Norway
d: 28 Sep 1876
p: Tonsvik, Norway

3 Aasta Karoline OLSEN
b: 4 Mar 1881
p: Tromso, Norway
d: 21 Jun 1976
p: Wheaton, Minnesota,

28
b:
d:

29
b:
d:

14 Lars HANSEN
b: abt 1816
p: Tromsosund ,Norway
m:
p:
d:
p: Tromsosund ,Norway

7 Kornelia Margrete LARSDATTER
b: 28 Dec 1852
p: Tromsosund ,Norway
d: 19 Apr 1933
p: Tromso, Norway

30
b:
d:

31
b:
d:

15 Anne P. ANDREASDATTER
b: abt 1823
p: Tromsosund ,Norway
d:
p: Tromsosund ,Norway

Prepared 2 Apr 2010 by:
Wayne G. Johnson
2000 Roy St. & Norwegian Crossing
PO Box 496
Beaver Bay, Minnesota 55601

1

Pedigree Chart

Chart no. 2

No. 1 on this chart is the same as no. 16 on chart no. 1

2 Apr 2010

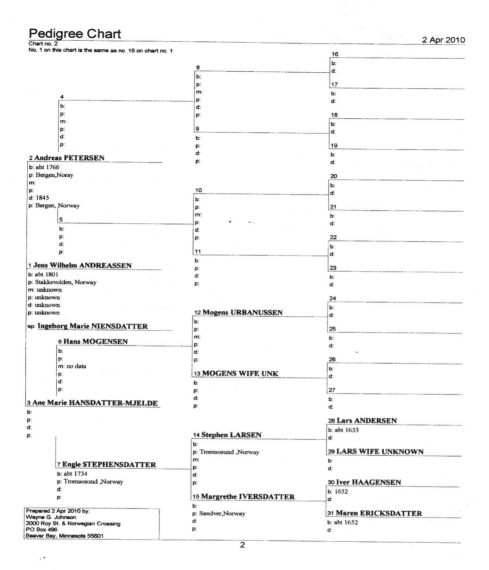

16
b:
d:

8
b:
p:
m:
p:
d:
p:

17
b:
d:

4
b:
p:
m:
p:
d:
p:

18
b:
d:

9
b:
p:
d:
p:

19
b:
d:

2 Andreas PETERSEN
b: abt 1766
p: Bergen,Noray
m:
p:
d: 1845
p: Bergen, Norway

20
b:
d:

10
b:
p:
m:
p:
d:
p:

21
b:
d:

5
b:
p:
d:
p:

22
b:
d:

11
b:
p:
d:
p:

23
b:
d:

1 Jens Wilhelm ANDREASSEN
b: abt 1801
p: Stakkevolden, Norway
m: unknown
p: unknown
d: unknown
p: unknown

24
b:
d:

sp: **Ingeborg Marie NIENSDATTER**

12 Mogens URBANUSSEN
b:
p:
m:
p:
d:
p:

25
b:
d:

6 Hans MOGENSEN
b:
p:
m: no data
p:
d:
p:

26
b:
d:

13 MOGENS WIFE UNK
b:
p:
d:
p:

27
b:
d:

3 Ane Marie HANSDATTER-MJELDE
b:
p:
d:
p:

28 Lars ANDERSEN
b: abt 1633
d:

14 Stephen LARSEN
b:
p: Tromsosund ,Norway
m:
p:
d:
p:

29 LARS WIFE UNKNOWN
b:
d:

7 Engle STEPHENSDATTER
b: abt 1734
p: Tromsosund ,Norway
d:
p:

30 Iver HAAGENSEN
b: 1652
d:

15 Margrethe IVERSDATTER
b:
p: Sandver,Norway
d:
p:

31 Maren ERICKSDATTER
b: abt 1652
d:

Prepared 2 Apr 2010 by:
Wayne G. Johnson
2000 Roy St. & Norwegian Crossing
PO Box 496
Beaver Bay, Minnesota 55601

2

Pedigree Chart

2 Apr 2010

Chart no. 3
No. 1 on this chart is the same as no. 18 on chart no. 1

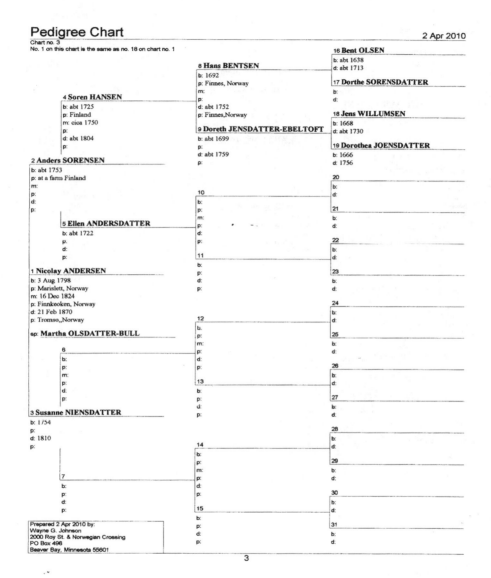

16 Bent OLSEN
b: abt 1638
d: abt 1713

8 Hans BENTSEN
b: 1692
p: Finnes, Norway
m:
p:
d: abt 1752
p: Finnes,Norway

17 Dorthe SORENSDATTER
b:
d:

4 Soren HANSEN
b: abt 1725
p: Finland
m: cica 1750
p:
d: abt 1804
p:

9 Doreth JENSDATTER-EBELTOFT
b: abt 1699
p:
d: abt 1759
p:

18 Jens WILLUMSEN
b: 1668
d: abt 1730

19 Dorothea JOENSDATTER
b: 1666
d: 1756

2 Anders SORENSEN
b: abt 1753
p: at a farm Finland
m:
p:
d:
p:

10
b:
p:
m:
p:
d:
p:

20
b:
d:

21
b:
d:

5 Ellen ANDERSDATTER
b: abt 1722
p:
d:
p:

11
b:
p:
d:
p:

22
b:
d:

23
b:
d:

1 Nicolay ANDERSEN
b: 3 Aug 1798
p: Marislett, Norway
m: 16 Dec 1824
p: Finnkeoken, Norway
d: 21 Feb 1870
p: Tromso,,Norway

sp: **Martha OLSDATTER-BULL**

12
b:
p:
m:
p:
d:
p:

24
b:
d:

25
b:
d:

6
b:
p:
m:
p:
d:
p:

13
b:
p:
d:
p:

26
b:
d:

27
b:
d:

3 Susanne NIENSDATTER
b: 1754
p:
d: 1810
p:

14
b:
p:
m:
p:
d:
p:

28
b:
d:

29
b:
d:

7
b:
p:
d:
p:

15
b:
p:
d:
p:

30
b:
d:

31
b:
d:

Prepared 2 Apr 2010 by:
Wayne G. Johnson
2000 Roy St. & Norwegian Crossing
PO Box 496
Beaver Bay, Minnesota 55601

3

443

Pedigree Chart

Chart no. 4

No. 1 on this chart is the same as no. 20 on chart no. 1

2 Apr 2010

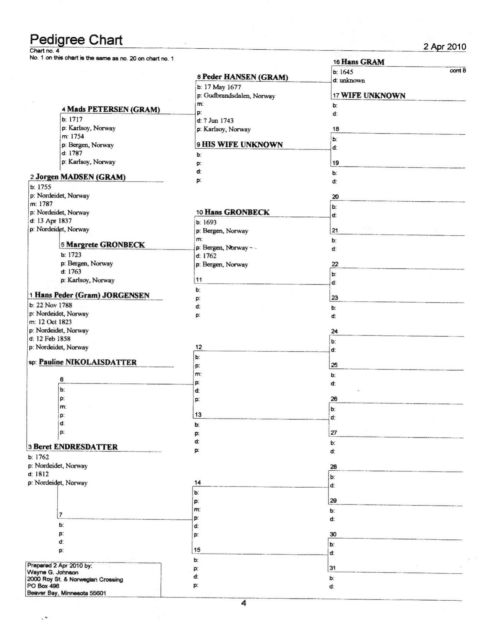

16 Hans GRAM
b: 1645
d: unknown
cont 8

17 WIFE UNKNOWN
b:
d:

8 Peder HANSEN (GRAM)
b: 17 May 1677
p: Gudbrandsdalen, Norway
m:
p:
d: ? Jun 1743
p: Karlsoy, Norway

4 Mads PETERSEN (GRAM)
b: 1717
p: Karlsoy, Norway
m: 1754
p: Bergen, Norway
d: 1787
p: Karlsoy, Norway

9 HIS WIFE UNKNOWN
b:
p:
d:
p:

2 Jorgen MADSEN (GRAM)
b: 1755
p: Nordeidet, Norway
m: 1787
p: Nordeidet, Norway
d: 13 Apr 1837
p: Nordeidet, Norway

10 Hans GRONBECK
b: 1693
p: Bergen, Norway
m:
p: Bergen, Norway
d: 1762
p: Bergen, Norway

5 Margrete GRONBECK
b: 1723
p: Bergen, Norway
d: 1763
p: Karlsoy, Norway

11
b:
p:
d:
p:

1 Hans Peder (Gram) JORGENSEN
b: 22 Nov 1788
p: Nordeidet, Norway
m: 12 Oct 1823
p: Nordeidet, Norway
d: 12 Feb 1858
p: Nordeidet, Norway

sp: **Pauline NIKOLAISDATTER**

6
b:
p:
m:
p:
d:
p:

12
b:
p:
m:
p:
d:
p:

13
b:
p:
d:
p:

3 Beret ENDRESDATTER
b: 1762
p: Nordeidet, Norway
d: 1812
p: Nordeidet, Norway

7
b:
p:
d:
p:

14
b:
p:
m:
p:
d:
p:

15
b:
p:
d:
p:

18
b:
d:

19
b:
d:

20
b:
d:

21
b:
d:

22
b:
d:

23
b:
d:

24
b:
d:

25
b:
d:

26
b:
d:

27
b:
d:

28
b:
d:

29
b:
d:

30
b:
d:

31
b:
d:

Prepared 2 Apr 2010 by:
Wayne G. Johnson
2000 Roy St. & Norwegian Crossing
PO Box 496
Beaver Bay, Minnesota 55601

4

Pedigree Chart

Chart no. 5
No. 1 on this chart is the same as no. 22 on chart no. 1

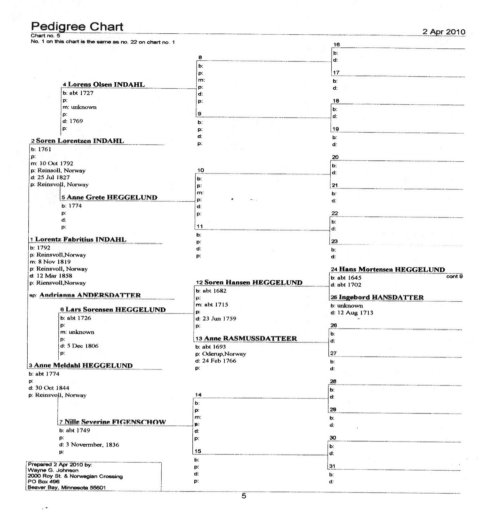

4 Lorens Olsen INDAHL
b: abt 1727
p:
m: unknown
p:
d: 1769
p:

2 Soren Lorentzen INDAHL
b: 1761
p:
m: 10 Oct 1792
p: Reinsoll, Norway
d: 25 Jul 1827
p: Reinsvoll, Norway

5 Anne Grete HEGGELUND
b: 1774
p:
d:
p:

1 Lorentz Fabritius INDAHL
b: 1792
p: Reinsvoll,Norway
m: 8 Nov 1819
p: Reinsvoll, Norway
d: 12 Mar 1858
p: Riensvoll,Norway

sp: **Andrianna ANDERSDATTER**

6 Lars Sorensen HEGGELUND
b: abt 1726
p:
m: unknown
p:
d: 5 Dec 1806
p:

3 Anne Meldahl HEGGELUND
b: abt 1774
p:
d: 30 Oct 1844
p: Reinsvoll, Norway

7 Nille Severine FIGENSCHOW
b: abt 1749
p:
d: 3 Novermber, 1836
p:

8
b:
p:
m:
p:
d:
p:

9
b:
p:
d:
p:

10
b:
p:
m:
p:
d:
p:

11
b:
p:
d:
p:

12 Soren Hansen HEGGELUND
b: abt 1682
p:
m: abt 1715
p:
d: 23 Jun 1759
p:

13 Anne RASMUSSDATTEER
b: abt 1693
p: Oderup,Norway
d: 24 Feb 1766
p:

14
b:
p:
m:
p:
d:
p:

15
b:
p:
d:
p:

16
b:
d:

17
b:
d:

18
b:
d:

19
b:
d:

20
b:
d:

21
b:
d:

22
b:
d:

23
b:
d:

24 Hans Mortensen HEGGELUND
b: abt 1645
d: abt 1702
cont 9

25 Ingebord HANSDATTER
b: unknown
d: 12 Aug 1713

26
b:
d:

27
b:
d:

28
b:
d:

29
b:
d:

30
b:
d:

31
b:
d:

Prepared 2 Apr 2010 by:
Wayne G. Johnson
2000 Roy St. & Norwegian Crossing
PO Box 496
Beaver Bay, Minnesota 55601

5

Pedigree Chart

Chart no. 6
No. 1 on this chart is the same as no. 26 on chart no. 1

2 Apr 2010

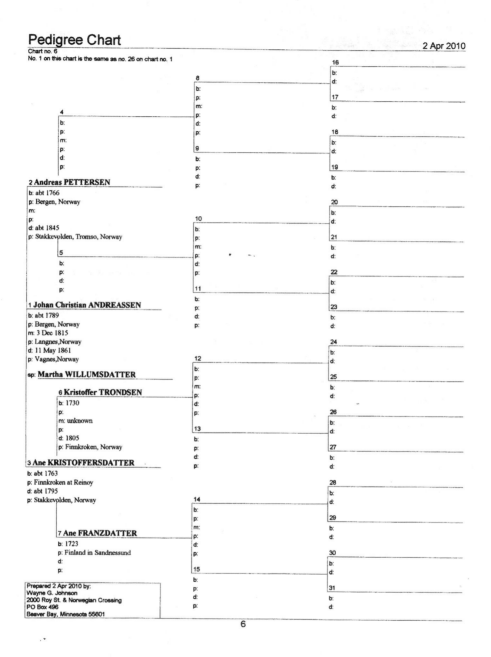

4
b:
p:
m:
p:
d:
p:

8
b:
p:
m:
p:
d:
p:

16
b:
d:

17
b:
d:

9
b:
p:
d:
p:

18
b:
d:

19
b:
d:

2 Andreas PETTERSEN
b: abt 1766
p: Bergen, Norway
m:
p:
d: abt 1845
p: Stakkevolden, Tromso, Norway

10
b:
p:
m:
p:
d:
p:

20
b:
d:

21
b:
d:

5
b:
p:
d:
p:

11
b:
p:
d:
p:

22
b:
d:

23
b:
d:

1 Johan Christian ANDREASSEN
b: abt 1789
p: Bergen, Norway
m: 3 Dec 1815
p: Langnes,Norway
d: 11 May 1861
p: Vagnes,Norway

sp: **Martha WILLUMSDATTER**

12
b:
p:
m:
p:
d:
p:

24
b:
d:

25
b:
d:

6 Kristoffer TRONDSEN
b: 1730
p:
m: unknown
p:
d: 1805
p: Finnkroken, Norway

13
b:
p:
d:
p:

26
b:
d:

27
b:
d:

3 Ane KRISTOFFERSDATTER
b: abt 1763
p: Finnkroken at Reinoy
d: abt 1795
p: Stakkevolden, Norway

14
b:
p:
m:
p:
d:
p:

28
b:
d:

29
b:
d:

7 Ane FRANZDATTER
b: 1723
p: Finland in Sandnessund
d:
p:

15
b:
p:
d:
p:

30
b:
d:

31
b:
d:

Prepared 2 Apr 2010 by:
Wayne G. Johnson
2000 Roy St. & Norwegian Crossing
PO Box 496
Beaver Bay, Minnesota 55601

6

446

Pedigree Chart

Chart no. 7
No. 1 on this chart is the same as no. 27 on chart no. 1

16 Jens WILLUMSEN-EBELTOFT
b: abt 1668
d: abt 1729

8 Willum JENSEN
b: abt 1701
p: Langnes, Norway
m: unknown
p:
d: abt 1760
p: Langnes, Norway

17 Dorothea JOENSDATTER
b: abt 1666
d: abt 1766

4 Jens WILLUMSEN
b: abt 1724
p:
m:
p:
d:
p:

18 Jorgen ADRIANSEN-FALCH
b: 1656
d: abt 1710

9 Adelus JORGENSDATTER-FALCH
b: abt 1697
p: Langnes, Norway
d: abt 1774
p: Langnes, Norway

19 Adsel SORENSDATTER
b: abt 1662
d:

2 Willum JENSEN
b: abt 1752
p: Sondre Langnes, Norway
m: abt 1784
p: Langnes, Norway
d: ? July 1820
p: Langnes, Norway

20 Hans THORSTENSEN
b:
d:

10 Torsten HANSEN
b:
p: Hegelund
m: unknown
p:
d:
p:

21 TORSTEN WIFE UNK
b:
d:

5 Martha TORSTENSDATTER
b: abt 1722
p: Hegelund
d: 1769
p: Langnes, Norway

22
b:
d:

11 WIFE UNKOWN
b:
p:
d:
p:

23
b:
d:

1 Martha WILLUMSDATTER
b: 9 Jan 1789
p: Langnes, Norway
m: 3 Dec 1815
p: Langnes,Norway
d: 11 May 1861
p: Stakkevolden, Tromso, Norway

sp: **Johan Christian ANDREASSEN**

24
b:
d:

12
b:
p:
m:
p:
d:
p:

25
b:
d:

6 Morten LARSEN
b: abt 1717
p: Denmark or Germany
m: 1755
p:
d: 1797
p: Trondhjem, Norway

26
b:
d:

13
b:
p:
d:
p:

27
b:
d:

3 Anne Birgiithe MORTENSDATTER
b: abt 1755
p: Renen,Norway
d: abt 1794
p: Langnes, Norway

28 Hans PEDERSEN
b: abt 1663
d: 1735

14 Ander HANSEN
b:
p:
m:
p:
d: 1747
p: Selnes, Norway

29 Golla PEDERSDATTER
b: abt 1665
d: 1756

7 Marith ANDERSDATTER
b: abt 1728
p: Bergen,Norway
d:
p:

30
b:
d:

15 ANDERS WIFE UNK
b:
p:
d:
p:

31
b:
d:

7

Pedigree Chart

Chart no. 8
No. 1 on this chart is the same as no. 16 on chart no. 4

2 Apr 2010

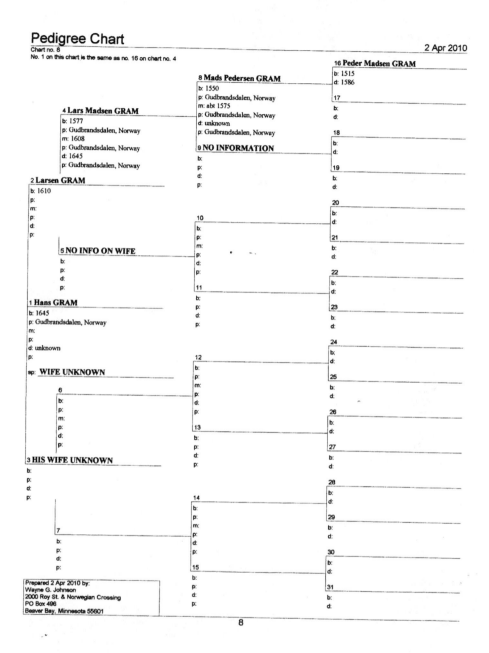

16 Peder Madsen GRAM
b: 1515
d: 1586

8 Mads Pedersen GRAM
b: 1550
p: Gudbrandsdalen, Norway
m: abt 1575
p: Gudbrandsdalen, Norway
d: unknown
p: Gudbrandsdalen, Norway

17
b:
d:

18
b:
d:

4 Lars Madsen GRAM
b: 1577
p: Gudbrandsdalen, Norway
m: 1608
p: Gudbrandsdalen, Norway
d: 1645
p: Gudbrandsdalen, Norway

9 NO INFORMATION
b:
p:
d:
p:

19
b:
d:

2 Larsen GRAM
b: 1610
p:
m:
p:
d:
p:

20
b:
d:

10
b:
p:
m:
p:
d:
p:

21
b:
d:

5 NO INFO ON WIFE
b:
p:
d:
p:

22
b:
d:

11
b:
p:
d:
p:

23
b:
d:

1 Hans GRAM
b: 1645
p: Gudbrandsdalen, Norway
m:
p:
d: unknown
p:

24
b:
d:

12
b:
p:
m:
p:
d:
p:

25
b:
d:

sp: **WIFE UNKNOWN**

6
b:
p:
m:
p:
d:
p:

26
b:
d:

13
b:
p:
d:
p:

27
b:
d:

3 HIS WIFE UNKNOWN
b:
p:
d:
p:

28
b:
d:

14
b:
p:
m:
p:
d:
p:

29
b:
d:

7
b:
p:
d:
p:

30
b:
d:

15
b:
p:
d:
p:

31
b:
d:

Prepared 2 Apr 2010 by:
Wayne G. Johnson
2000 Roy St. & Norwegian Crossing
PO Box 496
Beaver Bay, Minnesota 55601

8

Pedigree Chart

Chart no. 9
No. 1 on this chart is the same as no. 24 on chart no. 5

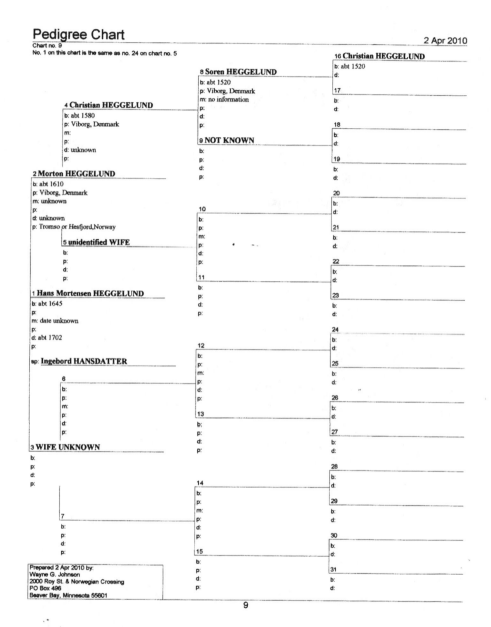

16 Christian HEGGELUND
b: abt 1520
d:

8 Soren HEGGELUND
b: abt 1520
p: Viborg, Denmark
m: no information
p:
d:
p:

17
b:
d:

18
b:
d:

4 Christian HEGGELUND
b: abt 1580
p: Viborg, Denmark
m:
p:
d: unknown
p:

9 NOT KNOWN
b:
p:
d:
p:

19
b:
d:

20
b:
d:

2 Morton HEGGELUND
b: abt 1610
p: Viborg, Denmark
m: unknown
p:
d: unknown
p: Tromso or Hesfjord,Norway

10
b:
p:
m:
p:
d:
p:

21
b:
d:

5 unidentified WIFE
b:
p:
d:
p:

22
b:
d:

11
b:
p:
d:
p:

23
b:
d:

1 Hans Mortensen HEGGELUND
b: abt 1645
p:
m: date unknown
p:
d: abt 1702
p:

sp: **Ingebord HANSDATTER**

24
b:
d:

12
b:
p:
m:
p:
d:
p:

25
b:
d:

6
b:
p:
m:
p:
d:
p:

26
b:
d:

13
b:
p:
d:
p:

27
b:
d:

3 WIFE UNKNOWN
b:
p:
d:
p:

28
b:
d:

14
b:
p:
m:
p:
d:
p:

29
b:
d:

7
b:
p:
d:
p:

30
b:
d:

15
b:
p:
d:
p:

31
b:
d:

Prepared 2 Apr 2010 by:
Wayne G. Johnson
2000 Roy St. & Norwegian Crossing
PO Box 496
Beaver Bay, Minnesota 55601

9

APPENDIX 11

Wayne Johnson's Biographical

Wayne G. Johnson

Wayne Gordon Johnson was born on 8 July 1921 on a farm in Artichoke Township near Ortonville, Minnesota. He was one of 14 children. His parents, Jentoft Christian Blom Johnson and Aasta Karoline Olsen had emigrated from Norway in 1907.

Wayne started his flying career in 1937 when, a farmer near Chokio, Minnesota, taught him to fly in a Curtiss Robin plane. He earned his flying lessons in exchange for farm chores while attending high school in Chokio. Spending over seventy years in the air as a pilot, he continued to fly well into his eighties.

On 8 December 1941, the day after the Japanese attack on Pearl Harbor, Johnson joined the Army Air Corps. After Cadet and Tactical training, and commissioned a 2nd Lieutenant, he was sent to China as a fighter pilot with General Claire Lee Chennault's famed *Flying Tigers*-14th Air Force. He flew the P-40 *Warhawk* and P-51 *Mustang* fighters in combat. For a lark, and not officially authorized, he flew the Japanese Aichi *Val* and *Jake* dive bombers at a Shanghai air field after the surrender. After the war he flew P-51s for the North Dakota Air National Guard while attending college and also did crop dusting in a Stearman by-plane. He has over 7,500 hours pilot time in over 60 different types of military and civilian aircraft with single and multi-engine land and sea ratings.

His most memorable combat mission was the first fighter strike on Japanese airdromes near Shanghai on 17 January 1945 when a flight of eight P-51 Mustangs from the 118th Tactical Reconnaissance *Black Lightning* Squadron, of which he was member, and eight P-51s from the 74th Fighter Squadron destroyed 94 Japanese aircraft on the ground and three in the air without loss of any U.S. planes. General Chennault, Commander of the *Flying Tigers*, said it was one of the most successful missions of the war.

1

Wayne Johnson is the Editor of the four volume history *Chennault's Flying Tigers,* designer and editor of the *Flying Tigers 2003 - 2007 Calendars.* He is the author of two privately published books, *The Trial of Christ,* where he analysis on the unfairness of the trial leading up to Christ's execution, and a *Sailor's War* based on the diary of his brother-in-law, Reo Knudson, who was wounded while serving on the battle ship *Tennessee* during the Japanese attack on Pearl Harbor on 7 December 1941.

He is past President and member of the Board of Directors of the *Flying Tigers* 14th Air Force Association. He served as Secretary of the *Flying Tigers* Museum Committee for the *Flying Tigers* exhibit at the Museum of Aviation, Warner Robins, Georgia. He helped design some of the exhibits at the Museum of Aviation, provided captions, historical material, and monitored the exhibits for historical accuracy. Johnson helped design the *Flying Tigers Memorial Monument* at the United States Air Force Museum Memorial Park in Dayton, Ohio; designed the *Flying Tigers* monument at New Park, Taipei, Taiwan; the *Flying Tigers* plaques for the Memorial Garden at the Air Force Academy in Colorado Springs; the *Flying Tigers* plaque for the Tomb of the Unknown at Arlington National Cemetery as well as the historical plaques for the National Air and Space Museum at Dulles International Airport. He was instrumental in securing a postage stamp honoring General Claire Chennault, commander of the *Flying Tigers,* in 1990.

Johnson has written numerous articles on aviation, and lectures widely, particularly on the role of the *Flying Tigers* in WWII, as well on other historical and legal matters. He is a member of the Air Force Association and a charter member of the Commemorative Air Force Association which was organized to preserve World War II aircraft and to operate a display museum as well as demonstrate WWII aircraft at air shows.

He helped form and is a charter member of the Lawyer-Pilots Association. He also helped organize and was the first president of the Flying Sportsman of North America.

2

Wayne Johnson graduated from the Chokio, Minnesota, high school in 1939 and received his higher education at Michigan Mining and Technology, North Dakota State University, University of Minnesota and the William Mitchell College of Law. He was admitted to the Minnesota bar in 1952. He is admitted to the practice of law in Minnesota and Wisconsin, United States District Courts, United States Circuit Courts of Appeal and the United States Supreme Court. He is a member of the of the American, Minnesota and Wisconsin Bar Associations, the American and Minnesota Trial Lawyers Associations, the Lawyer-Pilots Association, and the Minnesota City Attorneys Association

He has served as City Attorney for two cities for over 50 years, setting a record as the longest serving City Attorney not only in Minnesota, but in the United States. Among his awards are citations from the Minnesota State Bar Association *for leadership and unselfish participation in public affairs of the community, state and nation and those commendable personal qualities that characterize those who best exemplify the high ideals of the profession as an officer of the courts in the administration of justice; the* Wisconsin Bar Association for *50 Years of Distinguished Service and in recognition of special efforts in furtherance of the high standards and ideals of the legal profession dedicated to the public service,* the 11th Judicial District Bar Association *in recognition of 50 years of honorable service - setting an inspiring example of devotion to the duties of an Attorney and Counselor at law;* the Minnesota City Attorney's Association *for exceptional and dedicated public service;* the *Lifetime Achievement Award* from the Minnesota Trial Lawyers Association *for outstanding contributions and tireless efforts in promoting the public good.*

In 2004, he was awarded the prestigious *Douglas K. Amdahl Public Service Career Achievement Award* by the Public Service Section of the Minnesota Bar Association *in recognition if his dedication and commitment to public service and the public practice of law.* The award is named after the Honorable Douglas K. Amdahl, former Chief Justice of the Minnesota Supreme Court.

3

It is one of the highest awards made by the Minnesota State Bar Association.

Martindale-Hubbell, the international rating bureau for attorneys, gives Wayne Johnson an "a" *(very high)* rating for *Legal Ability* and a "v" *(very high) General Recommendation* that *embraces faithful adherence to ethical standards; professional reliability, and diligence.*

In 1968 he was named *Mr. Aviation of Minnesota* by the Governor and the State Department of Aeronautics for *exceptional service to aviation.* Other aviation awards include a *Certificate of Appreciation* from the Chinese Air Force in 1986 *In Recognition of Outstanding Personal and Professional Achievement in Military Aviation.* He was inducted into the *Minnesota Aviation Hall of Fame* in 2001. The Silver Bay Airport was re-named the *Wayne Johnson Airport* in August 2005, *in recognition of his contributions to aviation and community services.* Also in 2005, he was named an *Honorary Citizen* of Kunming, China, *for his services as a fighter pilot in the Flying Tigers of the 14th Air Force in China in World War II.*

Wayne Johnson is a life member of the Veterans of Foreign Wars, Loyal Order of Moose, Sons of Norway, U.S. Air Force Association, Commemorative Air Force Association and many other community and civic associations.

As a child of a poor farm family who struggled through the Great Depression, Wayne Johnson rose to a distinguished career in both the field of law and in aviation.

4